THE FUTURE OF EUROPE

The European Union is at a crossroads. Slowly recovering from a series of financial and economic crises, with trust fundamentally shaken by processes of disaggregation and increasingly nationalist politics, it is searching for new visions that are at once inspiring and workable. In its White Paper of 1 March 2017, the Commission proposed five non-exclusive options for the Future of Europe. As put by the Commission, the five scenarios are illustrative in nature to provoke thinking. They are not detailed blueprints or policy prescriptions. Likewise, they deliberately make no mention of legal or institutional processes – the form will follow the function.

This book takes the current state of the Union seriously. However, it aims to debate not only the political vision of Europe, but also the issue of legal integration beyond Brexit. Apart from addressing the institutional challenges for the EU, the contributions to this volume focus on two key areas: rule of law and security. Rule of law and security are not only paradigmatic for the future of Europe but are also closely connected to a particular vision of Europe based on 'integration through law'; a vision that has been strongly contested in recent years. The overarching question is: how can sustainable political and legal integration be achieved in Europe?

The volume builds on a conference organised by the Swedish Network for European Legal Studies in November 2017 and includes chapters by leading scholars in the field from the Nordic countries and wider Europe.

The Future of Europe

Political and Legal Integration Beyond Brexit

Swedish Studies in European Law
Volume 13

Edited by
Antonina Bakardjieva Engelbrekt
and
Xavier Groussot

•HART•
OXFORD • LONDON • NEW YORK • NEW DELHI • SYDNEY

HART PUBLISHING

Bloomsbury Publishing Plc

Kemp House, Chawley Park, Cumnor Hill, Oxford, OX2 9PH, UK

HART PUBLISHING, the Hart/Stag logo, BLOOMSBURY and the Diana logo are trademarks of Bloomsbury Publishing Plc

First published in Great Britain 2019

A catalogue record for this book is available from the British Library.

Library of Congress Cataloging-in-Publication data

Names: Bakardjieva Engelbrekt, Antonina, 1963- editor. | Groussot, Xavier, editor.

Title: The future of Europe : political and legal integration beyond Brexit / edited by Antonina Bakardjieva Engelbrekt and Xavier Groussot.

Description: Oxford [UK] ; Chicago, Illinois : Hart Publishing, an imprint of Bloomsbury, 2019. | Series: Swedish studies in European law ; volume 13 | Includes bibliographical references and index.

Identifiers: LCCN 2019008727 (print) | LCCN 2019008753 (ebook) | ISBN 9781509923311 (EPub) | ISBN 9781509923304 (hardback : alk. paper)

Subjects: LCSH: Rule of law—European Union countries. | Constitutional law—European Union countries. | Security, International—European Union countries. | European Union countries—Foreign relations. | European Union countries—Politics and government. | European Union—Great Britain. | Security, International—Great Britain. | European Union countries—Foreign relations—Great Britain. | Great Britain—Foreign relations—European Union countries.

Classification: LCC KJE5037 (ebook) | LCC KJE5037 .F88 2019 (print) | DDC 341.242/2—dc23

LC record available at https://lccn.loc.gov/2019008727

ISBN: HB: 978-1-50992-330-4
ePDF: 978-1-50992-332-8
ePub: 978-1-50992-331-1

Typeset by Compuscript Ltd, Shannon

Preface

IN 2017 THE European Union reached the respectful age of 60. The EU institutions were preparing for celebration, touting proudly the story of a unique Union that had brought 60 years of peace, prosperity and solidarity in Europe. In Rome, on 25 March 2017, the leaders of 27 Member States and of EU institutions signed the Rome declaration renewing their vows to continued unity and announcing the vision of a Union that is 'safe and secure, prosperous, competitive, sustainable and socially responsible'. However, amidst the celebrations, many were expressing concerns about the current state and the future of the Union, not least due to the conspicuously absent 28th Member State. More disquietingly even, maybe for the first time in the Union's venerable history, some were openly raising the question whether the European project had a future.

Probably in anticipation of these concerns, a few weeks before the day of the anniversary, the European Commission published its White Paper on the Future of Europe. The White Paper outlined five scenarios on how European integration could evolve in the years to come, and invited policy-makers, scholars and European citizens to reflect on the challenges ahead.

This edited volume is partly prompted by the Commission's White Paper. The book builds on a conference hosted by the Swedish Network for European Legal Studies on 17–18 November 2017. The conference brought together prominent legal scholars and political scientists and offered an opportunity to reflect on the fundamental conditions for sustainable political and legal integration in Europe with a special focus on rule of law and security. The express ambition with both the conference and the book has been to not allow the academic debate on the future of Europe to be overshadowed by the unfolding Brexit saga.

In this preface, we would like to extend our thanks to the authors for their insightful contributions and excellent cooperation throughout the publishing process. We would also like to thank all the speakers and panellists at the conference, including those who were not ultimately able to contribute to this book. Their conference presentations, together with the many incisive observations and comments from a competent and engaged audience, have helped clarify the thoughts and sharpen the arguments advanced in the book. Thanks are also due to the members of the steering group of the Network for their involvement in conceptualising the conference.

The practical arrangements for the conference were handled in an excellent manner by Network coordinator, now practising lawyer, Parasto Taffazoli, for which we are grateful. Finally, we would like to express our special thanks and appreciation to Network coordinator Marie Kagrell for her efficient and devoted editorial assistance.

Antonina Bakardjieva Engelbrekt
and Xavier Groussot

Contents

PART III
RULE OF LAW IN THE MEMBER STATES

PART IV
EPILOGUE

List of Contributors

Antonina Bakardjieva Engelbrekt is Professor of European Law at the Faculty of Law, Stockholm University and Chair of the Swedish Network for European Legal Studies. She was Torsten and Ragnar Söderberg Professor of Legal Science (2015–2018).

Graham Butler is Associate Professor of Law at Aarhus University, Denmark.

Paul Craig is Professor of English Law, St John's College, Oxford.

Massimo Fichera is Academy of Finland Research Fellow and Adjunct Professor in EU Law at the Faculty of Law, University of Helsinki.

Eduardo Gill-Pedro is Post-Doctoral Researcher at the Faculty of Law, Lund University.

Xavier Groussot is Professor of European Law and Dean for Research at the Faculty of Law, Lund University.

András Jakab is Professor of Austrian Constitutional and Administrative Law, University of Salzburg and Honorary Fellow, Pázmány Péter Catholic University, Budapest.

Anna Jonsson Cornell is Professor of Comparative Constitutional Law and Vice Dean of the Faculty of Law at Uppsala University.

Ulla Neergaard is Professor of EU Law at the University of Copenhagen.

Jürgen Neyer is Professor for the Institutional Order of the European Union at the European University Viadrina, Frankfurt (Oder).

Juha Raitio is Professor of European Law at the University of Helsinki and Adjunct Professor of European Law at the Universities of Lapland (Rovaniemi), Tampere and Turku.

Kaarlo Tuori is Professor Emeritus of Jurisprudence at Helsinki University.

Anna Zemskova is a PhD Candidate at the Faculty of Law, Lund University.

Table of Cases

ECJ/CJEU cases in numerical order

ECJ/CJEU cases in alphabetical order

Member State courts

Denmark

Finland

Germany

United Kingdom

Table of Legislation

Council Directives/Council and Parliament Directives

Council Framework Decisions

Council Regulations/Council and Parliament Regulations

Council Resolutions

Commission Communications

Commission Declaration

Commission Recommendation

Miscellaneous EU instruments

Member State legislation

Denmark

Hungary

Poland

United Kingdom

Table of Treaties

2000

2001

2004

2007

Introduction

Towards Sustainable Political and Legal Integration in Europe

Peering into the Future

ANTONINA BAKARDJIEVA ENGELBREKT AND XAVIER GROUSSOT

The European Union (EU) is at a crossroads. Worn out after a series of unprecedented crises, questioned and contested in its foundations, entwined in complex negotiations of the first ever exit of a major Member State, it is desperately in need of a new optimistic vision for its future. The past decade has, not surprisingly, generated gloomy analyses and predictions. Scholars and political commentators have scrambled to draw up one pessimistic scenario after another, ranging from stagnation and new crises to the very disintegration of the EU.[1]

To be sure, it is not easy to be optimistic at a time when the intellectual and political resources of the EU are being drained by the unfolding Brexit drama and by efforts to ensure basic compliance with commonly agreed decisions and policies in the face of the opportunistic behaviour of populist national governments. However, there is also a widespread feeling of urgency to look beyond the vagaries of the current political situation and reflect on the long-term choices that Europe is facing. The faults of the present institutional and legal set-up of the EU need to be identified, the possible consequences of alternative paths carefully weighed and the conditions for sustainable European integration spelled out.

This book is conceived as a scholarly reflection on the future of the EU, deliberately leaving the topic of Brexit aside. Whereas the Brexit theme is inevitably present in some of the contributions, our ambition has been to not let ourselves be absorbed by the current pains of deconstructing Britain's EU membership, but instead to mobilise scholarly rigour and imagination in thinking constructively of the future of the European political and legal order irrespective of potential exits from and entries into the EU.

[1] For a sample, see I Krastev, *After Europe* (Philadelphia, University of Pennsylvania Press, 2017); H Vollard, 'Explaining European Disintegration' (2014) 52 *Journal of Common Market Studies* 1142 and other publications cited in Neyer, ch 1 in this volume, n. 1.

The starting point for the book has been the European Commission White Paper of 2017 on the Future of Europe.[2] In this document, the Commission famously described five scenarios for the future of European integration. To this, Commission President Jean-Claude Juncker added his own 'sixth' scenario.[3] Whereas some of the scenarios differ little from the current state of the European project and could at best be described as preserving the status quo (or, less flatteringly, as muddling through), others are bolder and more ambitious. In its future-telling, the Commission has deliberately chosen not to get entangled in the detailed institutional and legal modalities underlying each scenario. As the White Paper puts it: 'The form will follow the function.'

In contrast to the White Paper, the contributions in this book are not directed at elaborating discrete scenarios for the future. Nor are they exclusively preoccupied by the topic of 'more' or 'less' Europe. Instead, the aim has been to critically approach a few overarching themes, which in our view are crucial for the sustainability of the European legal and political order. The chapters are grouped into three thematic clusters: (i) institutional and constitutional fundamentals of the EU; (ii) the rule of law and security; and (iii) the rule of law in the Member States.

The centrality that the rule of law *problématique* occupies in this book can of course be at least partly explained by the predominantly legal scholarly affiliation of the contributing authors. More importantly, however, the rule of law principle has been singled out in the White Paper of 2017, as well as in other EU policy documents, as being at the core of a community, whose Member States have committed to 'replace the use of armed forces by the force of law',[4] and respectively fundamental for any positive vision for the EU as a community of values.[5] Indeed, it is also our conviction that the rule of law as a constitutional value of the EU is crucial for sustaining mutual trust between Member States, national authorities and citizens in the EU. It is thereby indispensable to think more profoundly on the meaning of the rule of law principle in the context of the European integration project.

The focus on security is in turn prompted by the prominent place accorded to this theme in the White Paper of 2017 and, more generally, in the contemporary discourse on European integration. Security is often invoked as being a reserved domain for the nation state and an utmost expression of national sovereignty. However, it is also increasingly being brought forward as an area where the EU has a new and bigger role to play, giving reasons to speak of the 'securitisation' of European integration.[6] Security features prominently

[2] European Commission, *White Paper on the Future of Europe*, 2017, available at: https://ec.europa.eu/commission/sites/beta-political/files/white_paper_on_the_future_of_europe_en.pdf.

[3] Commission President Jean Claude Juncker, State of the Union Address 2017, available at: https://ec.europa.eu/commission/priorities/state-union-speeches/state-union-2017_en.

[4] European Commission (n 2) 6.

[5] See Commission President Jean Claude Juncker (n 3).

[6] See Gill-Pedro, ch 7 in this volume.

in the positive agenda for Europe, summarised by Commission President Juncker as 'a Europe that protects, a Europe that empowers and a Europe that defends'.[7] And in 2018, the Commission advanced a proposal for nothing less than a European Security Union. The complex ways in which this advancement in the domain of security both challenges and strengthens the rule of law in the EU is in our view worthy of sustained scholarly and political attention.

If we now turn to the individual contributions, the chapters in the *first* thematic cluster address some of the eternal institutional and constitutional questions of the European project, such as democracy, representation, the division of powers and rights. A common trait of all four chapters in this part of the volume is that the authors look into past experiences seeking to find keys to the future of European integration; we can speak of a sort of 'back to the future' approach.

The most daring dive into history is made by Jürgen Neyer (Chapter 1). Neyer notes the altogether pessimistic tone of recent EU scholarship and the expanding genre of disintegration studies. Although he acknowledges the long-heeded wisdom that history never repeats itself, he nevertheless argues that there are useful lessons to be drawn from past experiences, provided we recognise the limitations and risks of such historical parallels. In his chapter, he embarks on a journey into the history of past European political orders and examines the reasons for their eventual demise. His retrospective goes as far back as the Holy Roman Empire and includes the end of the Catholic hegemony in the early sixteenth century, the French Revolution of 1789 and the end of the Weimar Republic in 1933. Neyer identifies some striking similarities in the events and patterns of political behaviour that have led to the collapse of these political orders. The demise is typically preceded by periods of modernisation shocks and the dramatic reallocation of resources, triggering perceptions of relative depravations within large portions of the population followed by popular unrest. The other common trait is 'a dispersed structure of accountability, preventing a clear attribution of responsibility and competence to tackle the grievances of those feeling relatively deprived'. The third and final element is a culture of political ignorance of the ruling political elite, reinforcing their determination to preserve the political order without major compromises and adaptations. According to the author, this pattern can be discerned, albeit still in a less pronounced form, in the current political state of the EU.

A chief concern with the existing institutional and legal set-up of the EU should, according to Neyer, be that those most affected by the crises – both citizens and Member States – are not adequately represented in the most important political institutions of the EU order. The author thus approaches the familiar *topos* of EU's democracy deficit, yet gives it a different twist. Whereas the EU, at least at first glance, has institutional structures and principles in place that are

[7] Commission President Jean Claude Juncker (n 3).

designed to ensure accountability and representation, according to Neyer, the institutional set-up is (and with reference to Fritz Scharpf's influential analysis) skewed in favour of fostering liberalisation and not social integration. Neyer's appeal to current European political leadership is to transform the present EU political order by embracing social values and responding adequately to the grievances of the socially and economically deprived. He advances some concrete proposals for overcoming the prevalent system of 'organised unaccountability'. Some of the bold reform proposals he advances are: assigning to the European Parliament the competence of directly electing a European government, voting on a European budget and reallocating tax funds from the wealthy to the needy, and introducing European unemployment insurance. The proposals have a clear ideological tinge and aim at freeing Europe from its 'outdated neoliberalism and pushing it towards social democracy'. The author underlines the special responsibility of Germany, 'the indispensable nation', for carrying through a similar ambitious reform agenda. However, he does not offer a forecast as to the likelihood that his proposals will be followed at the practical political level. Overall, the chapter is inspired by the belief that only a socially balanced European society will provide for sustainable European integration.

In Chapter 2, Paul Craig also looks into the past, but his time perspective is much more limited and focused on the evolution of the institutional structure of the EU. At the centre of his analysis is again the question of the EU's democracy deficit, understood as a mismatch between voter power and political accountability. Generally, Craig shares much of the critique being levelled against the lack of adequate democratic representation and other flaws of the EU's institutional architecture. He briefly traces the transformation of the European Parliament from having only symbolic powers to achieving a close to co-equal status with the Council in the legislative process. However, despite this positive evolution, he concedes that the political reality is that voters still cannot directly affect a change of policy direction in the EU by removing the incumbents and replacing them with those espousing different policies ('throwing the scoundrels out'). However, the main objective of his analysis is not to join the chorus of critics, but rather to explore the question of who is to be held accountable for this unsatisfactory political status quo. His unequivocal answer to this question is: the Member States. The present disposition of EU institutional power is the result of successive Treaties, in which the principal players have been the Member States. This implies that the current institutional balance is one that the Member States have been willing to accept. The author shows through careful and dispassionate analysis that at every juncture when the opportunity for designing a more democratic EU has presented itself, Member State governments have opted to foreclose such choices and to retain their ultimate control through perpetuating the existing classical intergovernmental arrangements. Examples include the debates on a single EU president or on a reinforced European Council with a long-term president. In each and every respect, the blame for the imperfect, undemocratic and at times dysfunctional institutional structure of the EU is thus to be placed not on the European institutions or on the EU itself, but on the Member States. Naturally, to say that the Member States are the masters of the Treaties is almost a truism. Yet, this fact is easily forgotten when the balance sheet of the pros and cons of European integration is being drawn up. Member State governments (and not only of the recent populist brand) are often quick to assign the responsibilities for unsuccessful policies to the EU, thus deflecting internal political critique.

As to the possibility for alleviating the democratic deficit and ensuring a more adequate match between EU institutional decision-making structure and the precepts of democracy, Craig identifies four main constraints to such development: political, democratic, constitutional and substantive. Politically, he sees no prospect that the Member States would be willing to relinquish their control over the decision-making process. In terms of democratic constraints, he points out the double dimension of representation in the EU, namely of the people and of the Member States. Insistence on transferring more decision-making powers to the directly elected European Parliament implies vesting more trust in people's representation. However, a disregard of Member State representation is undesirable, politically highly unlikely and even potentially disruptive, generating radical anti-European sentiments. Constitutionally, the prospects of alleviating the democratic deficit are seriously constrained by the (over-)constitutionalisation of the Treaties, on the one hand, and by the selective competence accorded to the EU, on the other. In particular, the lack of EU competence in the crucial fields of taxation, welfare and redistributive policies puts a severe limitation on political choices. Finally, and with reference to Fritz Scharpf again, the substantive constraint flows from the asymmetry between the economic and the social, the single market being the prime domain of EU, while the social remaining in the ambit of the Member States. However, also in this respect, the main responsibility resides with the Member States.

In a sense, Craig's chapter can be read as a sobering and even disheartening response to the bold reform proposals advanced by Neyer. In essence, Craig's analysis demonstrates that there has been no lack of progressive visions and specific suggestions for constitutional and institutional transformations in direction towards greater accountability and real democracy. However, such attempts have notoriously failed, often as a consequence of Member State governments' open or covert obstruction. To expect that Member States will in the future change their behaviour is highly unlikely.

The next chapter of this thematic cluster (Chapter 3) addresses the central issue of EU competences by looking into the past, present and future of the EU flexibility clause (currently Article 352 of the Treaty on the Functioning of the European Union (TFEU)). In this chapter, Graham Butler tries to decipher to what extent the clause still has a role to play in the present institutional framework and distribution of competences in the EU. He traces the rise of the flexibility clause from an initial dormant state, through a dynamic and activist phase of more frequent and assertive legislative use of the clause, following the Paris Summit of 1972, to the gradual fall and rolling back of the clause from the 1980s onwards. The chapter captures an interplay between the EU legislator, extensively using the clause in the activist phase as an incubator of new competences (the environment, consumer protection, intellectual property (IP) rights) to be subsequently taken up into the Treaties, and the Court of Justice of the European Union (CJEU), generally confirming this activist stance through its jurisprudence. Correspondingly, in the phase of decline, a winding down of legislative use is matched by stricter control by the Court. Butler also vividly demonstrates how the interpretation and scope of the clause is influenced by the dynamic of Treaty change and the budding of new conferred competences, as well as by recalibrated wording of the clause with the Lisbon Treaty.

Although the amendment of the clause through the Lisbon Treaty prima facie suggests that its use should become broader and less controversial, Butler finds that the decline of the clause has in fact continued. The clause has in his view become narrower in scope compared to its predecessors and subject to stricter procedural requirements, not least subsidiarity control. Furthermore, national courts and legislators have not stayed passive, but have through a variety of mechanisms asserted their right to keep a national check on potential intensification of legislative use of the clause.

As regards the future, Butler does not predict any spectacular development in an expansionist direction. However, he also stresses, and generally praises, the remaining hidden potential of the clause to wake up to new unexpected vigour, should the political or constitutional evolution of the EU require so. The clause has thus served the EU well and remains a source of much-needed flexibility for the future.

Finally, in Chapter 4, Xavier Groussot and Anna Zemskova trace the role of rights and their spillover in the process of European integration. According to them, the rights-based vision of the future of Europe is problematic, given the irrefutable fact that EU rights have been politically and legally contested in recent years. The process of European integration begs one essential question: why are the rights so resilient in the process of European integration? Groussot and Zemskova's analysis has its starting point in the 'Ever Closer Union' clause enshrined in Article 1(2) of the Treaty on the European Union (TEU), which is viewed as reflecting the legacy of neofunctionalism. For them, the spillover of rights is driven at the general level by the clause and can thus be itself viewed as an integral part of the neofunctionalist legacy for explaining the process of European integration. The observed spillover of rights is a powerful phenomenon that acts as a trigger for facilitating European integration – even though, as in any system, there are obvious reverse processes in the form of spillback, specifically demonstrated by the limitation of individual rights during the economic crisis. According to the authors, the spillback of rights demonstrates their pliancy and their responsiveness to the persistent calls of effectiveness. It also explains why rights are so resilient in the process of European integration.

As shown in this chapter, the European rights are resilient since they constitute the privilege tools for ensuring the institutionalisation of the 'Ever Closer Union' clause through a process of rationalisation. In other words, 'Unity', 'Diversity' and 'Transparency' (the normative core values of Article 1(2) TEU) have been institutionalised by the EU Courts' case law on individual rights with the help of a complex network of legal principles, the most central among them being the autopoietic principle of EU administrative and constitutional law, namely the principle of proportionality. This network of principles tied to the application of rights tells us that the telos of European integration is not only about unity but also about diversity. In practice, it means that the effectiveness of EU law is not absolute and that there are situations in which it is accepted that EU law should yield and where national interests should prevail. In order to understand the resilience of rights in the process of European integration, it is also important to analyse their internal logic or 'voice'. Rights in EU law are founded on a functional logic epitomised by their own origin, structure and hermeneutic. The strength of the obligations and the concomitant functional logic of the European Court of Justice (ECJ) offer a plausible explanation regarding the resilience of 'rights' in the EU legal order. Yet the resilience of 'rights' in EU law can only be fully explained if it is connected in turn to the recognition of their functional acceptance at the domestic level by different epistemic communities representing private interests. This phenomenon constitutes the positive feedback loop of European rights in the process of European integration.

At the centre of the inquiries in the *second* thematic cluster are the questions of rule of law and security, the latter concept understood both more specifically as part of the EU's policy towards an Area of Freedom, Security and Justice (AFSJ) and, more broadly, as preserving the integrity and continued existence of the European liberal project.

In a first reflective and theoretical chapter (Chapter 5), Massimo Fichera advances the concept of 'discursive constituent power' and analyses its relation to European integration. The starting point in Fichera's discourse-theoretical analysis is the classical idea of the people as the constituent power from which a system of government derives its authority. He argues that transnational integration, and European integration in particular, does not renounce the idea of the people as constituent power. However, 'the people' is understood in a novel way, namely: (1) partly as 'mobile people', ie, a construction of people as moving from one place or another of the EU territory; and 2) partly as 'peoples' in the plural, ie, a construction of 'demoi' that is supposed to underpin the *process* of development of the EU as a polity. In both configurations, the security and fundamental rights discourses as discourses of power acquire particular relevance. In fact, for Fichera, the EU liberal project can only survive if it does not negate constituent power, but instead reinstates it as discursive constituent power through the self-justifying discourses of security and fundamental rights.

Consequently, Fichera believes that we should resist the temptation to characterise European integration as a process replacing constituent power with constitutional rights, on the one hand, and individual economic freedoms, on the other – or to view it as a primarily economic process; on the contrary, the political has never been really removed from the inner core of the process of European integration. However, as he states, discursive constituent power cannot escape the ambiguities and contradictions that are typical of the EU liberal project. The main reason for this is that the discourses of security and fundamental rights have been presented since the early stages of European integration as if they were neutral, whereas in fact they have always disguised a specific political direction. As a result, conflicts and tensions have been downplayed. From this perspective, security and fundamental rights as discourses of power express the interplay between the expansive trend of the EU machinery (for example, through the doctrine of primacy and the development of the internal market) and the resistance by Member States. It is through these discourses that the EU pursues a strategy of self-justification and self-empowerment accomplished in the name *of the peoples of Europe*.

In Chapter 6, Anna Jonsson Cornell investigates to what extent national security, understood as an EU constitutional law concept, presents a challenge to EU legal integration and what role it might play for the integration process in the future. The chapter outlines two meanings of national security as a constitutional law concept, namely: (i) national security as a competence-deciding concept; and (ii) national security as a justification for the derogation from and the restriction of fundamental rights protection. Although the difference between these two aspects is underlined, Jonsson Cornell notes that the dividing line is increasingly difficult to uphold. The overall ambition of the chapter is to map out how EU constitutional law deals with national security matters from a competence-deciding point of view in order to draw conclusions as to how it impacts on Member States' national security prerogative.

The chapter proceeds with an analysis of the concept of national security in the EU Treaties. Jonsson Cornell notes that Article 4(2) TEU is fairly clear as regards the national security exception. However, there is no clear understanding of the definition and scope of national security as a competence-deciding norm. At the same time, the expansive Court of Justice of the European Union (CJEU) jurisprudence on national security and public order as compelling reasons for limiting fundamental rights and freedoms prompts a conclusion that the scope of retained powers for national security purposes is very limited and restricted chiefly to institutional and organisational issues, together with operational (especially coercive) measures.

Turning to security in the EU policy towards AFSJ, Jonsson Cornell rightly points out that this area of legal integration still bears important traits of intergovernmentalism and state sovereignty even after the entry into force of the Lisbon Treaty and the removal of the pillar structure. Relying on Tuori, she emphasises that the 're-surfacing of state-sovereigntist concerns, reliance on the international law system, opt-ins and opt-outs, reflects [sic] an exceptionally high tension between the transnational, European and national'. The main tools for integration in AFSJ are coordination and cooperation, mutual recognition and legal harmonisation, in that order; thus, cooperation rather than integration remains the prevailing principle within this policy area.

In order to add to our understanding of how national security can be a driver for, or pose a hindrance to, EU legal integration Jonsson Cornell conducts two case studies. The first case study is on Schengen and the temporary closing of borders, while the second is on privacy rights in a national security context. The parallel study of these two cases is helpful to reveal if there are any differences as to how the concept of national security is understood, and hence what role it is allowed to play in different areas of European integration. The case studies show that in the Schengen context, national security as an EU constitutional law concept is given a broad understanding and the scope of the Member States' national security prerogative is correspondingly broad, both in terms of national security as a competence-deciding and a rights-restricting concept. In contrast, in the data retention and data processing context, the bar is set high in terms of rights protection, and the scope for claiming a national security exception is narrowed significantly.

Jonsson Cornell concludes that national security as an objective and interest can serve both as an accelerator and as a brake to EU legal integration. So far it has primarily served as an accelerator. Taking the political turmoil in Europe into account, especially the growing tendencies towards nationalism and the return to the nation state as the primary actor in the wake of the so-called migration crisis and Brexit, reaching the conclusion that the national security argument will serve to slow down EU legal integration in the future is not far-fetched. Still, the expansive understanding of national security, the lack of a clear national security competence-dividing norm, the growing impact of the Charter and the general constitutionalisation of EU law have so far had the effect that Member States' national security prerogative is shrinking and that rights protection to the benefit of individuals is increasing.

In a chapter partly commenting on Fichera's and Jonsson-Cornell's contributions (Chapter 7), Eduardo Gill-Pedro develops an independent theoretical framework for approaching the issue of security in the EU, building on the two concepts of 'community' (*communitas*) and 'immunity' (*immunitas*), as elaborated by the Italian philosopher Roberto Esposito. The point of Gill-Pedro's chapter is not to give a detailed exposition of Esposito's philosophy; rather, he aims at using the concepts advanced by Esposito and applying them as heuristic devices in order to think about the securitisation of the EU's area of freedom, security and justice. For Gill-Pedro, the EU deploys immunitarian logic to protect European integration from that which might threaten it. This results in a paradox. Indeed, we can understand the idea of European integration as imposing an obligation of community on the Member States, that is, as an obligation to be open to 'the other'. But this very idea of European integration is in turn deployed as the idea that justifies the immunitarian logic which imposes on Member States the obligation to identify and exclude 'the other'.

For Gill-Pedro, the 'special path' that justified the EU was that it acted as counter to such immunitarian logic. If instead the EU reinforces and legitimises immunitarian logic, then it may be the case that the peoples of Europe choose to deploy that logic not to immunise European integration, but instead to immunise ideas that they may consider more important and more relevant to them – the idea of their 'people', their 'nation' and their 'race'. Gill-Predro suggests that we are at a crossroads. If the EU continues to develop the logic of immunity in the service of the idea of European integration, but there are no meaningful processes by which the peoples of Europe can see themselves as authors of that integration, then the growing rift between the EU, as a political project, and its putative citizens becomes ever wider. By bringing in the importance of democracy in the EU security context, Gill-Pedro's chapter connects to the analyses of both Neyer and Craig in the first part of the book.

The *third* thematic cluster includes three chapters offering perspectives on European integration and the rule of law in individual Member States. The chapters remind us that probably the most decisive issue for the future of the European legal order is the EU's ability to guarantee the rule of law in its Member States and in all areas of EU policies. The first chapter in this part of the book (Chapter 8) is predominantly theoretical. In it, Juha Raitio presents the rich theoretical debate concerning the rule of law concept in Finland. He argues that nowadays in any EU Member State, the intellectual framework to approach the rule of law concept should be the 'triangle of democracy, human rights and rule of law'. For him, a 'thick' concept of rule of law would be the most balanced interpretation of rule of law not only in contemporary Finland but also within the EU as a whole. As shown in his chapter, in Finland, the interpretation of the rule of law principle is derived in constant reference and comparison to the Anglo-American concept of the rule of law and the German *Rechtsstaat* concept. Recently, the rule of law principle has also been considered from a global trade and comparative law viewpoint. Yet, there is in Raitio's view still reason to study the rule of law from a more theoretical point of view, since the concept, in particular in Scandinavian countries, has been questioned as being so vague and ambiguous that it had allegedly lost its meaning in legal argumentation. Provocatively, the concept has been compared to a 'rhetorical balloon'. Raitio does not find this sceptical view to be justified. He argues, in line with contemporary legal literature (and especially in the field of EU law), that one can refer to a 'thick' conception of rule of law, which contains both formal and material elements, including notably human and fundamental rights. Moreover, it is essential that the EU legal rule of law concept be interpreted in close contact with the democracy principle. Democracy cannot exist and human rights cannot be respected if the rule of law principle is not adhered to.

Turning more specifically to the situation in Finland, Raitio briefly reviews Finland's overall compliance with its EU law obligations, including the tendency of Finnish courts to follow CJEU preliminary rulings. He concludes that the country generally tends to respect its EU legal obligations and there are thus no significant problems as regards the rule of law or mutual trust from an EU law perspective.

A similarly positive assessment can hardly be found in the detailed and highly critical account of András Jakab on the situation of rule of law in Hungary (Chapter 9). The provocative title of Jakab's chapter, referring to the situation in post-socialist countries as one of 'institutional alcoholism', reflects his concern for societies which are experiencing the legacies of their authoritarian past and where those in power have a deeply problematic relationship with the very basic requirement of respect for law and for the constitutionally established decision-making process. Jakab's analysis is informed by institutionalist theory, where institutions are understood as formal rules, informal practices and narratives. He considers one of the major reasons for the systematic disrespect for the rule of law in post-socialist countries to reside in a formalist, rule-centred conception of law and a corresponding disregard for the actual, institutionalised, practice of law. In the prevailing narrative of the legal system, Jakab identifies the traces of the Marxist-Leninist theory of law, among others legal instrumentalism, ie, the view that law is an expression of the will of the ruling class, a preference for textual approaches to legal interpretation, the doctrine of unity of power instead of separation of powers and the belief that the force of international law is derived from national sovereignty and secondary to it.

Jakab describes the making of the Hungarian Constitution of 2010/11 from the perspective of institution-building, showing the mismatch between formal rules and actual practices. According to him, the institutionalist view of law advanced in the chapter yields two main findings: (i) that honest determination for achieving a radical institutional overhaul of a complete legal system is not sufficient and that such transformation can only be successful in the presence of external pressure; and (ii) that the reinforcement of substantive elements of a rule of law culture can be gradually achieved only if increased attention is paid to actual practices and narratives in the realm of legislation, on the application of the law and legal training. However, this requires political action and the adjustment of formal rules. In the Hungarian case, external pressure has decreased after the country's accession to the EU and political action is not to be expected, since it is not in the interest of the incumbent decision-makers. Hence, Jakab's bitter diagnosis is that overcoming the impasse seems unlikely for the time being.

A different 'national' story emerges from Ulla Neergaard's analysis of Danish 'exceptionalism' (Chapter 10). Neergaard traces Denmark's complex relationship with the EU, providing an overview of the many opt-outs and special arrangements surrounding the country's EU membership, such as: the EU citizenship opt-out, the Economic and Monetary Union (EMU) opt-out, the defence policy opt-out, the AFSJ opt-out, the 'second home' protocol and other areas of differentiation. From this analysis, a portrait emerges of a 'high-maintenance' Member State, which is often deviating from the commonly decided course of action, claiming individual and privileged treatment. To be sure, the regime Denmark has carved out for itself by way of special waivers and exceptions is a regime under the rule of law. This is confirmed in mutually agreed protocols and provisions. Nevertheless, this record of institutionalised exceptionalism seems to beg the question of whether the country is fully committed to its EU legal obligations, a question acquiring additional relevance in the aftermath of the *Ajos* saga featuring the largely disobedient behaviour of the Danish Supreme Court.

Yet Neergaard does not stop at providing a legal positivist analysis of Denmark's differential arrangements; she also looks behind the 'black letter' law and seeks to assess the actual practice and effects of the various instruments. Obviously, all the exceptions and special arrangements have been prompted by a fear of eroding national sovereignty and national identity. However, contrary to the dominant narrative, and surprisingly, the chapter shows that many of the opt-outs are subsequently mitigated in the process of implementation, sometimes to the extent of remaining only exceptions on paper. For instance, the opt-out on EU citizenship has practically no impact today. The opt-out on the EMU is certainly valid. However, Denmark follows consistently a fixed-exchange-rate policy vis-a-vis the euro, its (indirect) participation in the European Exchange Rate Mechanism has been long-lasting and compliant, it chose to join the Stability and Growth Pact in 1997 and the Treaty on Stability, Coordination and Governance in the EMU, and currently, joining the Banking Union is considered. As to the defence opt-opt, commentators note a permissive interpretation of the opt-out by Danish foreign policy-makers. Finally, despite the AFSJ opt-out, Denmark still contributes and participates in the cooperation within this policy area and to a much larger degree than anticipated.

In a way, Neergaard's inquiry into the 'bits and pieces' of Denmark's special regime provides a much-needed realistic perspective revealing more uniformity and compliance than is admitted by the Danish government and than is probably realised by the Danish public and even by some Danish politicians. Thus, according to Neergaard, the Danish situation may be seen as fitting well into the EU motto 'United in Diversity'. Moreover, according to all recent polls, the Danes are among the most eager supporters of remaining in the EU and a 'Dan-exit' is not a likely scenario at present.

In a chapter that serves as an epilogue to the book (Chapter 11), Kaarlo Tuori reflects on the dialectic relationship between European and Member States constitutionalism, seeking to resolve the tension between the two and to see whether they can be conceived as complementing or conflicting. Tuori makes two main points: first, the relationship between EU constitutionalism and Member State constitutionalism is not only about conflict, but is also about dialogue and cooperation, as well as complementarity; and, second, this relationship should not be discussed only within the juridical and political constitutions, but also within the sectoral constitutions, such as the economic, social and security constitutions.

Tuori elaborates his two points through criticism of two influential portrayals of EU constitutionalism and Member State constitutionalism: (i) constitutional pluralism, as conceived by Neil MacCormick[8] and developed by others; and (ii) the proposal to locate the constitutional aspect exclusively on the Member State side and approach the EU in terms of administrative law, as advanced by Peter Lindseth.[9] Tuori's concern with constitutional pluralists lies in their overblown emphasis on the conflictual nature of the relationship between European and Member State constitutionalism and their focus on what he calls the juridical constitution. Conversely, his discord with Lindseth concerns the use of a thick concept of democratic legitimacy, refusing to recognise the constitutional aspect of the EU and its legal system. Against these views, Tuori submits that in the European context, efforts to secure democratic constitutional legitimacy should be examined through the interaction between the transnational and national levels of constitutionalism (two-stage legitimation). In some crucial respects, European constitutionalism has been, and still is, parasitic in relation to national constitutionalism. Most importantly, this also holds for constitutional and democratic legitimacy. The fact that the general public has primarily confronted EU measures not directly, but indirectly, through the political and administrative institutions and the legal system of the respective Member State, has been crucial for the legitimacy that the EU and its individual policies have enjoyed among European citizenry. Along with the importance of sectoral constitutionalisation, the interaction between the transnational and national levels belongs to the features, which distinguish European from state constitutionalism. This interaction is vital for providing European institutions and policies with democratic legitimacy.

In Tuori's view, the legitimacy deficit, aggravated by the recent crises, cannot be mended through measures presupposing European citizenry – European demos – as a collective political agent. The solution lies instead in further strengthening the mechanisms of two-stage legitimation. The difficulty consists in reinforcing the influence of national democratic procedures while simultaneously avoiding nationalistic excesses, ensuring attention in national debates to the viewpoints of other Member States and the EU, and engaging national democracies in a constructive dialogue.

[8] N MacCormick, *Questioning Sovereignty: Law, State and Nation in the European Commonwealth* (Oxford, Oxford University Press, 1999).

[9] P Lindseth, *Power and Legitimacy: Reconciling Europe and the Nation-State* (Oxford, Oxford University Press, 2010).

As was stated at the outset, the objective of this book has not been to give an unequivocal answer to the much-debated question of 'more' or 'less' Europe; rather, the chapters in this volume demonstrate, each in its particular way, that such a dichotomy is simplistic and misguided. A more important objective that has steered the inquiry has been to identify conditions for and paths towards sustainable European political and legal integration – integration that would survive, and even be strengthened, by the inevitable crises that will arise in the future.

Probably not surprisingly, most of the chapters in the book highlight the importance of spelling out even more clearly the fundamental values on which the EU builds – democracy, the rule of law and fundamental rights. However, what the book also emphasises is that in the context of European integration, each of these fundamental values has to be redefined and reconceived, and can only be understood by taking into account the transnational character of the European project. This does not mean that the values are becoming malleable or devoid of content and meaning; rather, it implies that in a multi-faceted and diverse European polity, these values are inevitably contested and renegotiated in constant tension between the national and the European.

The chapters in this book outline and analyse various expressions of this tension: the horizontal and vertical dimensions of representation in the EU, discussed in Craig's chapter, the spillover and spillback of rights, traced by Groussot and Zemskova, the interplay between change and permanence, constitutive of the European liberal project as claimed by Fichera, the expansion and rolling back of the flexibility clause described by Butler, the role of national security as an accelerator and a brake of European integration, as pointed out by Jonsson Cornell, and ultimately the interplay between EU and Member State constitutionalism in Tuori's convincing conceptualisation.

Some of the examples given in the book point to the paradoxical nature of this tension, like the apparent coherence and loyalty achieved through differentiation in Neergard's account of Danish EU membership, the mutually reinforcing national and European dimensions of the rule of law in Ratio's account of the theoretical debate in Finland, and the need for external pressure for enhancing internal institution-building in Jakab's analysis of the rule of law in Hungary.

Certainly, the current protracted and multi-dimensional crisis in Europe has generated a sense of emergency which understandably prompts appeals for radical overhaul of the EU's institutional and constitutional set-up in direction that will lead to strengthening the democratic fundament of the EU and of adequate representation of the socially deprived in the EU political process, as powerfully argued by Neyer. And Gill Pedro is right to warn us that the growing tendency of 'securitisation' and of invoking 'immunity' in EU policy-making are in dire contradiction with the core idea of 'community' underlying the European project, and may dangerously feed nationalist and isolationist reactions.

Still, as noted by the Commission in its 2017 White Paper, the EU has always been at a crossroads. While acknowledging the graveness of the current situation, the chapters in this volume can nevertheless be read as giving grounds for moderate optimism. They seem to provide at least partial support for the 'evolutionary pragmatism' line of reasoning defended by scholars in the liberal intergovernmentalism string of European integration studies.[10] The key to the relative success of the European project has, at least until recently, resided in maintaining the tension between the Member States and the EU to a degree where it is productive and mobilises the enormous political and economic resources of a diverse polity. Rather than seeking legitimacy in a central source of authority, the strength of the EU has been in embracing the plurality of the peoples of Europe, as the legitimating force of a European democracy.[11] Therefore, as contended in many of the chapters in this book and as argued by influential scholars of European integration, rather than maintaining the mantra of an 'Ever Closer Union',[12] it is more promising for the EU to continue to heed the logo 'United in Diversity'.[13]

To be sure, there is today a more dramatic divergence in preferences and in models of economic and political governance across EU Member States, the fissures going along both the East/West and the South/North dimensions. There is likewise boiling dissatisfaction within broad portions of the population who feel left behind by the process of Europeanisation and globalisation – a dissatisfaction that nurtures anti-democratic, nationalist and populist politics. The long-term success of European political and legal integration therefore seems to depend on the EU's ability to contain rising illiberal regimes within the EU,[14] while converging more decisively around a vision for a socially just and sustainable European integration based on mutual trust, dialogue and a long-nurtured discipline of tolerance.[15]

REFERENCES

European Commission, *White Paper on the Future of Europe*, 2017, available at: https://ec.europa.eu/commission/sites/beta-political/files/white_paper_on_the_future_of_europe_en.pdf.

Joerges, C, 'How is a Closer Union Conceivable under Conditions of Ever More Socio-economic and Political Diversity? Constitutionalising Europe's *unitas in pluralitate*' (2018) 24 *European Law Journal* 257.

[10] A Moravcsik, 'Preferences, Power and Institutions in 21st-Century Europe' (2018) 56 *Journal of Common Market Studies* 1648.

[11] K Nicolaïdis, 'Braving the Waves? Europe's Constitutional Settlement at Twenty' (2018) 56 *Journal of Common Market Studies* 1614.

[12] See most recently Case C-621/18 *Wightman*, ECLI:EU:C:2018:999, paras 61 and 67.

[13] C Joerges, 'How is a Closer Union Conceivable under Conditions of Ever More Socio-economic and Political Diversity? Constitutionalising Europe's *unitas in pluralitate*' (2018) 24 *European Law Journal* 257; Nicolaïdis (n 11).

[14] S Meunier and MA Vachudova, 'Liberal Intergovernmentalism, Illiberalism and the Potential Superpower of the European Union' (2018) 56 *Journal of Common Market Studies* 1631.

[15] JHH Weiler, 'On the Power of the Word: Europe's Constitutional Iconography' (2005) 2 *ICON* 173.

Krastev, I *After Europe* (Philadelphia, University of Pennsylvania Press, 2017).
Lindseth, P, *Power and Legitimacy: Reconciling Europe and the Nation-State* (Oxford, Oxford University Press, 2010).
MacCormick, N, *Questioning Sovereignty: Law, State and Nation in the European Commonwealth* (Oxford, Oxford University Press, 1999).
Meunier, S and Vachudova, MA, 'Liberal Intergovernmentalism, Illiberalism and the Potential Superpower of the European Union' (2018) 56 *Journal of Common Market Studies* 1631.
Moravcsik, A, 'Preferences, Power and Institutions in 21st-Century Europe' (2018) 56 *Journal of Common Market Studies* 1648.
Nicolaïdis, K 'Braving the Waves? Europe's Constitutional Settlement at Twenty' (2018) *Journal of Common Market Studies* 1614.
Vollard, H 'Explaining European Disintegration' (2014) 52 *Journal of Common Market Studies* 1142.
Weiler, JHH, 'On the Power of the Word: Europe's Constitutional Iconography' (2005) 2 *ICON* 173.

Part I

Institutional and Constitutional Fundaments of the Union

1

Saving Liberal Europe Lessons from History

JÜRGEN NEYER

I. THE CHALLENGE

THE EUROPEAN UNION (EU) is in dire straits.[1] Southern Europe suffers under mass unemployment, East and West are unable to agree on migration, and illiberal populism is growing in importance all over the EU. Germany disagrees with France about the proper ways out of the crisis and Britain intends to leave the EU. A growing chorus of analysts speculate about the future of the EU and even announce a general crisis of liberalism.[2] Theorists of integration have discovered 'disintegration theory' as a new playing field.[3] The democratic deficit of the EU, its imperfect set-up of the common currency, the 'over-constitutionalisation' of its legal order and the underdeveloped nature of its political institutions are identified as major sources for the crisis.[4] None of this is wrong. There is significant evidence that the EU indeed suffers from multiple deficiencies and that it needs a major overhaul, probably even a relaunch of its operating system. However, what is missing in the literature so far is a historically grounded approach that makes use of the abundant historical lessons

[1] This chapter has benefited from discussion and input at the seminar of the Faculty of Law, Haifa University, 8 November 2017, the Center for German and European Studies, Haifa University, 9 November 2017 and the Viadrina Institute for European Studies, Frankfurt (Oder), June 2017. I am especially grateful to Jonathan Yovel, Eli Salzberger and Timm Beichelt for the invitation and their comments.

[2] *cf* I Krastev, *After Europe* (Philadelphia, University of Pennsylvania Press, 2017); H Brunkhorst, 'A Curtain of Gloom is Descending on the Continent: Capitalism, Democracy and Europe' (2017) 23 *European Law Journal* 335.

[3] H Vollard, 'Explaining European Disintegration' (2014) 52 *Journal of Common Market Studies* 1142; E Jones, 'Towards a Theory of Disintegration' (2018) 25 *Journal of European Public Policy* 440; D Hodson and U Puetter 'Studying Europe after the Fall' (2018) 25 *Journal of European Public Policy* 465.

[4] C Offe, *Europe Entrapped* (Cambridge, Polity Press, 2015); D Grimm, *The Constitution of European Democracy* (Oxford, Oxford University Press, 2017).

that Europe has on offer. Such an approach may shed new light on Europe's crisis and help to set it in context with the former crises of the political and legal order in Europe.

Historians themselves are sceptical in terms of drawing lessons from the past. It is often argued that history is not repetitive and that every historical case must be understood on its own terms. Drawing lessons from the past and identifying parallels among instances separated by hundreds of years are viewed with significant reservations. This chapter agrees that caution is an important scientific virtue, but also holds that caution must not be misunderstood as a general prohibition to compare across time, space and even cultures.[5] Across history, so the argument holds, we find strong evidence for the recurrence of a certain pattern of political conflict that has time and again invited social unrest, political mobilisation and finally the downfall of political orders. This pattern, as will be argued in the following sections, will recur today in Europe if we do not learn from history and implement the necessary steps to prevent it from happening again. The pattern begins with a modernisation shocks, ie, a phase of rapid social, economic, technological or cognitive change. Modernisation shocks are often accompanied by a reallocation of societal resources as some are more able to adapt than others and are quicker to reap the benefits of the new opportunities, whilst others are left behind. Modernisation is thus tightly connected to economic redistribution and to relative deprivation, ie, the subjective perception by people that they are receiving less than they deserve.[6] The second crucial and recurring element of a structure inviting the fall of political order is a dispersed structure of accountability, preventing a clear attribution of responsibility and competence to tackle the grievances of those feeling relatively deprived. If these two components meet with the third element, a political culture of ignorance, reinforcing the self-perception of the ruling class to legitimately maintain the contested order without any significant compromise, then we have all the elements in place that constitute the pattern of a highly delicate situation. It is a situation inviting social unrest and easily translating into political anger and even violence.

The EU of today resembles this situation to a significant degree. Right-wing populism has become a major political power in nearly all of Europe's parliaments. This challenges the very normative building blocks of the EU and resents

[5] Some of the most insightful books on understanding change and stability in political order have been written along these lines. See, eg, S Acemoglu and JA Robinson, *Why Nations Fail: The Origins of Power, Prosperity, and Poverty* (New York, Crown Publishers, 2012); J Diamond, *Collapse: How Societies Choose to Fail or Succeed* (New York, Viking Press, 2005); T Skocpol, *States and Social Revolutions: A Comparative Analysis of France, Russia and China* (Cambridge, Cambridge University Press, 1979).

[6] I Walker and HJ Smith, *Relative Deprivation: Specification, Development and Integration* (Cambridge, Cambridge University Press, 2001).

the liberal principles upon which the EU is established.[7] Human rights, free trade, the common currency and open borders are all contested policies under attack by illiberal parties. It is true that thus far, the new radical opposition, ranging from the French Front National and the German Alternative für Deutschland to the Hungarian Fidesz and the Polish PiS, has not used any violent means. And it is also true that most Europeans are still well aware that the benefits of integration by far outweigh its costs. However, if we ignore the lessons of the past, there is no guarantee that this will still be the case tomorrow. History has substantial lessons to offer, teaching us how easily fundamental opposition turns into violent protest.

The following sections present insights from a research project that has analysed four major crises of political order in European history. The downfall of the ancient Roman Republic, the end of Catholic hegemony in the early sixteenth century, the French Revolution of 1789 and the end of the Weimar Republic in 1933 have been selected for two reasons. First of all, they are the most prominent watersheds, separating well-established orders from major turmoil, and, second, they are the most distinct cases in terms of dominant cultures and philosophies as well as technological advancement. Notwithstanding their massive differences, all four cases have a number of distinctive features in common: a modernisation shock followed by massive social unrest, a widespread perception of relative deprivation, a political order of organised unaccountability and an ignorant political culture. In all four cases:

(1) unrest met with political ignorance on the part of the ruling elite,
(2) transformed into anger and violent mass mobilisation,
(3) split the elite in two opposing camps, and
(4) ultimately led to the downfall of the political order.

The most striking finding of these cases is not only the similarity of the pattern leading to the fall of political orders, but its parallels to the EU of today. We are again witnessing a modernisation shock,[8] we have clear evidence of growing socio-economic cleavages and relative deprivation,[9] we observe a European dysfunctional political order of limited accountability[10] and, last but not least,

[7] *cf* C Mudde, 'Europe's Populist Surge: A Long Time in the Making' (2016) 95 *Foreign Affairs* 25.

[8] There are numerous books detailing the practices and implications of the information revolution and the digital age. Good examples are H Fischer, *Digital Shock: Confronting the New Reality* (Montreal, McGill-Queen's University Press, 2006); M Castells, *End of Millennium*, 2nd edn (Oxford, Wiley-Blackwell, 2010).

[9] J Fisher and TM Smeeding, 'Income Inequality' (2016) *State of the Union: The Poverty and Inequality Report*, Stanford Centre on Poverty and Inequality, 32; B Milanovic, *Global Inequality: A New Approach for the Age of Globalization* (Cambridge, MA, Belknap Press of Harvard University Press, 2016).

[10] Y Papadopoulos, 'Accountability and Multi-level Governance: More Accountability, Less Democracy?' (2010) 33 *West European Politics* 1030; M Bovens, D Curtin and P t'Hart, *The Real World of EU Accountability: What Deficit?* (Oxford, Oxford University Press, 2010).

we have strong evidence of a dominant liberal political culture that finds it difficult to occupy common discursive ground with the rising forces of populism.[11] It is true that the intensity of conflict today is far from that of its historical predecessors and it is also hard to dispute that the Europe of today resembles a much fairer and more balanced order than was the case in ancient Rome, fifteenth-century Germany, eighteenth-century France or even the Weimar Republic. However, it is also true that globalisation is casting doubts on the power of liberalism to reintegrate economic activity and the political community of belonging. Massive impoverishment, political dislocation and a moral rift are threatening the very future of liberalism. Thus, the liberal order of today is far from being uncontested.[12] The final section of the chapter discusses the lessons to be drawn from history in order to stabilise the liberal order of Europe and to prevent the replication of earlier disruptions.

II. EUROPE IN HISTORICAL CONTEXT

A. Social Unrest

All four historical case studies of the fall of political order begin with a modernisation shock and new social cleavages. The beginning of the end of the ancient Roman Republic started with the Romans' victory in the Second Punic War. Following victory, the formerly small Roman world opened up to the wealth and the indulgence of some of the larger capitals in the Mediterranean world. Soldiers having spent all their lives on the fields surrounding Rome now walked the streets of Carthage and Alexandria, and learnt of unheard of lifestyles and ideas. Not less important, thousands of former enemies were enslaved and brought to work on the fields of the Roman nobility. The social consequences of this were severe. The new abundance of cheap labour combined with the economies of scale resulting from the now far larger lands owned by the nobility increased the competitive pressure on the large number of former soldiers who were returning to their small-scale fields. Over time, many of them were forced to give up their farms and to move to Rome in order to find a new source of income. They had, as a famous ancient source argues, conquered the world but lost their homes.[13] Social unrest grew and new social cleavages in Rome destabilised the social compromise that had been established in the early centuries of the Roman Republic.

[11] *cf* the contribution in R Wodak, M Khosravinik and B Mral, *Right-Wing Populism in Europe: Politics and Discourse* (London, Bloomsbury Press, 2013). The main thrust of the contributions is not about overcoming the reasons for right-wing populism, but how to combat it.

[12] See the debate in P Manent, 'The Crisis of Liberalism' (2014) 25 *Journal of Democracy* 131.

[13] TG Plutarch 8 f, translated by W Ax, W Lautemann and M Schlenke (eds), *Geschichte in Quellen* (Munich, Altertum, 1975) 471.

Quite similarly, the end of Catholic hegemony and the beginning of the Protestant movement was introduced by the combination of a new cognitive horizon opened up by the Renaissance and intensifying economic pressure in the fifteenth century on small farmers. Fewer and fewer farmers were ready to accept the leisurely lives of their Catholic priests at the same time as they had to fight ever harder for economic survival. When they were given the chance to read the Bible themselves, they started to understand that the lifestyle and the practices of the Church were directly opposed to the word of God. Many people lost belief in the righteousness of the Catholic clergy and even started to view the pope as evil instead of representing God on earth.[14]

The Enlightenment was no less of a shock for many people of the times. The ideas of Montesquieu, Locke and Rousseau undermined old justifications and destroyed the legitimacy of French absolutism. In addition, most farmers in the countryside and many citizens of Paris suffered as a result of a gravely unjust economic order in which a small aristocratic elite enjoyed spending a huge proportion of the wealth of society, whilst the overwhelming majority of the population were living on the breadline. Two-thirds of the rural population had to agree to additional labour on the aristocrats' fields in order to sustain themselves, while a full third suffered outright from starvation, even despite undertaking additional labour.[15]

The fall of the Weimar Republic was likewise introduced by immense progress and, at the same time, new social fragmentation. Refrigerators and radios, cars, planes and trains, and new ideas about basically everything began revolutionising the European world. At the same time, workers and employees were severely hit by hyper-inflation of 1923, and by the global economic crisis of the early 1930s. Many people lost their jobs and their savings, and dropped from experiencing a decent living into poverty and mass unemployment. The young German democracy failed to deliver on the promise of a better economic and social future that had accompanied the revolution of 1918. Frustrated by the incapacity of democracy to fulfil its promise of a better life, a majority of Germans turned their back on it and sought a better future by following either communism or fascism.[16]

It is true that the EU of today knows neither mass starvation nor any social cleavages of the same magnitude as in these historical cases. However, it is not

[14] Very instructive descriptions of the conditions and reasons leading to the fall of Catholic hegemony can be found in T Kaufmann, *Erlöste und Verdammte: Eine Geschichte der Reformation* (Munich, CH Beck, 2017).

[15] For excellent accounts of the French Revolution and the conditions leading up to it, *cf* J Willms, *Tugend und Terror: Geschichte der Französischen Revolution* (Munich, CH Beck, 2014); and E Schulin, *Die Französische Revolution* (Munich, CH Beck, 2004).

[16] Among the best accounts of the history of the Weimar Republic are E Kolb, *Die Weimarer Republik* (Munich, Oldenbourg Wissenschaftsverlag, 2002); A Rosenberg, *Geschichte der Weimarer Republik* (Hamburg, Europäische Verlagsanstalt, 1991); and H-U Wehler, *Deutsche Gesellschaftsgeschichte Bd. 4: Vom Beginn des Ersten Weltkrieges bis zur Gründung der beiden deutschen Staaten 1914–1949* (Munich, CH Beck 2008).

absolute but relative deprivation that motivates people to turn their back on political orders.[17] Just like its historical predecessors, the EU is today subject to a massive modernisation shock, this time constituted by technological innovation and globalisation. And we are again witnessing growing social discrepancies between rich and poor. Even more seriously, the very promise of the open society bringing with it prosperity and a better life for nearly everybody has become challenged. Post-Second World War Europe offered the promise of establishing the open society through a political re-embedding of the economic order.[18] Following the new Keynesian ideas, economics should never again be disembedded from politics, as was the case in the late nineteenth and early twentieth centuries. Social democracy was on the agenda of both moderate conservative and moderate socialist parties.

None of this true any longer. The Mediterranean Member States are facing mass unemployment and there is much talk of a 'lost generation'. Social inequalities are growing in nearly all Member States with a dynamic that is hard to reconcile with the promise of a better future for everybody. In addition, many Europeans today feel overwhelmed by the challenge of having to live up to an ever-faster process of adapting to the digital service economy and to the global division of labour. The success of the radical right in Europe is closely linked to these phenomena. The radical right promises a European world in which the state protects its national citizens from intense competition with other states and people. In the world of right-wing populism, citizens need no longer compete and adapt in order to deserve respect and good standing as a valued fellow. The great seductive potential of right-wing illiberalism lies in the concept of the nation and its implication that one is a decent fellow citizen if one carries the right passport.

B. The Institutional Order

All five cases given above (the four historical cases plus the EU) also show striking similarities in terms of political reaction. We can observe in all five cases a political order in which the most affected concerns are only marginally represented in the most important political institutions of the respective order. The Senate of the Roman Republic, to start with, knew no direct representation of the plebeians and only reacted to their concerns if individual senators identified with their cause. The Roman Republic was ultimately a republic in little more than name and had strong similarities to an aristocracy. The entire political order could only keep its fragile balance as long as the senators exploited their

[17] TR Gurr, *Why Men Rebel* (Princeton, Princeton University Press, 1970).

[18] JG Ruggie. 'International Regimes, Transactions, and Change: Embedded Liberalism in the Postwar Economic Order' (1982) 36 *International Organization* 379.

prominent positions with great self-restraint. After the Roman victory in the Second Punic War and the growing domestic clashes over the question of how to redistribute the conquered land, the self-restraint of the nobility and, following this, political peace broke quickly down. Social and economic concerns transformed into anger and violence.

The close nexus between the structure of representation and accountability on the one hand and the responsiveness of the political order to relevant concerns on the other hand is also obvious in the case of the sixteenth-century Reformation. The most important institution of the Catholic Church in Rome was the College of Cardinals. It was composed of senior ecclesiastical leaders who were all recruited from Italy or, in far lower numbers, from Spain. The cardinals were individually or collectively in charge of managing the important affairs of the Church and, most importantly, of electing the pope. German concerns were hardly represented in this body. Most of the cardinals cared only for their own business in Italy or Spain and perceived the territories north of the Alps as being backward and of very limited importance to their own affairs.

It goes without saying that the France of Louis XVI hardly performed better. Most of the important offices were sold to the nobility, and even the parliaments were for most of the eighteenth century bodies used for rubber stamping the directives of the king rather than sites of active policy-making or even opposition. In eighteenth-century France, the very idea of representation was in open contrast to the self-understanding of the times. The king claimed absolute power and being answerable to God only. Aristocrats partied rather than feeling an obligation to serve the country and its people. Societal grievances and concerns thus had hardly any institution to turn to. The irresponsibility of political institutions was thus firmly institutionalised in the *ancien régime*.

The case of the Weimar Republic is a little more complex. After 1918, Germany was a republic with a full-blown parliament and the rule of law. The government was appointed by the president of the republic, who was voted into office in general elections. However, dealing with the severe social and economic problems of the young German republic was not a matter of domestic policy alone. The Treaty of Versailles stipulated that Germany would have to transfer massive financial resources to the victors of the First World War in order to compensate them for the damage inflicted by its troops during the war. Although the burden imposed on Germany might have been fair and adequate taking into account the damage for which it was responsible, the reparations nevertheless overburdened the republic to the extent that it had no fair chance to meet the social expectations of the poorer parts of its population. The final blow was delivered following the Wall Street Crash in 1929. Although the national financial markets were already highly interdependent, they lacked any mechanism for preventing the spillover of the crisis from one state to the next. Global economic responsibility was still an unknown term and no institution or state was capable and willing to act as a lender of last resort.[19] Germany was severely dependent on foreign capital and was hard hit by the withdrawal of short-term capital. Unemployment skyrocketed in the following months and reached a level of more than 30 per cent in 1931. After having already suffered hyper-inflation and losing most of their savings in 1923, many people lost faith in the young republic and its democratic constitution. Democracy was apparently incapable of preventing millions of people from falling into poverty.

How is responsibility and accountability organised in the EU of today? Is the EU in significantly better shape and more resilient to political contestation? It only requires a quick look to realise that the EU's institutional order is far from convincing. The supranational layer of the EU is composed of a council, a parliament and a bureaucracy (the European Commission). At first glance, it seems to have all the bodies in place that are necessary for responding to the social challenges of Europe. Unfortunately, however, none of these bodies has the competence and the resources to bring about social asymmetries in Europe or only to adopt regulations with that effect. The EU's institutional and legal set-up is designed to foster liberalisation and not social integration.[20] All competences and resources for redistributive social policies are thus reserved for the Member States. Furthermore, the most affected Member States are subject to severe public debts and must comply with the rigid austerity mechanisms imposed by the Maastricht criteria and the European Stability Pact. Germany, as the economically most powerful Member State, insists on full compliance with the criteria. Structural reforms and not additional public expenditure are regarded as the proper means towards full employment and economic recovery. As a consequence, no one in Europe is in charge of meeting the social challenge. The European layer lacks the competences and the resources, the distressed states lack the power and the finances, and Germany lacks the political will to address the economic and social concerns of those most heavily affected by the new cleavages. It is hardly surprising that frustration with liberal Europe nowadays is widespread.

C. Political Culture

Inefficient structures can easily lead to massive frustration with outcomes if accompanied by a political culture that ignores policy deficiencies and even justifies the exclusion of social concerns. This is exactly the case in all of the four

[19] Very instructive analyses of the links between domestic and global politics in the 1930s are CP Kindleberger, *The World in Depression 1929–1939*, 2nd edn (Berkeley, University of California Press, 1986); and B Eichengreen, *Golden Fetters: The Gold Standard and the Great Depression, 1919–1939* (New York, Oxford University Press, 1992).

[20] FW Scharpf, 'Monetary Union, Fiscal Crisis and the Disabling of Democratic Accountability' in A Schäfer and W Streeck (eds), *Politics in the Age of Austerity* (Cambridge, Polity Press, 2013).

examples given in this chapter. Over the course of the second century BC, the Roman patricians lost much of their commitment to traditional Roman values and developed a self-understanding of power entrepreneurs who were responsible only to themselves. Marius, Sulla and, even more so, Pompeiius and Julius Cesar openly misused their public offices for the accumulation of wealth and personal power, without paying proper regard to the well-being of the Republic. When Caesar crossed the Rubicon and marched on Rome, he had no qualms in justifying the beginning of a civil war with personal reasons. He had been insulted by the Senate and was now looking to right a wrong inflicted on him personally. Political entrepreneurs like him were not atypical in those times. Personal glory and wealth became as important as serving the Republic had been 200 years earlier. Greed and striving for personal glory were the widely shared norms of political action.[21]

The self-serving behaviour of the political elite was not a phenomenon limited to the Roman patricians. The infamous Borgia family, which ruled the Catholic Church in the years before the Protestant movement came into being in the early sixteenth century, were similarly caught in a political culture of self-aggrandisement.[22] Machiavelli modelled his 'Principe', the ideal type of ruthless ruler, on the illegitimate son of the Borgia Pope Alexander VI. Cesare Borgia was famous for his many love affairs, for poisoning his opponents and for using all means available to expand the territory of the Roman Church. Serving their flock meant nothing more to the popes of the late fifteenth and the early sixteenth centuries than to increase their individual power and wealth, to expand the territory of the Vatican and to invest in new monuments that would impress their followers.

The French aristocracy of the eighteenth century was probably less ruthless but hardly less self-interested. The political culture of the elite was heavily influenced by the experience of the bloody civil wars of the sixteenth century and the ideas of Jean Bodin. In order to provide for a peaceful domestic order, Bodin argued that it was of the utmost importance that the king possessed absolute power. His legitimacy thus stemmed not from fair and equal representation or from social harmony, but from the establishment and enforcement of a monopoly of power. Thus, the king could not be subjected to any political scrutiny by his subjects, but was next to God and was answerable only to Him rather than any worldly body, person or group. It was clear that the very ideas of the Enlightenment, such as Montesquieu's suggestion that the spirit of all laws would have to be found in their contribution to a more reasonable society, were on an open collision course with the self-understanding of the king and his elite.

[21] 'Because of wealth, therefore, luxury and greed seized the youth: they gathered and consumed, did not treat their own carefully and desired foreign goods, shame and consideration, the divine and the human were the same to them, and measure and responsibility were foreign to them.' Sallust, Cat. 10,1–12,5, printed in K Bringmann, *Krise und Ende der römischen Republik* (Berlin, Akademie Verlag, 2003) 100–01.

[22] *cf* GJ Meyer *The Borgias: The Hidden History* (New York, Bantam Books, 2014).

The political culture of the Weimar Republic was no more helpful in overcoming the institutional deficiencies of the interwar order. From the very beginning, neither the communists and the socialists on the left of the political spectrum nor the monarchists on the right were on peaceful terms with the new democratic order. The left was dissatisfied with the meagre progress in terms of socialising big corporations and democratising the economy. On the right side of the political spectrum, the old gentry worked hard for the re-establishment of authoritarian rule and accepted the republican order only as long as the alternative was politically unfeasible. In this political climate of latent civil war among the opposing political factions, it was extremely hard to establish a political coalition that was strong enough to negotiate a politically and economically sustainable compromise with Germany's former enemies: France and the UK. France in particular was too afraid of a resurrection of German military power to relinquish the German reparations and to unconditionally withdraw its troops from German soil. In this complex combination of revenge, retaliation and incompatible ideas on the future of Germany, the German left and right were set on a collision course that left little room for the pragmatism necessary to prevent the fall of democracy.

There can be no doubt that the current European political elite is far less self-obsessed, greedy and ruthless than its historical predecessors. We can assume that the vast majority of European politicians today share a firm commitment to democratic principles and a belief in the rule of law. However, the EU's political culture is not too helpful in terms of compensating the institutional deficiencies of the European political order. The two most important bodies of the EU, the European Council and the Council of the EU, are composed of the heads of state, prime ministers and ministers of the Member States. They are accountable to national constituencies only and are firmly embedded in national political cultures, routines and perceptions of problem. A truly European political culture is thus hard to find in Brussels. As a consequence, all political discourse is centred on catering to the domestic interests of Member States and lacks the necessary identification with the integration process. European bureaucrats in the European Commission do not do much better. Although they often have a strong attachment to the integration project, they perceive themselves as 'guardians of the treaties' rather than political entrepreneurs. It is not any grand idea of developing the EU towards a truly political community, but the much more modest administration of the market that gives the Commission and its bureaucrats its identity.

We know today that neither the Roman Republic nor the Catholic hegemony, the French *ancien régime* or the Weimar Republic survived their institutional deficiencies and the ignorant political culture of their respective elites. The political cleavage between the Optimates and the Populares in Rome turned from competition into conflict and then into violence. It only ended after 100 years of civil war with the election of an emperor and the constitutionalisation of an openly authoritarian order. Likewise, the reform-oriented grievances of the early critiques of the Roman Church turned into a full-blown attack on the legitimacy of the pope, violent uprisings in many territories of the Holy Roman Empire and finally the consolidation of the new Protestant religion. The French *ancien régime* died under the guillotine and the Weimar Republic fell prey to Nazi fascism. All four cases are thus clear examples of modernisation shocks leading to social grievances that collided with irresponsible institutions and an ignorant political class. We can learn from all four cases that political orders trying to block change and to protect the status quo from necessary adaptations to social challenges will find it difficult to survive. The only thing that is constant in the course of history is change itself.

D. The Short-Sightedness of Policy-Making

This insight is common knowledge for most students of history. Early reforms might have spared the Roman Republic 100 years of civil war if the senators had only accepted thorough agricultural reform and a sharing of power with the people of Rome. The Catholic Church might still dominate European Christianity if it had refrained from building St Peter's Basilica and if Martin Luther and his followers had had no reason to object to the practices of selling indulgences. The German Weimar Republic might still exist if Chancellor Heinrich Brüning had opted for new social programmes and policies aimed at alleviating poverty and unemployment. None of this has happened. Why not? Why is it that political elites time and again so stubbornly refuse to implement the necessary reforms?

Policy conservatism and stubbornness are surely not related to lacking theoretical knowledge. The Roman senators of the first and second centuries BC and the popes of the fifteenth and sixteenth centuries were highly educated individuals. Likewise, Louis XV and Louis XVI knew of the social grievances and the mounting protests on the streets. All of them had access to the writings of philosophers and historians and the brightest scholars of the times. A more convincing reason for the foot-dragging of political elites than to assume simply foolishness[23] is provided by the fact that broad social reforms imply giving a voice to the marginalised and accepting the legitimacy of their cause. However, legitimacy opens the gates to participation in politics and thus easily leads to a reorganisation of authority and a loss of power of the ruling elite. If an elite is more focused on its personal power position than on the stability of the system as such, policies with a long-term rationality are obviously hard to implement. If they are perceived by the members of the ruling elite as undermining their individual positions, then they will most likely meet with open hostility.

[23] B Tuchman, *The March of Folly: From Troy to Vietnam* (New York, Knopf, 1984).

The inherent conservatism of ruling elites is a most important reason for the unlikeliness of major social reforms. A fair redistribution of land would have challenged the economic dominance of the Roman patricians. Similarly, the building of St Peter's Basilica was important in terms of providing the clients of the pope with resources and jobs, and the reforms of Turgot were perceived by the ruling French aristocracy as a step towards a new post-aristocratic regime. The same applies to policy change in the case of the Weimar Republic. Expansive social policy in the early 1930s would have meant confronting the French government's insistence on additional reparations Only a rather empathetic approach by the French government to its eastern neighbour would have prevented a new major international crisis. None of this was likely. All four examples highlight that the politically wise decision is often impossible to implement. Political orders do not fall for reasons that are unintelligible to the people of the times, but because of the constraints under which policy-making is conducted. Political short-term rationality and reasonable long-term policy-making often diverge sharply. Reforms remain unimplemented because they threaten to undermine the position of a ruling class. It is for this very reason that thorough reforms are often implemented only after a political order has been brought down and a new ruling class with a new constituency has come to power. There is much truth in the saying that no real social change has ever been brought about without a revolution.

Here again we can draw a number of striking similarities to the EU of today. Social cleavages grow in nearly all Member States, the financial straitjacket of the European Monetary Union (EMU) is causing mass unemployment in many Mediterranean Member States and the political order is heavily biased towards the governments of the Member States. This openly deficient state of the EU notwithstanding, we find hardly any voices promoting the necessary reforms. The recent reflections of the French President Emmanuel Macron to work towards a more balanced European social order and to reorganise the eurozone accordingly are being met with only very limited German enthusiasm. A European social policy or only the lowering of the discipline imposed by European austerity measures is not politically feasible in Germany. The ruling parties in Germany fear open protest from a significant number of their citizens if they were to use German taxpayers' money to support the Italian, Greek or Spanish economy, which is, in the eyes of many Germans, run by inefficient political parties and non-competitive economic structures.

III. A MORE SUSTAINABLE EUROPE

Europe is in urgent need of major reforms if it is to withstand the illiberal seduction of the Front National, the Alternative für Deutschland and of all the other new right-wing parties. It must overcome its one-sided economic bias and rediscover the social sensibility so necessary for long-term stability. Europe must become familiar again with an idea of liberalism that goes beyond market-making and the promotion of the four freedoms, and that is centred on the idea of social democracy. It is an idea of liberalism that is very much in line with liberal thinkers such as John Rawls, Amartya Sen and Martha Nussbaum. All three conceptualise the market as an instrument for the good society, ie, a social structure that pursues ethical goals. According to Rawls, social inequality is only just if and when it works to the benefit of the weakest in any given society.[24] Policies must not only be oriented towards maximising aggregate gross domestic product (GDP), but must also have a close eye on distributional implications. Europe can only be just if it produces fair outcomes. Europe can and also should learn from Amartya Sen. According to Sen, development should be understood as empowering citizens to develop their full individual potential.[25] Any society that supports exclusionary structures and that keeps citizens away from participating in the governance and culture of society is unjust. On the contrary, an active state is necessary which implements programmes aimed at broadening participation and social coherence. Finally, Europe will go a long way towards institutionalising a sustainable interpretation of liberalism if it integrates the suggestion by Martha Nussbaum that the weaker have a right to be at the centre of state policy and that the social cleavages in society are the most important obstacles on the way towards achieving a good society.[26]

Europe has to engage in a major overhaul of its political system if it is to take these suggestions seriously and if it accepts that only an economically balanced society is a politically sustainable society. The prevalent system of organised unaccountability needs to be overcome and replaced by a proper parliamentarian system allocating clear responsibilities and a competent centre of political authority.[27] The European political order of today is characterised by fragmented political authority and severe disempowerment of political competence. It has no single European political space, but must coordinate the political spaces of 28 Member States. Politics is thus too often driven by the domestic concerns of Member States and only rarely addresses European problems first. The outcome of this dysfunctional constitutional set-up is policy stagnation and organised irresponsibility. In the past, the architects of the European political order invested all of their optimism in the emergence of a European media and newspapers and the idea that a European public space would grow from the bottom up. We know today that this hope was futile. Citizens will not redirect their attention from the national to the European plane as long as the most important centres of political authority remain in the Member States. The only

[24] J Rawls, *Political Liberalism* (New York, Columbia University Press, 2005).

[25] A Sen, *The Idea of Justice* (New York, Belknap Press, 2009).

[26] M Nussbaum, *Frontiers of Justice: Disability, Nationality, Species Membership* (Cambridge, MA, Harvard University Press, 2006).

[27] J Neyer, 'Justified Multi-level Parliamentarism: Situating National Parliaments in the European Polity' (2014) 20(1) *Journal of Legislative Studies* 125.

convincing way to overcome the fragmentation of the European public space and for the establishment of a common site for the exchange of opinions, the shaping of preferences and, ultimately, the adoption of decisions is to empower the European Parliament.[28] If the European Parliament had the right to vote for a European government and to re-allocate resources from the wealthy to the needy, it would surely attract more public awareness. It would become the central site of a newly emerging European democracy with a fair chance to move beyond the mere administration of the common market. Europe needs a parliament with the right to adopt its own agenda, to initiate legislation and to decide on the levying and spending of taxes. Otherwise, it will remain stuck in its international past and will find it impossible to tackle and solve the problems that threaten the future of the EU.

The most pressing task for the new European Parliament is to free Europe from its outdated neoliberalism and to push the EU towards social democracy. The apolitical autonomy of the European Stability Mechanism and of the European Central Bank is anachronistic. This reflects a political strategy of policy insulation, shielding political decisions from parliamentary scrutiny. It imposes close budgetary discipline on national parliaments and runs contrary to any meaningful notion of parliamentary democracy. No less important, the legal codification of the Maastricht criteria straitjackets all Member States by forcing them to apply financial austerity policies with very limited positive effects for those who are already negatively affected by the social pressure of economic liberalisation.[29]

In order to counter social fragmentation and establish a meaningful counter-force to illiberalism, Europe needs a very different policy. It must take significant steps towards a European-wide redistributive scheme that supports those Member States that are incapable of implementing the structural reforms necessary for competing with the Member States in Northern Europe. Europe must come to accept that the idea of market forces pushing all Member States towards realising the same degree of competitiveness is a myth and will never become a reality. Greece and Sweden will not become similar countries in the foreseeable future. A sustainable common currency will thus need long-term financial flows from the more competitive to the less competitive Member States. The best option for implementing such an equalisation scheme would be the introduction of a form of European unemployment insurance.[30] The great advantage of this over direct transfers among the Member States would be to send a clear signal to all those negatively affected by Europeanisation that the

[28] B Crum, 'Parliamentary Accountability in Multilevel Governance: What Role for Parliaments in Post-crisis EU Economic Governance?' (2018) 25(2) *Journal of European Public Policy* 268.

[29] W Streeck, 'The Rise of the European Consolidation State' in H Magara (ed) *Policy Change under New Democratic Capitalism* (New York, Routledge, 2017).

[30] F Fichtner and P Haan, 'European Unemployment Insurance: Economic Stability without Major Redistribution of Household Incomes' (2014) 10 *DIW Economic Bulletin* 39.

EU cares for them. A form of European unemployment insurance would not support Member States' budgets, but would be built on direct transfers between the EU and those eligible. It would thus combine international financial equalisation with a clear signal to those who are for good reasons in opposition to unfettered liberalisation.

IV. THE INDISPENSABLE NATION – AND ITS RESPONSIBILITY

None of this will happen if it is not introduced or at least supported by Germany. Germany has become the uncontested leading nation of Europe. This was already the case in the EU of 28 Member States and will be even more so the case after Brexit. In the past, Germany has had a rather limited understanding of its role in Europe. It often covered the financial bill of additional steps of integration, but refrained from demanding a leading political role. However, what was good and important in the past is insufficient today. No major social policy initiatives will be launched and no redistributive scheme will be implemented if it is not supported by Germany and adopted by the German Bundestag. Neither the European Parliament nor the Council will take the lead in important decisions that are not coordinated with the German government or its ruling party. Already back in 2011, the former Polish Foreign Minister Radosław Sikorski called Germany the 'indispensable nation' of Europe. He was the probably the first Polish foreign minister who had good reasons to be more afraid of German inactivity than of German power.

A German government transforming its special responsibility for the integration process into an understanding of its European role as one of 'servant leadership'[31] is needed today. It should actively develop policy initiatives, lead Europe and get over with its past as a kind of oversized Switzerland. The proper role for the new Germany would be to trust its own ambitions and to design a post-crisis Europe. It should follow a policy which serves European and not national interests by investing in long-term policies that foster further integration. It is probably true that any German government living up to the standard of servant leadership and trying to finance redistributive European projects using German taxpayers' money would face an uphill struggle in doing so. Financial redistribution in favour of Mediterranean Member States is anything but popular in Germany. Majorities would thus be hard to organise and the project would most likely be opposed by a number of parties and even members of the ruling Christian Democratic Union (CDU). However, the same was true for many of the past reform projects that have never been realised. The French government in the late 1920s did not fight in the Assemblée Nationale

[31] L Mangasarian and J Techau, *Führungsmacht Deutschland: Strategie ohne Angst und Anmaßung* (Munich, dtv Verlagsgesellschaft, 2017).

for a moratorium on German reparations and stood by watching as the Weimar Republic went down. Pope Alexander VI insisted on building St Peter's Basilica and selling indulgences in Germany, and had to face growing Protestant opposition and finally the end of Catholic hegemony in Northern Europe. Louis XVI fired his reform minister Turgot due to growing aristocratic opposition and missed the probably last chance of the *ancien régime* to survive the growing social unrest in France.

It is one of the great tragedies of past European political orders that prudent policy is often in sharp contrast to the preferences of the ruling elite. The necessary and the easy often diverged sharply. It is here where political leadership is faced with its true challenge: to enact the right policies even if majorities reject them and to be ready to sacrifice one's own political future for the sake of the common good. One can only wish that the new German government will be strong and ambitious enough to meet this challenge and to revitalise the European promise of a better political future. Accepting leadership in Europe and transforming European market liberalism into social liberalism would be the proper policy resulting from the lessons of the past.

REFERENCES

Acemoglu, S and Robinson, JA, *Why Nations Fail: The Origins of Power, Prosperity, and Poverty* (New York, Crown Publishers, 2012).

Bringmann, K, *Krise und Ende der römischen Republik* (Berlin, Akademie Verlag, 2003).

Bovens, M, Curtin, D and t'Hart, P, *The Real World of EU Accountability: What Deficit?* (Oxford, Oxford University Press, 2010).

Castells, M, *End of Millennium*, 2nd edn, in *The Information Age: Economy, Society, and Culture Volume III* (Oxford, Wiley-Blackwell, 2010).

Diamond, J, *Collapse: How Societies Choose to Fail or Succeed* (New York, Viking Press, 2005).

Eichengreen, B, *Golden Fetters: The Gold Standard and the Great Depression, 1919–1939* (New York, Oxford University Press, 1992).

Fischer, H, *Digital Shock: Confronting the New Reality* (Montreal, McGill-Queen's University Press, 2006).

Fisher, J and Smeeding, TM, 'Income Inequality' (2016) *State of the Union: The Poverty and Inequality Report*, Stanford Centre on Poverty and Inequality 32.

Grimm, D, *The Constitution of European Democracy* (Oxford, Oxford University Press, 2017).

Gurr, TR, *Why Men Rebel* (Princeton, Princeton University Press, 1970).

Hodson, D and Puetter, U, 'Studying Europe after the Fall' (2018) 25 *Journal of European Public Policy* 465.

Jones, E, 'Towards A Theory of Disintegration' (2018) 25 *Journal of European Public Policy* 440.

Kaufmann, T, *Erlöste und Verdammte: Eine Geschichte der Reformation* (Munich, CH Beck, 2017).

Kindleberger, CP, *The World in Depression 1929–1939*, 2nd edn (Berkeley, University of California Press, 1986).
Kolb, E, *Die Weimarer Republik* (Munich, Oldenbourg Wissenschaftsverlag, 2002).
Krastev, I, *After Europe* (Philadelphia, University of Pennsylvania Press, 2017).
Manent, P, 'The Crisis of Liberalism' (2014) 25 *Journal of Democracy* 131.
Mangasarian, L and Techau, J, *Führungsmacht Deutschland: Strategie ohne Angst und Anmaßung* (Munich, dtv Verlagsgesellschaft, 2017).
Meyer, GJ, *The Borgias: The Hidden History* (New York, Bantam Books, 2014).
Milanovic, B, *Global Inequality: A New Approach for the Age of Globalization* (Cambridge, MA, Belknap Press of Harvard University Press 2016).
Mudde, C, 'Europe's Populist Surge: A Long Time in the Making' (2016) 95 *Foreign Affairs* 25.
Nussbaum, M, *Frontiers of Justice: Disability, Nationality, Species Membership* (Cambridge, MA, Harvard University Press, 2006).
Offe, C, *Europe Entrapped* (Cambridge, Polity Press, 2015).
Papadopoulos, Y, 'Accountability and Multi-level Governance: More Accountability, Less Democracy?' (2010) 33 *West European Politics* 1030.
Rawls, J, *Political Liberalism* (New York, Columbia University Press, 2005).
Rosenberg, A, *Geschichte der Weimarer Republik* (Hamburg, Europäische Verlagsanstalt, 1991).
Ruggie, JG, 'International Regimes, Transactions, and Change: Embedded Liberalism in the Postwar Economic Order' (1982) 36 *International Organization* 379.
Scharpf, FW, 'A Curtain of Gloom is Descending on the Continent: Capitalism, Democracy and Europe' (2017) 23 *European Law Journal* 335.
Schulin, E, *Die Französische Revolution* (Munich, CH Beck, 2004).
Sen, A, *The Idea of Justice* (New York, Belknap Press, 2009).
Skocpol, T, *States and Social Revolutions: A Comparative Analysis of France, Russia and China* (Cambridge, Cambridge University Press, 1979).
Tuchman, B, *The March of Folly: From Troy to Vietnam* (New York, Knopf, 1984).
Vollard, H, 'Explaining European Disintegration' (2014) 52 *Journal of Common Market Studies* 1142.
Walker, I and Smith, HJ, *Relative Deprivation: Specification, Development, and Integration* (Cambridge, Cambridge University Press, 2001).
Wehler, H-U, *Deutsche Gesellschaftsgeschichte Bd. 4: Vom Beginn des Ersten Weltkrieges bis zur Gründung der beiden deutschen Staaten 1914–1949* (Munich, CH Beck, 2008).
Willms, J, *Tugend und Terror: Geschichte der Französischen Revolution* (Munich, CH Beck, 2014).
Wodak, R, Khosravinik, M and Mral, B, *Right-Wing Populism in Europe: Politics and Discourse* (London, Bloomsbury Press, 2013).

2

The EU, Democracy and Institutional Structure

Past, Present and Future

PAUL CRAIG

I. INTRODUCTION

IT IS COMMONPLACE to bemoan the EU's democratic deficiencies, as attested to by the wealth of literature discussing the issue from a variety of perspectives. This chapter is not a literature review. On the contrary, it advances my own view on the issue, albeit one that is informed by existing scholarship. The ensuing analysis is predicated on the assumption that a principal, albeit not exclusive, cause for concern about EU democracy is the mismatch, or absence of fit, between voter power and political responsibility.

EU decision-making is structured in such a way that voters cannot determine the shape or direction of EU policy in the manner that occurs to a greater extent within Member States. Therefore, it is not possible in the EU for the electorate to remove the incumbents from office and replace them with a different political party that has a different set of policies. It is this malaise that underlies Weiler's critique of EU decision-making, captured in aphorismic terms by his affirmation of the centrality to democracy of the voters' ability to 'throw the scoundrels out'.[1] It is the same malaise that informs Maduro's critique, to the effect that the 'real EU democratic deficit is the absence of European politics',[2]

[1] JHH Weiler, U Haltern and F Mayer, 'European Democracy and its Critique' in J Hayward (ed), *The Crisis of Representation in Europe* (London, Frank Cass, 1995); JHH Weiler, 'Europe in Crisis – on "Political Messianism", "Legitimacy" and the "Rule of Law"' [2012] *Singapore Journal of Legal Studies* 248.

[2] M Maduro, 'A New Governance for the European Union and the Euro: Democracy and Justice' (2012) 11 *RSCAS Policy Paper* 1.

manifest in the lack of democratic political contestation about the content and direction of EU policy. Properly understood, these are but two sides of the same coin.

The ensuing discussion takes the same starting point as Weiler and Maduro. However, the direction of travel thereafter is rather different, insofar as we are concerned with an explanation and understanding of the status quo. The assumption, explicit or implicit, in much of the literature is that the fault for this malaise resides with the EU. The pattern of thought seems strikingly simple, shaped by the very cadence of language. This is most marked in the duality of meaning accorded to the phrase 'the EU's democratic deficit', which is used descriptively to capture the malaise adumbrated above and is deployed normatively to connote the fact that the fault resides with the EU, which is regarded as architect and author of the present reality.

The academic line of argument pursued thereafter flows naturally from the preceding duality of meaning. Given that the democratic shortcoming resides descriptively and normatively with the EU, democracy must therefore remain in the Member States, which are said to be the principal sites for democratic legitimation. Some of the literature on 'demoicracy' is grounded, in part at least, on such assumptions. The discussion that follows takes issue with this descriptive and normative link, and hence with the conclusions drawn therefrom.

It will be argued that the preceding link does not withstand examination. Insofar as there is a democratic deficit of the kind identified above, it flows from choices made expressly and repeatedly by the Member States over time as to the institutional structure for decision-making which they are willing to accept. These choices could have been different. There is no a priori block in this respect. On the contrary, there is no especial difficulty in devising an EU decision-making regime that would meet the democratic shortcomings outlined above. The EU itself is not blameless with respect to the mode of decision-making and nothing in the present chapter is predicated on that assumption. Improvements could doubtless be made in terms of the manner in which the principal EU institutions operate. This does not alter the fact that that the Treaty architecture that frames their respective powers, and the way in which they inter-relate, is the result of Member State choice, made and remade since the inception of the Community.

However, it will also be argued that there are four constraints to a fit between the EU's institutional decision-making structure and the precepts of democracy. The constraints are political, democratic, constitutional and substantive. The *political* constraint is predicated on the assumption that some form of parliamentary majoritarian regime would meet the democratic deficit articulated above, thereby ensuring a closer nexus between voter preferences and political responsibility. Yet, change of the kind that would meet the democratic infirmity thus conceived is very unlikely to occur, because the Member States will not accept it for the reasons explicated below. The *democratic* constraint is expressive of the fact that there is contestation as to whether such a parliamentary-type regime really is the most appropriate model for a polity such as the EU or whether a different form of democratic ordering would be better suited. The *constitutional* constraint denotes the fact that EU decision-making is limited by the very nature of the constituent Treaties. National constitutions constrain political choice. It is inherent in their very nature. The EU is no different in this respect in principle, in the sense that the founding Treaties form the architecture to which legislation made thereunder must conform. The difference is one of degree, but it is significant nonetheless, since the EU Treaties are far more detailed than any national constitution and hence the room for democratic policy choice is more circumscribed. The *substantive* constraint speaks to the democratic consequences of the imbalance between the economic and the social within the EU, as manifest in the original Treaties, and as a consequence of the EU's financial crisis.

II. INSTITUTIONAL STRUCTURE AND DEMOCRACY: THE PAST

The Community may only be 60 years old, but it is nonetheless easy to forget its institutional origins and the conception of democracy that existed (or not as the case may be) at the outset. The reality was that the original disposition of power in the Treaty of Rome saw little role for direct democratic input. The Assembly was accorded limited power and its only role in the legislative process was a right to be consulted where a particular Treaty article so specified. The principal institutional players were the Council and the Commission, but in many respects the Treaty of Rome placed the Commission in the driving seat in the development of Community policy. The Commission had the right of legislative initiative; it could alter a measure before the Council acted; its measurers could only be amended by unanimity in the Council;[3] it devised the overall legislative agenda; and it had a plethora of other executive, administrative and judicial functions. The message was that while the Council had to consent to proposed legislation, it was not easy for it to alter the Commission's proposal. The Commission might therefore have become something akin to a 'government' for the emerging Community.[4]

This vision accorded with, and was influenced by, Monnet's vision of Europe and by neofunctionalism. Monnet's conception of Europe was strongly influenced by the role of technocrats trained in the French Grands Ecoles. It served to explain the structure of the European Coal and Steel Community (ECSC), and the centrality of the High Authority therein, which embodied Monnet's technocratic approach. A corporatist style involving networks of interest groups was

[3] Article 250(1) EC.

[4] K Neunreither, 'Transformation of a Political Role: Reconsidering the Case of the Commission of the European Communities' (1971–72) 10 *Journal of Common Market Studies* 233.

the other legacy of Monnet's experience with planning authorities in France.[5] It was institutionalised in the ECSC in the form of the Consultative Committee. Integration was based on the combination of benevolent technocrats and economic interest groups, which would build transnational coalitions for European policy.[6] Monnet's strategy was thus for what has been termed elite-led gradualism.[7] The Assembly's powers within the ECSC were very limited.

The same general institutional structure was to be carried over to the European Economic Community (EEC): 'enlightened administration on behalf of uninformed publics, in cooperation with affected interests and subject to the approval of national governments, was therefore the compromise again struck in the Treaties of Rome'.[8] While Monnet favoured a democratic Community, 'he saw the emergence of loyalties to the Community institutions developing as a *consequence* of elite agreements for the functional organization of Europe, not as an essential *prerequisite* to that organization' (italics in original).[9]

Neofunctionalism was to be the vehicle through which Community integration, conceived of as technocratic, elite-led gradualism, combined with corporatist style engagement of affected interests, was to be realised. Neofunctionalism fitted neatly with Monnet's perception of the Community. Monnet and neofunctionalists also shared the same sense of legitimacy and democracy. For Monnet, and like-minded followers, the legitimacy of the Community was to be secured through outcomes, peace and prosperity. The ECSC was established in part to prevent a third European war. The EEC was created in large part for the direct economic benefits of a common market. Peace and prosperity were potent benefits for the people in the 1950s. Democracy was, by way of contrast, a secondary consideration, since it was felt that the best way to secure peace and prosperity was through technocratic elite-led guidance.

III. INSTITUTIONAL STRUCTURE AND DEMOCRACY: THE PRESENT

Prognostication as to the future is perilous at the best of times, more especially so in relation to an institution such as the EU. Exogenous shocks external to the EU, which are unforeseen and unforeseeable, can shatter the very best reasoned predictions. In a similar vein, endogenous change from within the EU can disrupt future visions that would otherwise be plausibly grounded, as attested to by the Catalonia problem in Spain, and electoral change in the Czech Republic,

[5] K Featherstone, 'Jean Monnet and the "Democratic Deficit" in the European Union' (1994) 32 *Journal of Common Market Studies* 149, 154–55.

[6] H Wallace, 'European Governance in Turbulent Times' (1993) 31 *Journal of Common Market Studies* 293, 300.

[7] W Wallace and J Smith, 'Democracy or Technocracy? European Integration and the Problem of Popular Consent' in Hayward (n 1) 140.

[8] ibid 143.

[9] M Holland, *European Community Integration* (New York, St Martin's Press, 1993) 16.

Austria and Italy in the legislative elections of 2017–18. While prediction is therefore fraught with difficulty, a necessary condition for any such exercise is to be cognisant of the rationale for the status quo. To forget the lessons of history is to invite the repetition of past mistakes or to predicate views as to future institutional change on assumptions that are unsustainable when viewed in historical perspective. The significance of this will be apparent in the ensuing discussion, which is premised on the institutional disposition of power that currently prevails.

Space constraints preclude a detailed analysis of the passage from the initial institutional division of power in the Treaty of Rome to the schema embodied in the Treaty of Lisbon.[10] Readers will be familiar with this and reference will be made to it in the subsequent analysis. Suffice it to say for the present that the European Parliament (EP) increased its power within the decision-making process. This occurred initially through the cooperation procedure, introduced by the Single European Act 1986, and then through the co-decision procedure in the Maastricht Treaty, as further strengthened by the Amsterdam Treaty. The EP attained something approximating co-equal status in the legislative process with the Council, as later recognised by the Treaty of Lisbon.[11] The European Council, as the ultimate repository of Member State power, also came to exercise an ever-increasing role in the decision-making process, both de facto and de jure, which was affirmed and strengthened in the Treaty of Lisbon.[12] The legal and political reality, as reflected in the Treaty of Lisbon, was an institutional decision-making process in which state interests still predominated and in which, notwithstanding the increase in the EP's power, the voters could not directly affect a change of policy direction in the EU by removing the incumbents and replacing them with those espousing different policies.

The Brexit discourse was conducted explicitly against the status quo and implicitly against assumptions concerning ascription of responsibility for the existing schema. Thus, the ills of the EU, whatsoever they might currently be, were conceived to be the responsibility of the EU, viewed in this respect primarily (but not solely) as the Commission, together with other 'powers' in Brussels. This is a great story, save for the fact that it bears little relation to reality. What is missing is considered discourse concerning the constitutional responsibility of the Member States for the status quo.

This is readily apparent in relation to the inter-institutional division of power within the EU. It is commonly acknowledged that the democratic deficit is a prominent feature of the EU's legitimacy problem, with the attendant implication, as noted in section I above, that it is not just a problem that besets the EU, but is the EU's fault. It is the EU qua real and reified entity that suffers from

[10] P Craig, 'Institutions, Power and Institutional Balance' in P Craig and G de Búrca (eds), *The Evolution of EU Law*, 2nd edn (Oxford, Oxford University Press, 2011) ch 3.

[11] Articles 14(1) and 16(1) of the Treaty on European Union [2007] OJ C306/1 (TEU).

[12] ibid art 15.

this infirmity, the corollary being that blame is cast on it. The EU is not blameless in this respect, but nor are the Member States, viewed collectively or individually. This is not to deny the existence of problems in this regard, the disjunction between political power and electoral accountability being an important facet of the democracy deficit argument.[13]

The issue is who bears responsibility for the status quo. This is all the more surprising given the sophisticated literature from international relations and political science concerning the relative influences of different players during periods of Treaty change, as well as in relation to the passage of EU legislation. The facts are not readily contestable, at least in relation to Treaty amendment. The stark reality is that the present disposition of EU institutional power is the result of successive Treaties in which the principal players have been the Member States. There may well be debate as to the relative degree of power wielded by Member States and the EU institutions in the shaping of EU legislation, but there is greater consensus on the fact that Member States have dominated at times of Treaty reform.[14]

Thus, insofar as the present arrangements divide EU policy-making both de facto and de jure between the Commission, Council, European Parliament and European Council, this is reflective of power balances that the Member States were willing to accept. This is readily apparent when considering the initial Treaty of Rome and any of the five major Treaty reforms since then. It is powerfully exemplified by the debates concerning institutional reforms in the Constitutional Treaty, which were taken over into the Treaty of Lisbon.[15] It was evident most notably in the battle as to whether the EU should have a single President who would be located in the Commission or whether a reinforced European Council should also have a long-term President.[16] It was apparent in

[13] Weiler, Haltern and Mayer (n 1); A Follesdal and S Hix, 'Why There is a Democratic Deficit in the EU: A Response to Majone and Moravcsik' (2006) 44 *Journal of Common Market Studies* 533; K Nicolaïdis, 'The Idea of European Demoicracy' in J Dickson and P Eleftheriadis (eds), *Philosophical Foundations of EU Law* (Oxford, Oxford University Press, 2012); K Nicolaïdis, 'Our European Demoi-cracy: Is this Constitution a Third Way for Europe?' in K Nicolaïdis and S Weatherill (eds), *Whose Europe? National Models and the Constitution of the European Union* (Oxford, Oxford University Press, 2003).

[14] G Marks, L Hooghe and K Blank, 'European Integration from the 1980s: State-Centric v Multiple-Level Governance' (1996) 34 *Journal of Common Market Studies* 341, 342; T Risse-Kappen, 'Exploring the Nature of the Beast: International Relations Theory and Comparative Policy Analysis Meet the European Union' (1996) 34 *Journal of Common Market Studies* 53; A Moravcsik, 'Preferences and Power in the European Community: A Liberal Intergovernmentalist Approach' (1993) 31 *Journal of Common Market Studies* 473; A Moravcsik, *National Preference Formation and Interstate Bargaining in the European Community, 1955–86* (Cambridge, MA, Harvard University Press, 1992); A Moravcsik, 'Negotiating the Single European Act: National Interests and Conventional Statecraft in the European Community' (1991) 45 *International Organization* 19; M Pollack, 'International Relations Theory and European Integration' *EUI Working Papers*, RSC 2000/55.

[15] P Norman, *The Accidental Constitution, The Making of Europe's Constitutional Treaty* 2nd edn (Brussels, EuroComment, 2005).

[16] P Craig, *The Lisbon Treaty: Law, Politics and Treaty Reform* (Oxford, Oxford University Press, 2010) ch 3.

the debates as to Council configurations and who would chair them. It was the frame within which the discourse took place concerning the number of Commissioners and the method of choosing them.

If blame is to be cast for the institutional status quo and for its democratic shortcomings, then it should principally be laid at the door of the creators of the scheme, the Member States, who must bear, both individually and collectively, constitutional responsibility for the status quo. The EU institutional disposition of power was the Member States' choice, which was made and reaffirmed over half a century. It was not foisted on them and it was not a fait accompli in relation to which they had no input. On the contrary, the Member States were, and remain, the institutional architects of the status quo.

IV. INSTITUTIONAL STRUCTURE AND DEMOCRACY: THE FUTURE – FOUR CONSTRAINTS

The preceding backdrop is a necessary condition for making plausible suggestions concerning the future disposition of inter-institutional power in the EU. It might be argued that reforms could alleviate the existing democratic disjunction between electoral power and political responsibility, and that the change whereby the Commission President was indirectly elected by reason of being the candidate of the party that secured most seats in the EP is a natural pointer in this direction. This could provide the foundation for true democratic contestation, whereby voters would be offered alternative political agendas for the EU, and their votes would truly determine the policy path for the next five years.

This could in theory happen. There are a range of democratic solutions available. It does not require some new masterplan of arrangements hitherto unknown to the world of democratic political architecture. A pretty detailed schema, premised on some form of parliamentary democratic regime, could be sketched out. Thus, to take one possible way forward, it would be possible to have a regime in which the people voted directly for two constituent parts of the legislature (the European Parliament and the European Council) and for the President of the Commission and the President of the European Council. It would be possible in theory to have the previous package, but only a single elected President for the EU as whole. It would be possible for the entire Commission to be reflective of the majority party in the EP and not just the President of the Commission. It would be possible for the EP to have a right of legislative initiative in tandem with that of the Commission. It is possible to devise such a schema with conditions devised to protect against the undesirable consequences of majoritarianism. The link between electoral power, substantive policy choice and accountability would be more visible and would be strengthened. There are necessary qualifications to this type of model, which will be addressed in section IV.B below, but it provides a useful starting point for discussion.

A. Political Constraints

i. Member States

The principal reason why nothing akin to the preceding model is likely to occur is that Member States are the main architects of Treaty change and they have never been willing to accept such a disposition of power. We must, as noted above, remember the past when planning the future. It is true that the choice between two Presidents and a single President for the EU was debated during the negotiations leading to the Constitutional Treaty. It is equally true that discourse concerning the election of the Commission President began in the 1980s. However, the broader reforms adumbrated above were not on the political agenda during the extensive negotiations concerning institutional power in 2003–4 that led to the Constitutional Treaty or in the subsequent discussions that culminated in the Treaty of Lisbon.

The reason why nothing akin to the preceding model has ever appeared in formal discussion of Treaty reform is not hard to divine. The Member States would lose power in relative and absolute terms. They would no longer be masters of the Treaty. The preceding model, or something akin thereto, would alleviate the democratic deficit as conceived in the preceding sense, but in doing so it would endow the elected majority in the EP, and the duly elected Presidents of the Commission and European Council, with a mandate and an authority to discharge the promised electoral pledges. This would be a fortiori so if the members of the Council were also directly elected. Such a regime would inevitably significantly circumscribe Member State room for manoeuvre. It would create a substantive path dependency as to the direction of policy and the priorities to be fulfilled.

Therefore, it is unsurprising that nothing akin to this has featured in serious political deliberations concerning the direction of institutional change within the EU. Viewed from this perspective, the democratic concession in the 2015 EP elections, known as the *Spitzenkandidaten* process, whereby the Commission President was imbued with greater legitimacy because he was supported by the dominant political party and canvassed as its candidate, could be accepted by the Member States because it did not fundamentally change the status quo ante. It did not create a path dependency towards a political agenda that committed the EU to a particular substantive set of reforms. It did not substantially undermine Member State power to set the pace and content of the EU agenda from within the European Council, and the Council. Moreover, the very fact that the other members of the Commission continued to be chosen by the Member States perforce limited the extent to which the Commission President, of whatever political persuasion, could shape the political agenda.

The preceding point is reinforced by the fact that the Member States have refused to confirm the continued application of the *Spitzenkandidaten* process in the 2019 elections.[17] The formal legal reality is that the European Council is only obliged to take account of the result in the European elections when it proposes its candidate for Commission President to the European Parliament.[18] The EP then votes on the candidate. The Commission and the EP, not surprisingly, pressed for the continuation of the *Spitzenkandidaten* process, arguing that it would increase public interest in EU affairs and thereby augment the democratic legitimacy of the outcome. However, the Member States were resistant to continuation of the schema, in part because the evidence indicated that only five per cent of voters went to the polls to influence the choice of Commission President, with little if anything to show in terms of increased voter turnout. They were also resistant to continuation of the 2015 regime on the ground that while it would strengthen the link between the Commission and the EP, this could damage the democratic legitimacy of the Commission President. The argument was that the *Spitzenkandidaten* system robbed the Commission President of the 'dual legitimacy' that would otherwise flow from approval by the democratically elected national leaders in the European Council, followed by that of the EP. While the European Council cannot, in formal terms, prevent the EP from operating the *Spitzenkandidaten* process, it can refuse to accept the candidate of the winning party as the automatic incumbent of the office of Commission President. Moreover, this would accord the Member States further leverage ex ante, in the sense that they could influence who is nominated as a candidate by the EP political parties.

The assertion of national control over the EU's inter-institutional architecture is further evident in Member State rejection of suggestions from Jean-Claude Juncker that the Commission President could be double-hatted, also functioning as Chair of European Council meetings. The Member States showed no appetite for this suggestion in the deliberations leading to the Constitutional Treaty, and their position in this respect has not altered in the interim. Member State control is evident yet again in the reluctance to move towards a smaller Commission, which would mean that not every state would have a commissioner all the time. While commissioners do not formally represent their country, the Member States are, nonetheless, reluctant to give up their own national in the Commission decision-making process. It is paradoxical that these outcomes are occurring when the UK is set to leave the EU, since the UK would applaud the reaffirmation of Member States' voices in EU decision-making.

[17] www.cer.eu/publications/archive/bulletin-article/2018/member-states-and-eu-taking-back-control.

[18] Article 17(7) TEU.

In addition, Member State opposition to reforms of the kind being considered here would not be confined to the executive branch of government. The same sentiment would be voiced by some national parliaments, which would not view with equanimity such institutional architecture, since it would be regarded as increasing the EU's legitimacy at the expense, inter alia, of national parliaments. Thus, while it suits the agenda of some political groupings in national parliaments to critique the EU's democratic credentials, they would, nonetheless, be resistant to change that alleviated such concerns if it thereby enhanced the EU's democratic legitimacy by providing the link between electoral power and political responsibility, with the consequence that the authority of national parliaments was thereby diminished.

Moreover, the diminution of state power that would be entailed by change of the kind mooted above would be constitutionally challenged in some countries, on the ground that the EU was truly becoming a super-state. Thus, while the German Federal Constitutional Court has repeatedly chided the EU in relation to its democratic credentials, it would likely be one of the national constitutional courts to decide that an institutional configuration of the kind set out above, which addressed the democratic deficit as presently understood, would not be compatible with German constitutional law. This was because such a change would mean that the EU was moving closer to a federal state, with the consequence that the Member States could no longer be regarded as the masters of the Treaty in the manner that existed hitherto.

The political constraints on alleviating the democratic deficit have been exacerbated by the rise in populism in some Member States. This is not the place to engage in discourse concerning the meaning and causes of populism;[19] this would require a paper or book in itself, and it would not be possible to do justice to the complexities of the argument in the context of this chapter. Suffice it to say the following for the present. Whatsoever one's views concerning the meaning and causes of populism, the effect thereof has been to render states more suspicious of 'external' authority and less inclined to accept choices that are not in accord with their own preferences. It is debatable whether this is an a priori consequence of populism, although it probably is. However, it is certainly a contingent consequence, so far as concerns the effect of populism in EU Member States. Given that this is so, such Member States are less likely to accept changes to the institutional architecture of EU decision-making which would diminish their power over the direction of EU policy.

[19] See, eg, J Judis, *The Populist Explosion: How the Great Recession Transformed American and European Politics* (New York, Columbia Global Reports, 2016); B Moffitt, *The Global Rise of Populism: Performance, Political Style, and Representation* (Stanford, Stanford University Press, 2016); J-W Müller, *What is Populism?* (Philadelphia, University of Pennsylvania Press, 2016); G de Búrca, 'Is EU Supranational Governance a Challenge to Liberal Constitutionalism?', *Social Science Research Network* 3105238, available at: https://lawreview.uchicago.edu/sites/lawreview.uchicago.edu/files/04%20deBurca_SYMP_Online.pdf.

ii. The EU

The EP would naturally favour change that would alleviate the democratic deficit. The increased conjunction between electoral power and political responsibility would enhance its power, more especially so if it resulted in the entire Commission bearing the political stamp of the dominant party in the EP. The setting of a truly EU electoral agenda, translated into political action by a Commission charged with the task of fulfilling the electoral mandate, would transform the EP's role as compared to the status quo. This would be further enhanced if there were EU political parties and if the EP were to gain a right of legislative initiative in addition to that of the Commission.

The Commission's perspective would likely be more equivocal, since such change would entail gains and losses when viewed from its institutional perspective. There would be gains, insofar as the EU would have greater legitimacy, which would reinforce its authority over existing categories of competence and facilitate the transfer of further power. The legitimacy of the Commission within such a schema would be augmented by reason of its electoral credentials. At the same time, there would be losses for the Commission, since change of the kind under consideration would reduce its room for setting the policy agenda and, in relative terms, would constrain the technocratic autonomy that it presently enjoys.

The European Council would likely fall at the other end of the spectrum. Its President is currently ensured presumptive support from the heads of the Member State by reason of the fact that they choose the incumbent after lengthy deliberation. There could be no such guarantee if the President of the European Council were to be directly elected. Moreover, the relative importance of the President would be likely to diminish if the current method of appointment were retained, but the Commission President were to be directly elected on a party political platform, more especially if other commissioners were similarly elected. The President of the European Council would henceforth be on the back foot, as compared to a Commission President invested with the authority to carry out the electoral programme. Furthermore, the heads of state within the European Council would be unlikely to view with equanimity an institutional regime in which the mode of intergovernmental adjustment were unduly constrained.

B. Democratic Constraints

When articulating the preceding model for change that would alleviate the democratic deficit, it was noted that the model would have to be qualified. It is now time to make good on that qualification.

The EU has always been grounded in two patterns of representation, the people being represented in the European Parliament, and state interests in the Council and European Council. Reforms to alleviate the democratic deficit by increasing the connection between electoral power and political responsibility focus primarily on the first mode of representation, the connection between voter choice, the EP and the shaping of the EU policy agenda.

However, the reality is that even if the broader package of reforms were adopted, it could not ensure that the people would exercise electoral control over the direction of EU policy, since the European Council would still be populated by heads of state, who would continue to have a marked influence over the policy agenda. The second mode of representation, via state interests, would perforce constrain the first, and this would be so even if the President of the European Council were to be elected. This is especially so, given the centrality of the European Council to agenda setting and the choice of priorities, such that nothing significant happens in the EU without its imprimatur.

It might be argued that there is nothing unusual in this respect, since it is a standard feature of national federal systems that there is duality of representation, the normal pattern being that state interests and those of the people are dealt with in different parts of the legislature. The duality does not prevent the offering of a coherent package to the electors. Therefore, the two modes of representation do not hinder the foundational democratic precept, viz that the voters choose who should represent them and the direction of policy, with the consequence that if parties fail to satisfy voter choice, they pay the price at the ballot box.

The national analogy is instructive, precisely because it is not replicated at the EU level. There is similarity insofar as both the EU and the federal systems are premised on two modes of representation: the people and the states. However, the similarity is superficial and conceals deeper differences. The reality is that there is a hierarchy between the two modes of representation, which do not naturally co-exist on an equal footing. In federal states, the paradigm is that representation of the people has primacy or that there is parity between such representation and that of the states. This does not hold true for the EU, where state representation through the Council and the European Council is more powerful than that of the people in the EP.

Thus, in federal parliamentary regimes, there are two component parts of the legislature, with the political agenda commonly set by the house elected by the people, with state interests, as represented in the other house, able to exert influence on the legislation. In federal presidential systems, such as the US, the balance of power between the elected houses may be different. However, this does not alter the point made here, because voters have a voice in relation to both houses, given that the incumbents are directly elected on party political tickets, whether Republican or Democrat, and also given that substantive policy will be set to some degree by the President, who is directly elected. A connection between voter choice and policy direction is thereby preserved.

The converse pertains as to the hierarchy between the two modes of representation in the EU. It is representation of state interests that is accorded primacy, both de jure and de facto, through the Council and the European Council, with representation of the people through the EP being secondary in this respect when viewed from an historical perspective. This is readily apparent in the Treaty provisions concerning the institutions,[20] which are reinforced by their practical modus operandi.

The reasons for the difference between the nation state and the EU in this respect are not hard to divine. The representation of state interests within a federal polity and within the EU is markedly different. Commonality of interest, shared identity and solidarity is considerably greater in the former than in the latter, and that is so notwithstanding the fact that there may be policy differences between regions within a federal state. Problems of domination of one state over another are, by way of contrast, considerably greater in the latter context than in the former, which serves to explain the attention given to voting rules and other mechanisms designed to alleviate this problem in the EU.

Therefore, it is important to view proposals to alleviate the EU's democratic deficit against the preceding backdrop. The reality is that such proposals entail a reordering of the hierarchy in the modes of representation as they pertain in the EU. Representation of the people is afforded elevated status, as manifest in the desire that voter choice be translated into political action such that the gulf between electoral power and political responsibility is eradicated or significantly diminished. This necessarily involves a reduction in the power wielded by the institutions that represent state interests.

It might be argued by way of response that this rebalancing is precisely what is intended, to which the counter is that the states are unlikely to accept the substantive path dependency and loss of power that would be attendant on this change. Alternatively, it might be argued that the alleviation of the democratic deficit can be accomplished without the rebalancing adumbrated above, to which the answer is that such an argument must be fleshed out in order to test its institutional and substantive veracity.

Concerns of an analogous nature have been expressed by Scharpf,[21] who argues that an unqualified majoritarian system would be problematic in the EU. He points out that constitutional democracies, such as Switzerland, Belgium and Canada, in which there is societal division, combined with structural majorities and minorities, often resort to 'consociational' or 'consensus democracy' with bicameral legislatures, super-majoritarian decision rules and the like to protect the interests of minority groups. While it is contestable whether the EU is characterised by the persistent, reinforcing cleavages that prevail in such countries, there is little doubt that some qualifications to majoritarianism would be required.[22]

> Present decision rules could of course be modified in some ways, perhaps to relax the Commission's monopoly of legislative initiatives. But they could not be replaced by a regime of straightforward majority rule without provoking disruptive political

[20] Articles 15–18 TEU.

[21] F Scharpf, 'After the Crash: A Perspective on Multilevel European Democracy' (2015) 21 *European Law Journal* 384, 395.

[22] ibid 395.

> conflicts and radical anti-European opposition in Member States whose national politico-economic and socioeconomic orders and values could be overridden by explicitly political decisions adopted by majorities of 'foreigners' in the European Parliament and in the Council. In other words, the explicit switch to majority rule would destroy the protection of persistent minorities that is presently ensured by the Community Method. And it could politicise European legislation in ways that might transform the largely dormant 'no-demos issue' of EU legitimacy into conflicts that could destroy the Union.

C. Constitutional Constraints

i. Constitutionalisation: Vertical and Horizontal Dimensions

The discussion thus far has been concerned with political constraints to change that would alleviate the democratic deficit, these coming largely from Member State opposition for the reasons adumbrated above. However, there is a further constraint as concerns reforms that would alleviate the democratic deficit, which would exist even if the Member States changed their view and were willing to embrace reform. The constraint flows from the constitutionalisation that attaches to all Treaty provisions. There is a duality to this constraint, which operates both vertically and horizontally.

The vertical dimension captures the effect of such constitutionalisation on relations between the Member States and the EU. It speaks to the limits placed on Member State action when the subject matter falls within the sphere of EU law. Foundational EU constitutional doctrines such as supremacy, direct effect and pre-emption kick in to constrict Member State action. This is so in relation to the vast majority of Treaty articles and much of the legislation enacted pursuant to the Treaty. Disquiet as to the limits thereby placed on Member State action is exacerbated by what is perceived to be the imbalance between the economic and the social within the EU, with the consequence that constitutionalised EU law can place severe limits on this balance at the Member State level.

The horizontal dimension of constitutionalisation addresses the confines thereby placed on political choice at the EU level. This dimension is especially important in relation to changes designed to alleviate the democratic deficit by increasing the connection between electoral power and political responsibility. All constitutions restrict choices that can be made via everyday politics. It is integral to the very nature of constitutions that they entail some pre-commitment, which confines choices that can be made thereafter, subject to any constitutional amendment. The limits may be procedural or substantive. The difference with respect to the EU is one of degree, not of kind, but it is significant nonetheless, since the constitutionalised EU Treaty is far more detailed than any national constitution. It still leaves room for some policy choice as concerns the direction of EU policy. Nevertheless, the EU Treaty limits the range of such choice that rival political parties can place before the electorate. There is much in the Treaty that constitutes substantive path dependency for the direction of EU policy, thereby limiting politicisation.

Concerns as to the preceding vertical and horizontal constraints have been voiced by scholars such as Grimm, who has focused on what he terms the democratic costs of constitutionalisation.[23] His central thesis is that the EU Treaties are over-constitutionalised, with the consequence that they are thereby taken off the agenda of normal politics, notwithstanding the fact that many such issues would be regarded as being within the province of ordinary law in Member States: 'in the EU the crucial difference between the rules for political decisions and the decisions themselves is to a large extent levelled'.[24] It is inherent in the nature of constitutions that they function as the framework for political decisions, with the consequence that elections 'do not matter as far as constitutional law extends'.[25] There may be too little constitutionalism, but there may also be too much, with the consequence that the democratic process is fettered.[26] While there are no universally applicable principles for determining the content of a constitution, the 'function of constitutions is to legitimise and to limit political power, not to replace it',[27] with the consequence that constitutions are a 'framework for politics, not the blueprint for all political decisions'.[28]

The EU Treaties fulfil many of the functions of national constitutions, specifying matters such as the inter-institutional distribution of power, the mode of law-making and the respective competence of the EU and Member States. They also go significantly beyond the remit of national constitutions, with the consequence that a wide range of matters become constitutionalised and taken off the agenda of normal politics. The effect of this is further enhanced by the constitutional doctrines of direct effect and supremacy, which transformed the four economic freedoms from 'objective principles for legislation into subjective rights of the market participants who could claim them against the Member States before the national courts'.[29]

This in turn meant that there were two modes of EU integration. The Treaty precepts could be advanced through legislation enacted by the EU institutions or they could be taken forward through judicial decisions, which were imbued with considerable force through direct effect and supremacy.[30] Member States had limited influence over the latter, and this was particularly important since

[23] D Grimm, 'The Democratic Costs of Constitutionalization: The European Case' (2015) 21 *European Law Journal* 460.
[24] ibid 470.
[25] ibid 463.
[26] ibid 464.
[27] ibid 465.
[28] ibid.
[29] ibid 467.
[30] J Weiler, 'The Community System: The Dual Character of Supranationalism' (1981) 1 *Yearbook of European Law* 267; J Weiler, 'The Transformation of Europe' (1991) 100 *Yale Law Journal* 2403, 2412–31; P Craig, 'Once upon a Time in the West: Direct Effect and the Federalization of EEC Law' (1992) 12 *Oxford Journal of Legal Studies* 453.

the lack of differentiation between the constitutional law level and the ordinary law level meant that the 'constitutionalisation of the treaties immunises the Commission and particularly the ECJ against any attempt by the democratically responsible institutions of the EU to react to the Court's jurisprudence by changing the law'.[31] For Grimm, the remedy was to limit the EU Treaties to their truly constitutional elements and downgrade other Treaty provisions that were not of a constitutional nature to the status of secondary law.

ii. Competence: Vertical and Horizontal Dimensions

Constitutionalisation is not the only constitutional constraint on political choice; it is also limited by the competence accorded to the EU. Political choices placed before the electorate in nation states are paradigmatically predicated on the state having plenary power. The assumption is that, subject to constitutional limits, the rival political parties can place a range of options before the electorate, which cover economic, social and political issues, broadly defined. This is the very lifeblood of normal politics, with contestation concerning matters such as economic redistribution, social welfare, health, crime and education featuring prominently on the electoral agenda. There is a vertical and a horizontal dimension to such limitations on competence as they pertain to the EU.

The most obvious dimension of competence is on the vertical plane insofar as it demarcates the respective spheres of authority of the EU and the Member States. It follows that, even assuming the Member States were willing to alleviate the democratic deficit by embracing political reordering of the kind set out above, the choices that rival political parties could place before the electorate are framed by the limits of EU competence. Therefore, it is not open to a political party to promise far-reaching change in terms of social welfare or economic redistribution, since the EU does not have competence over such matters, nor does it have the tax base from which to effectuate such change, it still being principally a regulatory state in this regard. Moreover, it is not open to a political party to promise far-reaching change on matters that are of prime concern to voters in national elections, such as education, health, crime and the like, since the EU's powers are limited in such areas.

However, there is a less obvious dimension of competence that resonates horizontally, insofar as it frames the exercise of political choice by the EU institutions when making EU policy. This is the consequence of the fact that not all heads of competence are created equal. The EU's power over different areas varies significantly, being dependent in part on whether the competence is exclusive, shared or complementary and in part on the fact that even within each such category, it is only by looking closely at the relevant Treaty

[31] Grimm (n 23) 471.

provisions that one can determine the real scope of EU power. There is therefore no 'boilerplate' that determines the nature of power possessed by the EU in the diverse areas that fall within, for example, shared competence. Moreover, the horizontal dimension to competence is manifest in the fact that the Treaties specify to some significant degree the hierarchy of substantive provisions, as attested to most notably by the dominance of the four freedoms. This perforce shapes the political choices that the EU institutions are able to make.

Furthermore, there are instances where there is a mismatch between the expectations of what the EU is expected to do and the limits of the competence accorded to it, as powerfully exemplified by the rule of law crisis. This may, in the medium term, prove to be the most serious of the crises faced by the EU. There is a rich and sophisticated literature on the topic, which explores the limits of the powers currently available to the EU and how they could be applied.[32] Moreover, there is a duality to the concept of national constitutional responsibility as it pertains to the rule of law crisis, most especially in Poland and Hungary. There is the fact that the principal responsibility for the crisis resides with the states that introduced the illiberal measures threatening the rule of law. There is the secondary responsibility that lies with the Member States collectively, as reflected in the Treaty provisions, which give expression to the limits of the controls over Member State action that they are willing to accept. The terms of Article 7 TEU set the parameters for such action and are predicated on the assumption that there will not be more than one misbehaving state at any point in time. The reality is that the EU is caught between a rock and a hard place or, if you prefer more classical illusions, between Scylla and Charybdis: it risks being damned for doing too little, criticised for being ineffectual or criticised for trying to do too much, and thereby straying into the terrain of domestic politics where it lacks competence.

[32] A von Bogdandy, M Kottmann, C Antpöhler, J Dickschen, S Hentrei and M Smrkolj, 'Reverse Solange: Protecting the Essence of Fundamental Rights against EU Member States' (2012) 49 *Common Market Law Review* 489; I Canor, 'My Brother's Keeper? Horizontal *Solange*: "An Ever Closer *Distrust* among the Peoples of Europe"' (2013) 50 *Common Market Law Review* 383; S Carrera, E Guild and N Hernanz, *The Triangular Relationship between Fundamental Rights, Democracy and the Rule of Law in the EU: Towards an EU Copenhagen Mechanism* (Brussels, Centre for European Policy Studies, 2013); A von Bogdandy and P Sonnevend (eds), *Constitutional Crisis in the European Constitutional Area: Theory, Law and Politics in Hungary and Romania* (Oxford, Hart Publishing, 2015); D Kochenov and L Pech, 'Monitoring and Enforcement of the Rule of Law in the EU: Rhetoric and Reality' (2015) 11 *European Constitutional Law Review* 512; J-W Müller, 'Should the European Union Protect Democracy and the Rule of Law in its Member States?' (2015) 21 *European Law Journal* 141; D Kochenov, 'EU Law without the Rule of Law: Is the Veneration of Autonomy Worth it?' (2015) 34 *Yearbook of European Law* 74; A Jakab and D Kochenov (eds), *The Enforcement of EU Law and Values: Methods against Defiance* (Oxford, Oxford University Press, 2016); C Closa and D Kochenov (eds), *Reinforcing the Rule of Law Oversight in the European Union* (Cambridge, Cambridge University Press, 2016).

D. Substantive Constraints

The fourth constraint on the exercise of democratic political choice is substantive. It is related to the constitutional constraint, but is nonetheless distinct, and hence warrants separate consideration. The balance between the economic and the social has been a contentious feature of the EEC since its inception and continues to be so. It is manifest in two ways.

i. The Economic and the Social: Core Treaty Provisions

Scharpf has long argued that the EU embodies an asymmetry between the economic and the social, such that the former is prioritised at the expense of the latter.[33] He contends that the EU is premised on asymmetrical treatment of the economic and social spheres. The economic order has predominated, as evidenced by the Treaty provisions and the primacy accorded to completion of the single market, with the attendant priority placed on market and competitive principles. Scharpf argued that it would have been possible, when the Treaty of Rome was framed, to have made the harmonisation of social protection a precondition for market integration, given that the welfare regimes of the original six Member States were relatively rudimentary and closer than they have since become.

If the Treaty of Rome had been cast in this form, then the debates at the EU level about the interplay between social protection and the market mechanism would have replicated similar discourse at the national level. Matters developed very differently. The Treaty focus was heavily on markets, with the consequence that there was a decoupling of economic integration and social protection. This led to constitutional asymmetry. Whereas at the national level, economic and social policy had the same constitutional status, it was economic policy that predominated at the EU level. The very predominance afforded to economic policy reduced the ability of Member States to influence their own economies or to 'realize self-defined socio-political goals'.[34]

The doctrines of direct effect and supremacy heightened these constraints. Scharpf argues that the Member States failed to recognise the impact of these twin doctrines, which laid the foundations for integration through law, whereby the Community courts could advance Treaty objectives if integration through legislation was not possible because of disagreement in the Council.[35]

[33] F Scharpf, 'Economic Integration, Democracy and the Welfare State' (1997) 4 *Journal of European Public Policy* 18; F Scharpf, 'The European Social Model: Coping with the Challenges of Diversity' (2002) 40 *Journal of Common Market Studies* 645; F Scharpf, 'Legitimate Diversity: The New Challenge of European Integration' in T Borzel and R Cichowski (eds), *The State of the European Union, Vol 6: Law, Politics and Society* (Oxford, Oxford University Press, 2003).

[34] Scharpf, 'The European Social Model' (n 33) 648.

[35] Scharpf (n 21) 386–87.

Negative integration through judicial decisions that deemed national laws to be inconsistent with the Treaty became the dominant mode of integration, until the new mode of harmonisation was introduced following the Single European Act 1986, thereby facilitating positive integration.

There came to be increasing pressure for the EU to play a greater role in social policy, thereby alleviating the constitutional imbalance between the market-making and market-correcting functions of a polity. This goes a long way towards explaining the inclusion of more heads of competence dealing with social policy, as well as development of the Structural Funds. Moreover, there were persistent efforts in the latter part of the last millennium to recast the single market in more holistic terms so as to include aspects of social and labour policy.[36]

However, Scharpf argued that it was not possible at the turn of the millennium for the EU to adopt the stance towards social policy that it had declined to take when the Treaty of Rome was signed. It was not possible to treat social welfare and protection through uniform rules applicable to all, because of the very diversity in welfare systems that existed within the Member States.[37] This was the rationale in part for the development of social policy through the open method of coordination (OMC).[38]

> Political parties and unions promoting 'social Europe' are thus confronted by a dilemma: to ensure effectiveness, they need to assert the constitutional equality of social protection and economic integration functions at the European level – which could be achieved either through European social programmes or through the harmonization of national social-protection systems. At the same time, however, the present diversity of national social-protection systems and the political salience of these differences make it practically impossible for them to agree on common European solutions. Faced by this dilemma, the Union opted for a new governing mode, the open method of coordination (OMC), in order to protect and promote social Europe.

These arguments are important. However, the following points are pertinent in this context. First, insofar as there is an imbalance between the economic and the social within the EU, this is the result of Member State choice, just as is the current institutional structure. It is of course true that judicial doctrines of direct effect and supremacy, as developed by the Court of Justice of the European Union (CJEU), have heightened this tension, but the fact remains that the centrality accorded to the four freedoms, and the relative weakness of the social as compared to the economic dimension, is reflective of what the Member

[36] P Craig, 'The Evolution of the Single Market' in C Barnard and J Scott (eds), *The Law of the Single European Market: Unpacking the Premises* (Oxford, Hart Publishing, 2002) ch 1; P Craig, 'The Community Political Order' (2003) 10 *Indiana Journal of Global Legal Studies* 79.

[37] Scharpf, 'The European Social Model' (n 33) 649–51.

[38] ibid 652.

States have been willing to accept, and the powers that it has been willing to accord, to a supranational polity. There is a paradox lurking here. The desire to preserve national sovereignty underpinned Member State reluctance to accord the EU power over social policy, yet the resulting predominance of the economic over the social within the EU impacted on Member State freedom to choose the balance between the economic and the social within the nation state.

Second, there is no doubt that the legal doctrines of direct effect and supremacy sharpened the cutting edge of the four freedoms, thereby further enhancing the economic dimension of the Treaties and the attendant negative integration resulting from the judicial doctrine. Nevertheless, Scharpf's argument, to the effect that the Member States were not cognisant of the significance of the legal doctrine, should be viewed with caution. Member States benefited from such judicial doctrine, insofar as it invested the Treaties and the rules made thereunder, with a peremptory force that they would otherwise have lacked. To put the same point in another way, these doctrines, as enforced by the EU courts, gave greater credibility to the commitments embodied in the Treaties.

ii. The Economic, the Social and the Political: EMU and the Financial Crisis

The financial crisis impacted significantly on the balance between the economic and the social, and more broadly on the political structure of decision-making in the EU. The effects were manifest at the EU level, insofar as the financial crisis meant that the EU's energies were concentrated on resolving the economic problems, with scant energy left for broader social policy. They were also manifest at the Member State level, since relief for debtor states was subject to conditionality requirements, which imposed strict austerity limits, with attendant implications for national social and welfare policy. Concerns in this respect were voiced by many commentators.

For Scharpf, the imbalance between the economic and the social was heightened by the financial crisis and the responses thereto.[39] This was, in part, because the eurozone regime, as it presently functions, exerts 'downward pressures on public sector functions and on wages – in the upswing to dampen the rise of external deficits and in the downswing to stimulate export-led recovery';[40] it was also in part because of what Scharpf regards as the far-reaching discretion afforded to the Commission under the EU legislation enacted to strengthen EU oversight of national fiscal policy after the crisis.[41]

Wilkinson, drawing on the motif of authoritarian liberalism, voiced the concern that 'democratic processes have been side-lined, albeit largely with the complicity of national political and economic elites, not to assert strong

[39] F Scharpf, *Governing in Europe: Effective and Democratic?* (Oxford, Oxford University Press, 1999); Scharpf (n 21).

[40] Scharpf (n 21) 391.

[41] ibid 392.

statehood but for the purpose of maintaining a project of economic integration said to depend on the success of the single currency'.[42] In a similar vein, he deprecates the fact that 'democratic authority is replaced by a combination of executive power and market rationality, defended by the perceived necessity of acting swiftly and bypassing public debate'.[43]

Similarly, Dawson and de Witte express disquiet at the way in which the financial crisis de facto shifted the substantive boundaries as to the intrusion of the EU into Member States 'by increasingly making in-roads in Member State autonomy in redistributive, fiscal and budgetary matters',[44] as manifest in the conditionality criteria imposed on debtor states. They too voice worry about the increased executive dominance in decision-making, with agenda setting being done to an ever-greater extent by the European Council. They acknowledge that the rationale for executive control in proposals for reform of the European Monetary Union (EMU) is that 'only executives and governments carry the competence, speed, credibility and legitimacy to mandate and direct significant EU intervention in core state powers such as fiscal policy'.[45] Nonetheless, they deprecate reform initiatives that further enhance executive power. Reform should, they argue, be such that the substantive direction of EU policy can be truly deliberated and contested,[46] thereby meeting a basic precept of political self-determination that 'government is conducted not just *for* but *by* the people' (italics in original).[47]

There is force in the preceding arguments. Thus, it is assuredly correct that the Commission has discretion pursuant to various regulations enacted following the financial crisis. However, the salient regulations were approved through the ordinary legislative procedure, with significant input from the EP as well as the Council, although the room for parliamentary involvement thereafter is limited.[48] Moreover, it is important not to be asymmetrical in this respect. It is the executives of the Member States that are very much in the driving seat when it comes to setting their national budget. They commonly exercise considerable discretion in this regard, such that it is difficult to ensure parliamentary accountability. There may be reasons why the national executive is willing to tolerate significant budgetary imbalance or feels powerless to address the issue. This can in turn have serious consequences for other Member States through the strain thereby placed on the euro. As such, the existence of Commission

[42] M Wilkinson, 'Authoritarian Liberalism in the European Constitutional Imagination: Second Time as Farce?' (2015) 21 *European Law Journal* 313, 315.

[43] ibid 327.

[44] M Dawson and F de Witte, 'Self-Determination in the Constitutional Future of the EU' (2015) 21 *European Law Journal* 371, 372.

[45] ibid 374.

[46] ibid 375.

[47] ibid 382.

[48] C Fasone, 'European Economic Governance and Parliamentary Representation: What Place for the European Parliament?' (2014) 20 *European Law Journal* 2.

discretion should be viewed in this light. Furthermore, the post-financial crisis legislative schema is premised on such Commission discretion, coupled with increased provision for national budgetary targets that can be policed by national legislatures more readily than hitherto.

V. INSTITUTIONAL STRUCTURE AND DEMOCRACY: THE PARADOX

There is a paradox of cause and effect in the EU's inter-institutional configuration of power as it presently exists and as it is likely to remain in the future. The cause captures the facts as set out hitherto. The Member States have shaped the present configuration of EU inter-institutional power, which is beset by a democratic deficit insofar as there is scant connection between the electoral vote and political power or responsibility, such that it is difficult for the voters to express a view as to the direction of EU policy that will be translated into action. Member States bear the principal responsibility for the status quo since they devised the current schema.

The effect captures the way in which we think about democratic legitimation in the EU. The infirmities in EU decision-making constitute the driver for the argument that EU legitimacy and democracy must be grounded in the Member States, not merely as one mode of representation within the EU. The argument becomes more 'visceral and foundational' in the sense that it is the Member States, and the national parliaments therein, that are regarded as the true bedrock of democracy. Their claims in this regard are grounded in the EU's democratic deficiencies, and this in turn is used to fuel the argument that such parliaments should participate in EU decision-making.

The paradox resides in the conjunction of cause and effect: Member State choice is central to the institutional architecture at the EU level and the democratic infirmity that is reflected therein. The infirmity cannot, by definition, be resolved at the EU level, given the nature of the choice thus made, with the consequence that the solution must be found elsewhere. The paradox is exacerbated by reason of the fact that, as argued above, most national parliaments would be in accord with their national executives in resisting change that would alleviate the democratic deficit within the EU, because of the effect that this could have on their own power. Thus, while 'a true political Union would involve not suppressing, but channelling and promoting meaningful conflict over the EU's substantive goals'[49] and while reinvigoration in this respect may be especially pertinent following the financial crisis, there is scant likelihood of this occurring.

It should be made clear that nothing in the preceding argument presumes the idea of a single demos for the entire EU; it is not predicated on the denial of

[49] M Dawson and F de Witte, 'Self-Determination in the Constitutional Future of the EU' (n 44) 382.

plurality in the political choices made by the EU; it does not rest on assumptions of a particular kind of federal order or anything akin thereto; it presumes no particular distribution of power between the EU and the Member States; and it is perfectly consistent with a role for national parliaments.

The paradox is, by way of contrast, simply reflective of the politics concerning the disposition of inter-institutional power as it has unfolded since the inception of the EEC. It is also reflective of normative assumptions as to the type of Community or Union that the Member States are willing to create, and the powers that they are content to invest in it. The enduring paradox persists: the refusal of Member States to allow institutional change that would alleviate the democratic deficiency in EU decision-making remains a principal cause of the malaise, the consequential effect being that the problem can only be addressed at the state level.

The paradox is all the more important because it comes with a 'political bite', which is doubly undermining for the EU. Member States prefer to offload blame concerning deficiencies in EU decision-making to the EU institutions themselves and divest themselves of responsibility. They do not readily concede their role as institutional architects of the status quo. Moreover, it is these very institutional deficiencies that serve to rob the EU of the legitimacy that it requires to tackle difficult social or economic issues. The EU is caught between a rock and a hard place, berated in equal measure for its over-attachment to the economic at the expense of the social, while being castigated for lacking the democratic legitimacy to make dispositive social or redistributive decisions.

REFERENCES

De Búrca, G, 'Is EU Supranational Governance a Challenge to Liberal Constitutionalism?', *Social Science Research Network* 3105238.

Canor, I, 'My Brother's Keeper? Horizontal *Solange*: "An Ever Closer *Distrust* among the Peoples of Europe"' (2013) 50 *Common Market Law Review* 383.

Carrera, S, Guild, E and Hernanz, N, *The Triangular Relationship between Fundamental Rights, Democracy and the Rule of Law in the EU: Towards an EU Copenhagen Mechanism* (Brussels, Centre for European Policy Studies, 2013).

Closa, C and Kochenov, D (eds), *Reinforcing the Rule of Law Oversight in the European Union* (Cambridge, Cambridge University Press, 2016).

Craig, P, 'Once Upon a Time in the West: Direct Effect and the Federalization of EEC Law' (1992) 12 *Oxford Journal of Legal Studies* 453.

——. 'The Evolution of the Single Market' in C Barnard and J Scott (eds), *The Law of the Single European Market, Unpacking the Premises* (Oxford, Hart Publishing, 2002).

——. 'The Community Political Order' (2003) 10 *Indiana Journal of Global Legal Studies* 79.

——. *The Lisbon Treaty, Law, Politics and Treaty Reform* (Oxford, Oxford University Press, 2010).

——. 'Institutions, Power and Institutional Balance' in P Craig and G de Búrca (eds), *The Evolution of EU Law*, 2nd edn (Oxford, Oxford University Press, 2011).

Dawson, M and de Witte, F, 'Self-Determination in the Constitutional Future of the EU' (2015) 21 *European Law Journal* 371.

Fasone, C, 'European Economic Governance and Parliamentary Representation: What Place for the European Parliament?' (2014) 20 *European Law Journal* 2.

Featherstone, K, 'Jean Monnet and the "Democratic Deficit" in the European Union' (1994) 32 *Journal of Common Market Studies* 149.

Follesdal, A and Hix, S, 'Why There is a Democratic Deficit in the EU: A Response to Majone and Moravcsik' (2006) 44 *Journal of Common Market Studies* 533.

Grimm, D, 'The Democratic Costs of Constitutionalization: The European Case' (2015) 21 *European Law Journal* 460.

Holland, M, *European Community Integration* (New York, St Martin's Press, 1993).

Jakab, A and Kochenov, D (eds), *The Enforcement of EU Law and Values: Methods against Defiance* (Oxford, Oxford University Press, 2016).

Judis, J, *The Populist Explosion: How the Great Recession Transformed American and European Politics* (New York, Columbia Global Reports, 2016).

Kochenov, D, 'EU Law without the Rule of Law: Is the Veneration of Autonomy Worth it?' (2015) 34 *Yearbook of European Law* 74.

Kochenov, D and Pech, L, 'Monitoring and Enforcement of the Rule of Law in the EU: Rhetoric and Reality' (2015) 11 *European Constitutional Law Review* 512.

Maduro, M, 'A New Governance for the European Union and the Euro: Democracy and Justice' RSCAS Policy Paper 2012/11, 1.

Marks, G, Hooghe, L and Blank, K, 'European Integration from the 1980s: State-Centric v. Multiple-Level Governance' (1996) 34 *Journal of Common Market Studies* 341.

Moffitt, B, *The Global Rise of Populism: Performance, Political Style, and Representation* (Stanford, Stanford University Press, 2016).

Moravcsik, A, 'Negotiating the Single European Act: National Interests and Conventional Statecraft in the European Community' (1991) 45 *International Organization* 19.

——. *National Preference Formation and Interstate Bargaining in the European Community, 1955–86* (Cambridge, MA, Harvard University Press, 1992).

——. 'Preferences and Power in the European Community: A Liberal Intergovernmentalist Approach' (1993) 31 *Journal of Common Market Studies* 473.

Müller, J-W, 'Should the European Union Protect Democracy and the Rule of Law in its Member States' (2015) 21 *European Law Journal* 141.

——. *What is Populism?* (Philadelphia, University of Pennsylvania Press, 2016).

Neunreither, K, 'Transformation of a Political Role: Reconsidering the Case of the Commission of the European Communities' (1971–72) 10 *Journal of Common Market Studies* 233.

Nicolaïdis, K 'Our European Demoi-cracy: Is This Constitution a Third Way for Europe?' in K Nicolaïdis and S Weatherill (eds), *Whose Europe? National Models and the Constitution of the European Union* (Oxford, Oxford University Press, 2003).

——. 'The Idea of European Demoicracy' in J Dickson and P Eleftheriadis (eds), *Philosophical Foundations of EU Law* (Oxford, Oxford University Press, 2012).

Norman, P, *The Accidental Constitution, The Making of Europe's Constitutional Treaty*, 2nd edn (Brussels, EuroComment, 2005).

Pollack, M, 'International Relations Theory and European Integration' (2000) 55 *EUI Working Papers*, RSC.

Risse-Kappen, R, 'Exploring the Nature of the Beast: International Relations Theory and Comparative Policy Analysis Meet the European Union' (1996) 34 *Journal of Common Market Studies* 53.
Scharpf, F, 'Economic Integration, Democracy and the Welfare State' (1997) 4 *Journal of European Public Policy* 18.
——. *Governing in Europe: Effective and Democratic?* (Oxford, Oxford University Press, 1999).
——. 'The European Social Model: Coping with the Challenges of Diversity' (2002) 40 *Journal of Common Market Studies* 645.
——. 'Legitimate Diversity: The New Challenge of European Integration' in T Borzel and R Cichowski (eds), *The State of the European Union, Vol. 6: Law, Politics and Society* (Oxford, Oxford University Press, 2003).
——. 'After the Crash: A Perspective on Multilevel European Democracy' (2015) 21 *European Law Journal* 384.
Von Bogdandy, A, Kottmann, M, Antpöhler, C, Dickschen, J, Hentrei, S and Smrkolj, M, 'Reverse Solange: Protecting the Essence of Fundamental Rights against EU Member States' (2012) 49 *Common Market Law Review* 489.
Von Bogdandy, A and Sonnevend, P (eds), *Constitutional Crisis in the European Constitutional Area: Theory, Law and Politics in Hungary and Romania* (Oxford, Hart Publishing, 2015).
Wallace, H, 'European Governance in Turbulent Times' (1993) 31 *Journal of Common Market Studies* 293.
Wallace, W and Smith, J, 'Democracy or Technocracy? European Integration and the Problem of Popular Consent' in J Hayward (ed), *The Crisis of Representation in Europe* (London, Frank Cass, 1995).
Weiler, J 'The Community System: The Dual Character of Supranationalism' (1981) 1 *Yearbook of European Law* 267.
——. 'The Transformation of Europe' (1991) 100 *Yale Law Journal* 2403.
Weiler, JHH, 'Europe in Crisis: On "Political Messianism", "Legitimacy" and the "Rule of Law"' (2012) *Singapore Journal of Legal Studies* 248.
Weiler, JHH, Haltern, U and Mayer, F, 'European Democracy and its Critique' in J Hayward (ed), *The Crisis of Representation in Europe* (London, Frank Cass, 1995).
Wilkinson, M, 'Authoritarian Liberalism in the European Constitutional Imagination: Second Time as Farce?' (2015) 21 *European Law Journal* 313.

3

The EU Flexibility Clause is Dead, Long Live the EU Flexibility Clause

GRAHAM BUTLER

I. INTRODUCTION

SPECIFYING WITH ABSOLUTE precision where the line is between EU and Member States competences has always been difficult. This may have been due to the fact that the legal basis for EU legislation has had an ostentatious history, and while the EU has been in possession of powers beyond those which are specifically conferred, ever so discreetly, in the flexibility clause (hereinafter 'the clause'), Article 352 of the Treaty on the Functioning of the European Union (TFEU) has provided a means that goes beyond the treaties' confines. The clause is known by many names: the residual competence clause; a discretionary power; the implied power; the open-ended power; the elastic clause; a constitutional blank cheque; a lacunae-filling provision; the general enabling power; an open provision; the special normative instrument; the catch-all provision; the residual power; the elastic provision; the general authorisation power; the hive of legislative expansion; the competence reservoir; *la petite revision*; and many more. Whatever its designation or array of aliases,[1] it is a remarkable element of EU law that has to be looked at in full.

One of the prevailing themes on the clause in scholarship is trying to foresee its limits, as opposed to its potential. This is a natural course of contemplation, given that abstractly, the clause is boundless. However, what becomes apparent from observing the clause is its double dynamic: first, the willingness of the EU legislature to make use of it as a basis for EU legislation, before then rolling back; and, second, the degree to which the Court of Justice of the European Union (hereinafter 'the Court') has permitted its use within the confines of the treaties as a whole, before also rolling back. From its wild days of extensive use

[1] Articles I-18 of the Treaty establishing a Constitution for Europe [2004] OJ C310/01 called what is today art 352 the 'flexibility clause', so this is the name that will be used in this chapter.

to its time of slowly becoming more dormant, it has led to a varied legislative and judicial interpretation. In light of this conundrum, this chapters attempts to determine what the future has in store for the EU's clause, and it is argued that the clause still has a purpose, but only if used fittingly and sparingly.

II. THE FLEXIBILITY CLAUSE

If politics is the art of the possible, then European integration has had to be the attempt of the daring. The very creation of the EU's original incarnation, the European Coal and Steel Community (ECSC), was an exercise of integration by a cohort of the willing, and to do that, it required some level of elasticity. Today's clause, Article 352 TFEU, has its origins in Article 95 of the ECSC Treaty and, at present, a corresponding provision is also included in the Euratom Treaty.[2] For comparison's sake, the US has its own clause – the necessary and proper clause – which can be equated with Article 352 TFEU.[3]

Whilst the clause has been in situ since the very founding of the EU, its use has experienced both ups and downs. Merely because it has been tucked away towards the end of the treaties does not mean it can be discounted; in fact, its potential as a legal basis for *any* legislation has meant attention has rightly focused on it. Over time, it has seen changing legislative practice and judicial consideration, and its capacity for legislative expansion has become apparent in a twofold manner: first, by legislative adoption and later disavowal; and, second, with judicial approval at first, before later being clamped down upon.

The EU acts on the basis of the principle of conferred powers. The wording of the treaties have stated specific conferral of competence and, if strictly construed, it ensures that the EU does not act beyond its conferred set of competences. By contrast, the clause is the exception, for it has allowed the exact legislative powers conferred upon the EU to be extended beyond those provided for. The clause through Article 352 TFEU is the EU's own built-in expansion mechanism,[4] which has formally reduced the scope for a strict reading of Article 5 of the Treaty on European Union (TEU), which sets out the framework for competence conferral, thus relaxing the understanding of strictly conferred competences. As a result, it has the ability to provide for legislative means beyond the stringent confines of explicitly conferred competence and be a legal

[2] Article 203 of the Euratom Treaty: 'If action by the Community should prove necessary to attain one of the objectives of the Community and this Treaty has not provided the necessary powers, the Council shall, acting unanimously on a proposal from the Commission and after consulting the European Parliament, take the appropriate measures.' There are two subtle distinctions. For its use in the Euratom Treaty, the European Parliament only has to be consulted and national parliaments do not have to be notified. See A Södersten, *Euratom at the Crossroads* (Cheltenham, Edward Elgar Publishing, 2018) 70.

[3] R Schütze, *European Union Law*, 2nd edn (Cambridge, Cambridge University Press 2018) 235.

[4] Article 352 TFEU and Declarations Nos 41 and 42, as they presently stand, are set out in full at the end of this chapter.

basis for extensive legislative power. This, naturally, raised questions as to just how far the clause had reached.

A. Opposing Angles

The clause allows for EU legislation to emanate in fields where there is no explicit legal basis. It thus opens up two differing perspectives. Viewed one way, broadly, it represents the full reach of EU competence, or competence at its feasible limit. It is a general power, where other specific powers are not adequate. It has been seen as the idyllic way to integrate beyond what the treaties provide and has been understood as being an effective instrument in order to ensure the EU legal order is not overly rigid, allowing for the process of integration through law to be made more operative.

On the other hand, narrowly, the clause may be perceived as having the potential to be too broad, exceeding the conferred competence that has been granted elsewhere in the treaties. The restrictive view of the clause was that it was to be a concession to the otherwise strictly conferred fields of competence. This construal would mean that Article 352 TFEU can only be invoked as an ancillary, incidental or minor supplementary legal basis for EU legislation. In theory, this would mean that the clause would not have received as much scholarly attention as it has to date. However, such a narrow reading has not been the reality and, instead, has at different junctures in the history of the clause been used to different extents. As construed, it represents 'the weakest point in the limiting function of the current division of power'.[5]

The infrequent use of the clause in the EU's earliest days was conventional, for the treaties were ambitious, but the exercise of powers was cautious at first. However, the middle road is that the clause would act alongside the specific powers conferred and in a manner that does not totally undermine the general scheme of the treaties. Read this way, there had to have been limits to the scope of the clause.

B. Conceivable Custom

There are two circumstances where the clause could be used in practice. Firstly, as a means of supplementing the conferred powers; and secondly, as a way of going into new areas beyond the conferred powers. The conferred powers of the EU are 'purpose bound',[6] and so the clause could be seen to be a misuse

[5] A von Bogdandy and J Bast, 'The Vertical Order of Competences' in A von Bogdandy and J Bast (eds), *Principles of European Constitutional Law* (Oxford, Hart Publishing, 2006) 362.

[6] G Bebr, *Development of Judicial Control of the European Communities* (The Hague, Martinus Nijhoff Publishers, 1981) 117.

of the legal basis if objectives are pursued incorrectly. Despite being bound up by the quagmire of being an instrument of political harmony through the unanimity requirement in the Council, it has been used for both major and minor elements of EU policy: from the introduction of the euro currency as part of the third stage of the Economic and Monetary Union (EMU)[7] to the 'Europe for Citizens' programme run by the Commission.[8]

What makes the clause worthy of further consideration for the future is how it has had different uses in the course of its history. Whilst there are some limits to the use of Article 352 TFEU as a 'catch-all' clause, the boundaries have not been entirely clear. In the early years of the EU's existence, the clause was not used, which may be attributed to two principle reasons: first, that it may not have been needed – the explicit, albeit limited legal bases served the needs of the EU legislature well; and, second, there was a potential fear of what precedent its use might set. Yet, over time, the clause was given widespread usage and evolved into a sufficiently elastic legal basis. The era in which the clause was utilised the most can be called its rise.

III. THE RISE OF THE FLEXIBILITY CLAUSE

At present, there are significant constraints imposed on the use of the clause. Yet it was not always this way, and the rise of the clause is a germane illustration of the EU's legislative process at work. The main reason the clause came into being was that historically, there had only been a limited range of competences conferred upon the EU. Therefore, contemplation had to be made first about its plausible use.

A. Consideration and Activation

Given the clause's exceptional status, there was uncertainty as how to handle or manage it at first. There was a period of time before the rise of the clause where it was considered 'destined to remain a dead letter'.[9] However, according to another later reading, there had been 'long-standing readiness among the Member States acting unanimously in Council to assert a broad reach to the [EU] legislative competence'.[10] Prior to the 1970s, the uses of the clause were

[7] Council Regulation (EC) No 1103/97 of 17 June 1997 on Certain Provisions Relating to the Introduction of the Euro [1997] OJ L162/1.

[8] Council Regulation (EU) No 390/2014 of 14 April 2014 Establishing the 'Europe for Citizens' Programme for the Period 2014–2020 [2014] OJ L115/3.

[9] P Pescatore, *The Law of Integration: Emergence of a New Phenomenon in International Relations, Based on the Experience of the European Communities* (Leiden, AW Sijthoff, 1974) 41. However, he did recognise that 'recourse to [the] provision is becoming more and more significant'.

[10] S Weatherill, 'Competence Creep and Competence Control' (2004) 23 *Yearbook of European Law* 1, 6.

few and far between. Nevertheless, by the late 1960s, the Commission was cautiously exploring circumstances where the clause could be used as a legal basis.[11] It is also of interest to note the subject matter for which the clause was used preceding this period. For example, a matter relating to the customs union and the free movement of goods availed of the clause in 1968,[12] given the potential inadequacy of the explicit legal bases in the treaties at that time. In addition, it was also used as a basis for regulating trade in agricultural products pre-enlargement.[13]

In the initial phase of European legal integration, the conferred powers that were explicitly granted for the adoption of EU legislation were sufficient, by and large, to achieve the aims of the treaties. The special nature of the clause required that there had to be a genuine need to utilise it. Yet, for no great reason other than to kick-start a new programme of legislation, the Paris Summit of 1972 paved the way for greater use of the clause, opening up its potential for realisation. At this 'point of departure',[14] the Member States expressed the will to 'make the widest possible use of all the dispositions of the Treaties, including Article [352 TFEU]'.[15] As a result, when the clause began to be utilised, it was given a maximalist reading. This reinvigoration of legislative competence was recognition that the effects of the Empty Chair Crisis had now passed and marked a turn towards the 'reinterpretation' of the clause,[16] whereby the subsidiary role that the clause was meant to have took centre-stage. This rise of the clause, in turn, raised doubts that, in practice, it posed a risk to the conferred or enumerated powers specifically set out elsewhere in primary law.

B. The Broad Scope of the Flexibility Clause

Political impetus for the use of the clause commenced at a vigorous rate. There was a quantifiable increase in EU legislation having its legal basis resting on the clause, thus exceeding the traditional understanding of the conferred competence provisions in the treaties. An added impulse for assertive usage of the clause by the EU legislature arose out of a case questioning the possibility to use the clause as an appropriate legal basis. The changed political interpretation

[11] IE Schwartz, 'Article 235 and Law-Making Powers in the European Community' (1978) 27 *International and Comparative Law Quarterly* 614.

[12] Regulation (EEC) No 803/68 of the Council of 27 June 1968 on the Valuation of Goods for Customs Purposes [1968] OJ L148/6.

[13] H Smit and P Herzog, 'Article 235' in H Smit and P Herzog (eds), *The Law of the European Community: A Commentary on the EEC Treaty*, vol 6 (New York, Matthew Bender, 1976) 6-316.

[14] R Schütze, 'Dynamic Integration: Article 308 EC and Legislation "in the Course of the Operation of the Common Market": A Review Essay' (2003) 23 *Oxford Journal of Legal Studies* 333, 335.

[15] 'Statement from the Paris Summit (19 to 21 October 1972)'.

[16] V Engström, 'How to Tame the Elusive: Lessons from the Revision of the EU Flexibility Clause' (2010) 7 *International Organizations Law Review* 343, 352.

of the clause, as being more open, would have to be judicially tested and was initially affirmed by the Court.

In *Massey-Ferguson*, the Court stated that even though other articles of the treaties could be construed widely, there was 'no reason why the Council could not legitimately consider that recourse to the procedure of Article [352 TFEU] was justified in the interest of legal certainty'.[17] Thus, for the sake of completeness, the clause could be used to complement existing legal bases. The Court went further than what was perhaps anticipated,[18] given that the clause could then be used in an expansive manner. This would have the significance of the EU legislature not trying to over-rely on specific legal bases through erroneous interpretation. Read another way, *Massey-Ferguson* was the Court giving licence to the EU legislature to avail itself of the clause for legislative purposes, even though a maximalist construal of explicit legal bases may have sufficed.

However, *Massey-Ferguson* did not address the full breadth of matters relating to the clause; it merely brought some clarity about what the 'necessary' proviso of the clause was to mean. Importantly, the case left open the question of how sufficient the alternative legal bases had to be. Still, the case was the confirmation that the EU legislature wanted from a legal standpoint for the initial use of the clause. This clarification by the Court meant new legislative opportunities, without worrying that the EU did not possess the sufficient competences for adopting legal acts. If interpreted expansively, *Massey-Ferguson* opened up a scenario whereby nearly anything could fall within the clause's reach. Problematically, it meant the 'absence of … judicial control in the process of 'mutating' [EU] competences'.[19] Moreover, it was the first time when using the clause as a general competence, in addition to a specific competence, came before the Court and the legality of such use had to be assessed.

In many ways, *Massey-Ferguson* confirmed the obvious – that the use of the clause was as intended by the drafters of the treaties – and was affirmed by the Member States at the aforementioned Paris Summit of 1972. This stance by the Court on the legal basis of EU legislation, which was seen more generally in its early days, has in the literature been conceptualised as a form of 'active passivism'.[20] It can be seen as a milestone in the rise of the clause, for it marked a period of 'judicial indifference as to the [EU] legislator's preferences.[21]

[17] Case C-8/73 *Hauptzollamt Bremerhaven v Massey-Ferguson GmbH* [1973] ECLI:EU:C:1973:90, para 4.

[18] A Tizzano, 'The Powers of the Community' in *Thirty Years of Community law* (Luxembourg, Office for Official Publications of the European Communities, 1983) 56.

[19] R Schütze, 'Organized Change towards and "Ever Closer Union": Article 308 EC and the Limits to the Community's Legislative Competence' (2003) 22 *Yearbook of European Law* 79, 87.

[20] M Cappelletti, M Seccombe and J H H Weiler, 'Integration through Law: Europe and the American Federal Experience: A General Introduction' in M Cappelletti, M Seccombe and JHH Weiler (eds), *Integration Through Law: Europe and the American Federal Experience*, vol 1 (Berlin, De Gruyter, 1986) 34.

[21] Schütze (n 19) 99.

Had the Court arrived at the opposite conclusion – that the clause was unsuitable for use as an additional legal basis – it would have killed the evolution of the clause at this stage; instead, the judgment led to the continued rise of the clause. The Advocate General in the case noted that 'one cannot see what damage to the public interest has been caused by the adoption of such a measure on the basis and under the procedure of Article [352 TFEU]' and even though it was a 'more complicated procedure, [it had] nevertheless attained the desired objective'.[22]

C. The Extensiveness of the Clause

The clause was subsequently used as a basis for the adoption of EU legal acts which 'by virtue of their general effect and direct application, are in effect regulations',[23] conferring new powers to the EU that otherwise had not been specifically granted. This led to the adoption of EU legislation in new fields of policy where the EU had no express competence to legislate. The clause was used so extensively that it brought about competence for the EU in 'some rather unlikely corners'.[24] By the early millennium, it was claimed the clause provided a legal basis for over 700 EU legal acts.[25]

Many of the policies in the present treaties with explicit legal bases were borne out of the clause, before later on being bestowed their own provision. One such policy area was the environment.[26] However, even when environmental policy received its own legal basis, with a basic provision for EU legislation in environmental law and its ties to the internal market, measures could still be adopted on the basis of the clause, used in addition to the express competence provision, in a combined manner.[27]

[22] Opinion of Advocate General Trabucchi in Case C-8/73 *Hauptzollamt Bremerhaven v Massey-Ferguson GmbH* [1973] ECLI:EU:C:1973:76, 914.

[23] P Mengozzi, *European Community Law from the Treaty of Rome to the Treaty of Amsterdam* (The Hague, Kluwer Law International, 1999) 81.

[24] S Weatherill, 'Beyond Preemption? Shared Competence and Constitutional Changes in the European Community' in David O'Keeffe and PM Twomey (eds), *Legal Issues of the Maastricht Treaty* (London, Chancery, 1994) 15.

[25] G de Búrca and B de Witte, 'The Delimitation of Powers between the EU and its Member States' in A Arnull and D Wincott (eds), *Accountability and Legitimacy in the European Union* (Oxford, Oxford University Press, 2003) 217.

[26] Examples include Council Decision of 11 June 1981 on the Conclusion of the Convention on Long-Range Transboundary Air Pollution (81/462/EEC) [1981] OJ L171/11 and Council Decision of 12 June 1986 on the Conclusion of the Protocol to the 1979 Convention on Long-Range Transboundary Air Pollution on Long-Term Financing of the Cooperative Programme for Monitoring and Evaluation of the Long-Range Transmission of Air Pollutants in Europe (EMEP) (86/277/EEC) [1986] OJ L181/1.

[27] A Nollkaemper, 'The European Community and International Environmental Co-operation: Legal Aspects of External Community Powers' (1987) 14 *Legal Issues of Economic Integration* 55, 58.

In addition, EU intellectual property (IP) law, an extensive discipline in its own right, has its origins in the clause.[28] Trademark law was the first dimension of IP to see the use of Article 352 TFEU,[29] before later finding its own basis in today's Article 118 TFEU. Agencies of the EU were also established upon the clause,[30] although some were later founded upon other legal bases.[31] The clause was even utilised for the conclusion of international agreements during the period of its rise.[32] The ascendency of the clause led to it being a powerful legal basis for EU legislation. However, this trend did not last long.

IV. THE FALL OF THE FLEXIBILITY CLAUSE

The interpretation of law over time is naturally subject to modification. What is a distinguishing feature of the clause is that legislative and judicial actors at EU level have both altered their stance down through the years. Once the clause had found its true purpose in being a legal basis not explicitly foreseen in the treaties, its status came under interrogation. The incomplete nature of specific competences in the EU was largely supplemented by the clause. With extensive use, questions arose as to whether the clause amounted to *kompetenz-kompetenz* – a power to acquire new competences in an inherent fashion,[33] for it eventually began to be seen as a means of skirting around the formal amendment of the treaties.[34] However, a number of events led to its decline and eventual fall.

The clause itself is specifically provided for in the EU treaties and therefore its existence itself should not prove to be problematic, but legitimate questions can be asked of *how* it is utilised. Accordingly, if 1972 and 1973 saw the rise of the clause, it was 1986 and 1987 that marked the period of its fall. Two reasons

[28] K Lenaerts, I Maselis and K Gutman in J Tomasz Nowak (ed), *EU Procedural Law*, 3rd edn (Oxford, Oxford University Press, 2014) 700.

[29] Council Regulation (EC) No 40/94 of 20 December 1993 on the Community Trade Mark [1993] OJ L11/1.

[30] For three examples over time, see Council Regulation 3245/81/EEC of 26 October 1981 Setting up a European Agency for Co-operation [1981] OJ L328/1; Council Regulation (EC) No 2965/94 of 28 November 1994 Setting up a Translation Centre for Bodies of the European Union [1994] OJ L314/1; Council Regulation (EC) No 168/2007 of 15 February 2007 Establishing a European Union Agency for Fundamental Rights [2007] OJ L53/1.

[31] For example, the European Union Institute for Security Studies (EUISS) and the European Union Satellite Centre (SatCen) are founded upon a CFSP legal basis.

[32] For example, Council Decision of 3 March 1975 Concluding the Convention for the Prevention of Marine Pollution from Land-Based Sources (75/437/EEC) [1975] OJ L194/5; Council Decision of 25 July 1977 Concluding the Convention for the Protection of the Mediterranean Sea against Pollution and the Protocol for the Prevention of the Pollution of the Mediterranean Sea by Dumping from Ships and Aircraft (77/585/EEC) [1977] OJ L240/1.

[33] R Schütze, 'EU Competences: Existence and Exercise' in D Chalmers and A Arnull (eds), *The Oxford Handbook of European Union Law* (Oxford, Oxford University Press, 2015) 79.

[34] Schütze (n 19) 84.

can be seen as to why the clause began to fall out of favour: expanded specific legal bases and judicial curbing. When the Single European Act (SEA) came about, it included new policy fields and the extension of qualified majority voting (QMV) as two distinctive features. This had indirect knock-on consequences for the clause, for it could have been perceived as no longer needed for EU legislation in certain policy fields.

However, with the SEA, evasively, there was the new possibility for Member States in the Council to insist that the clause was to be included as a legal basis for legislation, given that this would in practice mean a veto would be held by Member States, thus circumventing the possibility of QMV and steering legislation towards continued unanimity. At this juncture, the question of legislative powers and the scope of legal basis arrived before the Court, having to retest the scope of the clause and to see if the *Massey-Ferguson* approach was still relevant.

A. The Narrower Scope of the Flexibility Clause

The question about the use of the clause in light of the SEA arose in *Generalised Tariff Preferences*.[35] If the *Massey-Ferguson* guidance on the clause was non-interventionist in relation to the EU legislature's choice of legal basis to achieve an objective of the EU, then *Generalised Tariff Preferences* was anything but. The Advocate General had 'grave doubts' as to how widely the Court may understand what the objectives of the treaty were,[36] and the Court said that the 'the choice of the legal basis for a measure may not depend simply on an institution's conviction as to the objective pursued[,] but must be based on objective factors which are amenable to judicial review'.[37] Consequently, in a sharp turn of events, the Court ruled that: 'It follows from the very wording of Article [352 TFEU] that its use as the legal basis for a measure is justified only where no other provision of the Treaty gives the [EU] institutions the necessary power to adopt the measure in question.'[38] Therefore, the clause could not be used blindly by the EU legislature. Hence, from that point onwards, if pre-existing, specific legal bases for the conclusion of a legal act can be utilised alone, then these must be used, and the clause cannot be added in circumstances where it is not necessary.

This judgment, particularly the point that the clause 'may be used as the legal basis for a measure only where no other provision of the Treaty gives the

[35] Case C-45/86 *Commission v Council* [1987] ECLI:EU:C:1987:163 (hereinafter '*Generalised Tariff Preferences*').

[36] Opinion of Advocate General Lenz in Case C-45/86 *Commission v Council* [1987] ECLI:EU:C:1987:53, 1512.

[37] *Generalised Tariff Preferences* (n 35) para 11.

[38] ibid para 13.

[EU] institutions the necessary power to adopt it', was swiftly affirmed in subsequent case law.[39] The outcome in *Generalised Tariff Preferences* clearly bears the hallmarks of the warnings heeded in the Opinion of the Advocate General in *Massey-Ferguson*. There it was said that 'it would certainly be against the spirit of the system created by the Treaty if the Commission or the Council were to consider it necessary to act on the basis of Article [352 TFEU] in a case where other provisions of the Treaty already clearly provide suitable powers of action'.[40]

If the SEA and *Generalised Tariff Preferences* led to the slow decline of the potential of the clause, contributing to the start of its fall, then the Treaty of Maastricht and *Opinion 2/94* were further contributors to such a waning. The Treaty of Maastricht saw the introduction of a swath of new competences, in addition to QMV being extended even further, and the gradual introduction of subsidiarity. Building upon the *Generalised Tariff Preferences* judgment, *Opinion 2/94* attempted to define the exterior scope of the clause.

Post-1973, the opening-up of the clause had paved the way for the legislature to 'bypass the need' to amend the treaties.[41] Recognising this issue, *Opinion 2/94* placed limits on EU legislative power, even on a conferred basis, leading to an understanding that the clause could not always be used. Specifically, the Court held that the clause:

> [I]s designed to fill the gap where no specific provisions of the Treaty confer on the [EU] institutions express or implied powers to act, if such powers appear none the less to be necessary to enable the [EU] to carry out its functions with a view to attaining one of the objectives laid down by the Treaty. That provision, being an integral part of an institutional system based on the principle of conferred powers, cannot serve as a basis for widening the scope of [EU] powers beyond the general framework created by the provisions of the Treaty as a whole and, in particular, by those that define the tasks and the activities of the [EU]. On any view, Article [352 TFEU] cannot be used as a basis for the adoption of provisions whose effect would, in substance, be to amend the Treaty without following the procedure which it provides for that purpose.[42]

[39] Case C-350/92 *Spain v Council* [1995] ECLI:EU:C:1995:237 (hereinafter '*Medicinal Products*') para 26; Case C-271/94 *Parliament v Council* [1996] ECLI:EU:C:1996:133 (hereinafter '*Edicom*') para 13; Case C-94/94 *United Kingdom v Council* [1996] ECLI:EU:C:1996:431 (hereinafter '*Working Time Directive*') para 48; Case C-268/94 *Portugal v Council* [1996] ECLI:EU:C:1996:461 (hereinafter '*Development Cooperation*') para 21; Case C-22/96 *Parliament v Council* [1998] ECLI:EU:C:1998:258 (hereinafter '*IDA*') para 22; and Case C-436/03 *Parliament v Council* [2006] ECLI:EU:C:2006:277 (hereinafter '*European Cooperative Society*') para 36.

[40] Opinion of Advocate General Trabucchi in *Massey-Ferguson* (n 22) 914.

[41] T Konstadinides, 'Drawing the Line between Circumvention and Gap-Filling: An Exploration of the Conceptual Limits of the Treaty's Flexibility Clause' (2012) 31 *Yearbook of European Law* 227, 229.

[42] *Opinion 2/94*, Accession by the Community to the European Convention for the Protection of Human Rights and Fundamental Freedoms [1996] ECLI:EU:C:1996:140, paras 29 and 30.

With the EU wishing to accede to the European Convention on Human Rights (ECHR) and there being no specific legal basis to do so, the EU attempted to use the clause. However, viewed one way, the 'weight of the modification of the human rights regime' exceeded the scope of the clause.[43] Thus, the ruling of the Court confirmed that the clause cannot be utilised by the EU legislature where an alternative option to achieve a particular aim would be to amend the treaties and that the clause had to be interpreted in line with the principle of conferred powers. The *Opinion 2/94* bombshell put firm limits on the scope of the clause and perhaps even rolled it back to a provision with minimalistic intent.

With this outer reach of the clause now being developed judicially, it can be noted that there was nothing to stop the Court from saying the same thing at any previous occasion when questions about the scope of the clause arose. The epiphany the Court had at this juncture might be difficult to grasp, but chronologically speaking, *Opinion 2/94* could be seen as a direct response to the German Constitutional Court's *Maastricht* judgment,[44] ensuring that the clause did not *in itself*, by its mere existence, confer powers on the EU legislature. Furthermore, it could be argued that the Court sought to define its own understanding of what the visible limits to the clause were, thereby ensuring that no national court was doing the Court's work. Alternatively, *Opinion 2/94* could be interpreted as merely a claim of autonomy[45] in the same way that *Opinion 2/13* was.[46] For all the critique of *Opinion 2/94*, it nonetheless also gave hesitant backing to the clause in principle, stating that it is 'an integral part of an institutional system',[47] despite its not being able to be deployed in the particular instance. Therefore, whilst it was still possible to use the clause, the conditions and prospects for its use changed dramatically. Not only had the SEA and the Treaty of Maastricht lessened the need for relying on the clause, but also procedurally, there were now some judicially imposed obstacles to its use.

Despite the treaty changes to tighten the use of the clause and the Court's jurisprudence that put limits on it being deployed as a legal basis, the clause still had purpose. Commentators have noted that '[c]ontrary to what may have been expected, there [was] not … any decrease' in the use of the clause immediately following *Opinion 2/94* and the Treaty of Maastricht.[48] This might put

[43] N-L Arold Lorenz, X Groussot and G Thor Petursson, *The European Human Rights Culture: A Paradox of Human Rights Protection in Europe?* (Leiden, Martinus Nijhoff Publishers, 2014) 223.

[44] BVerfG, Cases 2 BvR 2134/92 & 2159/92 *Manfred Brunner and Others v The European Union Treaty* [1994] 1 CMLR 57.

[45] Konstadinides (n 41) 236.

[46] *Opinion 2/13*, Accession of the European Union to the European Convention for the Protection of Human Rights and Fundamental Freedoms [2014] ECLI:EU:C:2014:2454. See L Halleskov Storgaard, 'EU Law Autonomy versus European Fundamental Rights Protection: On Opinion 2/13 on EU Accession to the ECHR' (2015) 15 *Human Rights Law Review* 485.

[47] Opinion 2/94 (n 42) para 30.

[48] CF Bergström and J Almer, 'The Residual Competence: Basic Statistics on Legislation with a Legal Basis in Article 308 EC', Swedish Institute for European Policy Studies (SIEPS) (2002) 3.

the claim of the fall of the clause into question, yet the numbers alone do not tell the full story. In fact, whilst numerically its use was constant, substantively the clause moved away from internal market law-making and began a reorientation towards institutional and external policy fields. Article 352 TFEU shares similar traits to another treaty provision – Article 216 TFEU – which serves as the legal basis for the EU to enter into international agreements. Both are objective-orientated and are non-specific with respect to just how far they can be stretched. However, external relations was the 'least justifiable' use of the clause,[49] particularly when considering the types of legislation adopted, including development cooperation and emergency aid.

The subsequent Treaty of Amsterdam did nothing materially to alter the clause. The Treaty inserted certain aspects of social policy into primary law, thus providing a new legal basis for legislation that had been previously adopted under the clause.[50] However, it also led to the Laeken Declaration, a pronouncement of the heads of government meeting as the European Council, expressing misgivings about the way in which the clause had been utilised by the Member States themselves through the EU legislative process. More specifically, the Declaration raised concerns about the 'encroachment upon the exclusive areas of competence of the Member States',[51] but without recognition that each member of the Council possessed a veto power.

B. Detaching the Internal Market

The Treaty of Lisbon made a number of amendments to the clause, chiefly of a functional nature. The changes meant that the clause was no longer to apply with respect to the internal market alone, but more broadly 'to attain one of the objectives set out in the Treaties'.[52] This subtle but important change in wording has led to something particular about the understanding of the clause, as well as about the very essence of what the EU is about. The dropping of the internal market proviso from the clause was not overtly significant, as the legislature never strictly adhered to that limitation beforehand in any case. However, the amendment did introduce 'sharper conceptual boundaries'.[53] Sceptically, binding the clause to the common market constituted 'limits that lack[ed] precision',[54]

[49] A Dashwood, 'Article 308 EC as the Outer Limit of Expressly Conferred Community Competence' in C Barnard and O Odudu (eds), *The Outer Limits of European Union Law* (Oxford, Hart Publishing, 2009) 40.

[50] S van Raepenbusch and D Hanf, 'Flexibility in Social Policy' in B de Witte, D Hanf and E Vos (eds), *The Many Faces of Differentiation in EU Law* (Antwerp, Intersentia, 2001) 76.

[51] European Council, 'Presidency Conclusions: European Council Meeting in Laeken, 14–15 December 2001, SN 300/1/01 REV 1', 22.

[52] Article 352(1) TFEU.

[53] Schütze (n 19) 113.

[54] S Weatherill, 'Better Competence Monitoring' (2005) 30 *European Law Review* 23, 24.

and the EU's overall aims had well and truly gone beyond economic objectives achieved through the market. According to one view, the 'realignment … reflect[s] … the Union as no longer restricted to a narrow common market objective'.[55] One observer noted how the term 'common market', rather than being read literally as a narrow definition, could also be seen as 'a term of art'.[56] Furthermore, in hindsight, it was 'hard to see how … worthy activities could honestly be said to have manifested itself in the course of operation of the common market',[57] citing some external relations examples, including financial relief, food aid and technical assistance programmes, that were based on the clause.

Instead of speaking of internal market objectives, the clause in its amended version authorises action 'within the framework of the policies defined in the Treaties', inclining the reader to see the imposition of a limitation on its use. Yet the precise formulation of the clause on this particular point had never been a problem in relation to adopting legislation, Accession to the ECHR had nothing to do with the internal market, and *Opinion 2/94* did not even mention this as an obstacle. Therefore, it is fair to say that while delimiting the use of the clause, the Court did embrace how widespread it may be used, if done correctly. Thus, the current Article 352 TFEU reflects the contemporary practice of the clause.[58] Even with specific legal bases, the internal market provisions are not sufficient in themselves to further the internal market, and despite the clause today being of 'little significance',[59] it can still be utilised to give effect to the basic freedoms, such as the free movement of goods.[60] Given the fact that the legal order of the EU has been evolutionary, this textual change can be welcomed, since to continue to link the clause with just one aspect of EU law like the internal market would have implied that the EU should continue to distance itself from reality.

C. Subsidiarity

Subsidiarity in EU law has received mixed reactions, both theoretically and substantively, yet the Treaty of Lisbon sought to increase its prevalence in EU primary law even further, with the intention of ensuring a wider inclusion

[55] A Rosas and L Armati, *EU Constitutional Law: An Introduction* (Oxford, Hart Publishing, 2012) 26.

[56] Dashwood (n 49) 36.

[57] A Dashwood, 'The Limits of European Community Powers' (1996) 21 *European Law Review* 113, 123.

[58] Konstadinides (n 41) 243.

[59] S Weatherill, *The Internal Market as a Legal Concept* (Oxford, Oxford University Press, 2017) 13.

[60] For example, an EU regulation to provide a means of removing obstacles on the basic of action/inaction by Member States has relied upon the clause. See Council Regulation (EC) No 2679/98 of 7 December 1998 on the Functioning of the Internal Market in Relation to the Free Movement of Goods among the Member States [1998] OJ L337/8.

of democratic legal actors. Subsidiarity forms the basis of providing input legitimacy in the activation of the clause, which, for much of its life, did not require the consent of the European Parliament. The Parliament only had to be consulted and had no veto power; instead, the control over the legal basis was exercised by unanimity within the Council. Now within Article 352(1) TFEU, the Treaty of Lisbon requires the consent of the Parliament to be attained before the clause is invoked. This elevation of the European Parliament's role means that Member States are not the only veto holders for the use of the clause.

Article 352(2) TFEU now also ensures the Commission shall 'draw national [p]arliaments' attention to proposals' based on the clause. This information right accorded to national parliaments constitutes a considerable democracy promotion and an effort to respect enhanced levels of subsidiarity. With the involvement of national parliaments and recognition that the clause is an 'exceptional use of EU legislative power',[61] the obligation falls on the Commission to formally notify national legislatures. This is a change which, while bringing political processes closer to the use of the clause, intended to add a greater democratic element by linking it to the newly introduced early warning mechanism.[62] However, the additional informative exercise that the Commission must now take in informing national parliaments, as per Article 352(2) TFEU, is not strong enough that it equates to a consent power, but is merely a right for national parliaments to be informed.

A number of national parliaments have already objected to the use of the clause,[63] demonstrating that the added subsidiarity is already having its intended effect. Whilst one way of interpreting the involvement of national parliaments in the application of the clause may be that it is mere symbolism,[64] there is also a more formal legal consideration. This sizeable subsidiarity effort has been selected over an alternative option of increased judicial control. There is thus the danger that this inclusion of national parliaments may 'affect the perception of the EU as an autonomous supranational actor',[65] thereby potentially undermining the EU legislative process. Furthermore, it hypothetically adds to the length of time that would be needed for legislation to be adopted under the clause, which, by some understandings, was intended to be an agreed-upon legal basis along the same timeline as any other legal basis in the treaties.

[61] P Craig, *The Lisbon Treaty: Law, Politics, and Treaty Reform* (Oxford, Oxford University Press 2011) 184.

[62] For recent work on the early warning mechanism in place, see K Granat, *The Principle of Subsidiarity and its Enforcement in the EU Legal Order: The Role of National Parliaments in the Early Warning System* (Oxford, Hart Publishing, 2018).

[63] F Fabbrini and K Granat, '"Yellow Card, But No Foul": The Role of the National Parliaments under the Subsidiarity Protocol and the Commission Proposal for an EU Regulation on the Right to Strike' (2013) 50 *Common Market Law Review* 115, 136.

[64] A Wetter Ryde, 'Mapping out the Procedural Requirements for the Early Warning Mechanism' in A Jonsson Cornell and M Goldoni (eds), *National and Regional Parliaments in the EU-Legislative Procedure Post-Lisbon: The Impact of the Early Warning Mechanism* (Oxford, Hart Publishing, 2017) 73.

[65] Engström (n 16) 371.

D. Annexed Declarations

The Intergovernmental Conference that led to the adoption of the Treaty of Lisbon also adopted two Declarations.[66] It has not been sufficiently clarified to date how the new Declarations annexed to the treaties would be interpreted by the Court, as Article 352 TFEU appears to be shaped as a narrower legal basis. However, what can be noted is how the Declarations should be read alongside the clause itself. On the face of it, they do not appear to have limited the clause in any real substantive manner, particularly given the treaties' wide-ranging ambitions. Furthermore, Declaration No 42 appears to be verifying the current state of the Court's jurisprudence, most prominently *Opinion 2/94*, thereby trying to ensure no return to the laissez-faire type of judgments such as *Massey-Ferguson*.

Even with the two declarations in place, the revised clause, prima facie, appears as an easier provision to utilise,[67] despite the reduced need to avail of it. However, its post-Lisbon use has been considerably less controversial than its pre-Lisbon use,[68] implying it has become narrower in scope compared to its predecessors and subject to stricter procedural requirements.[69] The procedural safeguards imposed on the use of the clause in the post-Lisbon era may have acted too much as a deterrent to its use, rather than safeguarding its proper and intended potential use. Thus, it appears that the Treaty of Lisbon has contributed to ensuring the ever-prolonging decline and fall of the clause. This notwithstanding, the Treaty has not done much to allay fears of the clause continuing to be a means of the EU accumulating competence.[70] Procedurally, the clause is much tighter and in reality, its use has declined to a mere trickle. Post-Lisbon, only a few legislative acts have been adopted that rely upon the clause.[71]

E. National Judicial Responses to the Flexibility Clause

The very problem with the clause was that it could be seen as being too successful in fulfilling its intended aims. Additional legal bases were added to the

[66] Declarations no. 41 and 42. See the Appendix to this chapter.

[67] J Nergelius, *The Constitutional Dilemma of the European Union* (Groningen, Europa Law Publishing, 2009) 53.

[68] P Craig, 'Competence: Clarity, Conferral, Containment and Consideration' (2004) 29 *European Law Review* 323, 341.

[69] J-C Piris, *The Lisbon Treaty: A Legal and Political Analysis* (Cambridge, Cambridge University Press, 2010) 144.

[70] Rosas and Armati (n 55) 26.

[71] Two examples include Council Regulation (EU) No 216/2013 of 7 March 2013 on the Electronic Publication of the Official Journal of the European Union [2013] OJ L69/1; and Council Regulation (EU) 2015/496 of 17 March 2015 Amending Regulation (EEC, Euratom) No 354/83 as Regards the Deposit of the Historical Archives of the Institutions at the European University Institute in Florence [2015] OJ L79/1.

treaties over time to ensure recourse was not made time and again to the clause, guaranteeing that it did not become a general competence provider. With EU law and policy heading in an ever-greater number of directions, scapegoats inevitably had to be found by the naysayers. In that light, the clause could be seen as the 'primary culprit of creeping legislative expansion'.[72] One of the principal reasons it can thus be singled out for is its very stature. For many years, its premise was vague and its application by political actors was discretionary.[73] Accordingly, the suspicion with which it has been viewed seeped down to national legal actors. Pushback has taken place on legal and political plains, and in an elongated power play, national supreme and constitutional courts have not all been silent, and legislative actors at the national and subnational levels have voiced concerns over the clause.

With this backdrop, the clause has been subject to national litigation and arguably it has been national judicial systems that have put up the strongest case against the use of the clause in the EU. The judiciary of the original six Member States showed a well-known resistance to certain aspects of the nature of EU law,[74] particularly the clause in question. This was long before enlargement, but it has been hypothesised that resistance may just as well have been in existence in other Member States,[75] albeit in a more contained manner. The German Constitutional Court's *Maastricht* judgment called the clause a 'competence to round-off the Treaty'.[76] In other words, the *kompetenzerweiterungsvorschrift*[77] and the same national court's *Lisbon* judgment made a dynamic reading of the clause. It stated that the use of the clause:

> [C]onstitutionally requires ratification by the German Bundestag and the Bundesrat on the basis of … [the German] Basic Law'. In addition, '[t]he German representative in the Council may not express formal approval on behalf of … Germany … as long as these constitutionally required preconditions are not met.[78]

This insistence on German legislative exercise of consent to be given to the German executive is nothing more than a national legal matter. However, from

[72] L Miller, 'European Contract Law after Lisbon' in D Ashiagbor, N Countouris and I Lianos (eds), *The European Union after the Treaty of Lisbon* (Cambridge, Cambridge University Press, 2012) 240.

[73] B Guastaferro, 'The European Union as a Staatenverbund? The Endorsement of the Principle of Conferral in the Treaty of Lisbon' in M Trybus and L Rubini (eds), *The Treaty of Lisbon and the Future of European Law and Policy* (Cheltenham, Edward Elgar, 2012) 121.

[74] From the German Constitutional Court, see FC Mayer, 'Defiance by a Constitutional Court – Germany' in A Jakab and D Kochenov (eds), *The Enforcement of EU Law and Values: Ensuring Member States' Compliance* (Oxford, Oxford University Press, 2017). However, this likely stretched to other legal actors within the state.

[75] B Davies, *Resisting the European Court of Justice: West Germany's Confrontation with European Law, 1949–1979* (Cambridge, Cambridge University Press, 2012) 203.

[76] *Manfred Brunner and Others v The European Union Treaty* (n 44) para 99.

[77] The 'extension of competence provision' or 'competence extension provision', depending on one's translation.

[78] BVerfG, Cases 2 BvE 2/08, 5/08, 1010/08, 1022/08, 1259/08 and 182/09 '*The Lisbon Judgment*' ECLI:DE:BVerfG:2009:es20090630.2bve000208, para 328.

the point of view of EU law, the fact that extending the EU's competence base may lead to a lesser role for national parliaments is not contrary to EU law, but merely a natural outcome. What is unusual about this *Lisbon* judgment is that it insists that the German legislature, at the national level, ratify the use of the clause. This is odd, given that in practice, for 'the adoption of secondary law … national parliamentary approval is not normally required under the EU Treaties'.[79] Whether such power plays by national courts are worthy activities or a mere hobby-horse of jurists eminently in pursuit of power and legitimacy is debatable, but they leave no one any wiser with respect to how to interpret and apply the clause. It thus remains an open question as to whether national courts' concerns with the clause have in fact made the EU legislature rethink the use of the clause in the current age.

F. National Legislative Responses to the Flexibility Clause

However, it has not just been national courts that were interested in the clause, but regional and national legislatures too. Subnational entities in Member States would be key proponents in this regard, given that they, alongside national lawmakers, have the most to lose by widening EU competence. The German Länder have been proponents of the abolition of the clause,[80] but this has not been considered a realistic proposal by the real decision-makers. In the UK, domestic legislation has been passed to the effect that there is an authorisation mechanism in place in the national legal order as a way of control over executive action by the government acting in the Council. This is a Member State, internally, building in its own safeguards, withholding its own consent when its national government decides on the use of the clause in the Council. The European Union Act 2011 specifies that '[a] Minister of the Crown may not vote in favour of or otherwise support an Article 352 [TFEU] decision',[81] without an Act of Parliament, unless it fits into one of the defined exemptions catered for by that domestic statute.[82]

Whilst this Act has furthered the UK's 'zeal for control over EU decisions',[83] it is far from alone. One of the reasons offered for this was to prevent members

[79] P Kiiver, 'The Lisbon Judgment of the German Constitutional Court: A Court-Ordered Strengthening of the National Legislature in the EU' (2010) 16 *European Law Journal* 578, 583.

[80] A von Bogdandy and J Bast, 'The Federal Order of Competences' in von Bogdandy and Bast (eds) (n 5) 300.

[81] Section 8(1) ('Decisions under Art 352 of TFEU') of the European Union Act 2011 (Act of Parliament) (c 12) 2011.

[82] Section 8(6) setting out the exceptions includes, based on the clause: equivalent measures already adopted; if it renews a legal act already adopted; extends a legal act to a new EU or non-EU Member States; repeals an existing legal act adopted; or consolidates an existing legal act.

[83] P Craig, 'The European Union Act 2011: Locks, Limits and Legality' (2011) 48 *Common Market Law Review* 1915, 1918.

of the government from 'go[ing] native' in Council meetings.[84] In fact, whilst national legislative actions similar to those in the UK have been evidently taken in a small number of Member States, this is not fully reflective of the bigger picture; rather, many national governments are 'still alert' as to the use of the clause.[85] However, another reason is the simple fact that national parliaments have been left behind in the process of European integration and through such a limited measure, they can self-exercise a form of subsidiarity control.

The above-mentioned national legal act in the UK has similarities to how the German situation post-*Lisbon* judgment manifested itself, except that the UK acted via national legislation, whereas the German reaction came in the form of a judicial ruling. However, in both instances, the national governments of these Member States now have strong national checks on the use of the clause by their national parliaments, which in turn can be used for leverage in an attempt to secure other concessions on other policies at the EU level. Some years on, the British practice stemming from the European Union Act 2011 has emerged in a peculiar way. All forthcoming decisions in the Council for the adoption of EU legislation based upon the clause are grouped together in what is known as a 'European Union (Approvals) Act',[86] which is adopted annually.[87] Ultimately, going forward, each Member State maintains the right to keep a national check on any future legislative expansion using the clause.

V. THE FUTURE OF THE FLEXIBILITY CLAUSE

The legislative use and judicial interpretation of the flexibility clause have gradually elucidated what it can and cannot be used for. The clause once served as the 'locus of true expansion' of EU powers,[88] but the expansionary period of EU law is well and truly over. Thus, the fall of the clause has been evident, with its limited use today, yet the clause still has the potential to become expansive if legislators so decide. As eloquently put, the clause stated that 'in the absence of internal powers, the Council may, subject to the conditions and in accordance with the procedure specified in Article [352 TFEU], create such powers if they are 'necessary' for the attainment of an objective of the [EU] … to attain

[84] R Schütze, *European Union Law* (Cambridge, Cambridge University Press, 2015) 234.

[85] T Konstadinides, 'The Competences of the European Union' in R Schütze and T Tridimas (eds), *Oxford Principles of European Union Law*, vol 1 (Oxford, Oxford University Press, 2018) 210.

[86] HM Government, 'Review of the Balance of Competences between the United Kingdom and the European Union: Semester 4: Subsidiarity and Proportionality' (HM Government, 2014) 26.

[87] European Union (Approvals) Act 2013 (Act of Parliament) (c 9) 2013; European Union (Approvals) Act 2014 (Act of Parliament) (c 3) 2014; European Union (Approvals) Act 2015 (Act of Parliament) (c 37) 2015; European Union (Approvals) Act 2017 (Act of Parliament) (c 35) 2017. It should be noted that there was no Act in 2016.

[88] JHH Weiler, 'The Transformation of Europe' (1991) 100 *Yale Law Journal* 2403, 2443.

one of its objectives, affirm[ing] its own competence'.[89] The clause's standalone basis was, theoretically, to be capped by prescribing that its use was linked with 'necessity' – a supposedly limiting provision.

Whilst the clause has existed in one form or another throughout the entire period of the EU's existence, it went largely unrestrained by the Court as a basis for legislative measures for most of its reign until *Generalised Tariff Preferences*,[90] when its use in addition to another more specific legal basis was first questioned. The narrowing-down of the clause continued, with the Court stating in *International Convention on the Harmonized Commodity Description and Coding System* that '[t]he fact that the contested decision may affect another measure which is based on [Article 352 TFEU] does not necessarily imply recourse to that provision as a legal basis'[91] and thus seeing the role of explicitly conferred legal bases. This meant that a specific legal basis must take precedence over a general legal basis, such as the clause.

For the future of Europe, it is important to determine whether the clause still has a meaningful role to play in the EU legal order and whether it still has the possibility to adapt to arising circumstances as it did in the past. In the modern age, it 'scarcely lead[s] to the extension of competences',[92] and the question is therefore, if the *flexibility* clause has become more *inflexible*, what use may it have for the future and how might the clause fit into the EU's constitutional evolution. If the dynamism of how it was exploited previously is intercepted, given legal and political considerations, then what role can we envision for the clause?

A. Mandatory or Optional

In recent times, the Court clarified in *Pringle* that the clause does not impose any burden upon the EU[93] and cannot be utilised by parties as a means of forcing a response from the EU legislature to whatever situation is before it. As the Court stated as far back as *ERTA*, the 'appropriate measures' aspect of Article 352 TFEU does not equate to an obligation for it to be used, but merely 'confers … an option' upon the legislature to act,[94] reaffirming the discretionary

[89] Opinion of Advocate General Tizzano in Joined Cases C-466-469/98, C-471-2/98, and C-475-6/98 *Commission v United Kingdom and Others* [2002] ECLI:EU:C:2002:63 (hereinafter '*Open Skies*') para 48.

[90] *Generalised Tariff Preferences* (n 35).

[91] Case C-165/87 *Commission v Council* [1988] ECLI:EU:C:1988:458 (hereinafter '*International Convention on the Harmonized Commodity Description and Coding System*') para 17.

[92] U Everling, 'The European Union as a Federal Association of States and Citizens' in von Bogdandy and Bast (eds) (n 5) 716.

[93] Case C-370/12 *Thomas Pringle v Government of Ireland and Others* [2012] ECLI:EU:C:2012:756, para 67.

[94] Case C-22/70 *Commission v Council* [1971] ECLI:EU:C:1971:32 (hereinafter '*ERTA*') para 95.

nature of the clause. Therefore, it has to be asked just how *flexible* the flexibility clause is.

Article 352 TFEU does have an 'outer limit',[95] as demonstrated by the Court in *Opinion 2/94*,[96] whereby the Court said that it cannot be used instead of treaty amendment. However, the Court did not eliminate recourse to the clause altogether. In the *Erasmus* case, it stated that the clause could be utilised by the Council if it was its '[u]nequivocal … conviction' that another legal basis was insufficient,[97] provided that it was necessary and the other legal basis did not suit the measure. The Court found that the addition of the clause was allowed, even though the legislation contained only 'some research aspects'.[98] This in turn has raised new questions about what is to be viewed as 'necessary', as set out in the treaties. The Treaty of Lisbon did not make an attempt at bringing any clarity to this point of ponder, so the test remains the same as before.

B. Non-uses

In the aftermath of *Opinion 1/09*,[99] in which the Court prevented the establishment of a European Patent Court based on the legal text before it, the use of the clause was not considered sufficient for achieving the desired outcome,[100] and consequently enhanced cooperation under Article 20 TFEU was to be used instead. This demonstrates that enhanced cooperation has thereby offered an alternative legal basis for going beyond the explicitly conferred competences of the EU as per the treaties, and may be used as a general legal basis, in the same way that the clause has been.

It would appear that one of the strengths of the clause is its ability to provide a basis for dealing with unanticipated developments as they arise. However, the challenges the EU faced over the last decade dealing with financial and migration issues brought about an array of encounters, for which the clause served little to no purpose in terms of providing legal solutions. Recourse was instead made to international law, demonstrating that the clause fell short in times of need. In addition, as the clause is seeing its demise, there has been a rise and acceleration in the use of non-EU treaties. This is not in itself new, for the Schengen arrangement was initially formed outside of the EU legal structures.

[95] S Weatherill and P Beaumont, *EU Law*, 3rd edn (London, Penguin 1999) 370.

[96] *Opinion 2/94* (n 42).

[97] Case C-242/87 *Commission v Council* [1989] ECLI:EU:C:1989:217 (hereinafter '*Erasmus*') para 39.

[98] K Lenaerts, 'Constitutionalism and the Many Faces of Federalism' (1990) 38 *American Journal of Comparative Law* 205, 218.

[99] *Opinion 1/09*, European and Community Patents Court [2011] ECLI:EU:C:2011:123.

[100] B de Witte and T Martinelli, 'Treaties between EU Member States as Quasi-instruments of EU Law' in M Cremona and C Kilpatrick (eds), *EU Legal Acts: Challenges and Transformations* (Oxford, Oxford University Press, 2018) 184.

However, many of the non-EU treaties will eventually have to be incorporated into the EU legal order at a future juncture.

To take one example, the European Stability Mechanism (ESM) will have to be incorporated into EU law at a later stage. However, whether this will be done through formal treaty amendment or by the clause remains to be seen. The Commission has openly pondered such a choice, stating:

> While it would not be excluded to integrate the ESM … under the current Treaties, via a decision pursuant to Article 352 TFEU … it appears that, given the political and financial importance of such a step and the legal adaptations required, that avenue would not necessarily be less cumbersome than operating an integration of the ESM through a change to the EU Treaties.[101]

However, a consideration that the Commission does not discuss is Declaration No 41, which appears to exclude the use of the clause for EMU purposes.[102] Thus, the clause is a less viable option for incorporation of the ESM into EU law than a formal treaty amendment, given this conundrum and the doctrine set out in *Opinion 2/94*.

The clause is also not a manner in which a Member State may leave the EU, for this is provided for in Article 50 TEU, but perhaps might be considered suitable for other deeds, such as withdrawal from the euro currency, as was seriously contemplated by a Member State at one juncture. There are no mechanisms for exiting 'optional policies' such as the single currency. Yet, the viability of the clause for non-permanent measures would likely come up against the judiciary's view of the clause, for it has to date only been used for permanent legislation and not for ad hoc temporary scenarios.

C. Optimal Use

The intense use of the flexibility clause implies that, over time, policy areas have emerged that were not foreseen (or at the very least acknowledged) by the treaties and their drafters. For the earlier years, the use of the clause suited the wants of Member States, but in contemporary Europe, it no longer does so. Still, however, the best use of the clause is arguably when it is complementing other existing, explicit legal bases.

The use of the clause for adopting legislative measures has the inherent problem that it does not provide a legal basis that is specifically provided by EU primary law. Such use thus lacks a 'higher level of political legitimacy'[103] that

[101] Communication from the Commission, 'A Blueprint for a Deep and Genuine Economic and Monetary Union: Launching a European Debate' COM [2012] 777 Final, 34.

[102] Furthermore, in light of *Pringle*, formal treaty amendment appears as the more viable option. See B de Witte and T Beukers, 'The Court of Justice Approves the Creation of the European Stability Mechanism outside the EU Legal Order: *Pringle*' (2013) 50 *Common Market Law Review* 805, 834.

[103] Weiler (n 88) 2435.

might otherwise be afforded a legislative matter that has an ingrained treaty basis. Yet using the clause for supplementary purposes is still possible,[104] which bodes well for its longevity. With it being able to be read in a minimalist,[105] maximalist and everything-in-between manner, the imprecise scope of the clause can cause consternation. If it was intended that the clause was only to be utilised 'to attain one of the objectives set out in the Treaties', then this potential restraining effect of linking it to the EU's objectives has truly failed, for the objectives of the EU are an open-ended construct and are themselves ever-expanding.

The use of Article 352 TFEU during the pillars stage of European integration, between the post-Maastricht and pre-Lisbon era, was curtailed by the very constitutional design of the treaties. The clause was only able to be used for achieving the objectives of the EU set down in the then First Pillar – the Community objectives. It could not be used for the attainment of objectives of the Second Pillar (Common Security and Defence Policy (CFSP)) or the Third Pillar (Area of Freedom, Security and Justice (AFSJ)). The EU's foreign policy through CFSP has never been included in its scope, which is hardly surprising, given that the CFSP provisions have been sufficiently flexible in any case.[106]

The limited number of cases before the Court dealing with the scope of the clause can partly be attributed to the fact that unanimity is needed, and therefore the likely actors to challenge the legal basis of legislation would have had to consent to its use in the first place. The only remaining legal actors with sufficient *locus standi* to challenge measures may be other EU institutions such as the European Parliament, as it did in *European Cooperative Society*.[107] However, given that the Treaty of Lisbon now provides the Parliament with a consent power, such circumstances are less likely to be challenged before the judiciary.

D. What Next in the Law?

What makes the clause so appealing as an instrument of study is its ability to adjust to arising political needs. If the clause is ever utilised again as it was in the past, a solution will be found, such as granting a specific legal basis in future treaties, as has been the practice to date. Ingenuity, creativity and assertion will be necessary elements of legal thinking if it is ever to be deployed in

[104] Case C-166/07 *Parliament v Council* [2009] ECLI:EU:C:2009:499 (hereinafter '*International Fund for Ireland*') paras 41, 67 and 69.
[105] On judicial minimalism, see G Butler, 'In Search of the Political Question Doctrine in EU Law' (2018) 45 *Legal Issues of Economic Integration* 329.
[106] Articles 23–46 TEU. More specifically, see art 24(1) TEU. See also G Butler, *Constitutional Law of the EU's Common Foreign and Security Policy: Competence and Institutions in External Relations* (Oxford, Hart Publishing, 2019).
[107] *European Cooperative Society* (n 39).

the future. Given the history of the clause, it might be questioned whether it has been the ground for implied power at all or, rather, an individual contrivance for EU legislation. If the clause is to be separated and argued to have been a standalone legal basis, used as it was immediately post-*Massey Ferguson*, then any other construal of the clause would have ensured that it would never have risen as it did.

One of the anomalies regarding the clause has been that despite its decreased use as a legal basis, concerns about its scope have still not been fully alleviated. It could therefore be said that as long as the clause continues to exist, its critics will continue to lament it. Whilst some may call for it to be deleted altogether,[108] it has continued to exist. However, if future treaty change were to be undertaken and Article 352 TFEU were to be put under the microscope again, some modest proposals could be put forward. This may include specifically linking Article 5 TEU, the current basis of competence conferral, with Article 352 TFEU, the clause, by ensuring their reference to each other, for it is to a certain extent peculiar that the two have never been formally linked.

It is the Member States themselves that sought to use the clause to its maximum capabilities for the purposes of legislative expansion. Yet in light of the journey that the clause has taken, it is challenging to envisage a scenario where there would be a return to a similar widespread use. The Commission, which has a keenness for moving as much EU decision-making to be made by QMV, will only propose legislation based on the clause in limited circumstances, given its unanimity nature.

The clause is one of the declining number of legal bases in the treaties where unanimity voting is required in the Council. This minority status is even specifically protected, as it cannot be amended through the simplified revision procedure provided in Article 48(7) TEU, given that Article 353 TFEU states that it does not apply to the clause. This has the intended effect of ensuring that the unanimity element of the clause remains sacrosanct. Whatever method of interpretation of the clause is used in the future, whether liberal or conservative, the consent of all Member States will still be needed.

The Court has seen no reason to alter its stance on Article 352 TFEU from its reasoning provided in *Generalised Tariff Preferences* that specific legal bases are preferred over general legal bases. Yet in retrospect, it can be asked whether the Court ought to have reined in the clause earlier. In its history, there have been tenuous uses of the provision.[109] Prior to *Generalised Tariff Preferences*,

[108] Attributable to unnamed Member States, 'The European Convention: The Secretariat: Report from Chairman of Working Group V "Complementary Competencies" to Members of the Convention. Subject: Final Report of Working Group V (CONV 375/1/02 REV 1)' 14.

[109] Even recently, the establishment of the EU's Fundamental Rights Agency (FRA) in 2007 was founded upon the clause, with insubstantial links to the internal market, when that was an applicable provision. Council Regulation (EC) No 168/2007 of 15 February 2007 Establishing a European Union Agency for Fundamental Rights [2007] OJ L53/1.

the EU legislature availed itself of the clause as a legal basis independent of specific legal bases as a means of wielding strong legislative power. Upon mature reflection, this can be questioned given that legislative use of Article 352 TFEU in situations in which competence was not conferred explicitly meant that the breadth of the treaties grew ever wider, thus circumventing the very limits placed on the EU. Sensibly, therefore, the modern practice is a much more appropriate use of the clause. On the other hand, the Court 'reining in' the clause may have been difficult, for it may in actual fact have borne the risk of defeating the very purpose for which the clause was intended. Despite changes of the treaties, the parties have never attempted to seriously codify the Court's jurisprudence on the clause, with the most obvious link being the similarities between *Opinion 2/94* and Declaration No 42 annexed to the treaties post-Lisbon.

The Court has also obfuscated the clause on occasion. In *Kadi I*,[110] it chose to focus on other matters[111] rather than clarify how Article 352 TFEU could be used conjunctively with other legal bases during the pillars era. Yet, it has been said that the clause both 'represents and defines' the limits of the scope of the EU treaties.[112] As a result, it is perfectly reasonable to suggest treaty amendments as the proper means of going beyond the confines of the treaties. Nonetheless, this might be implausible. Even if the EU had no flexibility clause, there would have been the additional legal risk that legal bases would be used that would be incorrect and, in some cases, wholly inappropriate.

In future incarnations of the EU treaties, the clause might have a different location. For example, during the drafting that led to the draft Constitutional Treaty, consideration was given to relocating the clause from the end of the TFEU to being included earlier in the treaties, within a general title on competence.[113] This never occurred and the clause is still tucked away in Article 352 TFEU. However, this is an insight into what future reform may look like. In addition, expanding the Opinion procedure found in Article 218(11) TFEU,[114] by way of extending this ex ante judicial control to the clause, has been another reform considered,[115] in which Member States that are hesitant on the use of the clause might be reassured by having legal certainty provided. Despite the discussion, no action has been taken so far on extending the Opinion procedure.

[110] Joined Cases C-402/05 P and C-415/05 P *Kadi and Al Barakaat International Foundation v Council and Commission* [2008] ECLI:EU:C:2008:461.

[111] Konstadinides (n 41) 248.

[112] R Schütze, *From Dual to Cooperative Federalism: The Changing Structure of European Law* (Oxford, Oxford University Press, 2009) 142.

[113] 'The European Convention' (n 108) 16.

[114] For more on the Opinion procedure conducted by the Court in an ex ante manner, see G Butler, 'Pre-ratification Judicial Review of International Agreements to Be Concluded by the European Union' in M Derlén and J Lindholm (eds), *The Court of Justice of the European Union: Multidisciplinary Perspectives* (Oxford, Hart Publishing, 2018).

[115] 'The European Convention' (n 108) 16.

VI. LONG LIVE THE FLEXIBILITY CLAUSE

Legal bases for specific policy areas have been a defining feature of the principle of conferral on the basis of which the EU operates. However, in order to ensure that the treaties have not been overly rigid, it has been necessary since the earliest premise of European integration to grant the legislator a flexibility clause for its modus operandi. With that, there has been no legislative, judicial or academic consensus on how the clause is to be used. For that reason, it remains a captivating provision of EU primary law, for it has always been a means of European integration and will continue to be.

The flexibility clause's political journey has come full circle, from the Paris Summit of 1972 of making maximum use of it to the modern era of minimum use of it. Judicially, the voyage has been similar, from a relaxed to strict allowance of the clause. Today, there is a more cautious legislature and a more assertive judiciary. Given how the treaties have developed, it is unlikely that the legislature and judiciary will return to a laissez-faire approach to the use of the clause anytime soon, but that is not to say they never will. Just because its use has declined significantly, its fallback availability means that it may again become a functional legal tool for the future of Europe.

The EU's treaties have to be adept at ensuring it is able to cope with contemporary challenges. If the last few years have demonstrated anything, it is that the treaties as a whole have not been enough. Turbulences from different angles – internal Member State fractions, global political winds and changes in international power – have all placed the European integration project under strain. And yet the EU's flexibility has and will continue to be subjected to perennial questioning of its nature, scope, use, and limits. Having said that, the most recent decade has not seen many legal acts adopted based on the clause. The potential responsiveness of the clause to provide the means of filling out the objectives of EU law has therefore fallen flat when it was needed the most.

A. The Tenet of Flexibility

The constitutional law of polities always fails to fully envisage the circumstances that may come within its purview. This is all the more valid for the EU, which is focused on integration of many kinds. In such a light, the orthodoxy of flexibility is eminently sensible. Whilst certainty as regards the appropriate legal basis for EU legislation is highly desirable, it is in practice difficult to accomplish, for 'complete clarity and predictability are simply not possible', given the political nature of processes leading to the adoption of new legislation.[116]

[116] P Koutrakos, 'Legal Basis and Delimitation of Competence in EU External Relations' in M Cremona and B De Witte (eds), *EU Foreign Relations Law: Constitutional Fundamentals* (Oxford, Hart Publishing, 2008) 197.

In addition, it would 'have been impossible to fix definite limits leaving no room for expansion' of the EU's competence and potential actions.[117]

It can be said with some certainty that the flexibility clause overreached on at least a few occasions well beyond the purposes for which it was intended. A 'gap' in the treaties to be filled by the clause might have been a misnomer, since a 'gap' is merely a lack of competence. The limits of the clause not being taken fully to heart meant that it lost an element of its legitimacy. Yet at the same time, a narrow interpretation of the clause may be a contradiction. In practice, the routine for the use of the clause has been corrected.[118] Therefore, the clause could be edging towards dormancy.

The imprecision of the clause as a credible legal basis has led to its rise and subsequent fall. When it became used by the EU legislature, it was subject to cursory judicial review, and today it is rarely used by the legislature. Yet if it were to be used, it would be subject to detailed judicial review. With the *Generalised Tariff Preferences* judgment and *Opinion 2/94* from the Court, the substantive elements of the *Massey-Ferguson* judgment were left behind. Thus, the pre-SEA era was no longer tolerable from a legal standpoint. If the use of the clause is ever picked up again, new judicial authority will be needed, determining whether previous jurisprudence such as *Generalised Tariff Preferences* and *Opinion 2/94* are still valid.

B. Promise and Potential

The clause once lived up to some people's promise and then some. As long as the clause is present, the temptation of expanding its potential scope will make it an attractive provision for integration-minded actors. Too wide a reading of the clause undermines competences actually conferred. The clause came to 'define the boundaries' of the EU legislature's competence,[119] yet it is, to some extent, still a 'problem child'.[120] As a legal basis, it is a 'culprit' of being difficult to limit[121] and it has been subject to intense judicial scrutiny when it was challenged as a legal basis.

With its fall occurring through expanded specific legal bases and tighter judicial attitude towards its use, the clause is no match for its former self. However, in light of its declining use, this should not be confused with an imminent

[117] R Monaco, 'The Limits of the European Community Order' (1976) 1 *European Law Review* 269, 276.

[118] Dashwood (n 49) 44.

[119] Schütze (n 19) 101.

[120] E Fahey, 'Does the Emperor Have Financial Crisis Clothes? Reflections on the Legal Basis of the European Banking Authority' (2011) 74 *Modern Law Review* 581, 594.

[121] S Weatherill, 'Competence and Legitimacy' in C Barnard and O Odudu (eds), *The Outer Limits of European Union Law* (Oxford, Hart Publishing, 2009) 19.

elimination of the clause. At one stage, a more precise delimitation of the clause may have been wanted by some actors; however, this would have defeated its innate purpose. A complete gutting of the clause has not happened because it would be fanatical to do so, for sensible legal reasoning is strongly inclined towards the retention of the clause. Even under intense scrutiny, it has withstood any true intentions of ever seeing it removed from the EU legal order altogether. If there had been no clause, the EU would most likely have developed in a different way. Furthermore, given that it was utilised, an early judicial rebuttal of it might have been viewed as an interference with a political choice, which the Court did not have a strong enough reason to prevent.

C. No Imminent Expansion

The expansion of the EU's competences has been a result of a conferral of competences arising from explicit legal bases and the clause. Other, more distant and less precise terms have contributed in the name of the spirit of the constitutional framework of the EU, but to a far lesser extent.[122] The EU legislature has undeniably read beyond the literal interpretation of the treaties when looking for competence, yet it would be a magnification of the truth to say this has been legally erroneous. Incorrect illustrations have labelled the clause as having the potential to 'deprive the Member States of almost all their functions'.[123] This is misleading, particularly given the more restrictive scope of the provision in recent times and the fact that there is still a unanimity requirement for its use. The aforementioned attempts by national courts and legislatures to pick a fight with the EU's clause have been relatively limited.

Despite additional legal bases being added progressively at the major intergovernmental conferences, the clause has still continued to retain a purpose. It is worth recalling why the clause has existed at all – to ensure that the objectives of the EU are able to be achieved if the explicit powers conferred are too narrow or insufficient. In that sense, the clause has been necessary for the EU to continue to address the circumstances before it. There is still no settlement on what the clause is to do in the future, but it is now accepted that the clause has legal and political limitations on how it can be operated. Amendment to the flexibility clause and its predecessors has only been undertaken lightly, and so wholescale

[122] For example, the 'ever closer Union' point, which is often contended as being the raison d'être of EU law and policy, has had a limited effect in the Court's case law. It could even have said to have no profound effect in the name of expanding EU powers. See P Cruz Villalón, 'Within and without "Ever Closer Union"' in T Giegerich, D C Schmitt and S Zeitzmann (eds), *Flexibility in the EU and beyond: How Much Differentiation Can European Integration Bear?* (Baden-Baden, Nomos, 2017) 459.

[123] TC Hartley, *Constitutional Problems of the European Union* (Oxford, Hart Publishing, 1999) 96.

revisions can be deemed improbable. Whilst the Treaty of Lisbon made significant strides to improve the clause through clarity and additional established safeguards, the clause can still be used broadly if the Member States so decide. Therefore, the clause is no absolute safeguard of Member State competences[124] and has a future in the EU legal order.

D. Concluding Remarks

There is no doubt that Article 352 TFEU has been useful for furthering the ideals of European integration through law, but its wild years are over. It would have been unreasonable to expect the drafters to envisage every particular sectoral area that would see EU action and thus its own legal basis, and so having a built-in flexibility mechanism was logical. The sheer breadth of different legal bases in the treaties today means resort to the catch-all clause as a legal instrument is no longer needed in the same way as it once was. However, changes brought about by additional revisions have also contributed to its demise.

Striving for a form of constitutional perfection for the EU is a folly, for whilst such a notion exists in theory, this is far removed from the European actuality. Even a more grounded reality of a constitutional settlement is beyond the means of the possible in the present era. Instead, as has long been the case, an acceptance of an 'unfinished' constitutional system will have to prevail.[125] It is the Member States in the Council that chose to give rise to the clause and it is the same Member States that have also undermined it. EU policies are a mixture of static and fluid beings, but there are still areas of policies where conferral of competence to the EU has not occurred. For the future of Europe, flexible primary law is needed, entailing unconventional measures, including the clause, to ensure the EU's longevity.

APPENDIX

Article 352 TFEU

1. If action by the Union should prove necessary, within the framework of the policies defined in the Treaties, to attain one of the objectives set out in the Treaties, and the Treaties have not provided the necessary powers, the Council, acting unanimously on a proposal from the Commission and

[124] B de Witte, 'Exclusive Member State Competences: Is There Such a Thing?' in S Garben and I Govaere (eds), *The Division of Competences between the EU and the Member States: Reflections on the Past, the Present and the Future* (Oxford, Hart Publishing, 2017) 70.

[125] See F Snyder, 'The Unfinished Constitution of the European Union: Principles, Processes and Culture' in JHH Weiler and M Wind (eds), *European Constitutionalism beyond the State* (Cambridge, Cambridge University Press, 2003).

after obtaining the consent of the European Parliament, shall adopt the appropriate measures. Where the measures in question are adopted by the Council in accordance with a special legislative procedure, it shall also act unanimously on a proposal from the Commission and after obtaining the consent of the European Parliament.

2. Using the procedure for monitoring the subsidiarity principle referred to in Article 5(3) of the Treaty on European Union, the Commission shall draw national Parliaments' attention to proposals based on this Article.
3. Measures based on this Article shall not entail harmonisation of Member States' laws or regulations in cases where the Treaties exclude such harmonisation.
4. This Article cannot serve as a basis for attaining objectives pertaining to the common foreign and security policy and any acts adopted pursuant to this Article shall respect the limits set out in Article 40, second paragraph, of the Treaty on European Union.

Declaration (No 41) on Article 352 TFEU

The Conference declares that the reference in Article 352(1) of the Treaty on the Functioning of the European Union to objectives of the Union refers to the objectives as set out in Article 3(2) and (3) of the Treaty on European Union and to the objectives of Article 3(5) of the said Treaty with respect to external action under Part Five of the Treaty on the Functioning of the European Union. It is therefore excluded that an action based on Article 352 of the Treaty on the Functioning of the European Union would only pursue objectives set out in Article 3(1) of the Treaty on European Union. In this connection, the Conference notes that in accordance with Article 31(1) of the Treaty on European Union, legislative acts may not be adopted in the area of the Common Foreign and Security Policy.

Declaration (No 42) on Article 352 TFEU

The Conference underlines that, in accordance with the settled case law of the Court of Justice of the European Union, Article 352 of the Treaty on the Functioning of the European Union, being an integral part of an institutional system based on the principle of conferred powers, cannot serve as a basis for widening the scope of Union powers beyond the general framework created by the provisions of the Treaties as a whole and, in particular, by those that define the tasks and the activities of the Union. In any event, this Article cannot be used as a basis for the adoption of provisions whose effect would, in substance, be to amend the Treaties without following the procedure which they provide for that purpose.

REFERENCES

Arold Lorenz, N-L, Groussot, X and Thor Petursson, G, *The European Human Rights Culture: A Paradox of Human Rights Protection in Europe?* (Leiden, Martinus Nijhoff Publishers, 2014).

Bebr, G, *Development of Judicial Control of the European Communities* (The Hague, Martinus Nijhoff Publishers, 1981).

Bergström, CF and Almer, J, 'The Residual Competence: Basic Statistics on Legislation with a Legal Basis in Article 308 EC', Swedish Institute for European Policy Studies (SIEPS), 2002.

Beukers, T, 'The Court of Justice Approves the Creation of the European Stability Mechanism outside the EU Legal Order: *Pringle*' (2013) 50 *Common Market Law Review* 805.

Butler, G, 'In Search of the Political Question Doctrine in EU Law' (2018) 45 *Legal Issues of Economic Integration* 329.

——. 'Pre-ratification Judicial Review of International Agreements to Be Concluded by the European Union' in M Derlén and J Lindholm (eds), *The Court of Justice of the European Union: Multidisciplinary Perspectives* (Oxford, Hart Publishing, 2018).

——. *Constitutional Law of the EU's Common Foreign and Security Policy: Competence and Institutions in External Relations* (Oxford, Hart Publishing, 2019).

Cappelletti, M, Seccombe, M and Weiler, JHH, 'Integration through Law: Europe and the American Federal Experience: A General Introduction' in M Cappelletti, M Seccombe and JHH Weiler (eds), *Integration through Law: Europe and the American Federal Experience*, vol 1 (Berlin, De Gruyter, 1986).

Craig, P, 'Competence: Clarity, Conferral, Containment and Consideration' (2004) 29 *European Law Review* 323.

——. 'The European Union Act 2011: Locks, Limits and Legality' (2011) 48 *Common Market Law Review* 1915.

——. *The Lisbon Treaty: Law, Politics, and Treaty Reform* (Oxford, Oxford University Press 2011).

Cruz Villalón, P, 'Within and without "Ever Closer Union"' in T Giegerich, DC Schmitt and S Zeitzmann (eds), *Flexibility in the EU and Beyond: How Much Differentiation Can European Integration Bear?* (Baden-Baden, Nomos, 2017).

Dashwood, A, 'The Limits of European Community Powers' (1996) 21 *European Law Review* 113.

——. 'Article 308 EC as the Outer Limit of Expressly Conferred Community Competence' in C Barnard and O Odudu (eds), *The Outer Limits of European Union Law* (Oxford, Hart Publishing, 2009).

Davies, B, *Resisting the European Court of Justice: West Germany's Confrontation with European Law, 1949–1979* (Cambridge, Cambridge University Press, 2012).

De Búrca, G and de Witte, B, 'The Delimitation of Powers between the EU and its Member States' in A Arnull and D Wincott (eds), *Accountability and Legitimacy in the European Union* (Oxford, Oxford University Press, 2003).

De Witte, B, 'Exclusive Member State Competences: Is There Such a Thing?' in S Garben and I Govaere (eds), *The Division of Competences between the EU and the Member States: Reflections on the Past, the Present and the Future* (Oxford, Hart Publishing, 2017).

De Witte, B and Martinelli, T, 'Treaties between EU Member States as Quasi-instruments of EU Law' in M Cremona and C Kilpatrick (eds), *EU Legal Acts: Challenges and Transformations* (Oxford, Oxford University Press, 2018).

Engström, V, 'How to Tame the Elusive: Lessons from the Revision of the EU Flexibility Clause' (2010) 7 *International Organizations Law Review* 343.

Everling, U, 'The European Union as a Federal Association of States and Citizens' in A von Bogdandy and J Bast (eds), *Principles of European Constitutional Law* (Oxford, Hart Publishing, 2006).

Fabbrini, F and Granat, K, '"Yellow Card, But No Foul": The Role of the National Parliaments under the Subsidiarity Protocol and the Commission Proposal for an EU Regulation on the Right to Strike' (2013) 50 *Common Market Law Review* 115.

Fahey, E, 'Does the Emperor Have Financial Crisis Clothes? Reflections on the Legal Basis of the European Banking Authority' (2011) 74 *Modern Law Review* 581.

Granat, K, *The Principle of Subsidiarity and its Enforcement in the EU Legal Order: The Role of National Parliaments in the Early Warning System* (Oxford, Hart Publishing, 2018).

Guastaferro, B, 'The European Union as a Staatenverbund? The Endorsement of the Principle of Conferral in the Treaty of Lisbon' in M Trybus and L Rubini (eds), *The Treaty of Lisbon and the Future of European Law and Policy* (Cheltenham, Edward Elgar, 2012).

Hartley, TC, *Constitutional Problems of the European Union* (Oxford, Hart Publishing, 1999).

Kiiver, P, 'The Lisbon Judgment of the German Constitutional Court: A Court-Ordered Strengthening of the National Legislature in the EU' (2010) 16 *European Law Journal* 578.

Konstadinides, T, 'Drawing the Line between Circumvention and Gap-Filling: An Exploration of the Conceptual Limits of the Treaty's Flexibility Clause' (2012) 31 *Yearbook of European Law* 227.

——. 'The Competences of the European Union' in R Schütze and T Tridimas (eds), *Oxford Principles of European Union Law*, vol 1 (Oxford, Oxford University Press, 2018).

Koutrakos, P, 'Legal Basis and Delimitation of Competence in EU External Relations' in M Cremona and B de Witte (eds), *EU Foreign Relations Law: Constitutional Fundamentals* (Oxford, Hart Publishing, 2008).

Lenaerts, K, 'Constitutionalism and the Many Faces of Federalism' (1990) 38 *American Journal of Comparative Law* 205.

Mayer, FC, 'Defiance by a Constitutional Court – Germany' in A Jakab and D Kochenov (eds), *The Enforcement of EU Law and Values: Ensuring Member States' Compliance* (Oxford, Oxford University Press, 2017).

Mengozzi, P, *European Community Law from the Treaty of Rome to the Treaty of Amsterdam* (The Hague, Kluwer Law International, 1999).

Miller, L, 'European Contract Law after Lisbon' in D Ashiagbor, N Countouris and I Lianos (eds), *The European Union after the Treaty of Lisbon* (Cambridge, Cambridge University Press, 2012).

Monaco, R, 'The Limits of the European Community Order' (1976) 1 *European Law Review* 269.

Nergelius, J, *The Constitutional Dilemma of the European Union* (Groningen, Europa Law Publishing, 2009).
Nollkaemper, A, 'The European Community and International Environmental Co-operation: Legal Aspects of External Community Powers' (1987) 14 *Legal Issues of Economic Integration* 55.
Pescatore, P, *The Law of Integration: Emergence of a New Phenomenon in International Relations, Based on the Experience of the European Communities* (Leiden, AW Sijthoff, 1974).
Piris, J-C, *The Lisbon Treaty: A Legal and Political Analysis* (Cambridge, Cambridge University Press, 2010).
Rosas, A and Armati, L, *EU Constitutional Law: An Introduction* (Oxford, Hart Publishing, 2012).
Schütze, R, 'Dynamic Integration: Article 308 EC and Legislation "in the Course of the Operation of the Common Market": A Review Essay' (2003) 23 *Oxford Journal of Legal Studies* 333.
——. 'Organized Change towards and "Ever Closer Union": Article 308 EC and the Limits to the Community's Legislative Competence' (2003) 22 *Yearbook of European Law* 79.
——. *From Dual to Cooperative Federalism: The Changing Structure of European Law* (Oxford, Oxford University Press, 2009).
——. 'EU Competences: Existence and Exercise' in D Chalmers and A Arnull (eds), *The Oxford Handbook of European Union Law* (Oxford, Oxford University Press, 2015).
——. *European Union Law* (Cambridge, Cambridge University Press, 2015).
——. *European Union Law*, 2nd edn (Cambridge, Cambridge University Press 2018).
Schwartz, IE, 'Article 235 and Law-Making Powers in the European Community' (1978) 27 *International and Comparative Law Quarterly* 614.
Smit, H and Herzog, P, 'Article 235' in H Smit and P Herzog (eds), *The Law of the European Community: A Commentary on the EEC Treaty*, vol 6 (New York, Matthew Bender, 1976).
Snyder, F, 'The Unfinished Constitution of the European Union: Principles, Processes and Culture' in JHH Weiler and M Wind (eds), *European Constitutionalism beyond the State* (Cambridge, Cambridge University Press, 2003).
Södersten, A, *Euratom at the Crossroads* (Cheltenham, Edward Elgar, 2018).
Tizzano, A, 'The Powers of the Community' in *Thirty Years of Community law* (Luxembourg, Office for Official Publications of the European Communities, 1983).
Van Raepenbusch, S and Hanf, D, 'Flexibility in Social Policy' in B de Witte, D Hanf and E Vos (eds), *The Many Faces of Differentiation in EU Law* (Antwerp, Intersentia, 2001).
Von Bogdandy, A and Bast, J, 'The Vertical Order of Competences' in A von Bogdandy and J Bast (eds), *Principles of European Constitutional Law* (Oxford, Hart Publishing, 2006).
Von Bogdandy, A and Bast, J, 'The Federal Order of Competences' in A von Bogdandy and J Bast (eds), *Principles of European Constitutional Law*, 2nd edn (Oxford, Hart Publishing, 2009).
Weiler, JHH, 'The Transformation of Europe' (1991) 100 *Yale Law Journal* 2403.
Weatherill, S, 'Beyond Preemption? Shared Competence and Constitutional Changes in the European Community' in D O'Keeffe and PM Twomey (eds), *Legal Issues of the Maastricht Treaty* (London, Chancery, 1994).

——. 'Competence Creep and Competence Control' (2004) 23 *Yearbook of European Law* 1.
——. 'Better Competence Monitoring' (2005) 30 *European Law Review* 23.
——. 'Competence and Legitimacy' in C Barnard and O Odudu (eds), *The Outer Limits of European Union Law* (Oxford, Hart Publishing, 2009).
——. *The Internal Market as a Legal Concept* (Oxford, Oxford University Press, 2017).
Weatherill, S and Beaumont, P, *EU Law*, 3rd edn (London, Penguin, 1999).
Wetter Ryde, A, 'Mapping out the Procedural Requirements for the Early Warning Mechanism' in A Jonsson Cornell and M Goldoni (eds), *National and Regional Parliaments in the EU-Legislative Procedure Post-Lisbon: The Impact of the Early Warning Mechanism* (Oxford, Hart Publishing, 2017).

4

The Resilience of Rights and European Integration

XAVIER GROUSSOT AND ANNA ZEMSKOVA

I. INTRODUCTION: THE POSSIBILITY OF THE STATUS QUO

THE WHITE PAPER of the Commission on the Future of Europe delivered last year has relaunched the discussion on integration through law within the context of the Treaty of Lisbon by proposing five scenarios.[1] In particular, President Jean-Claude Juncker in his State of the Union speech of September 2017 proposed a sixth scenario for the Future of Europe based on three 'unshakeable principles': freedom, equality and the rule of law.[2] This strong rights-based vision of the future of Europe is, arguably, not unproblematic given the irrefutable fact that EU rights have been politically and legally contested in recent years. To go this way would not change much in the present operation of the EU legal order and would, in fact, merely confirm a choice of the status quo for the future of European integration. To go this way would also lead to the possible endorsement of the argument that rights may degenerate into mere 'talks' and, as a result, be used for the legitimation of the status quo.[3]

This possible '(non)-tournant' of the process of European integration begs one essential question that we intend to answer in this chapter: why are the rights so resilient in the process of European integration? Our reflection has its starting point in the 'Ever Closer Union' clause enshrined in Article 1(2) of the Treaty on European Union (TEU), which is here viewed as reflecting the legacy of neofunctionalism. Article 1(2) TEU has sadly once again come under

[1] White Paper on the Future of Europe: Avenues for Unity for the EU at 27, Brussels, 1 March 2017. The five scenarios are the following: 1) carrying on; 2) nothing but the single market; 3) those who want more do more; 4) doing less more efficiently; and 5) doing much more together.

[2] President Jean-Claude Juncker's State of the Union Address 2017, Brussels, 13 September 2017.

[3] See K Günther, 'The Legacies of Injustice and Fear: A European Approach to Human Rights and Their Effects on Political Culture' in P Alston (ed), *The EU and Human Rights* (Oxford, Oxford University Press, 1999) 117. Günther considers that the degeneration is facilitated by the abuse of human rights for other purposes (economic or political) or the ideological use of human rights for the legitimation of the status quo (at 143).

the spotlight of European (dis)integration due to the Brexit referendum and the well-known point made by David Cameron that the EU and its Member States should annihilate the 'Ever Closer Union' clause. Our main argument in this chapter is that the resilience of rights is intimately connected to Article 1(2) TEU and its constitutional spirit. This chapter is divided into two parts. The first part analyses the spillover of rights into the EU legal order by taking a historical perspective and by explaining the institutionalisation of the 'Ever Closer Union' clause by the judicial branch (section II). The second part looks at the concept of rights and their internal logic (their 'voice') from a functionalist and analytical perspective (section III).

II. THE SPILLOVER OF RIGHTS

A. The Legacy of Neofunctionalism and Rights (in the Light of Article 1(2) TEU)

Article 1(2) TEU includes the so-called 'Ever Closer Union' clause and states:

> This Treaty marks a new stage in the process of creating an ever closer union among the peoples of Europe, in which decisions are taken as openly as possible and as closely as possible to the citizen.

This clause is the cradle of two significant theories which explain the process of European integration: legal pluralism (a theory of legal integration);[4] and neofunctionalism (a theory of political integration).[5]

The hallmark of neofunctionalism developed by Ernst B Haas is based on the idea of 'spillover' of policies in various sectors of the EU.[6] Neofunctionalism describes a process 'whereby political actors in several distinct national settings are persuaded to shift their loyalties, expectations, and political activities, towards a new and larger center, whose institutions possess or demand jurisdiction over the pre-existing national states'.[7] And just like the

[4] See M Avbelj and J Komárek, *Constitutional Pluralism in Europe and Beyond* (Oxford, Hart Publishing, 2012).

[5] See A Moravcsik, 'The European Constitutional Compromise and the Neofunctionalist Legacy' (2005) 12 *Journal of European Public Policy*, 349, 351. As put by Moravcsik: 'The EU's current constitutional status quo appears stable and normatively attractive. Beyond incremental changes in policy, it is difficult to imagine functional pressures, institutional pressures, or normative concerns upsetting the stability of the basic constitutional equilibrium in Europe today. There is thus a tension between the optimistic rhetoric of "ever closer union" – itself in part a legacy of Haasian neofunctionalism – what we might call a "European Constitutional Compromise" (or, if you are British, "European Constitutional Settlement"). While a bias in favour of "ever closer union" continues to suffuse EU scholarship, distorting our understanding of European integration, empirical analysis of the broader importance of the EU in European politics, global affairs, and democratic theory might do better to begin by acknowledging the existence of this political equilibrium. Today the central debate in the EU is not about how to continue on the road to further integration, but about precisely where to stop – a debate for which neofunctionalism is ill-equipped.'

[6] EB Haas, *The Uniting of Europe* (Standford, Stanford University Press, 1958).

[7] ibid 12.

'Ever Closer Union' clause, its essence is founded on the belief that Europe is a society not in being but in becoming, what we can call the belief in 'Everism' – 'Everism' being literally coded in the European DNA by Article 1(2) TEU since the Treaty of Rome.[8] We think that an organic version of neofunctionalism offers a viable general theory of European integration and can also be used to understand the process of legal integration (at the macro-level) and the resilience of rights in the EU (at the micro-level).

Already in 1993, Burley (Slaughter) and Mattli in their seminal article 'Europe before the Court: A Political Theory of Legal Integration' rely on neofunctionalism to explain the process of legal integration in the EU.[9] They consider that the neofunctionalist theory provides a convincing and parsimonious explanation of legal integration.[10] At its core is the idea that law functions as a mask for politics, ie, acting as a 'functional domain' to avoid the head-on conflicts of political interests.[11] They also view the European Court of Justice (ECJ) as elaborating a pro-community constituency of private individuals by giving them a direct stake in the promulgation and implementation of EU law, notably through the creation of the direct effect doctrine.[12] Alec Stone Sweet considers that their theory shows that the European courts are sensitive to the interests of private actors and that constitutionalisation enhances the effectiveness of EU law as feedback loops were constituted (this is an integral part of the spillover effect). In his words:

> Constitutionalization enhanced the effectiveness of EU law, which attracted litigation brought by private actors; more litigation meant more preliminary references which, in turn, generated the context for a nuanced, intra-judicial dialogue between the ECJ and national judges on how best to accommodate, and empower, one another; and, as the domain of EC law, and of the ECJ's jurisprudence expanded, this dialogue intensified, socialising more into the system, encouraging more use. The dynamics embody those of the 'virtuous circle' which is at the heart of judicialization.[13]

Notably, this dynamic of integration is particularly visible in the fields of EU individual rights, where private actors and European citizens have been able to benefit from the direct effect doctrine by relying in front of the European

[8] See recital 1 of the preamble of the European Economic Community (EEC) Treaty: 'Determined to establish the foundations of an ever closer union among the European peoples'. See also R McCrea, 'Forward or Back: The Future of European Integration and the Impossibility of the Status Quo' (2017) 23 *European Law Journal* 66, 91. As put by McCrea, 'Ever Closer Union' was not just a phrase, as Mancini suggested; 'it is deep in the DNA of the EU and may be an existential condition for the effectiveness and viability of the EU and its future. The methods of integration chosen by those who founded the EEC mean that it is very difficult to call a halt to the integration process, but the drop in political support for further integration raises acute dilemmas for the Union by creating demand for just such a stop'.

[9] A-M Burley and W Mattli, 'Europe before the Court: A Political Theory of Legal Integration' (1993) 47 *International Organization* 41, 72–73.

[10] ibid 43.

[11] ibid 44, 72–73.

[12] ibid 60.

[13] See A Stone Sweet, 'The European Court of Justice and the Judicialization of EU Governance' (2010) 5 *Living Reviews in European Governance* 16.

courts on the many individual rights enshrined both in the Treaties and also elaborated by the ECJ at the end of the 1960s through the theory of general principles of EU law.[14] This spillover of rights is obviously boosted by the entry into force of the EU Charter of Fundamental Rights in 2009, which logically increases the litigation before the courts based on individual rights. However, in order to be viable and in light of the economic crisis,[15] neofunctionalism will have to offer a theoretical framework that allows not only for further integration but also disintegration.[16] It is important to note in that respect that the economic crisis has led to an increased level of integration to the detriment of the protection of individual rights (a clear spillback of rights).[17] Moreover, according to Ronan McCrea, the EU is today in a 'Catch 22' situation, since the spillover and integration through law have not only helped to accomplish a remarkable level of integration, but also produced the need for further integration that may be politically impossible.[18] For him, a standstill is not a viable option and either further integration or disintegration is required.[19] In that regard, the theory of legal pluralism here offers an interesting framework since, as argued by Ben Rosamond, the affiliation to pluralism forms an integral part of the *Uniting of Europe* (the original work by Haas, the father of neofunctionalism).[20] Indeed, as already stressed before, the shift of loyalty from the periphery to the centre happens in a legal pluralist milieu where, as put by Haas, 'the end result is a new political community super-imposed over the pre-existing ones'.[21] Viewed in the light of (legal) pluralism, neofunctionalism is not an obsolete theory.[22] On the contrary, in our view, it constitutes an appropriate lens to be relied on in order to understand the process of political and legal integration in Europe.

[14] See X Groussot, *General Principles of Community Law* (Groningen, Europa Law Publishing, 2006).

[15] A Niemann and D Ioannou, 'European Economic Integration in Times of Crisis: A Case of Neofunctionalism?' (2015) 22 *Journal of European Public Policy* 196.

[16] PC Schmitter, 'Ernst B Haas and the Legacy of Neofunctionalism' (2005) 12 *Journal of European Public Policy* 255.

[17] See below, section III.B.

[18] McCrea (n 8) 91.

[19] ibid 92.

[20] B Rosamond, 'The Uniting of Europe and the Foundation of EU Studies: Revisiting the Neofunctionalism of Ernst B Haas' (2006) 13 *Journal of European Public Policy* 237.

[21] See n 7 above.

[22] See also E B Haas, *The Uniting of Europe* (Notre Dame, University of Notre Dame Press, 2004). The theory was considered to be obsolete a first time in 1965 with the so-called policy of the empty chair adopted by the de Gaulle government. There was a rebirth of the theory with the Delors Commission at the end of the 1980s and the beginning of the 1990s. Haas mentioned in the last edition of *The Uniting of Europe* published after his death in 2003 that the theory was no longer obsolete. Indeed, the integration momentum as a solution to the economic crisis offers fertile ground to the rebirth of the theory. See also W Sandholtz and A Stone Sweet, 'Neofunctionalism and Supranational Governance' in E Jones et al (eds), *The Oxford Handbook of the European Union* (Oxford, Oxford University Press, 2012) 1–19.

It is worth underlining that the ECJ, in the pre-Lisbon era, explicitly relied in *Pupino* on the 'Ever Closer Union' clause to develop the scope of individual rights in EU law within (at the time) the third pillar; an area where the jurisdiction of the ECJ under Article 35 EU was less extensive than under the EC Treaty. Interestingly, the ECJ ruled that:

> Irrespective of the degree of integration envisaged by the Treaty of Amsterdam in the process of creating an ever closer union among the peoples of Europe within the meaning of the second paragraph of Article 1 EU, it is perfectly comprehensible that the authors of the Treaty on European Union should have considered it useful to make provision, in the context of Title VI of that treaty, for recourse to legal instruments with effects similar to those provided for by the EC Treaty, in order to contribute effectively to the pursuit of the Union's objectives.[23]

Through the use of Article 1(2) TEU and in the name of ensuring an effective application of the EU's objectives, the ECJ has extended by itself its jurisdiction to protect individual rights. This is a spillover of individual rights and its general principles in the context of EU law by relying on the 'Ever Closer Union' clause, which imposes on Member States and institutions a duty of mutual loyalty outside the scope of Article 10 EC (now Article 4(3) TEU).[24]

Though the reliance on the 'Ever Closer Union' clause is rare in ECJ case law, it made another remarkable appearance in *Opinion 2/13* on the EU's accession to the European Convention on the Protection of Human Rights and Fundamental Freedoms (ECHR). In order to come to the conclusion that there was no need for accession at the time, the ECJ emphasised the so-called special and essential characteristics of the EU. In that respect, it stated that:

> EU law is characterised by the fact that it stems from an independent source of law, the Treaties, by its primacy over the laws of the Member States and by the direct effect of a whole series of provisions which are applicable to their nationals and to the Member States. These essential characteristics of EU law have given rise to a structured network of principles, rules and mutually interdependent legal relations linking the EU and its Member States, and its Member States with each other, which are now engaged, as is recalled in the second paragraph of Article 1 TEU, in a

[23] Case C-105/03 *Criminal Proceedings against Maria Pupino* [2005] ECLI:EU:C:2005:386, para 36.

[24] See Opinion of AG Kokott in Case C-105/03 *Criminal Proceedings against Maria Pupino* [2005], ECLI:EU:C:2004:712, paras 25–26. Accordingly: 'That is apparent from an overview of the provisions of the Treaty on European Union. Article 1 EU lays down the objective of creating a new stage in the process of achieving an ever closer union among the peoples of Europe, on the basis of which relations between the Member States and between their peoples can be organised in a manner demonstrating consistency and solidarity. That objective will not be achieved unless the Member States and institutions of the Union cooperate sincerely and in compliance with the law. Loyal cooperation between the Member States and the institutions is also the central purpose of Title VI of the Treaty on European Union, appearing both in the title – Provisions on Police and Judicial Cooperation in Criminal Matters – and again in almost all the articles.'

> 'process of creating an ever closer union among the peoples of Europe …' Also at the heart of that legal structure are the fundamental rights recognised by the Charter.[25]

We can see here the legacy of neofunctionalism as inherent to the reasoning of the Court. The EU is clearly still becoming – at least from the ECJ's perspective.

B. European Rights History X

One of the active agents of the enhancement of the 'Ever Closer Union' clause through different channels, which are sometimes hidden, are the European (fundamental, human, individual or economic etc) rights that have paved a peculiar path to the European Olympus. Concealed at first, they found opportunities to strengthen their position, staying resilient to backsliding developments and becoming one of the constitutive forces driving the European project forward.[26] In order to understand the actual role and potential of rights in the EU, it is necessary to take a look at their history that can be described as a story of hiding, brotherhood and experience – the experience of integration.

Initially, fundamental rights were invisible chameleons that derived their growing significance from other constitutive elements permeating the new legal order. The economic freedoms underpinning the overarching objectives of the European project,[27] the uniting common value of the rule of law[28] and the general principles encapsulating and shaping the EU law edifice,[29] inspired by the constitutional traditions common to the Member States and international instruments,[30] have at different stages of the existence of the EU all been used as a mask for deepening European integration through the promotion of the fundamental rights that the Treaties initially did not explicitly envisage, leaving this specific domain to adjudication by the ECJ. This fact partially explains why the concepts of fundamental and individual rights are so blurred and undefined in the EU legal order: the problematic genesis of the rights might be rooted not in the internal market rationality,[31] but allegedly in the rationality of the rights themselves.

[25] *Opinion 2/13* [2014] ECLI:EU:C:2014:2454, paras 167–69.

[26] G de Búrca, 'The Language of Rights and European Integration' in G More and J Shaw (eds), *New Legal Dynamics of European Union* (Oxford, Oxford University Press, 1996) 6.

[27] C Harding, 'Economic Freedom and Economic Rights: Direction, Significance and Ideology' (2018) 24 *European Law Journal* 24.

[28] See art 2 TEU.

[29] T Tridimas, *The General Principles of EC Law* (New York, Oxford University Press, 1999) 3.

[30] X Groussot, *Creation, Development and Impact of the General Principles of Community Law: Towards a Jus Commune Europaeum?* (Gothenburg, Intellecta docusys, 2005) 40.

[31] M Bartl, 'Internal Market Rationality: In the Way of Re-imagining the Future' (2018) 24 *European Law Journal* 99.

The decisive influence exercised by the economic freedoms on the emergence of the fundamental rights in the EU in their specific form cannot be ignored[32] – the initial operational framework of the EU envisaged the creation of the single market, but did not prescribe a moral dimension in the form of fundamental rights.[33] This lacuna led to a dynamic development of the obligational nature of rights in the EU consisting in the fact that rights emerged as a tool for enforcement of the obligations enshrined in the Treaties.[34] Yet the evolution of the European project could not help producing spillover effects that resulted in 'moralising' the economic goals through the enhancement of fundamental rights in both the economic and social spheres. The onset of one of the most powerful instruments created to ensure the protection of the rights of individuals, the doctrine of direct effect, is evidential in this respect. The iconic case of *Van Gend en Loos*[35] not only established the mechanism guarding the rights of the individuals, but also served as an effective tool of European integration with the help of which EU law penetrates national legal systems[36] and provides for unity in the universe of diversity. With the help of the 'magical triangle',[37] individuals became a driving force of the integration process ensuring successful unifying interconnection between the EU and Member States' legal orders.

The obligational characteristic of the rights in the EU was not only restricted to obligations stemming from positive law, but also drew inspiration from the unwritten principles that advanced fostering rights that were deemed to have a promising future. The early case law that dates back to 1969, namely *Stauder*,[38] demonstrates this pattern. Another essential component of the interplay of common European values put forward as an agent advocating for respecting fundamental rights is the rule of law. Rights pursue shielding individuals from the abuse of power exercised by public authorities[39] as well as safeguarding the rule of law.[40] The recent judgment in *Juízes Portugueses* from the ECJ[41] is a

[32] M Bartl, 'Internal Market Rationality, Private Law and the Direction of the Union: Resuscitating the Market as the Object of the Political' (2015) 21 *European Law Journal* 573.

[33] De Búrca (n 26) 6.

[34] HCH Hofmann and C Warin, 'Identifying Individual Rights in EU Law', University of Luxembourg Law Working Paper No 004-2017, 17 July 2017, 2.

[35] JHH Weiler, '*Van Gend en Loos*: The Individual as Subject and Object and the Dilemma of European Legitimacy' (2014) 12 *International Journal of Constitutional Law* 94.

[36] S Robin-Olivier, 'The Evolution of Direct Effect in the EU: Stocktaking, Problems, Projections' (2014) 12 *International Journal of Constitutional Law* 166.

[37] A Vauchez, 'Integration-through-Law', Contribution to a Socio-history of EU Political Commonsense, EUI Working Papers RSCAS 2008/10, 1.

[38] Case 29/69 *Stauder* [1969] ECLI:EU:C:1969:57, para 7: 'Interpreted in this way the provision at issue contains nothing capable of prejudicing the fundamental human rights enshrined in the general principles of community law and protected by the court.'

[39] J Bengoetxea, 'Rights (and Obligations) in EU Law' in Jones et al (n 22) 6.

[40] T Konstadinides, *The Rule of Law in the European Union: The Internal Dimension* (Oxford, Hart Publishing, 2017) 29.

[41] Case C-64/16 *Associação Sindical dos Juízes Portugueses* [2018] ECLI:EU:C:2018:117.

perfect example of the inter-relation between the rule of law, which is ready to lend a shoulder to EU values in need,[42] and fundamental rights at risk of falling into decay. However, the 'hiding' of fundamental rights in the EU has always been intertwined with efforts for providing an effective centralising force that could enhance European integration more prominently. We are now referring to the Charter of Fundamental Rights of the European Union, whose status has altered from being a non-binding document[43] into one of the constitutive elements of EU primary legislation, betokening a new phase in the process of European integration.[44] The Charter of Fundamental Rights can be undoubtedly considered a jewel in the crown of European rights history that provided a stabilising foundation for individuals to acknowledge their rights and freedoms not just as ephemeral concepts lacking any potential force, but reflecting the shared values of the EU that are to be safeguarded. The Charter does not nullify the achievements in the sphere of fundamental rights accrued by extensive jurisprudence of the ECJ before it gained legal force.[45] On the contrary, it accumulates the obtained experience and creates a basis for further development without freezing the expansive dynamic of rights reflected in the ongoing evolution of the case law of the ECJ.[46]

This brings us to the third element underpinning the growth of fundamental rights – experience: the experience of integration that saturates the European project throughout its existence by means of the work of the Court. The adjudication of the ECJ has played a major role in shaping the understanding and the enforceability of the rights without shifting the values of the EU. On the contrary, the Court has been rediscovering existing rights, acting as a stabilising force while manoeuvring between conflicting interests.[47] Nevertheless, the process of facilitating fundamental rights has varied in its intensity in different dimensions of the European project. That might be seen more explicitly through the lens of sectoral constitutionalisation advanced by Kaarlo Tuori.[48] Even though the visible progress of rights protection might seem to be fluctuating in the various fields, the uniting factor of this process consists in the constant development of safeguarding the fundamental rights both before and

[42] Article 2 TEU – 'respect for human rights' is one of the values on which the EU is founded; see also Preamble of TEU.

[43] J Dutheil de la Rochère, 'The EU Charter of Fundamental Rights, Not Binding But Influential: The Example of Good Administration' in A Arnull, P Eeckhout and T Tridimas (eds) *Continuity and Change in EU Law: Essays in Honour of Sir Francis Jacobs* (Oxford, Oxford University Press, 2008) 157–58.

[44] K Lenaerts, 'Exploring the Limits of the EU Charter of Fundamental Rights' (2012) 8 *European Constitutional Law Review* 375.

[45] Hofmann and Warin (n 34) 11–14.

[46] For a further analysis of this point, see section II.C below.

[47] See section II.A above for a more detailed analysis; and see also S de Vries, 'Balancing Fundamental Rights with Economic Freedoms According to the European Court of Justice' (2013) 9 *Utrecht Law Review* 170.

[48] See K Tuori, *European Constitutionalism* (Cambridge, Cambridge University Press, 2015).

after the Charter of Fundamental Rights came into force. This trait constitutes the golden thread of European integration serving as a link between the past and the present. It is sufficient to take a quick look at the sectoral expansion of fundamental rights in the case law of the Court. The decisive voice of the Court in *Schmidberger*[49] in 2003, advocating for the observance of fundamental rights in the context of economic freedoms and outweighing the overarching objective of the European project, highlights the permeating spirit of rights in the EU. In the same vein, the lack of a cross-border element in case *Ruiz Zambrano*[50] created no hindrance for the individuals to exercise the rights granted to them on the basis of their status as EU citizens. The tendency of protection of fundamental rights that cannot be derogated in the light of clashes with public international law (like in *Kadi I*),[51] or in the context of a relationship that can be considered to be falling outside the scope of EU law (like in *Åkerberg Fransson*)[52] or falling within the competence of the European Court of Human Rights (ECtHR) (like in *Menci*)[53] proves to strengthen a rationalised movement of pushing forward European integration with the support of fundamental rights that is becoming more and more multi-faceted nowadays.[54]

C. The Institutionalisation of the 'Ever Closer Union' Clause

Institutionalisation is the process by which rules are elaborated, applied and construed by those who live under them.[55] The 'Ever Closer Union' clause has been institutionalised in Europe by the case law of the ECJ and the national courts through a widespread process of rationalisation. To understand this process, it is worth looking again at the text and rationales of Article 1(2) TEU. This provision, which can be traced back to the origins of the Treaty of Rome,[56] is in fact based on two meta-principles: on the one hand, the principle of unity

[49] Case C-112/00 *Schmidberger* [2003] ECLI:EU:C:2003:333.

[50] Case C-34/09 *Gerardo Ruiz Zambrano* [2011] ECLI:EU:C:2011:124; see also K Lenaerts, 'EU Citizenship and the European Court of Justice's "Stone-by-Stone" Approach' (2015) 1 *International Comparative Jurisprudence* 1.

[51] Cases C-402/05 P and C-415/05 P *Yassin Abdullah Kadi and Al Barakaat International Foundation v Council of the European Union and Commission of the European Communities* [2008] ECLI:EU:C:2008:461.

[52] Case C-617/10 *Åkerberg Fransson* [2013] ECLI:EU:C:2013:105.

[53] Case C-524/15 *Criminal Proceedings against Luca Menci* [2018] ECLI:EU:C:2018:197.

[54] See section II.C below for further analysis of this.

[55] See A Stone Sweet et al, 'The Institutionalization of European Space' in A Stone Sweet et al (eds) *The Institutionalization of Europe* (Oxford, Oxford University Press, 2001) 6–7.

[56] See Moravcsik (n 5) 349. Neofunctionalism is seen as a framework rather than a theory with the 'Ever Closer Union' clause at its heart. This principle has been enshrined since the origins of the EEC in the 'ever closer union of peoples' clause that reflects both the unity ('closer union') and diversity ('the peoples') of the ongoing European project. The disappearance with the Treaty of Lisbon of the 'Unity and Diversity' clause (enshrined in art I-8 of the Constitutional Treaty) was not a fatal blow to the core principle of constitutional heterarchy and tolerance.

('closer union') and diversity ('the peoples'); and, on the other hand, the principle of transparency ('decisions are taken as openly as possible'). In EU law, it is argued that these two meta-principles have been institutionalised by the Court's case law on individual rights with the help of a complex network of legal principles.

At the general level, the expansion of transparency and proportionality in EU law lies at the heart of the development of EU individual rights. As shown by Shapiro, there was an emergent concern and common distrust in the Europe of the 1980s and 1990s as to the place and role of EU technocracy.[57] The principle of transparency was seen as a magic solution to eliminate this concern and to restore the trust of the European citizens in the bureaucratic system.[58] This tendency has implied setting increasing limits on national administrative *discretion* and shaping a certain 'judicialisation' of administrative procedure across Europe.[59] The phenomenon of the limitation of *discretion* at the national level by EU law was driven by the adjudicative application of the principles of equivalence and effectiveness, which can also be viewed as 'the foundation stones of EU administrative law'.[60]

A similar process can also be detected in relation to the principle of proportionality, where the ECJ has boosted its dissemination by inviting courts to undertake a stricter review of *discretionary* administrative decisions.[61] Traditionally speaking, the use of this principle to review Member State legislation has been much more rigorous than its application against EU legislation. According to Tridimas, 'the principle is applied as a market integration mechanism and the intensity of review is much stronger'.[62] In relation to the 'economic freedoms', it protects the citizen against Member States' actions that impose obligations, restrictions and penalties causing a heavy obstacle to one of the economic freedoms.[63] In the early 1980s, the principle of proportionality was

[57] See M Shapiro, 'The Institutionalization of the European Administrative Space' in Stone Sweet et al (n 55) 94.

[58] ibid 97–98.

[59] D Kelemen, *Eurolegalism: The Transformation of Law and Regulation in the European Union* (Cambridge, MA, Harvard University Press, 2011).

[60] ibid 54.

[61] ibid. Kelemen in *Eurolegalism* (n 59) considers that 'the ECJ has also encouraged the spread across Europe of a proportionality test for discretionary administrative decisions – demanding that national courts assess whether an administrative measure imposed a burden on the individual suitable, necessary, and proportional to the objective sought … By spreading the principle of proportionality across the EU, the ECJ has invited courts to engage in stricter judicial scrutiny of discretionary administrative decisions'.

[62] T Tridimas, 'Proportionality in Community Law: Searching for the Appropriate Standard of Scrutiny' in E Ellis (ed), *The Principle of Proportionality in the Laws of Europe* (Oxford, Hart Publishing, 1999) 65. Tridimas considers that the principle of proportionality is the most often relied-upon principle in litigation (at 66) and the most effective tool of review (at 69).

[63] Case 16/78 *Choquet* [1978] ECLI:EU:C:1978:210, 2302; Case 796/79 *Testa* [1980] ECLI:EU:C:1980:163, 1997; Case 203/80 *Casati* [1981] ECLI:EU:C:1981:261, 2618; and Case 261/81 *Rau* [1982] ECLI:EU:C:1982:382, 3972.

largely used against Member States attempting to derogate from one of the economic freedoms. The principle thus constituted an instrument of economic integration. Then, at the end of the 1980s, the principle spilled over into the context of fundamental rights. The *Wachauf* case, which established an obligation for the Member States to respect fundamental rights in implementing EU law, paved the way for human rights actions concerning national measures derogating from it.[64] After the entry into force of the EU Charter of Fundamental Rights and the Treaty of Lisbon, the principle of proportionality is also applied with a stronger intensity at the institutional level,[65] whereas its use at the national level is much more nuanced than before due to the application of the horizontal clauses of the EU Charter of Fundamental Rights (notably Articles 52(1) and Article 53 and Article 4(2) TEU). This new interpretative shift is indeed closer to the text of Article 1(2) TEU. The principle of proportionality is not only the main tool for economic integration; it is also the keystone for European integration *tout court* viewed and understood as a spillover phenomenon. It is, in that sense, that it constitutes *the* autopoietic principle of EU law and, as a result, the engine of 'integration through rights'. Proportionality is a self-reproducing principle that nourishes at the macro-level on other principles (such as mutual recognition, transparency and fundamental rights) and reproduces at the micro-level (individual case level) the telos of the 'Ever Closer Union' clause. This is so that its capsules or agents are the many individual rights to be found in the EU legal order.

The telos of European integration is not only about unity but also about diversity. In practice, this means that the effectiveness of EU law is not absolute and that there are situations in which it is accepted that EU law should yield and where the national interests should prevail. Sophie Robin-Olivier in 2014 elegantly showed the recent evolution of the doctrine of direct effect towards a more flexible and less self-centred (no effectiveness *à tout prix*) principle.[66] The latest case law of the ECJ clearly shows this potential for diversity of the doctrine of direct effect or what we can call the 'diversity of effectiveness'. This 'diversity of effectiveness' is in our view very well illustrated by the 'rights' jurisprudence of the ECJ on the use of national standards of protection of fundamental rights (the so-called *Melloni* doctrine)[67] and the constitutional exceptions to the application of the principle of mutual trust in the context of the European Arrest Warrant (the so-called *Aranyosi* doctrine).[68]

[64] Case 5/88 *Wachauf* [1989] ECLI:EU:C:1989:321.

[65] See J Kokott and C Sobotta, 'The Evolution of the Principle of Proportionality in EU Law: Towards an Anticipative Understanding?' in S Vogenauer and S Weatherill (eds), *General Principles of Law: European and Comparative Perspectives* (Oxford, Hart Publishing, 2017) 167–78.

[66] Robin-Olivier (n 36) 187.

[67] Case C-399/11 *Melloni* [2013] ECLI:EU:C:2013:107.

[68] Joined Cases C-404/15 and C-659/15 PPU *Aranyosi and Robert Căldăraru* [2016] ECLI:EU:C:2016:198.

As to the *Melloni* doctrine, it has been reiterated and applied (though the ECJ does not explicitly mention Article 53 of the Charter) in the so-called *Taricco II* case, a preliminary reference from the Italian Constitutional Court in the context of criminal tax law and fundamental rights.[69] The ECJ granted a broad margin of discretion to Italy by not disapplying the higher standard of protection afforded at the national level by the Criminal Code. The ECJ balanced the protection of fundamental rights with the principle of effectiveness of EU law (as encapsulated by Article 325 of the Treaty on the Functioning of the European Union (TFEU)). In the end, the Italian state was free to provide that rules on the definition of offences and the determination of penalties form part of substantive criminal law, since they were not impeding the primacy, unity and effectiveness of EU law.[70] It follows from *Taricco II* that the effectiveness of EU law is clearly not absolute and the primacy of EU law is conditional in the field of EU individual rights. In the end, this interpretation is in line with the logic of the 'Ever Closer Union' clause.

In a similar vein, the ECJ has limited the effectiveness of the principle of mutual trust with the *Aranyosi* doctrine.[71] In *Aranyosi*, the Court ruled that where the executing judicial authority finds that there exists, for the individual who is the subject of a European Arrest Warrant, a real risk of inhuman or degrading treatment under Article 4 of the EU Charter, the execution of that warrant must be postponed.[72] Notably, this conclusion was based on the logic of *Opinion 2/13*, where the Court sees a tension between the automaticity (effectiveness) of mutual trust and the Draft Agreement for the Accession of the EU to the ECHR.[73] This obligation of mutual trust is jeopardised by accession, which is liable to upset the balance in the EU and undermine the autonomy of EU law.[74] Mutual trust is particularly present in the Area of Freedom, Security and Justice (AFSJ), where the Member States are required to assume, except in exceptional circumstances, that all the other Member States comply with EU law and particularly with the fundamental rights recognised by EU law.[75] Recently, the ECJ

[69] Case C-42/17 *Criminal Proceedings against MAS and MB* [2017] ECLI:EU:C:2017:936, para 47: 'In that respect, the national authorities and courts remain free to apply national standards of protection of fundamental rights, provided that the level of protection provided for by the Charter, as interpreted by the Court, and the primacy, unity and effectiveness of EU law are not thereby compromised (judgment of 26 February 2013, *Åkerberg Fransson*, C-617/10, EU:C:2013:105, paragraph 29).'

[70] ibid paras 45–49.

[71] See K Lenaerts, '*La vie après l'avis*: Exploring the Principle of Mutual (Yet Not Blind) Trust' (2017) 54 *Common Market Law Review* 805.

[72] Cases C-404/15 and C-659/15 PPU *Aranyosi and Robert Căldăraru* [2016] ECLI:EU:C:2016:198, para 98.

[73] *Opinion 2/13* (n 25) para 191.

[74] ibid para 194.

[75] See, to that effect, the judgments in Cases C-411/10 and C-493/10 *NS and Others* [2011] EU:C:2011:865, paras 78–80; and Case C-399/11 *Melloni* [2013] ECLI:EU:C:2013:10, paras 37 and 63. This obligation based on automaticity may also conflict with the case-by-case analysis

has had to deal with the developments of the *Aranyosi* doctrine in the explosive Polish context of the reform of the judiciary. In *Ministry for Justice and Equality*, the ECJ was asked whether, in order for the executing judicial authority to be required to postpone the execution of a European Arrest Warrant, it has to find, first, that there are deficiencies in the Polish system of justice amounting to a real risk of breach of the right to a fair trial and, second, that the person concerned is exposed to such a risk, or whether it is sufficient for it to find that there are deficiencies in the Polish system of justice, without having to ascertain that the individual concerned is exposed thereto.[76] This new development confirms the application of the *Aranyosi* doctrine in the context of fair trial and the rule of law.[77] In so ruling, the ECJ has confirmed the reality of the 'virtuous circles' of diversity and conditional effectiveness in the case law of the ECJ in the area of mutual trust.

III. (RIGHTS AND) OBLIGATIONS IN EU LAW

A. Obligations and Interests in EU Law: A Functional Approach to Rights

Bengoextea wrote an enlightening article entitled on 'Rights (and Obligations) in EU Law'.[78] This article approaches the general issue of 'rights' from an analytical perspective and claims that the notion and logic of 'rights' require closer scrutiny. Surprisingly, there is a paucity of research on the concept of 'rights' from an analytical perspective in EU law.[79] What is the internal logic of 'rights' in EU law? And is it enough to explain their resilience by reference only to their internal logic?

In any case, in analytical jurisprudence, the concept of rights must always be studied in tandem with the reverse side of the coin – its dark side: the concept of obligations (or duties).[80] It is argued in this chapter that the obligations

used in ECtHR cases to determine a breach of human rights. See, eg, *Tarakhel v Switzerland* App no 29217/12 (ECtHR, 4 November 2014); and *Sneersone and Kampanella* App No 14737/09 (ECtHR, 12 July 2011).

[76] See Opinion of Advocate General Tanchev in Case C-216/18 PPU *Minister for Justice and Equality* [2018] ECLI:EU:C:2018:517, para 9.

[77] ibid paras 47–48.

[78] See Bengoetxea (n 39).

[79] See WN Hohfeld, 'Fundamental Legal Conceptions as Applied in Judicial Reasoning' (1917) 26 *Yale Law Journal* 710; R Alexy, *A Theory of Constitutional Rights* (New York, Oxford University Press, 2002); J Bengoetxea, *The Legal Reasoning on the European Court of Justice* (Oxford, Oxford University Press, 1993); Bengoetxea (n 39); N MacCormick and O Weinberger, *An Institutional Theory of Law: New Approaches to Legal Positivism* (Dordrecht, Springer, 1986), in particular 93–109; and A Peczenik, *On Law and Reason* (Dordrecht, Springer, 2009).

[80] See C Warin, 'Individual Rights under Union Law: A Study on the Relation between Rights, Obligations and Interests in the Case Law of the Court of Justice' (Doctoral thesis, University of Luxembourg, 2017). Warin describes the EU concept of individual rights as an original blend of influences. The originality of the EU concept is that it is the result of a hybridisation process between the objective and subjective legality control (see 44–49).

(or duties) in EU law are extremely strong. As seen in the previous section and in contrast to the US approach to rights,[81] the focus of the ECJ in rights adjudication is on assessing the legitimacy or proportionality of Member States' collective interests when derogating from EU law. In other words, the Court's attention does not lie on the analysis of the definitional breach of the right, but instead on the definitional scope of the obligation framed by EU law and its Treaty objectives now listed in Article 3 TEU after the entry into force of the Treaty of Lisbon.[82] This approach to rights is very banal[83] or administrative and is akin to the model of the French Conseil d'État, where the court acts as the protector of the prerogatives of the administration.[84] This objective or functional approach comes, in a way, as no surprise, given the historical *main mise* of French administrative law on the EU system of judicial review.[85]

The existence of XXL obligations stimulated and enforced by the ECJ and the national courts may explain – but only in part – why the rights are so resilient within the process of European integration. In that sense, it is also vital to take account of the private interests of the various epistemic communities in order to fully understand their resilience in the judicialisation of the EU legal order.[86] Is it not the case that the *Van Gend en Loos* doctrine has put two sets of actors in the epicentre of EU law: the courts and the individuals?[87] Therefore, it is essential to analyse the concept of rights from both sides. From the Court's perspective, it is clear that the ECJ relies on a functional or purposive approach to rights, consistently elaborating or interpreting them in light of the objectives of the Treaty (and most notably in light of the effectiveness of EU law). In that sense, the Court is the guardian of the effectiveness of EU law and ensures the promotion of unity and coherence of the EU legal order. The constant and dense reliance on the method of teleological interpretation confirms such an argument. This is so in relation both to the creation of individual rights and to their interpretation.

Indeed, the teleological interpretation appears closely related to the gap-filling function attributed to the ECJ in the elaboration of individual rights as general principles, which accordingly must be compatible with the structure and objectives of the Community.[88] This method of interpretation may also be denominated by the expression 'effet utile'. This term might suggest that the Court should interpret the law in the light of its own wishes and should

[81] See M Tushnet, 'An Essay on Rights' (1982) 62 *Texas Law Review*, 1363, 1371–72.

[82] The list of objectives was enshrined in art 2 EU before the entry into force of the Lisbon Treaty.

[83] M Koskenniemi, 'The Effect of Rights on Political Culture' in P Alson (ed), *The EU and Human Rights* (Oxford, Oxford University Press, 1999) 99.

[84] See A Mestre, *Le Conseil d'État, protecteur des prérogatives de l'administration* (Paris, Librairie Générale de Droit et de Jurisprudence, 1972).

[85] See, eg, art 263 TFEU.

[86] Stone Sweet (n 13).

[87] Weiler (n 35).

[88] Case 11/70 *Internationale Handelsgesellschaft* [1970] EU:C:1970:114, para 4.

therefore be cautiously used.[89] This interpretation is also often referred to as 'effective interpretation of Treaty obligations' and places the emphasis on the function, which the Treaty has to undertake, while taking into consideration the various political, economic and social facts that surround the functioning of the Treaty. As argued by Bredimas, the functional interpretation performs two functions: first, it is used as a method against the clear text and manifest intention of the legislator; and, second, it constitutes a method to fill the gaps.[90] In the end, this implies that individual rights are formulated and interpreted in the light of the objectives (purposes) of the Treaty. From a theoretical point of view, one may resort to Alexy's definition of teleological interpretation.[91] To put it in a nutshell, the state of affairs determines the validity of the norm.[92] In the elaboration of individual rights through the doctine of general principles of law, it can be said that the objectives of the EU (eg, effectiveness) make up the very state of affairs.[93]

This reading is supported by *Opinion 2/13*, where the ECJ in full court stated that:

> The autonomy enjoyed by EU law in relation to the laws of the Member States and in relation to international law requires that the interpretation of those fundamental rights be ensured within the framework of the structure and objectives of the EU.[94]

The Court, going further in the logic of European integration, even considered that:

> The pursuit of the EU's objectives, as set out in Article 3 TEU, is entrusted to a series of fundamental provisions, such as those providing for the free movement of goods, services, capital and persons, citizenship of the Union, the area of freedom,

[89] H Schermers, *Judicial Protection in the EC* (Deventer, Kluwer, 1976) 13. Following the same line of reasoning, Arnull argued that 'the purposive or teleological approach … is controversial one for those who are accustomed to seeing judges accord greater weight seem surprising in which the legislature has chosen to express itself': A Arnull, *The European Union and its Court of Justice*, (Oxford, Oxford University Press, 1999) 515.

[90] A Bredimas, 'Methods of Interpretation and Community Law' (1978) *European Studies in Law* 20, 70. See also Schermers (n 89). The author considers the existence of three purposes: promotion of the objectives; prevention of unacceptable rules; and filling gaps (at 13).

[91] R Alexy, *A Theory of Legal Argumentation: The Theory of Rational Discourse as Theory of Legal Justification* (Oxford, Clarendon Press, 1989) 243.

[92] In relation to the general principles, one may wonder to which 'very state of affairs' a particular principle is considered as valid. The principle (R) can only be justified and thus elaborated if and only if it does not contravene to the 'very state of affairs' (Z).

[93] See M Lasser, 'Anticipating Three Models of Judicial Control, Debate and Legitimacy: The European Court of Justice, the Cour de Cassation and the United States Supreme Court', Jean Monnet Working Paper 1/03. Effectiveness and uniformity may be defined as meta-purposes (meta-teleological style of reasoning or meta-teleological policy arguments), i.e purposes, values or policies underlying the EU and its legal structure interpreted as a whole (ibid 44). The author concluded that the ECJ's interpretative technique is therefore orientated towards developing a proper legal order, namely one that would be sufficiently certain, uniform and effective (ibid 54).

[94] *Opinion 2/13* (n 25) para 170. See, to that effect, *Internationale Handelsgesellschaft mbH* (n 88) para 4; and *Yassin Abdullah Kadi and Al Barakaat International Foundation* (n 51) paras 281–85.

> security and justice, and competition policy. Those provisions, which are part of the framework of a system that is specific to the EU, are structured in such a way as to contribute – each within its specific field and with its own particular characteristics – to the implementation of the process of integration that is the *raison d'être* of the EU itself.[95]

In other words, the ECJ still believes in the main rationale of the 'Ever Closer Union' clause under Article 1(2) TEU, ie, that EU law is becoming, as the essence of the EU legal order and as the alpha motive for defining and explaining the integrative momentum. The approach taken here by the full Court is outrageously (neo)functionalist.

It is argued in this chapter that the strength of the obligations and the concomitant functional logic of the ECJ offer a plausible explanation regarding the resilience of 'rights' in the EU legal order. Yet the resilience of 'rights' in EU law can only be fully explained if it is connected in turn to the recognition of their functional acceptance at the domestic level by different epistemic communities representing private interests. As already explained in section II of this chapter, the individuals (private persons or undertakings and even their lawyers)[96] have an interest in ensuring that the stakes they draw from EU law are effectively protected in national courts.[97] These feedback loops explain the success and genius of this regional legal system as the individuals act as the agents of EU law or, to paraphrase the expression of Weiler, act as a 'legal vigilante'.[98] In the end, the various epistemic communities promote the spillover of rights and the development of its corollary, ie, the principle of effectiveness, by invoking rights before national courts through the use of the doctrine of direct effect.

In addition, the belief in *les bienfaits* of the direct effect of individual rights has been romanticised and neutralised by legal doctrine. This has been done particularly by the so-called school of the 'Law of Integration', which views the law in general and EU law in particular as a coherent and unified system.[99] EU law was transformed into a compelling tool to promote the goals of European integration.[100] For instance, Ami Barav explained the use of

[95] *Opinion 2/13* (n 25) para 171. Please compare the wording of art 3 TEU, which does not include the word 'effectiveness', and art 2 EU (pre-Lisbon).

[96] See A Vauchez, *Brokering Europe: Euro-Lawyers and the Making of a Transnational Polity* (Cambridge, Cambridge University Press, 2015).

[97] See Robin-Olivier (n 36) 187–88.

[98] Weiler (n 35) 103.

[99] See P Pescatore, *Le droit de l'intégration* (Leiden, Sijthoff, 1972). See also W Hallstein, *Europe in the Making* (London, Allen & Unwin, 1972). Hallstein stated that: 'The European Community is a remarkable legal phenomenon. It is a creation of law; it is a source of law; and it is a legal system' (at 30).

[100] See also L Azoulai, '"Integration through law" and Us' (2016) 14 *International Journal of Constitutional Law* 452. According to Azoulai, the law of integration was also conceived of as a practical device. It was part of a strategy to compel legal and political minds to promote the goals of integration.

direct effect for developing the spillover of EU law in different substantive areas of EU law by referring to the now-famous formula from *effet utile* to *effet consequence*.[101] In a similar logic, Rodriguez Iglesias, the former President of the ECJ, considered that the elaboration of the unwritten individual rights by the Court by relying on the general principles was not an act of judicial activism because it was strictly judicial. In those instances, the law is viewed as the unique point of reference. It is in fact perceived and understood as a cold and neutral object, and not as an agent with a partisan agenda.

B. Supranational Integration and Effectiveness

In studying European constitutionalism and the process of integration, we consider that it must be examined in terms of its interaction with Member States' constitutionalism.[102] As confirmed many times by the ECJ, the structure of EU law not only requires the Member States to respect individual rights when they are implementing EU law, but also that the interpretation of those rights be ensured within the framework and objectives of the EU.[103] This structural approach founded on respect for the sacrosanct principle of effectiveness is nowadays subject to strong contestation. How is the ECJ coping with this criticism in its case law on individual rights?

The contestation of 'EU rights' is both juridical and political. On the one hand, national courts, especially the highest instance courts, have reacted to the activism of the ECJ in the fields of EU fundamental rights. To study this juridical contestation is in our view necessary in order to fully understand the concept of 'rights' in the EU transnational context.[104] It appears impossible to analyse the concept of 'EU rights' without studying their relationship with the

[101] See M Shapiro, *Courts: A Comparative and Political Analysis* (Chicago, University of Chicago Press, 1981).

[102] See K Tuori, *European Constitutionalism* (Cambridge, Cambridge University Press, 2015). Sectoral constitutionalism draws a distinction in EU law between the economic, social and security constitution. Such a threefold dichotomy is particularly useful when analysing the concept of EU individual rights and gauging the impact of these rights in specific areas of EU law and in the Member States. See also K Tuori, ch 11 in this volume. According to Tuori, Peter Lindseth in *Power and Legitimacy* refuses to recognise the constitutional aspect of the EU and its legal system. Lindseth uses 'constitutionalism' in a thick normative sense, referring to vital elements of the American notion of a constitutional democracy and the European notion of a democratic *Rechtsstaat*, such as democracy and fundamental rights. Such a thick concept of constitutionalism reflects the persistent dominance of the state template in constitutional theory and, hence, risks blocking the view to the specificity of European constitutionalism. It focuses on the juridical and political constitutions, and tends to neglect sectoral constitutionalisation, a distinct feature of European constitutionalism which corresponds to the basic teleological policy orientation of the EU and its law.

[103] *Opinion 2/13* (n 25) paras 170–71.

[104] K Tuori, 'Transnational law: On Legal Hybrids and Perspectivism' in M Maduro et al (eds), *Transnational Law: Rethinking European Law and Legal Thinking* (Cambridge, Cambridge University Press, 2014) 11.

national level. Dawson even argues that it is especially those contested rulings in the field of European human rights law that will overcome the democratic deficit.[105] Recent years have seen the emergence of a strong legal reaction of the highest national courts to the rulings of the ECJ on EU rights – eg, *Rasmussen* (by the Danish Supreme Court and reacting to a ruling of the ECJ on horizontal direct effect of EU rights)[106] and *Taricco II* (a preliminary question put forward by the Italian Constitutional Court, but reacting to a previous ruling of the ECJ in *Taricco*)[107] constitute vivid examples of this trend. The two rulings of the ECJ have in common a glorification of the principles of effectiveness vis-a-vis national rights. In *Rasmussen*, the ECJ strongly confirmed the application of the horizontal direct effect doctrine of individual rights. In *Taricco*, the ECJ set aside a provision of Italian criminal law in the name of EU effectiveness without considering the high standard of protection afforded by the national rights.[108] The ECJ has two choices in terms of answering these national reactions: either it does not listen to the calls and pursues its 'integration policy' by infusing more effectiveness; or it listens to the calls and reduces the level of effectiveness by diffusing the constitutional conflicts through, for instance, the help of Article 53 of the Charter, Article 4(2) TEU or the granting of broad discretion to the Member States.

During the years of economic crisis and the pre-Brexit situation, when David Cameron argued vehemently for the eradication of the 'Ever Closer Union' clause in Article 1(2) TEU and commented at the same time in the UK newspapers on the *Dano* ruling[109] of the ECJ, the Luxembourg jurisprudence in relation to individual rights was in a state of limbo. On the one hand, the case law on citizenship – in the spotlight of the media – was narrowed to such an extent that many questioned the fundamental status of EU citizenship.[110] On the other hand, the ECJ was able to produce from time to time some judicial *coups d'éclat* – probably in order to keep the flame of effectiveness alive, but

[105] See M Dawson, 'Re-generating Europe through Human Rights? Proceduralism in European Human Rights Law' (2013) 14 *German Law Journal* 651,658. See also J Habermas, 'On the Internal Relation between the Rule of Law and Democracy' in C Cronin and P de Greiff (eds), *Habermas: The Inclusion of The Other: Studies in Political Theory* (Cambridge, MA, MIT Press, 1998). The theory of Habermas comes in handy for this part of the analysis; indeed, Habermas sees independent courts as vital in a constitutional democratic setting.

[106] Case C-441/14 *Dansk Industri (DI), Acting on Behalf of Ajos A/S* [2016] ECLI:EU:C:2016:278.

[107] *Criminal Proceedings against MAS and MB* (n 69).

[108] The rulings of the ECJ related to the interpretation of art 53 of the Charter must also be explored since this horizontal provision allows the ECJ to pacify the potential conflict with the national court by relying on the national fundamental right instead of the EU right. The contestation of EU fundamental rights is also political and targets the very nature and function of these rights. In the end, it is a contestation of the (liberal) model of integration through (EU) law.

[109] Case C-333/13 *Dano* [2014] ECLI:EU:C:2014:2358.

[110] K Hyltén-Cavallius, 'EU Citizenship at the Edges of Freedom of Movement' (Doctoral thesis, University of Copenhagen, 2017); see in particular section 5.4.3 in relation to the problematic application of the genuine enjoyment test (at 252–55).

with the clear and present risk to see the national courts reacting to its *trop plein* of effectiveness. The judicial strategy of the ECJ was in fact to put money both on the red (unity) and the black (diversity), but the strategy was also to put a little bit more money on the black as, exemplified in section II when discussing the 'diversity of effectiveness'.

Opinion 2/13 and its ode to the effectiveness of EU law came as a turning point in a political climate galvanised by the *legal* resolution of the economic crisis through an increased process of integration. Arguably, these two events mark, to a certain extent and least for some, the revival in the strong belief in functionalism and the law of integration. The State of the Union speech delivered by Juncker in 2017 is a perfect exemplification of such a shift in the process of integration. The rule of law and the 'rights' (the so-called sixth scenario) are back in business again to ensure the golden future of Europe. The legal repercussions are in our view clearly visible in two high-profile cases delivered in 2018 by the Grand Chamber of the ECJ: *Vera Egenberger* and *Relu Adrian Coman*. In *Vera Egenberger*, the ECJ emphasised the full effectiveness of Articles 21 and 47 of the Charter.[111] In doing so, it stated in relation to Article 21 of the Charter very powerfully that the prohibition of all discrimination on the grounds of religion or belief is mandatory as a general principle of EU law and is sufficient in itself to confer on individuals a right that they may rely on as such in disputes between them in a field covered by EU law.[112] In a similar vein and in relation to Article 47 of the Charter, the Court held that this provision on the right to effective judicial protection is sufficient in itself and does not need to be made more specific by provisions of EU or national law to confer on individuals a right which they may rely on as such.[113] In *Relu Adrian Coman*, the ECJ precluded the competent authorities of the Member State, of which the EU citizen is a national, from refusing to grant that third-country national a right of residence in the territory of that Member State on the ground that the law of that Member State does not recognise marriage between persons of the same sex. For the ECJ, an obligation to recognise such marriages for the sole purpose of granting a derived right of residence to a third-country national does not undermine the national identity or pose a threat to the public policy of the Member State concerned.[114] A national measure that is liable to obstruct the exercise of freedom of movement for persons may be justified only where such a measure is consistent with the fundamental rights guaranteed by the Charter.[115] The logic in *Relu Adrian Coman*, like in

[111] Case C-414/16 *Vera Egenberger* [2018] ECLI:EU:C:2018:257, para 82.
[112] ibid para 76. This case confims the doctrine of horizontal effect without referring to *Ajos/Rasmussen*.
[113] ibid para 78.
[114] Case C-673/16 *Relu Adrian Coman and Others* [2018] ECLI:EU:C:2018:385, para 46.
[115] Case C-165/14 *Alfredo Rendón Marín* [2016] EU:C:2016:675, para 66.

Vera Egenberger, is based on effectiveness, since it appears clear in this case that the right of residence must be granted to a third-country national who is a family member, since the effectiveness of the citizenship of the EU would otherwise be impaired.[116]

The last part of our study enters into the domain of 'the political'.[117] It focuses on the study of the contestation of the concept of rights – a contestation which is part of the broader questioning of the positive force of the law.[118] This powerful contestation is quite a recent one in Europe and can be found in the writings of many authors such as Scharpf, Joerges and Somek, or more recently Isiksel, Urbina and Bartl.[119] Though this powerful contestation is multi-form in nature, it embeds a common and crucial denominator: the critique of liberalism. For instance, in her book *Europe's Functional Constitution* from 2016, Isiksel makes the claim that the core of the European constitution is founded on the *finalité économique*.[120] In a book from 2017, *A Critique of Proportionality and Balancing*, Urbina attacks the main judicial tool of liberalism in the European case law: the principle of proportionality.[121] Another influential claim was made by Somek in his book *Individualism*.[122] For him, the ECJ case law eroded the safeguards of democracy and promoted a radical form of authoritarian materialism. His thesis enshrines an interesting critique of Tocquevillian homogeneity, market holism and the judicial endorsement of mobility also marked by the absence of a theory of justice. It is a critique of European democracy as a liberal society. Weiler criticises the growth of fundamental rights in Europe as shifting original EU values, which bend duties and responsibilities of individuals towards the community, to a self-centred approach of individualism.[123] In 2018, Bartl put forward the thesis that the 'strange non-death of internal market rationality' may explain the reason why the European project has not spilled over to the more robust forms

[116] ibid para 74 and see also para 36; a derived right of residence of a third-country national exists in principle only when it is necessary in order to ensure that an EU citizen can exercise effectively his or her rights to move and reside freely in the EU.

[117] For the growing of 'the political', see J Dickson and P Elefheriadis (eds), *Philosophical Foundations of European Union Law* (Oxford, Oxford University Press, 2012).

[118] See Azoulai (n 100).

[119] See above for A Somek, T Isiksel and F Urbina. See for F Scharpf, 'The Double Asymmetry of European Integration or: Why the EU Cannot Be a Social Market Economy', MPIfG Working Paper 09/12. For C Joerges, see 'Law and Politics in Europe's Crisis: On the History of the Impact of an Unfortunate Configuration' (2014) 21 *Constellations* 249.

[120] T Isiksel, *Europe's Functional Constitution: A Theory of Constitutionalism beyond the State* (Oxford, Oxford University Press, 2016).

[121] F Urbina, *A Critique of Proportionality and Balancing* (Cambridge, Cambridge University Press, 2017).

[122] A Somek, *Individualism: An Essay on the Authority of the European Union* (Oxford, Oxford University Press, 2007).

[123] JHH Weiler, 'Taking (Europe's) Values Seriously' in R Hofmann and S Kadelbach (eds), *Law beyond the State* (Frankfurt, Campus Verlag, 2016) 141.

of solidarity.[124] According to her, the success of neoliberal discourse is located in the interaction of the EU institutional design and the ideological consensus around neoliberal rationality.[125]

All these criticisms of the liberal Europe based on the 'rule of rights' challenge the models of the law of integration and integration through law[126] to the point of raising the question as to whether these models are in fact exhausted. Forty years ago, Pescatore showed *con brio* that legal integration has led to 'the creation of stable structures capable of standing up to the assault of crisis and the erosion of time'. As put by Baquero Cruz, 'perhaps he wouldn't write that today'.[127] Or perhaps, particularly taking into consideration recent developments as to the rise of effectiveness as illustrated in this section, he would still write it.[128] This chapter has shown that the story of the resilience of rights in the process of European integration is also the story of the resilience of effectiveness. The ebbs and flows of the rights follow the ebbs and flows of effectiveness scrupulously in line with the text of Article 1(2) TEU, the 'Ever Closer Union' clause. And the only way to stop this process of integration is to get rid of the 'Ever Closer Union' clause. There is no other alternative. Ideally hoping for a less self-centred and less self-referential system, the reality is marked by an overconstitutionalisaton of the EU legal order through the spillover of rights.[129] The EU rights are resilient in the both senses of the term, in the sense that they are resistant and pliant. They are resilient since they operate in line with the text of Article 1(2) TEU and are faithfully interpreted, in this respect, by the ECJ. As shown in this chapter, the EU rights may show certain limits in the process of European integration,

[124] Bartl (n 31) 108. See also C Crouch, *The Strange Non-death of Neoliberalism* (Cambridge, Polity Press, 2011); and W Davies, *The Limits of Neoliberalism: Authority, Sovereignty and the Logic of Competition* (London, Sage, 2014).

[125] Bartl (n 31) 114.

[126] The key difference between integration through law (ITL) and the law of integration is that ITL views the law both as an object and as an agent. As put by Azoulai (n 100) 455: 'Unlike the law of integration, the ITL project started as an effort to understand, rather than hide, the contradictions of the integration process, i.e. an effort to analyze the "resilience" of the integration process in the face of recurring crises within and outside.'

[127] J Baquero Cruz, 'What's Left of the Charter: Reflections on Law and Political Methodology' (2008) 15 *Maastricht Journal of European and Comparative Law* 65.

[128] See Azoulai (n 100) 450. The most prominent representative of this vision of the Rechtsgemeinschaft today is Martin Selmayr, the Head of the European Commission President's Cabinet, who interprets this tradition in a rather narrow way by considering the EU as a legalistic construction (see Martin Selmayr, The Foundation of a European Law Institute: The Planting of a Little "Apple Tree" for a European Legal Culture', 1 June 2011, www.europeanlawinstitute.eu/fileadmin/user_upload/p_eli/_3__Martin_Selmayr.pdf.

[129] D Grimm, *The Constitution of European Democracy*, (Oxford, Oxford University Press, 2017). Grimm points out the overconstitutionlisation of European integration. In relation to rights, it is possible to describe the EU rights as liquid or water. Indeed, the EU rights are nurturing and eroding at the same time the national judicial *terrain* (see in that respect, P Caro de Sousa, 'Normative and Institutional Dimensions of Rights' Adjudication around the World', 17 April 2018, www.dx.doi.org/10.2139/ssrn.3164407). In that respect, it should not be forgotten that too much water kills the flower.

but the rule of law is never too far away to fill the gaps left over by the limits of rights adjudication.

C. The Rule of Law as a Mask, Again

The role of the rule of law has varied throughout the existence of the European project, fluctuating between a stance of a passive constitutive element deemed to be inherent in every legal order that supports and enhances the idea of democracy and protection of fundamental rights, and an active driving force facilitating the development of the European project. Yet, facing the criticism of being described as a 'rhetoric balloon'[130] or an 'empty slogan',[131] the rule of law nowadays demonstrates its capacity to position itself as a powerful principle able to combine different facets that saturate the European project and, under pressure from extreme scenarios that the EU is facing, to continue acting as a uniting element fostering the European integration.

The operational functionality of the rule of law can be seen as a mask that the Court puts on to facilitate the progress of the European project: once the principle is applied as a 'secret' coverage for transmitting the special agenda, it transforms into a mask, while at the same time shielding it from other conflicting objectives – the analogy applied to law as an instrument regulating an interplay between law and politics in the integration processes from the neofunctionalistic perspective.[132] Initially the rule of law acted as a common value[133] agreed upon by Member States that reached a consensus on finding a balanced solution to the rule of the iron fist[134] representing the core antagonist of the principle – arbitrariness.[135] Despite the fact that the rule of law has not

[130] F Sterzel, *Rättsstaten – Rätt, Politik och Moral: Seminarium 5 oktober 1994* (Stockholm, Rättsfonden, 1996) 21.

[131] JN Shklar, 'Political Theory and the Rule of Law' in AC Hutcheson and P Monahan (eds) *The Rule of Law: Ideal or Ideology* (Toronto, Carswell, 1987) 1.

[132] A-M Burley and W Mattli, 'Europe before the Court: A Political Theory of Legal Integration' (1993) 47 *International Organization* 41, 72–73.

[133] See art 2 TEU and also the text of art 263 TFEU (originally art 173 EC). The rule of law in the EU is rooted in the concept of limited governance and judicial review. See also art 31 of the European Coal and Steel Community (ECSC): 'to ensure the rule of law in the application and interpretation of the present Treaty and of the regulations for its execution'. For clear links in the case law between rule of law and judicial review, see also recently *Minister for Justice and Equality* (n 76) para 51.

[134] White Paper on the Future of Europe: Reflections and Scenarios for the EU27 by 2025, the European Commission, COM (2017) 2025, 1 March 2017.

[135] M Krygier, 'Transformations of the Rule of Law: Legal, Liberal, Neo-', conference paper, 4. See also SA Scheingold, *The Rule of Law in European Integration: The Path Schuman Plan* (New Haven, Yale University Press, 1965), in particular the section on supranationalism and judicial review (at 3–17). In his book, which seems to have been written way ahead of his time, Scheingold shows the strong connection between the rule of law and the theory of limited governance through judicial review. It is for the court to translate the expansive logic of sector integration into standard for gauging the decisions of the high authority. Effectiveness and the respect of transpersonal end are at the core of the court's judicial review.

been expressly defined in the Treaties, being left as a principle stemming from the common constitutional traditions of the Member States, it united them on the intrinsic aspects of circumscribing the public powers by law and the impartial independent courts[136] that are to provide the judicial review of acts of the public authorities[137] of both the EU and Member States and to guarantee the legally constrained exercise of the public powers.

As a common value, the rule of law has also served as an implicit driving force for European integration, gradually demonstrating its force more vividly. Starting off from the confirmation of Member States' loyalty to the principle,[138] underpinned by a possibility of invoking the so-called 'nuclear option',[139] it continued to remind the EU and the Member States of the fact that the measures adopted by them cannot escape judicial review, ensuring the conformity and unity with primary law as the rule of law constitutes the foundation of the EU.[140] In *Les Verts*, the Court highlighted an essential component crucial for European integration that constituted enhancing the development of the European project without eroding the balance between the EU institutions and Member States in the context of the internal dimension of the rule of law in the EU.[141] Over the course of time, the 'backbone of any modern constitutional democracy'[142] cemented its status of a 'primary constitutional principle'[143] that cannot be neglected in the ambit of public international law as well. The *Kadi I* case reaffirmed the EU legal order as an autonomous legal system guarding the protection of human rights that cannot be undermined by an international agreement.[144] The recourse to the rule of law in this case brings us to one of the most crucial facets that this principle entails: while aiming at striking the balance between a core constitutional value and effective international measures,[145] the rule of law is being used as a mask for protection of

[136] Communication from the Commission to the European Parliament and the Council, 'A New EU Framework to Strengthen the Rule of Law', COM (2014) 158 final/2, 4.

[137] S Peers and M Costa, 'Court of Justice of the European Union (General Chamber) Judicial Review of EU Acts after the Treaty of Lisbon; Order of 6 September 2011, Case T-18/10 Inuit Tapiriit Kanatami and Others v. Commission & Judgment of 25 October 2011, Case T-262/10 Microban v. Commission' (2012) 8 *European Constitutional Law Review* 91; GF Mancini and DT Keeling, 'Democracy and the European Court of Justice' (1994) 57 *Modern Law Review* 181.

[138] See Preamble to the TEU.

[139] Article 7 TEU; see also D Kochenov and L Pech, 'Monitoring and Enforcement of the Rule of Law in the EU: Rhetoric and Reality' (2016) 11 *European Constitutional Law Review* 516; M Ovádek, 'The Rule of Law in the EU: Many Ways Forward But Only One Way to Stand Still?' (2018) 40 *Journal of European Integration* 498.

[140] Case 294/83 *Parti Ecologiste 'Les Verts'* [1986] ECLI:EU:C:1986:166, para 23.

[141] Konstadinides (n 40) 55.

[142] Communication from the Commission to the European Parliament and the Council, 'A New EU Framework to Strengthen the Rule of Law' COM (2014) 158 Final/2, 1.

[143] L Pech, 'The Rule of Law as a Constitutional Principle of the European Union', Jean Monnet Working Paper Series No 4/2009, 28 April 2009, 56.

[144] *Yassin Abdullah Kadi and Al Barakaat International Foundation* (n 51) para 316.

[145] J Kokott and C Sobotta, 'The *Kadi* Case: Constitutional Core Values and International Law – Finding the Balance?' (2012) 23 *European Journal of International Law* 1024.

fundamental rights and strengthening their vulnerable position when targeted by a political interaction,[146] or in emergency circumstances that should not diminish the level of protection of rights.[147] This tendency has not been incidental. The recent judgment of the ECJ in *Portuguese Judges*[148] demonstrates the expanding role of the rule of law directed at not just confirming the necessity of safeguarding fundamental rights, but going further and expanding the scope of their protection in the external dimension of the rule of law between the EU and the Member States. The independence and impartiality of the judiciary have always been constitutive elements of the rule of law capable of imposing legal constraints on public powers.[149] The budgetary austerity measures in question adversely affected, among others, the judiciary branch of Portugal and were described as undermining the principle of judicial independence enshrined in both the TEU[150] and the Charter of Fundamental Rights.[151] As is well known, the tools and mechanisms enacted as a reaction to the financial crisis claim to pursue effectiveness that is also deemed to further the integration process. However, striving for effectiveness quite often seems to be achieved at the expense of legality[152] and encroaching on the rights of individuals.[153] It is remarkable that the Court pointed out the obligational nature of the rule of law reflected in Article 19(1) TEU, which expresses a duty imposed on the Member States to provide remedies to ensure effective legal protection in the fields covered by EU law. The Court underpinned this reasoning by reference to Articles 2 and 4(3) TEU, without recourse to the Charter of Fundamental Rights whose applicability depends upon the necessity of the measure in question to be implementing EU law.[154] This approach is crucial in the context of the cases dealing with challenging the legality of measures adopted as a response to the consequences of the financial crisis, where the issue of the origin of the measures quite often constitutes the core of cases[155] and plays a decisive role in terms of

[146] K Lenaerts, 'The *Kadi* Saga and the Rule of Law within the EU' (2014) 67 *SMU Law Review* 707, 715.

[147] Opinion of AG Poiares Maduro in *Yassin Abdullah Kadi and Al Barakaat International Foundation* (n 51) paras 35, 45 and 53.

[148] Case C-64/16 *Associação Sindical dos Juízes Portugueses* [2018] ECLI:EU:C:2018:117.

[149] TRS Allan, *Constitutional Justice: A Liberal Theory of the Rule of Law* (Oxford, Oxford University Press, 2003) 1.

[150] Article 19(1) TEU.

[151] Article 47 of the Charter of Fundamental Rights.

[152] F Costamagna, 'The Court of Justice and the Demise of the Rule of Law in the EU Economic Governance: The Case of Social Rights', Working Paper for 'Reconciling Economic and Social Europe: Values, Ideas and Politics REScEU', 8.

[153] L Ginsborg 'The Impact of the Economic Crisis on Human Rights in Europe and the Accountability of International Institutions' (2017) 1 *Global Campus Human Rights Journal* 101.

[154] Article 51(1) of the Charter of Fundamental Rights.

[155] Cases C-8/15 P to C-10/15 P *Ledra Advertising Ltd and Others* [2016] ECLI:EU:C:2016:701; Cases C-105/15 P to C-109/15 P *Konstantinos Mallis and Others* [2016] ECLI:EU:C:2016:702; see also S Laulhe Shaelou and A Karatzia, 'Some Preliminary Thoughts on the Cyprus Bail-in Litigation: A Commentary on *Mallis* and *Ledra*' (2018) 43 *European Law Review* 249.

whether action can be potentially brought at a European level or not.[156] The expansive interpretation of the obligation to adhere to the rule of law might be seen as giving ground to competence-creep criticism.[157] However, the choice of the Court shows the potential of the principle to confirm not only the rule of law, but ultimately the rule of rights whose protection shall be guarded at both the EU and the national levels. This aspect requires even more attention not only in light of the austerity measures aimed at restoring financial stability in the severely affected Member States that have been in the spotlight of the courts' adjudication in recent years,[158] but also in the context of the developing scenarios in Poland and Hungary,[159] which demonstrate worrying signs of decay of the principle that need to be urgently addressed.[160]

Not surprisingly, the rule of law is viewed as a promising salvation for the future development of the European project, representing the sixth scenario suggested by Juncker.[161] Apparently, this constitutional principle, and an acknowledged European value, has a capacity to enhance the achievement of an 'Ever Closer Union' by reinstalling the sense of mutual trust and belonging in the EU blurred by such cases as *Pringle* and *Dano*,[162] proving to be more than just an 'institutional ideal'[163] that lacks an operational potential.

IV. CONCLUSION: THE IMPOSSIBILITY OF THE STATUS QUO

The spillover of rights is driven at the general level by the 'Ever Closer Union' clause enshrined in Article 1(2) TEU. And it is in this context that the spillover of rights can be viewed as an integral part of the legacy of neofunctionalism

[156] A Poulou, 'Austerity and European Social Rights: How Can Courts Protect Europe's Lost Generation?' (2014) 15 *German Law Journal* 1145, 1173.

[157] Konstadinides (n 40) 30.

[158] F Fabbrini, 'The Euro-Crisis and the Courts: Judicial Review and the Political Process in Comparative Perspective' (2014) 32 *Berkeley Journal of International Law* 64, 64–65.

[159] The European Parliament supported the EU Commission's proposal to trigger art 7 TEU in relation to Poland; see www.europarl.europa.eu/news/en/press-room/20180226IPR98615/rule-of-law-in-poland-parliament-supports-eu-action. See also the Opinion of AG Tanchev for a pending case: *Minister for Justice and Equality* (n 76). The Committee on Civil Liberties, Justice and Home Affairs approved the draft proposal for a Council decision to enact art 7 TEU in relation to Hungary that was subsequently approved by the European Parliament on 12 September 2018: www.europarl.europa.eu/news/en/press-room/20180906IPR12104/rule-of-law-in-hungary-parliament-calls-on-the-eu-to-act.

[160] KL Scheppele and L Pech, 'What is Rule of Law Backsliding?' *VerfBlog*, 2 March 2018, www.verfassungsblog.de/what-is-rule-of-lawbacksliding; L Pech and S Platon, 'Rule of Law Backsliding in the EU: The Court of Justice to the Rescue? Some Thoughts on the ECJ Ruling in *Associação Sindical dos Juízes Portugueses*', 13 March 2018, www.eulawanalysis.blogspot.com/2018/03/rule-of-law-backsliding-in-eu-court-of.html.

[161] Juncker (n 2).

[162] Azoulai (n 100) 458–59.

[163] G Palombella, 'The Rule of Law as an Institutional Ideal' in L Morlino and G Palombella (eds), *The Rule of Law and Democracy: Internal and External Issues* (Leiden, Brill, 2010).

for explaining the process of European integration. The observed spillover of rights is a powerful phenomenon that acts as a trigger for facilitating European integration – even though, as in any system, there are obvious shortcomings in the form of spillback, specifically demonstrated by the limitation of individual rights during the economic crisis. They do not impair the integrational process as the rights in the EU possess a potential for accumulating the forces through other instruments available in the EU legal order that allows them to foster the European project, despite distress that can be acknowledged at first sight. In fact, the spillback of rights demonstrates their pliancy and their responsiveness to the persistent calls of effectiveness. It also explains why rights are so resilient in the process of European integration. As has been shown in this chapter, the European rights are resilient since they constitute the privilege tools for ensuring the institutionalisation of the 'Ever Closer Union' clause through a process of rationalisation. In other words, 'Unity', 'Diversity' and 'Transparency' (the normative core values of Article 1(2) TEU) have been institutionalised by the courts' case law on individual rights with the help of a complex network of legal principles, the central principle being *the* autopoietic principle of EU administrative and constitutional law, namely proportionality. This network of principles tied to the application of rights tells us that the telos of European integration is not only about unity but also about diversity. In practice, it means that the effectiveness of EU law is not absolute and that there are situations in which it is accepted that EU law should yield and where national interests should prevail. To understand the resilience of rights in the process of European integration, it is also important to analyse their internal logic or voice. Rights in EU law are founded on a functional logic epitomised by their own origin, structure and hermeneutic. The strength of the obligations and the concomitant functional logic of the ECJ offer a plausible explanation regarding the resilience of 'rights' in the EU legal order. Yet the resilience of 'rights' in EU law can only be fully explained if it is connected in turn to the recognition of their functional acceptance at the domestic level by different epistemic communities representing private interests. This phenomenon constitutes the positive feedback loop of European rights in the process of European integration.

REFERENCES

Alexy, R, *A Theory of Legal Argumentation: The Theory of Rational Discourse as Theory of Legal Justification* (Oxford, Clarendon Press, 1989).

——. *A Theory of Constitutional Rights* (New York, Oxford University Press, 2002).

Allan, TRS, *Constitutional Justice: A Liberal Theory of the Rule of Law* (Oxford, Oxford University Press, 2003).

Arnull, A, *The European Union and its Court of Justice* (Oxford, Oxford University Press, 1999).

Avbelj, M and Komárek, J, *Constitutional Pluralism in Europe and Beyond* (Oxford, Hart Publishing, 2012).

Azoulai, L, '"Integration through Law" and Us' (2016) 14 *International Journal of Constitutional Law* 452.
Baquero Cruz, J, 'What's Left of the Charter: Reflections on Law and Political Methodology' (2008) 15 *Maastricht Journal of European and Comparative Law* 65.
Bartl, M, 'Internal Market Rationality: In the Way of Re-imagining the Future' (2018) 24 *European Law Journal* 99.
Bengoetxea, J, *The Legal Reasoning on the European Court of Justice* (Oxford, Oxford University Press, 1993).
Bengoetxea, J, 'Rights (and Obligations) in EU Law' in E Jones et al (eds), *The Oxford Handbook of the European Union* (Oxford, Oxford University Press, 2012).
Bredimas, A, 'Methods of Interpretation and Community Law' (1978) *European Studies in Law* 20.
Burley, A-M and Mattli, W, 'Europe before the Court: A Political Theory of Legal Integration' (1993) 47 *International Organization* 41.
Crouch, C, *The Strange Non-death of Neoliberalism* (Cambridge, Polity Press, 2011).
Davies, W, *The Limits of Neoliberalism: Authority, Sovereignty and the Logic of Competition* (London, Sage, 2014).
Dawson, M, 'Re-generating Europe through Human Rights? Proceduralism in European Human Rights Law' 14 *German Law Journal* 651.
De Búrca, G, 'The Language of Rights and European Integration' in G More and J Shaw (eds), *New Legal Dynamics of European Union* (Oxford University Press, 1996).
De Vries, S, 'Balancing Fundamental Rights with Economic Freedoms According to the European Court of Justice' (2013) 9 *Utrecht Law Review* 170.
Dickson, J and Elefheriadis, P (eds), *Philosophical Foundations of European Union Law* (Oxford, Oxford University Press, 2012).
Dutheil de la Rochère, J, 'The EU Charter of Fundamental Rights, Not Binding But Influential: the Example of Good Administration' in A Arnull, P Eeckhout and T Tridimas (eds), *Continuity and Change in EU Law: Essays in Honour of Sir Francis Jacobs* (Oxford, Oxford University Press, 2008).
Fabbrini, F, 'The Euro-Crisis and the Courts: Judicial Review and the Political Process in Comparative Perspective' (2014) 32 *Berkeley Journal of International Law* 64.
Ginsborg, L, 'The Impact of the Economic Crisis on Human Rights in Europe and the Accountability of International Institutions' (2017) 1 *Global Campus Human Rights Journal* 101.
Grimm, D, *The Constitution of European Democracy* (Oxford, Oxford University Press, 2017).
Groussot, X, *Creation, Development and Impact of the General Principles of Community Law: Towards a Jus Commune Europaeum?* (Gothenburg, Intellecta docusys, 2005).
——. *General Principles of Community Law* (Groningen, Europa Law Publishing, 2006).
Günther, K, 'The Legacies of Injustice and Fear: A European Approach to Human Rights and Their Effects on Political Culture' in P Alston (ed), *The EU and Human Rights* (Oxford, Oxford University Press, 1999).
Haas, EB, *The Uniting of Europe* (Stanford, Stanford University Press, 1958).
——. *The Uniting of Europe* (Notre Dame, University of Notre Dame Press, 2004).
Habermas, J, 'On the Internal Relation between the Rule of Law and Democracy' in C Cronin and P de Greiff (eds), *Habermas: The Inclusion of the Other: Studies in Political Theory* (Cambridge, MA, MIT Press, 1998).
Hallstein, W, *Europe in the Making* (London, Allen & Unwin, 1972).

Harding, C, 'Economic Freedom and Economic Rights: Direction, Significance and Ideology' (2018) 24 *European Law Journal* 24.
Hofmann, HCH and Warin, C, 'Identifying Individual Rights in EU Law', 17 July 2017, University of Luxembourg Law Working Paper No 004-2017.
Hohfeld, WN, 'Fundamental Legal Conceptions as Applied in Judicial Reasoning' (1917) 26 *Yale Law Journal* 710.
Hyltén-Cavallius, K, 'EU Citizenship at the Edges of Freedom of Movement' (Doctoral thesis, University of Copenhagen, 2017).
Isiksel, T, *Europe's Functional Constitution: A Theory of Constitutionalism Beyond the State* (Oxford, Oxford University Press, 2016).
Joerges, C, 'Law and Politics in Europe's Crisis: On the History of the Impact of an Unfortunate Configuration' (2014) 21 *Constellations* 249.
Kelemen, D, *Eurolegalism: The Transformation of Law and Regulation in the European Union* (Cambridge, MA, Harvard University Press, 2011).
Kochenov, D and Pech, L, 'Monitoring and Enforcement of the Rule of Law in the EU: Rhetoric and Reality' (2016) 11 *European Constitutional Law Review* 516.
Kokott, J and Sobotta, C, 'The *Kadi* Case: Constitutional Core Values and International Law – Finding the Balance?' (2012) 23 *European Journal of International Law* 1024.
——. 'The Evolution of the Principle of Proportionality in EU Law: Towards an Anticipative Understanding?' in S Vogenauer and S Weatherill (eds), *General Principles of Law: European and Comparative Perspectives* (Oxford, Hart Publishing, 2017).
Konstadinides, T, *The Rule of Law in the European Union: The Internal Dimension* (Oxford, Hart Publishing, 2017).
Koskenniemi, M, 'The Effect of Rights on Political Culture' in P Alston (ed), *The EU and Human Rights* (Oxford, Oxford University Press, 1999).
Laulhe Shaelou, S and Karatzia, A, 'Some Preliminary Thoughts on the Cyprus Bail-in Litigation: A Commentary on *Mallis* and *Ledra*' (2018) 43 *European Law Review* 249.
Lenaerts, K, 'Exploring the Limits of the EU Charter of Fundamental Rights' (2012) 8 *European Constitutional Law Review* 375.
——. 'The *Kadi* Saga and the Rule of Law within the EU' (2014) 67 *SMU Law Review* 707.
——. 'EU Citizenship and the European Court of Justice's "Stone-by-Stone" Approach' (2015) 1 *International Comparative Jurisprudence* 1.
——. 'La vie après l'avis: Exploring the Principle of Mutual (Yet Not Blind) Trust' (2017) 54 *Common Market Law Review* 805.
MacCormick, N and Weinberger, O, *An Institutional Theory of Law: New Approaches to Legal Positivism* (Dordrecht, Springer, 1986).
Mancini, GF and Keeling, DT, 'Democracy and the European Court of Justice' (1994) 57 *Modern Law Review* 181.
McCrea, R, 'Forward or Back: The Future of European Integration and the Impossibility of the Status Quo' (2017) 23 *European Law Journal* 66.
Mestre, A, *Le Conseil d'État, protecteur des prérogatives de l'administration* (Paris, Librairie Générale de Droit et de Jurisprudence, 1972).
Moravcsik, A, 'The European Constitutional Compromise and the Neofunctionalist Legacy' (2005) 12 *Journal of European Public Policy* 349.
Niemann, A and Ioannou, D, 'European Economic Integration in Times of Crisis: A Case of Neofunctionalism?' (2015) 22 *Journal of European Public Policy* 196.

Ovádek, M, 'The Rule of Law in the EU: Many Ways Forward But Only One Way to Stand Still?' (2018) 40 *Journal of European Integration* 498.
Palombella, G, 'The Rule of Law as an Institutional Ideal' in L Morlino and G Palombella (eds), *The Rule of Law and Democracy: Internal and External Issues* (Leiden, Brill, 2010).
Pech, L, 'The Rule of Law as a Constitutional Principle of the European Union', 28 April 2009, Jean Monnet Working Paper Series No 4/2009, 56.
Peczenik, A, *On Law and Reason* (Dordrecht, Springer, 2009).
Peers, S and Costa, M, 'Court of Justice of the European Union (General Chamber) Judicial Review of EU Acts after the Treaty of Lisbon; Order of 6 September 2011, Case T-18/10 *Inuit Tapiriit Kanatami and Others v. Commission* & Judgment of 25 October 2011, Case T-262/10 *Microban v. Commission*' (2012) 8 *European Constitutional Law Review* 91.
Pescatore, P, *Le droit de l'intégration* (Leiden, Sijthoff, 1972).
Poulou, A, 'Austerity and European Social Rights: How Can Courts Protect Europe's Lost Generation?' (2014) 15 *German Law Journal* 1145.
Robin-Olivier, S, 'The Evolution of Direct Effect in the EU: Stocktaking, Problems, Projections' (2014) 12 *International Journal of Constitutional Law* 166.
Rosamond, B, 'The Uniting of Europe and the Foundation of EU Studies: Revisiting the Neofunctionalism of Ernst B. Haas' (2006) 13 *Journal of European Public Policy* 237.
Sandholtz, W and Stone Sweet, A, 'Neofunctionalism and Supranational Governance' in E Jones et al (eds), *Oxford Handbook of the European Union* (Oxford, Oxford University Press, 2012).
Shklar, JN, 'Political Theory and the Rule of Law' in AC Hutcheson and P Monahan (eds), *The Rule of Law: Ideal or Ideology* (Toronto, Carswell, 1987).
Shapiro, M, *Courts: A Comparative and Political Analysis* (Chicago, University of Chicago Press, 1981.
——. 'The Institutionalization of the European Administrative Space' in A Stone Sweet et al (eds), *The Institutionalization of Europe* (Oxford, Oxford University Press, 2001).
Scheingold, SA, *The Rule of Law in European Integration: The Path Schuman Plan* (New Haven, Yale University Press, 1965).
Schermers, H, *Judicial Protection in the EC* (Deventer, Kluwer, 1976).
Schmitter, PC, 'Ernst B. Haas and the Legacy of Neofunctionalism' (2005) 12 *Journal of European Public Policy* 255.
Somek, A, *Individualism: An Essay on the Authority of the European Union* (Oxford, Oxford University Press, 2007).
Sterzel, F, *Rättsstaten – Rätt, Politik och Moral: Seminarium 5 oktober 1994* (Stockholm, Rättsfonden, 1996) 21.
Stone Sweet, A, 'The European Court of Justice and the Judicialization of EU Governance' (2010) 5 *Living Reviews in European Governance* 16.
Stone Sweet, A et al, 'The Institutionalization of European Space' in A Stone Sweet et al (eds) *The Institutionalization of Europe* (Oxford, Oxford University Press, 2001).
Tridimas, T, 'Proportionality in Community Law: Searching for the Appropriate Standard of Scrutiny' in E Ellis (ed), *The Principle of Proportionality in the Laws of Europe* (Oxford, Hart Publishing, 1999).
——. *The General Principles of EC Law* (New York, Oxford University Press, 1999).

Tushnet, M, 'An Essay on Rights' (1982) 62 *Texas Law Review*, 1363.

Tuori, K, 'Transnational law: On Legal Hybrids and Perspectivism' in M Maduro et al (eds), *Transnational Law: Rethinking European Law and Legal Thinking* (Cambridge University Press, 2014) 11.

——. *European constitutionalism* (Cambridge, Cambridge University Press, 2015).

Urbina, F, *A Critique of Proportionality and Balancing* (Cambridge, Cambridge University Press, 2017).

Vauchez, A, *Brokering Europe: Euro-lawyers and the Making of a Transnational Polity* (Cambridge, Cambridge University Press, 2015).

Warin, C, 'Individual Rights under Union Law: A Study on the Relation between Rights, Obligations and Interests in the Case Law of the Court of Justice' (Doctoral thesis, University of Luxembourg, 2017).

Weiler, JHH, 'Van Gend en Loos: The Individual as Subject and Object and the Dilemma of European Legitimacy' (2014) 12 *International Journal of Constitutional Law* 94.

——. 'Taking (Europe's) Values Seriously' in R Hofmann and S Kadelbach (eds), *Law Beyond the State* (Frankfurt, Campus Verlag, 2016).

Part II

Rule of Law and Security

5

Discursive Constituent Power and European Integration

MASSIMO FICHERA

I. INTRODUCTION

THE IDEA OF constituent power has always been controversial in constitutional studies. Yet, despite its highly contested nature, the intensification of the process of constitutionalisation in the second part of the twentieth century has contributed to its resurgence, at least in its popular version. Renewed attempts to derive the authority of a system of government from the decision taken by the constituent power (in particular, the people) acquire a peculiar significance in light of the wave of populism across the European Union (EU). Once again, we are faced with crucial questions as regards the process of European integration. Is there a constituent power in the EU? And, if so, does it come from the people? From Bodin's idea of sovereignty as 'the highest power of command', the final instance of coercion, to Paine and Sieyes' notion of sovereignty as the power to found and to constitute, multiple approaches can be adopted. These approaches tend to convey the image of an unconstrained and undivided force, either in its repressive attitude or in its creative assertiveness. However, they seem increasingly unsuitable for the current conceptual landscape of transnational integration. This difficulty is confirmed by recent efforts to locate the constituent power in the international community, which may also, at best, be doubted.

This chapter seeks to unravel a different scenario, one in which a form of *discursive* constituent power emerges from the interstitial tissue of the EU. From this angle, all ambiguities and contradictions of the EU liberal project may be laid open. In particular, this chapter follows a discourse-theoretical line of research and adopts as its starting point a dual conception of 'The People': (1) as 'mobile people', ie, a construction of people as moving from one place to another of the EU territory; and (2) as 'peoples' in the plural, ie, a construction of 'demoi' that is supposed to underpin the *process* of development of the EU as a polity. It will be shown that in both configurations, the security and fundamental rights discourses as discourses of power are much more relevant than may seem to be the case. Section II introduces the notion of discursive constituent power and identifies European integration as a process constantly in search of justification. Section III instead analyses security and rights as self-justifying discourses of power, and advocates a move away from self-referentiality.

II. DISCURSIVE CONSTITUENT POWER

Amendment has always been a prominent feature of the process of European integration,[1] as confirmed by the number of amending Treaties that have been signed and ratified after the Treaty of Rome.[2]

Change and permanence are thus interwoven in the European liberal project of integration in such a way that 'change could only mean increase and enlargement of the old'.[3] I would like to characterise this feature of adaptation to change, of permanence in the face of threats with the expression 'security of the European project'. Security, interpreted in its broadest meaning, is not mere stability. It possesses an existential connotation and is never guaranteed once and for all. Rather, it oscillates and is shaped by its own opposite, *in*security, in a constant interplay. Whenever the foundational values of any polity are questioned by an excessively high number of opponents, the very existence of the polity is at stake.[4] Founding a polity thus means also attempting to secure its long-term survival, and constituent power plays a key role in this process – although its configuration needs to rely upon a mechanism of lawful authorisation.

Yet, any effort to articulate limits to constituent power by linking it to a supposedly pre-existing binding law is pointless.[5] The only way for constituent power to find a source of legitimacy is to be bound to a form of extra-judicial normativity, whilst maintaining its factual dimension. In other words, the nature of constituent power should be recognised as simultaneously political *and* legal.[6]

[1] It is not by chance that the Preamble of the Treaty on the European Coal and Steel Community (ECSC) already referred to an 'organized and vital Europe' and 'the foundation of a broad and independent community among peoples'. See eur-lex.europa.eu; and L van Middelaar, *The Passage to Europe* (New Haven, Yale University Press, 2011) 17–18.

[2] As is well known, the Merger Treaty (which entered into force on 1 July 1967), the Single European Act (1 July 1987) and the Treaties of Maastricht (1 November 1993), Amsterdam (1 May 1999), Nice (1 February 2003) and Lisbon (1 December 2009).

[3] H Arendt, *On Revolution* (New York, Penguin, 2006) 193–94.

[4] M Fichera, 'Security Issues as an Existential Threat to the Community' in M Fichera and J Kremer (eds), *Law and Security in Europe: Reconsidering the Security Constitution* (Cambridge, Intersentia, 2003) 85, 92.

[5] E-W Böckenförde, 'The Constituent Power of the People: A Liminal Concept of Constitutional Law' in *Constitutional and Political Theory: Selected Writings* (Oxford, Oxford University Press, 2017) 169, 184.

[6] C Mortati, 'La teoria del potere costituente' (1972) 1 *Studi sul potere costituente e sulla riforma costituzionale dello Stato- Raccolta di Scritti* 12–14 employs the notion of 'normative fact', ie, a fact

In fact, in the past, three forms of establishment of a new constitutional order have been distinguished: illegal, a-legal and legal.[7]

Although these are general observations, they may apply to specific scenarios. In particular, the foundation of the EU as a polity faces similar paradoxes and conundrums, especially as regards the configuration of a constituent power. The questions are often: (1) whether and how such constituent power can be configured at the transnational level and who effectively holds it; (2) what rationality the EU liberal project follows; and (3) what makes the EU liberal project *secure*. The following pages will address these questions gradually. To sum up the arguments made in the following pages, I would like to argue that transnational integration, in particular European integration, does not renounce the idea of people as constituent power. European integration is constitutional integration, insofar as it does not displace the-people-as-constituent-power, but makes an idiosyncratic use of it within both a political and a legal framework.

First of all, in order to grasp the nature of constituent power in the EU, we need to keep in mind that the EU project of integration is a liberal project. In other words, as it develops the ideas of a common internal market and the rule of law, the EU draws inspiration from the classic liberal aspiration to ensure the peaceful co-existence of people(s) and allow individuals to fulfil their life projects as best they can. Whilst regarded with suspicion by several versions of liberalism, the-people-as-constituent-power acts as a powerful rhetorical device if viewed from a particular angle of liberal thought.[8] The liberal-democratic idea of attributing *pouvoir constituant* to the people as the subject of the founding act[9] and therefore the author of a radical break from the past – especially an authoritarian arrangement – is intimately connected to individual empowerment and the security of a polity. This happens in two ways. First, the abolition of pre-existing structures, a break of the status quo, is normally justified through a reference to individual freedom.[10] Second, a liberal legal system legitimises itself through the construction of an idea of 'people', which, however, is fictitious.

which contains within itself its own law and the guarantees of its persistence in the future. However, the normativity of constituent power depends on the extent to which it is perceived as binding: see V Crisafulli, *Lezioni di diritto costituzionale* (Padua, CEDAM, 2000) 106.

[7] S Romano, 'L'instaurazione di fatto di un ordinamento costituzionale e la sua legittimazione' in *Scritti minori* (Milan, Giuffré, 1950) 110.

[8] For this strand of liberal thought, see, eg, T Paine, 'Rights of Man' in E Foner (ed), *Paine: Collected Writings*, (New York, Library of America, 1995), 579 (identification of constituent power with the 'people'). In the post-absolutist era, others have located constituent power in the more or less equivalent 'nation': E Sieyès, *Qu'est-ce le Tiers état?*, ed R Zapperi (Paris, Librarie Droz, 1970).

[9] However, conceptions of constituent power not bound to the idea of people are also possible (eg, political parties, ruling elite and monarch). See J Colón-Ríos, 'Five Conceptions of Constituent Power' (2014) 130 *Law Quarterly Review* 306; P de Vega, *La reforma costitucional y la problemática del poder constituyente* (Madrid, Tecnos. 1985) 233; C Mortati, 'Voce Costituzione (dottrina generale)' in *Enciclopedia del diritto* (Milan, Giuffré, 1961) 163 ff; J Bryce, 'Flexible and Rigid Constitutions' in *Studies in History and Jurisprudence* (Oxford, Oxford University Press, 1901) 129.

[10] C Möllers, 'Pouvoir Constituant – Constitution – Constitutionalisation' in A von Bogdandy and J Bast (eds), *Principles of European Constitutional Law* (Oxford, Hart Publishing, 2006) 183, 186.

A 'people' does not really exist, or does so only retroactively, *post factum*, in such a way that only an act of force, as it were, founds the law.[11] In a sort of 'vicious circle', as often observed, no people is authorised to constitute a polity *before* the actual polity is constituted.[12] This holds true at the transnational level just as it does at the national level.

The argument illustrated in this chapter is that, during the process of European integration, it is possible to trace the development of a *discursive* constituent power. In other words, the idea of 'people' is constructed through the discourses of security and fundamental rights. How does this happen?

The argument goes as follows. The notion of constituent power is strictly related to the notion of sovereignty as creative power, ie, the power to constitute, to found – as opposed to sovereignty as coercive or repressive power.[13] This productive, creative dimension of sovereign power, as an original power that simultaneously grounds a constitutional order from within and generates it from the outside, has been often associated with 'the people' by some of the earlier theorists of liberal constitutionalism, as noted earlier.[14] However, constituent power does not consist merely in the exercise of a specific type of power by a people at any given moment; it also *constitutes* people as an entity that did not exist beforehand.[15] The consideration of the self-constituting nature of this power leads to a deeper reflection on the problem of attribution of acts to a collective subject. As Lindahl points out, 'the attribution of legislation to a collective is first and foremost an act of *self*-attribution, that is, an act by which the members of a community recognise legislative acts as acts of their *own* community'.[16] Self-constitution and self-attribution inevitably indicate that the object of our discussion is ultimately an act of self-empowerment. Yet, at this point, there emerges one of the several paradoxes associated with constituent power. For if this is really an act of self-empowerment, how can we

[11] J Derrida, 'Declarations of Independence' (1986) 15 *New Political Science* 7, 10.

[12] See, eg, H Lindahl, 'The Paradox of Constituent Power: The Ambiguous Self-Constitution of the European Union' (2007) 20 *Ratio Juris* 485. For the expression 'vicious circle', see R Carré de Malberg, *Contribution á la Théorie Générale de l'État* (Paris, Librairie de la société du Recueil Sirey, 1922) 494.

[13] For the conceptualisation of sovereignty as the power of command, see J Bodin, *On Sovereignty* (Cambridge, Cambridge University Press, 1992); see also later works, eg, J Austin, *The Province of Jurisprudence Determined* (London, John Murray, 1832).

[14] J Locke, *The Second Treatise of Government: An Essay Concerning the True, Original, Extent and End of Civil Government* (Cambridge, Cambridge University Press, 1991) 366–67; Paine, 'Rights of Man' (n 8) 579; Sieyès (n 8) 180–91; C Mortati, 'Appunti sul problema delle fonti del potere costituente' (1946) 1 *Rassegna di diritto pubblico* 26. More recently, see also A Negri, *Insurgencies: Constituent Power and the Modern State* (Minneapolis, University of Minnesota Press, 1999) 2, where constituent power is defined as 'the source of production of constitutional norms – that is, the power to make a constitution and therefore to dictate the fundamental norms that organize the powers of the state. In other words, it is the power to establish a new juridical arrangement, to regulate juridical relationships within a new community'.

[15] M Loughlin, 'The Concept of Constituent Power' (2014) 13 *European Journal of Political Theory* 218, 229.

[16] Lindahl (n 12) 491.

attribute it to a fictitious subject that did not exist beforehand and whose existence is constantly debated – namely the *European* people? What are the limits of constituent power, if any?

In an attempt to go beyond the mere opposition between the reduction of law to mere originary fact and the configuration of constituent power as fully inherent in the constituted order, Negri argues that constituent power poses a 'radical question' and, 'insofar as it constitutes the political from nothingness, is an expansive principle'.[17] Negri's intention is to emphasise the creative dimension of constituent power as 'first decision' by pointing to its 'original radicalness' or 'radical openness', ie, its ability to open a number of 'grounding, innovative, linguistic and constitutional possibilities'.[18] However, in doing so, he defines constituent power as a pure 'act of choice', which necessarily stands in opposition to sovereignty as an act of repression, and is linked indissolubly with an absolutistic interpretation of democracy and the image of a continuum between law, revolution and constitution.[19] In other words, 'the question is not to limit constituent power, but to make it unlimited', because, in the end, 'the process started by constituent power never stops'.[20]

This approach helps us to highlight, once again, the interplay between change and permanence, which is constitutive of the European liberal project. At the same time, however, Negri fails to analyse further the relationship between limited and unlimited. For only if we view the potential for constituent power to act simultaneously as a challenge and an incentive for liberal constitutionalism will we be able to consider more thoroughly the latter's contradictions. As a matter of fact, constituent power does not dissolve once it has been exercised, but 'remains alongside and above the constitution'.[21] However, unlike the voluntaristic interpretation that follows from Sieyès, I argue that the ambiguity of EU liberal constitutionalism resides in the fact that, being unable to eliminate constituent power, it has safeguarded the interplay between change and permanence (the security of the European project) by disguising constituent power – the truly political dimension of the process of integration – in the form of the security and fundamental rights discourses. This is important, especially once we recognise the significance of constituent power as a legal power.[22] The argument above highlights the opacities of the meta-rationale of security, which operates at the same time to silence constituent power and (re-)activate it. On the one hand, security is pursued by preserving and promoting the core

[17] Negri (n 14) 16.
[18] ibid 20.
[19] ibid 22–24.
[20] ibid 24.
[21] C Schmitt, *Constitutional Theory* (Durham, NC, Duke University Press, 2008) 125–26: 'Every genuine constitutional conflict, which involves the foundations of the comprehensive political decision itself, can … only be decided through the will of the constitution-making power itself.'
[22] C Schmitt, *The Nomos of the Earth* (New York, Telos, 2003) 82–83 (referring to M Hauriou, *Précis de droit constitutionnel* (Paris, Librairie de la société du Recueil Sirey, 1923) 284).

values of the European project, as perceived by a more or less extended section of the society. Yet, this also implies that the formulation of these values must correspond to some degree to the interpretive, legislative and administrative practices which take place in that society. On the other hand, the risk is that security relies on a self-referential imagery, which does not open up a space for other realities. Essentially, constitutional regeneration across the decades cannot be truly accomplished by restricting the space for alternative visions of liberal democracy.

Because, in the long term, through a progressive erosion of the legitimacy of its claims,[23] this restrictive operation could endanger the EU liberal project, the latter has ensured its own continuity by relying on crisis. This is not a new phenomenon; in fact, especially in the twentieth century, liberalism in its most progressive version has relied upon *continuous* crisis to strengthen its appeal and consolidate support for an enlarged state.[24] In a sense, the EU liberal project – a project that purports to go beyond the traditional paradigm of state sovereignty – has carried out a similar strategy since the beginning. Crises produce exceptions, which make it necessary to invoke the constituent power in its disguised form in order to change the existing state of affairs. Yet, and most importantly, this invocation is always already made *from within* the legal system. It is a rhetorical device, employing the creative force of the-people-as-constituent-power *as if this were a real entity*. This is how the security of the European project is promoted. Thus, the EU liberal project can only survive if it does not negate constituent power, but reinstates it as *discursive* constituent power through the self-justifying discourses of security and fundamental rights. Consequently, I believe we should resist the temptation to characterise European integration as a process replacing constituent power with constitutional rights, on the one hand, and individual economic freedoms, on the other[25] – or to view it as a primarily economic process.[26] On the contrary, the political has never been really removed from the inner core of the process of European integration.[27] Although, on the face of it, political power was supposed to be

[23] See already F Scharpf, 'Democratic Policy in Europe' (1996) 2 *European Law Journal* 136.

[24] P Starr, *Freedom's Power: The History and Promise of Liberalism* (Cambridge, Basic Books, 2007) 8.

[25] See instead MA Wilkinson, 'The Reconstitution of Post-War Europe: Liberal Excesses, Democratic Deficiencies' in MW Dowdle and MA Wilkinson (eds), *Constitutionalism beyond Liberalism* (Cambridge, Cambridge University Press, 2017) 38, 51–59.

[26] See, eg, K Tuori, *European Constitutionalism* (Cambridge, Cambridge University Press, 2015) 26–28, where the author argues that, while the political and juridical constitution have enjoyed constitutive primacy, the economic constitution has enjoyed functional primacy. The distinction between constitutive and functional primacy is not entirely clear, especially if it is argued that 'European integration has been primarily an economic project, and in spite of the expansion of EU activities into new policy domains, economic integration retains a dominant position' (ibid 26).

[27] F Scharpf, 'Legitimacy in the Multi-level European Polity' in P Dobner and M Loughlin (eds), *The Twilight of Constitutionalism* (Oxford, Oxford University Press, 2010) 89, where the EU is defined as a polity possessing liberal credentials, but lacking republican credentials: is this not

confined within the national sphere,[28] in practice, transnational market integration has disguised a macro-political agenda which could only operate effectively if it was kept behind the curtains.[29] Similarly, the creation of an Economic and Monetary Union (EMU) – by relying on the principle of price stability and an independent central bank with limited powers (the European Central Bank (ECB)) – has removed an important element of Member States' autonomy away from the national sphere of action by placing it within a clearly political ordo-liberal transnational framework of governance.[30]

The ever-present political dimension of European integration, far from being *limited by* the security and fundamental rights discourses, is instead *expressed through* them. These discourses have contributed to constructing two ideas of 'people-as-constituent-power'. The first idea is that of 'mobile people', a category of people that are supposed to benefit from EU free movement rights. They circulate from one country to another mostly to satisfy professional ambitions or their aspirations for a better life – or to receive a service. The second idea is that of 'peoples' in the plural: as the imagery of a unified people constantly conflicts with the reality of the European diversified landscape, the powerful depiction of 'peoples', conceived as states and citizens at the same time, is a recurring object of study for EU scholarship.[31] As has been observed recently: 'The presupposition of a European people, as the collective subject of the European legal order does not exclude the continued presupposition of European peoples, in the plural, as the collective subjects of national legal orders.'[32] Discursive constituent power is thus a powerful tool for the justification of the EU liberal project; however, before analysing how this occurs, I will look more closely at its dynamic and conflictual nature. The position adopted here thus dissociates itself from that part of normative legal theory that either relegates constituent

eminently a matter of political self-design that affects the development of all sectors of EU law? (ibid, 93).

[28] J Weiler, 'The Transformation of Europe' (1992) 100 *Yale Law Journal*, 2403.

[29] M Bartl, 'Internal Market Rationality, Private Law and the Direction of the Union: Resuscitating the Market as the Object of the Political' (2015) 21 *European Law Journal* 572, 578.

[30] K Tuori and K Tuori, *The Eurozone Crisis: A Constitutional Analysis* (Cambridge, Cambridge University Press, 2014).

[31] K Nicolaïdis, 'The Idea of European Demoicracy' in J Dickson and P Eleftheriadis (eds), *Philosophical Foundations of European Union Law* (Oxford, Oxford University Press, 2012) 247; K Nicolaïdis, 'European Democracy and its Crisis' (2013) 51 *Journal of Common Market Studies* 351; R Bellamy, '"An Ever Closer Union among the Peoples of Europe": Republican Intergovernmentalism and Democratic Representation within the EU' (2013) 35 *Journal of European Integration* 499. Habermas has recently evoked a similar image of 'double constituting authority' or a constituent power shared between the European citizens, on the one hand, and of the European peoples of the different Member States, on the other. The heterarchical relationship between European citizens and European peoples would be a key feature of the founding process. See J Habermas, 'Democracy in Europe: Why the Development of the EU into a Transnational Democracy is Necessary and How it is Possible' (2015) 21 *European Law Journal* 546, 554; J Habermas, *The Crisis of the European Union: A Response* (Cambridge, Polity Press, 2012) esp 28–44.

[32] Lindahl (n 12) 494.

power outside the legal domain to the sphere of the political or believes it is a redundant concept.[33] Normativists sometimes label as 'negatively prescriptive political theories' those theories that deny that law's authority derives from the intrinsic qualities of legal orders and, by so doing, do not answer clearly the question whether such authority is internal or external to law.[34] Since it is argued here that this paradox is expressed by way of a fiction, taking place through discourses operating within the EU legal order, the approach followed here is not strictly decisionist either.

Scholars in the past have sought to find a middle way between normativism and decisionism by means of the so-called *relational* approach. Relationalism proposes to understand the political space as a space of unresolved conflicts and of a constant dialectic between closure and openness.[35] As a result, there emerges a tension between the sovereign exercise of constituent power and the way in which sovereign authority is expressed once political power is institutionalised. In other words, it is possible to identify in the moment of foundation a symbolic act, by means of which a multitude of people come together as a group: this act will inevitably involve the use of some degree of force. However, force and conflicts do not vanish with this symbolic transcendental act, but persist during the constitutional development of a polity. The reason for this state of affairs is that the institutional arrangement designed in a given historical and political context never corresponds to the actual decisional authority of the institutions. From a relationalist perspective, power resides 'neither in "the people" nor in the constituted authorities; it exists in the relation established between constitutional imagination and governmental action'.[36] One implication of this dynamic approach is that constituent power does not emerge merely at the foundational moment, only to disappear or remain concealed in some obscure location; rather, constituent power continues to operate within a polity and, by doing so, it preserves the political space as an open space of contestation. This amounts to configuring polity-building – in our case, EU polity-building – as a disputed process, which does not respond to the logic of communicative rationality.[37] However, relationalism does not take seriously the consequences of its reasoning. For, once we recognise the deeply conflictual nature of constituent power as a 'living power', we should also be prepared to admit that any claim by a part to act on behalf of a whole is fictitious.[38] No constituent claim can be universal

[33] D Dyzenhaus, 'Constitutionalism in an Old Key: Legality and Constituent Power' (2012) 1 *Global Constitutionalism* 229.

[34] ibid 233–34.

[35] Loughlin (n 15) 228.

[36] ibid 231.

[37] MA Wilkinson, 'Political Constitutionalism and the European Union' (2013) 76 *Modern Law Review* 191, 208.

[38] See the interpretation of Machiavelli's thought on constituent power in F del Lucchese, 'Machiavelli and Constituent Power: The Revolutionary Foundation of Modern Political Thought' (2017) 16 *European Journal of Political Theory* 3, 12.

because there is no homogeneous will. And yet, in order for this claim to be legitimate, it needs to be represented *as if* it were universal. It will be an all-inclusive, all-encompassing claim, but it will nevertheless always be a partial claim. The EU liberal project exemplifies these ambiguities because, whilst putting forward its claim to universality, it always already draws a line between those who should be included and those who should be excluded.[39]

Given the partial nature of any constituent claim, there cannot be any metaphysically unified people endowed with sovereign authority.[40] The reason is that, just like any other polity, if not more than any other polity, the EU polity is fragmented and heterogeneous. What is more, the tension between the constituted arrangement within the EU polity and the open-ended range of alternatives which are theoretically available for the exercise of constituent power cannot be reduced to mere disagreement; rather, such tension can and should always open the way for alternatives, which are situated beyond the purely liberal paradigm that has been followed so far. Thus, *discursive* constituent power contributes to a process of constant change, which could theoretically allow for possibilities of development outside the existing ones. However, the practical exercise of such power is affected by the tendency of the EU liberal project to 'neutralise' the security and fundamental rights discourses. This does not mean merely converting political disputes into technicalities, as has instead been argued.[41] The political is still present, *en travesti*, as noted earlier, in such a way that security and fundamental rights appear as universalistic and all-embracing, whereas they are in reality always partial, addressed to particular categories of people in particular contexts.

One important consequence of these remarks is that the conflictual features of discursive constituent power are revealed in their basic factuality. European integration unrolls as a process which is constantly in search of a justification. However, as crises produce breaks in the continuity of integration, the-people-as-constituent-power is appealed to time and again in order to support the strategic moves made by the EU institutions.

As will be shown in the next section, in the earlier stages of European integration, the political, inherently conflictual nature of EU constitutional claims was disguised in the form of a seemingly neutral market (economic-technocratic) integration,[42] mostly negative integration,[43] which pursued the

[39] M Fichera, 'Sketches of a Theory of Europe as an Area of Freedom, Security and Justice' in M Fletcher, E Herlin-Karnell and C Matera (eds), *The European Union as an Area of Freedom, Security and Justice* (Oxford, Routledge, 2017) 34, 41.

[40] Wilkinson (n 37) 207.

[41] A Cohen, 'Constitutionalism without Constitution: Transnational Elites between Mobilisation and Legal Expertise in the Making of a Constitution for Europe (1940s–1960s)' (2007) 32 *Law and Social Enquiry*, 109.

[42] E Haas, *The Uniting of Europe* (Stanford, Stanford University Press, 1958).

[43] See, eg, Case C-120/78 *Cassis de Dijon* [1979] ECR 649.

aim of 'the decoupling of politics and economics'[44] (which, as already seen, followed an eminently political agenda in reality). This state of affairs seems increasingly difficult to maintain in the current historical-political climate, as the process of constitutionalisation reaches a more advanced stage, in which the probability of conflict between different levels of governance and geopolitical areas is growing.[45] The building up of the Area of Freedom, Security and Justice (AFSJ) is clearly representative of such an advanced stage of integration.

III. THE DISCOURSES OF SECURITY AND FUNDAMENTAL RIGHTS

Communication is exchanged not only by mere text, but also by 'all kinds of linguistically mediated practices in terms of speech, writing, images, and gestures that social actors draw upon in their production and interpretation of meaning'.[46] From this perspective, discourses and power are mutually constitutive: discourses produce and strengthen power, but also undermine it, being at the same time an instrument and an effect of it.[47] Discourses of power can thus also be constitutive of a polity, while being constantly in tension or overlapping with each other. They shape meanings, condition actors' behaviour and choices, and correspond to rhetorical strategies that dominate in a given historical context. The reason is that processes of production and interpretation of texts, as well as the social conditions within which they are generated, and other social practices, such as courts' rulings or other jurisdictional acts, are indicative of specific patterns or relations of power.[48] The meta-rationale of the security of the European project – which, as noted earlier, conveys the existential implications of the EU enterprise – is articulated in security and fundamental rights as discourses of power. These discourses are constitutive of the EU as a polity because it is through them that the interaction between the EU institutions, as well as between the institutional apparatus and the citizens, takes place. They contribute to shaping a reality that is an integral part of the EU legal order. 'Discourses' are interpreted here as different from 'narratives', as the latter are (sometimes competing) forms of interpretation of reality employed to explain or justify events and/or to support specific policies.[49] The object of this analysis

[44] G Majone, *Rethinking the Union of Europe Post-crisis: Has Integration Gone Too Far?* (Cambridge, Cambridge University Press, 2014) 149–78.

[45] M Fichera, 'Law, Community and *Ultima Ratio* in Transnational Law' in M Fichera, S Hänninen and K Tuori (eds), *Polity and Crisis: Reflections on the European Odyssey* (Farnham, Ashgate, 2014) 189.

[46] J Torfing, 'Discourse Theory: Achievements, Arguments, and Challenges' in D Honneth and J Torfing (eds), *Discourse Theory in European Politics: Identity, Policy and Governance* (New York, Palgrave MacMillan, 2005) 1, 6.

[47] M Foucault, *The History of Sexuality: Vol I. The Will to Knowledge* (London, Penguin, 1998) 101.

[48] N Fairclough, *Language and Power* (Harlow, Longman, 1989) 26.

[49] RR Krebs, *Narrative and the Making of US National Security* (Cambridge, Cambridge University Press, 2015).

is, instead, essentially a daily practice that is embedded in the very process of formation of a polity. By observing such practice, it is almost inevitable to point out how, regardless of our personal judgement, dominance may be enacted and reproduced by subtle, routine, everyday forms of text and talk that appear 'natural' and quite 'acceptable'.[50] Clearly, the main focus here is on that type of social power that is exercised by entrenched elites or specific sectors of society. Yet, this is not storytelling with heroes and villains, but something more akin to a *Bildungsroman* with an open *finale*.

The security and fundamental rights discourses have emerged since the early stages of European integration. As regards fundamental rights, contrary to what many commentators argue,[51] their relevance has been high long before explicit provisions were inserted into the Treaties. In reality, as noted by de Búrca, a Comité d'études pour la constitution européenne ('a self-selected group of lawyers, scholars, activists, and national parlamentarians') had already been set up in 1952 with the aim of drafting a Constitution for a European Political Community (EPC).[52] Many solutions adopted in the draft articles were either adopted later or even more advanced than the current system for the protection of fundamental rights. Later, an Ad Hoc Assembly, composed (at the formal request of governments) of politicians selected from the six ECSC states and chaired by Henry Spaak (President of the ECSC), established a Constitutional Committee, which drafted the EPC Treaty.[53] Although the EPC project failed and no explicit fundamental rights clause was introduced into the Treaty establishing the European Economic Community (hereinafter the EEC Treaty), several hints contained in the latter point to the constant development of them as a discourse; for example, the Preamble's aspiration 'to lay the foundations of an ever closer union among the peoples of Europe' and the provision of direct elections to the European parliament are an indication in this sense.[54] As is well known, this implied 'the establishment of institutions endowed with sovereign rights, the exercise of which affects Member States and also their citizens'.[55]

In addition, an embryonic form of the discourses of security and fundamental rights was already present in the Manifesto of Ventotene, which is regarded

[50] TA van Djik, 'Principles of Critical Discourse Analysis' (1993) 4 *Discourse & Society* 249, 254.

[51] See, eg, A Tizzano, 'The Role of the ECJ in the Protection of Fundamental Rights' in A Arnull, P Eeckhout and T Tridimas (eds), *Continuity and Change in EU Law: Essays in Honour of Sir Francis Jacobs* (Oxford, Oxford University Press, 2008) 126; P Pescatore, 'The Context and Significance of Fundamental Rights in the Law of the European Communities' (1981) 2 *Human Rights Law Journal* 295; K Lenaerts and E de Smijter (eds), 'A "Bill of Rights" for the European Union' (2001) 38 *Common Market Law Review* 273; FG Jacobs, 'Human Rights in the European Union: The Role of the Court of Justice' (2001) 26 *European Law Review* 331; S Besson, 'The European Union and Human Rights: Towards a Post-national Human Rights Institution' (2006) 6 *Human Rights Law Review* 323.

[52] G de Búrca, 'The Road Not Taken: The EU as a Global Human Rights Actor' (2011) 105 *American Journal of International Law* 649, 654.

[53] ibid 659–62.

[54] ibid 666–67.

[55] Preamble to the Treaty of Rome, 25 March 1957.

as the first symbolic step towards the unification of Europe. The commonality of the European peoples is emphasised in the Manifesto several times, as 'either all together they will submit to Hitler's dominion, or all together they will enter a revolutionary crisis after his fall'.[56] The goals of the Manifesto of Ventotene are crystal-clear. It aims to encourage 'the emancipation of the working classes and the realisation for them of more humane living conditions' precisely because 'modern civilisation has taken as its specific foundation the principle of liberty'.[57] During the 'revolutionary crisis', the Ventotene movement 'derives the vision and security of what must be done not from a previous consecration of what is yet to be the popular conscience, but the knowledge of representing the deepest necessities of modern societies'. The new project is thus presented as a movement that *precedes* popular conscience (ie, the self-awareness of the future 'peoples of Europe') and, even more than that, aims *to shape this conscience* by constructing a discourse centred on the inevitability of the coming-together in the face of existential threats. By proceeding in this direction and creating the necessary conditions for individual freedom, the movement will 'evolve towards increasing comprehension of the new order, even though moving through eventual and secondary political crises, and acceptance of it by the population'.[58] Here, rather tellingly, the idea of crisis emerges almost as a constitutive element in the progressive establishment of the EC/EU. Once the conditions for individual freedom have been realised (through the rights discourse), 'the population' will accept the new order and retroactively gain self-awareness as the collective subject of the European legal order.

The input provided by these ideas later produced the image of a 'European family', which would 'dwell in peace, in safety and in freedom'[59] and realise a Coal and Steel Community as 'the first concrete foundation of a European federation indispensable to the preservation of peace'.[60] Whilst not employing this overtly federalist tone, the Court of Justice of the European Union (CJEU), as is well known, fabricated the doctrines of direct effect and primacy in order to emphasise, on the one hand, the autonomy of the EC/EU legal order as regards both international law and domestic law and, on the other, its effectiveness within the internal legal orders.[61] Thus, the importance of the first, foundational cases of EC/EU law lies not only in their 'constitutional' significance, but also in the contribution they gave to the development of the intertwined

[56] Manifesto of Ventotene (1941), www.cvce.eu/content/publication/1997/10/13/316aa96c-e7ff-4b9e-b43a-958e96afbecc/publishable_en.pdf, 7.

[57] ibid 8 and 2 respectively.

[58] ibid 11.

[59] Winston Churchill's Speech, Zurich University, 19 September 1946.

[60] Robert Schuman, Declaration of 9 May 1950.

[61] Case C-26/62 *Van Gend en Loos* [1963] ECLI:EU:C:1963:1; Case C-6/64 *Costa v Enel* [1964] ECLI:EU:C:1964:66.

security and fundamental rights discourses from the perspective of autonomy and effectiveness/uniformity. In particular, *Van Gend en Loos* and *Costa v ENEL* flow from the 'speciality' of the EU legal order, which, on the one hand (*Van Gend*), empowers individuals – the fundamental rights discourse – and, on the other hand (*Costa*), empowers the EU legal order itself – the security discourse. These rulings are part of a set of 'pre-dictions' and 'retro-dictions', from which not only the strategic moves of the main actors but also their semantic patterns have formed a judicial framework of principles that have crystallised at the foundations of the EU polity.[62] Even the principles of autonomy and effectiveness/ uniformity[63] (as well as loyalty, proportionality and subsidiarity, and the notion of common constitutional traditions) are expressions of the security discourse, which is articulated in two directions.

First, the EU project can only be secure if EU law is capable of producing effects at the domestic level, which benefit EU citizens uniformly. As a result, national provisions, even those having a constitutional character, cannot undermine the unity and effectiveness of EU law.[64] Second, the autonomy claimed by the EC/EU legal order is both normative and institutional, and, as will be seen below, is often the result of the robust interpretive role performed by the CJEU, which has defended it vigorously in its case law. In fact, it has been correctly argued that the CJEU in these cases interpreted the Treaties as a material constitution; however, the related contention that no normative autonomy can be attached to popular constituent power as the source of the constitution should be reconsidered.[65] As already noted, while there was no physical 'people' at the origins, an idea of 'people' (or 'peoples') has been relentlessly constructed from the very beginning of the process of European integration.[66]

Yet, it is worth recalling, once again, that the foundational stages of European integration were not immune from either crisis or conflict. On the one hand, setbacks to the process of the establishment of the Common Market (initially through harmonisation or even unification of national laws) made the task of Europhile legal experts far from harmonious. As has been documented, *Van Gend en Loos* and *Costa v ENEL* themselves were subject to conflicting interpretations, even at the moment that the respective decisions

[62] A Vauchez, 'The Transnational Politics of Judicialization: *Van Gend en Loos* and the Making of the EU Polity' (2010) 16 *European Law Journal* 1, 5–6.

[63] See, eg, Case 43/75 *Defrenne v Sabena (No 2)* [1976] ECLI:EU:C:1976:56; Case 41/74 *Van Duyn v Home Office* [1974] ECLI:EU:C:1974:133; Joined Cases C-6/90 and C-9/90 *Francovich v Italy* [1991] ECLI:EU:C:1991:428.

[64] Case 11/70 *Internationale Handelsgesellschaft* [1970] ECLI:EU:C:1970:114, para 3; Case C-409/06 *Winner Wetten* [2010] ECLI:EU:C:2010:503, para 61; Case C-416/10 *Križan* [2013] ECLI:EU:C:2013:8, para 70.

[65] As, instead, maintained by Tuori (n 26) 54–55.

[66] This is true even of alternative projects, eg, the failed Fouchet Plan (1961) (which pursued a more intergovernmental agenda). The plan aimed to build up a 'Europe of Peoples' and, of course, in its art 2 emphasised the need to protect human rights, fundamental rights and democracy.

were taken. On the other hand, as disagreements and crises characterised the 1960s, these rulings were crucial in bolstering the integrating, almost missionary role of the CJEU.[67]

Interestingly, following the *Van Gend en Loos* and *Costa v Enel* line, the security and fundamental rights discourses from the perspective of autonomy and effectiveness/uniformity are very much present in an intervention by Walter Hallstein, the President of the EEC, at a session of the European Parliament discussing the Dehousse Report in 1965.[68] In this intervention, Hallstein interprets the CJEU as claiming that: 'Community law and the municipal laws of the Member States are different legal systems. Each in itself is autonomous in the legal sense and therefore subject only to the conditions of elaboration and validity that are proper to it.'[69] From the autonomy of the EC/EU legal order stems its special nature as an order based on a 'constitution' legitimating a set of rules which are directly applicable in the Member States. According to Hallstein, if such a system were not autonomous and therefore complied with the norms of international law, 'its mission would be seriously jeopardised, and even finally frustrated', for in cases of conflict between EC/EU law and incompatible national law, the latter or the former would prevail, depending on whether the national legal system where the conflict takes place is dualist or monist.[70] European law must therefore gain its 'rightful place' and 'ensure what every system of law must ensure: security'.[71] What is more: 'The fundamental rights of the citizen are not being restricted as a result of the activity of Community bodies but in fact considerably enlarged.'[72] On the occasion of the formal completion of the Customs Union, the European Commission went even further and made it clear that once the hostility between France and Germany had been settled, the moment had come 'to call the young and creative forces of Europe' to move forward because 'political integration' must aim at establishing a 'pacific order'.[73]

In the 1970s, in response to the geopolitical crises of the time, as well as the oil crisis and the fall of the Bretton Woods system (1973), the energy crisis (1979) and the related stagflation (which exacerbated the hostility towards 'foreign workers' in European countries and caused many immigrant workers to return to their home countries in the South),[74] renewed attempts to advance

[67] Vauchez (n 62) 7-22.

[68] 'Rapport Général de Fernand Dehousse, membre de l'Assemblée Parlementaire Européenne', 30 April 1960.

[69] Address by Professor Walter Hallstein in the debate on the Dehousse Report (*Primacy of Community Law over Municipal Law of the Member States*), European Parliament, June Session 1965, 3, http://aei.pitt.edu/view/year/1965.creators_name.html.

[70] ibid 7.

[71] ibid 13.

[72] ibid 12.

[73] Declaration by the Commission on the Occasion of Achievement of the Customs Union on 1 July 1968, EC Bull 7-1968, 6–8.

[74] T Judt, *Postwar: A History of Europe since 1945* (London, Vintage, 2010) 457.

European integration were made.[75] A proposal was tabled by West German Chancellor Helmut Schmidt to create a 'European Monetary System' (EMS), a system of fixed bilateral exchange rates that would commit the participants to economic rigour in the name of the stability and anti-inflationary priorities set by Germany.[76] Moreover, the Tindemans Report insisted that a common defence policy should be drawn up, democratic legitimacy enhanced and the powers of the European Commission strengthened.[77] Couched in the language of crisis, the Report argues that European peoples, whilst in favour of closer links with each other, are concerned about new values which are 'scarcely mentioned by the Treaties' – this, in turn, requires the completion of the 'unfinished structure' of the EU and to 'enshrine in a legal text all the changes which have been gradually made', including the protection and recognition of fundamental rights.[78]

An innovative push towards a set of concrete measures of further integration came from a number of documents published in the 1980s. A 1984 Communication from the European Commission, for example, '[c]onsidering that it is essential that the Community should respond to the expectations of the people of Europe' (in this particular case, we might add, 'mobile people') suggested adopting a European passport, a single document for the movement of goods, the abolition of immigration and customs formalities for travellers within the internal frontiers, and a system of equivalence for qualifications.[79] These concrete measures are part of a broader canvas seeking, once again, to rely on the image of 'European peoples' sharing the values of respect for human rights and the rule of law, peace and an ever closer Union. These aims are enshrined in the 1984 draft Treaty Establishing the European Union, which, inter alia, contains important provisions on citizenship, fundamental rights and free movement.[80]

In this context, security and fundamental rights as discourses of power express the interplay between the expansive trend of the EU machinery (for example, through the doctrine of primacy and the development of the internal market) and the resistance by Member States. At the substantive level, concerns

[75] See already the Davignon Report (foreign policy), which at point 5 promotes a 'united Europe' based on 'the respect of liberty and the rights of man' to be attained 'thanks to the political will of the peoples': *Bulletin of the European Communities* 11, November 1970.

[76] Judt (n 74) 461.

[77] European Commission Report to the European Union by L Tindemans, *Bulletin of the European Communities*, Supplement 1/76. As is well known, the first direct elections to the European Parliament took place in 1979.

[78] ibid 11–13 and 26–27. See, similarly, European Commission Report, *Bulletin of the European Communities*, Supplement 5/75, eg, 25–27; Joint Declaration on Fundamental Rights by the European Parliament, the Council and the Commission (1977) OJ C103/1 (27 April).

[79] Communication from the Commission to the Council, 'A People's Europe: Implementing the Conclusions of the Fontainebleau European Council' COM (1984) 446 Final, Brussels, 24 September. Statements on fundamental rights and free movement are also contained in Rhodes European Council, Conclusions of the Presidency, 2–3 December 1988, SN 4443/1/88.

[80] Draft Treaty Establishing the European Union, 14 February 1984 (eg, arts 4 and 44 on sanctions in the case of serious and persistent violation of democratic principles or fundamental rights by one Member State).

have often been raised as regards the implications of the doctrine of primacy for the national standards of protection of fundamental rights.[81] Similarly, for a long time, the EU has been characterised by a tension between its internal market rationale and its citizenship rationale. The individual right component has been a key aspect of EC/EU law rhetoric.[82]

It is in this light that the developments of the case law of the CJEU should be considered. As is well known, the idea that the EU legal order has a constitutional character has been repeatedly emphasised by the Court in its case law.[83] However, precisely because of the concerns deriving from the above-mentioned tension between the transnational and the national level, from the 1970s onwards, the fundamental rights discourse has been a necessary legitimacy- and autonomy-enhancing tool, as part of the Court's weaponry. A constant effort to boost the EU's credentials as a distinct creature of transnational law has led to an assertion of autonomy, on the one hand, vis-a-vis its Member States[84] and, on the other, vis-a-vis international law.[85] Such autonomy implies that the interpretation of fundamental rights that lie at the core of the EU legal system be ensured in line with its structure and objectives.[86] These moves may be interpreted as part of the EU ongoing strategy of self-justification and self-empowerment accomplished *in the name of the peoples of Europe* through the security and fundamental rights discourses.

The same discourses resurface time and again in official speeches in times of crisis. The EU liberal project cannot be interrupted because people demand it. The *finalité* of European integration – sometimes overtly federalist, often leaving little space for reflexivity – requires simultaneously further enlargement and reinforced cooperation because any alternative solution would lead to self-destruction and 'would demand a fatal price above all of our people'.[87] Correspondingly, even in the face of seemingly overwhelming financial distress, 'the ECB is ready to do whatever it takes to preserve the euro', which is, as a result, 'irreversible'.[88] The reason for this zealous defence of the European

[81] A von Bogdandy and S Schill, 'Overcoming Absolute Primacy: Respect for National Identity under the Lisbon Treaty' (2011) 48 *Common Market Law Review* 1417.

[82] J Weiler, 'Individual and Rights: The Sour Grapes' (2010) 21 *European Journal of International Law* 277.

[83] See, eg, Case C-294/83 *Les Verts v Parliament* [1986] ECLI:EU:C:1986:166; *Opinion 1/91 Draft EEA Agreement* [1991] ECLI:EU:C:1991:490.

[84] Case 29/69 *Stauder v City of Ulm* ECLI:EU:C:1969:57; *Internationale Handelsgesellschaft* (n 64); Case 4/73 *Nold v Commission* [1974] ECLI:EU:C:1974:51. More recently, see Case C-399/11 *Melloni* [2013] ECLI:EU:C:2013:107.

[85] Joined Cases C-402/05 and 415/05 *Kadi and Al-Barakaat* [2008] ECLI:EU:C:2008:46; C-160/09 *Ioannis Katsivardas- Nikolaos Tsitsikas* [2010] ECLI:EU:C:2010:293.

[86] *Internationale Handelsgesellschaft* (n 64) para 3; *Kadi and Al-Barakaat* (n 85) paras 281–85.

[87] Speech by Joschka Fischer at Humboldt University, Berlin, 12 May 2000: 'From Confederacy to Federation: Thoughts on the Finality of European Integration', 3–5.

[88] Speech by Mario Draghi, President of the European Central Bank, at the Global Investment Conference in London, 26 July 2012: 'the only way out of this present crisis is to have more Europe, not less Europe'.

Sonderweg is that, ultimately, a government must offer its citizens 'physical and economic security', as well as protect liberty and individual rights.[89] This means that 'Europe' must not only protect its citizens, but must also 'empower' them and 'preserve the European way of life'.[90] Needless to say, this way of life corresponds to the ideal of the rule of law.

The system of protection of equality and rule of law as provided by the EU is premised upon the functioning of the security and fundamental rights discourses, ensuring the survival and further development of the EU project. This is why the principle of sincere cooperation demands that Member States ensure the application of and respect for EU law within their own territories – hence the commitment to taking any appropriate measure to ensure fulfilment of the obligations deriving from the Treaties or the acts of the EU institutions.[91] Of course, according to Article 51(1) of the Charter of Fundamental Rights (CFR), EU fundamental rights bind Member States only when they implement EU law. Moreover: (a) domestic standards of protection of fundamental rights cannot prejudice either the standards provided by the CFR or the principles of primacy, unity and effectiveness of EU law; and (b) Article 53 CFR cannot be interpreted as meaning that a Member State may disapply EU law that is in compliance with the CFR when fundamental rights protected by that Member State's constitution are at stake.[92] In order to secure the uniform interpretation and application of EU law, fundamental rights may be restricted for the purposes of achieving the objectives set out by the Treaties,[93] above all the establishment of a common market,[94] or the stability of the financial system.[95] In fact, as regards those rights in the CFR which correspond to the rights guaranteed by the ECHR, the power conferred upon Member States by Article 53 ECHR (which considers the standards of protection ensured by the ECHR as a minimum

[89] Speech by Mario Draghi, President of the European Central Bank, at the 'Teatro Sociale' in Trento, 13 September 2016, 1 ('De Gasperi' award ceremony).

[90] State of the Union Address by Jean-Claude Juncker, President of the European Commission, Strasbourg, 14 September 2016: 'Towards a Better Europe: A Europe that Protects, Empowers and Defends'. See also speech by Mario Draghi, President of the European Central Bank, at the joint ECB and Banka Slovenije Conference on the occasion of the tenth anniversary of the adoption of the euro, Ljubljana, 2 February 2017: 'Security through Unity: Making Integration Work for Europe'.

[91] Article 4(3) of the Treaty of the European Union [2007] OJ C306/1 (TEU). See also CJEU *Opinion 1/09* [2011] ECLI:EU:C:2011:123 para 68.

[92] *Melloni* (n 84) paras 58–60.

[93] *Internationale Handelsgesellschaft* (n 64) para 4, where the CJEU ruled that the protection of fundamental rights, 'whilst inspired by the constitutional traditions common to the Member States, must be ensured within the framework of the structures and objectives of the Community'.

[94] For example, in Case C-5/88 *Wachauf* ECLI:EU:C:1989:321, para 18, the CJEU pointed out that 'fundamental rights … are not absolute … but must be considered in relation to their social function', so that 'restrictions may be imposed on the exercise of those rights, in particular in the context of the organisation of a common market, provided that those restrictions correspond in fact to objectives of general interest pursued by the Community and do not constitute, with regard to the aim pursued, a disproportionate and intolerable interference, impairing the very substance of those rights'.

[95] Case C-62/14 *Gauweiler and Others v Deutscher Bundestag* ECLI:EU:C:2015:400.

standard) is only limited 'to that which is necessary to ensure that the level of protection provided for by the Charter and the primacy, unity and effectiveness of EU law are not compromised'.[96] Besides, it is in light of the interplay between the security and fundamental rights discourses that the CJEU held that the draft agreement for the accession to the ECHR would affect 'the specific characteristics of EU law and its autonomy' and would therefore not be compatible with Article 6 (2) TEU.[97]

It is in the nature of the above-mentioned discourses to find strength in themselves – in their own circularity and sense of inevitability. The EU polity, according to these discourses, needs a market, because it needs a market.[98] A similar sense of self-referentiality may be detected in classic integration through law arguments[99] as well as in all those arguments relying on the 'Ever Closer Union' motto and confusing the process with the outcome.[100]

However, the risk is that the self-justificatory nature and circularity of such discourses – the self-referentiality of the meta-rationale of security – leads to a blind alley and potential self-destruction. For example, monetary union itself was considered to be necessary in order to complete the single market, but simultaneously it was argued that monetary union could only be fully beneficial as long as the single market was completed.[101] Analogously, EMU was initially supposed to promote deeper integration and lead to a political union, even though the details of any form of political integration – starting from a sound coordination of fiscal policies – were far from being agreed upon by the very Member States that launched EMU.[102] As long as neither a fully operating single market nor a fully fledged EMU supported by a political union exist, the EU polity is bound to be fragile and thus exposed to threats'. Security and insecurity are, in fact, always tied up together. The former can never, conceptually, do away with the latter. You can only claim you are 'secure' against a threat named at any one time, and yet that very threat undermines your claim.

Precisely for this reason, and as a remedy against self-referentiality, the EU ought not to appear as a 'mechanical necessity imposed by the logic of

[96] CJEU *Opinion 2/13* para 189, ECLI:EU:C:2014:2454.

[97] ibid para 200.

[98] Analogous self-referential reasoning can be found in other contexts. For example, in ECJ Joined Cases C-138/17, 146/17, 150/17, 174717 and 222/17 *EU v Gascogne* ECLI:EU:C:2018:1013, the Court dismissed the argument that the right to an independent and impartial tribunal was prejudiced by having the EU represented by the CJEU in a judgment before the CJEU.

[99] Pescatore, *Law of Integration* (1974); M Cappelletti, M Seccombe and J Weiler (eds), *Integration through Law: Europe and the American Federal Experience* (Berlin, de Gruyter, 1985) vol 1, Book 1; however, for a revised approach, see D Augenstein, *'Integration through Law' Revisited: The Making of the European Polity* (Farnham, Ashgate, 2012).

[100] As noted in G Majone, 'The European Union Post-Brexit: Static or Dynamic Adaptation?' (2017) 23 *European Law Journal* 9, 18.

[101] Majone (n 44) 29–30.

[102] ibid 50.

integration; in other words, a public debate of what type of Europe responds to the democratic demands of the Member States is better than a sterile debate about more or less Europe.[103] In fact, what I call the 'heterarchical paradigm' is better suited than other paradigms to address the current state of affairs,[104] as long as this paradigm allows some degree of openness to agonistic conflict and contestation.[105]

IV. CONCLUSIONS

The process of European integration has been characterised by the emergence of a dual conception of 'The People': on the one hand, 'mobile people', ie freely moving individuals and, on the other, 'peoples' in the plural, which would constitute the basis for the process of development of the EU as a polity. Both ideas are the result of a construction of people-as-constituent-power through the security and fundamental rights discourses. As crises produce breaks in the continuity of integration, the-people-as-a constituent power is appealed to time and again to promote further integration and constitutionalisation. However, discursive constituent power cannot escape the ambiguities and contradictions that are typical of the EU liberal project. The main reason for this is that the discourses of security and fundamental rights have been presented since the early stages of European integration as if they were neutral, whereas in fact they have always disguised a specific political direction. As a result, conflicts and tensions have been downplayed. From this perspective, security and fundamental rights as discourses of power express the interplay between the expansive trend of the EU machinery (for example, through the doctrine of primacy and the development of the internal market) and the resistance by Member States. It is through these discourses that the EU pursues a strategy of self-justification and self-empowerment accomplished *in the name of the peoples of Europe.*

REFERENCES

Arendt, H, *On Revolution* (New York, Penguin, 2006).
Augenstein, D, *'Integration through Law' Revisited: The Making of the European Polity* (Farnham, Ashgate, 2012).
Austin, J, *The Province of Jurisprudence Determined* (London, John Murray, 1832).
Avbelj, M and Komarek, J (eds), *Constitutional Pluralism and Beyond* (Oxford, Hart Publishing, 2012).

[103] M Maduro, A New Governance for the European Union and the Euro: democracy and justice, EUI RSCAS Policy Paper 2012/11.

[104] See, eg, M Avbelj and J Komarek (eds) *Constitutional Pluralism and Beyond* (Oxford, Hart Publishing, 2012).

[105] For theories of agonistic pluralism, see, eg, C Mouffe, 'Deliberative Democracy or Agonistic Pluralism?' (1999) 66 *Social Research* 745.

Bartl, M, 'Internal Market Rationality, Private Law and the Direction of the Union: Resuscitating the Market as the Object of the Political' (2015) 21 *European Law Journal* 572.

Bellamy, R, '"An Ever Closer Union among the Peoples of Europe": Republican Intergovernmentalism and Demoicratic Representation within the EU' (2013) 35 *Journal of European Integration* 499.

Besson, S, 'The European Union and Human Rights: Towards a Post-national Human Rights Institution' (2006) 6 *Human Rights Law Review* 323.

Bodin, J, *On Sovereignty* (Cambridge, Cambridge University Press, 1992).

Bryce, J, 'Flexible and Rigid Constitutions' in *Studies in History and Jurisprudence*, vol 1 (Oxford, Oxford University Press, 1901).

Böckenförde, E-W, 'The Constituent Power of the People: A Liminal Concept of Constitutional Law' in *Constitutional and Political Theory: Selected Writings* (Oxford, Oxford University Press, 2017).

Cappelletti, M, Seccombe, M and Weiler, J (eds), *Integration through Law: Europe and the American Federal Experience* (Berlin, de Gruyter, 1985).

Carré de Malberg, R, *Contribution á la Théorie Générale de l'État*, vol 2 (Paris, Librairie de la société du Recueil Sirey, 1922).

Cohen, A, 'Constitutionalism without Constitution: Transnational Elites between Mobilisation and Legal Expertise in the Making of a Constitution for Europe (1940s–1960s)' (2007) 32 *Law and Social Enquiry* 109.

Colón-Ríos, J, 'Five Conceptions of Constituent Power' (2014) 130 *Law Quarterly Review* 306.

Crisafulli, V, *Lezioni di diritto costituzionale*, vol 1 (Padua, CEDAM, 2000).

De Búrca, G, 'The Road Not Taken: The EU as a Global Human Rights Actor' (2011) 105 *American Journal of International Law* 649.

De Vega, P, *La reforma costitucional y la problemática del poder constituyente* (Madrid, Tecnos, 1985).

Del Lucchese, F, 'Machiavelli and Constituent Power: The Revolutionary Foundation of Modern Political Thought' (2017) 16 *European Journal of Political Theory* 3.

Derrida, J, 'Declarations of Independence' (1986) *New Political Science* 7.

Dyzenhaus, D, 'Constitutionalism in an Old Key: Legality and Constituent Power' (2012) 1 *Global Constitutionalism* 229.

Fairclough, N, *Language and Power* (Harlow, Longman, 1989).

Fichera, M, 'Security Issues as an Existential Threat to the Community' in M Fichera and J Kremer (eds), *Law and Security in Europe: Reconsidering the Security Constitution* (Cambridge, Intersentia, 2003).

——. 'Law, Community and *Ultima Ratio* in Transnational Law' in M Fichera, S Hänninen and K Tuori (eds), *Polity and Crisis: Reflections on the European Odyssey* (Farnham, Ashgate, 2014).

——. 'Sketches of a Theory of Europe as An Area of Freedom, Security and Justice' in M Fletcher, E Herlin-Karnell and C Matera (eds), *The European Union as an Area of Freedom, Security and Justice* (Abingdon, Routledge, 2017).

Foucault, M, *The History of Sexuality: Vol. I. The Will to Knowledge* (London, Penguin, 1998).

Habermas, J, *The Crisis of the European Union: A Response* (Cambridge, Polity Press, 2012).

——. 'Democracy in Europe: Why the Development of the EU into a Transnational Democracy is Necessary and How it is Possible' (2015) 21 *European Law Journal* 546.
Hauriou, M, *Précis de droit constitutionnel* (Paris, Librairie de la société du Recueil Sirey, 1923).
Jacobs, FG, 'Human Rights in the European Union: The Role of the Court of Justice' (2001) 26 *European Law Review* 331.
Judt, T, *Postwar: A History of Europe since 1945* (London, Vintage, 2010).
Krebs, RR, *Narrative and the Making of US National Security* (Cambridge, Cambridge University Press, 2015).
Lenaerts, K and de Smijter, E, 'A "Bill of Rights" for the European Union' (2001) 38 *Common Market Law Review* 273.
Lindahl, H, 'The Paradox of Constituent Power: The Ambiguous Self-Constitution of the European Union' (2007) 20 *Ratio Juris* 485.
Locke, J, *The Second Treatise of Government: An Essay Concerning the True, Original, Extent and End of Civil Government* (Cambridge, Cambridge University Press, 1991).
Loughlin, M, 'The Concept of Constituent Power' (2014) 13 *European Journal of Political Theory* 218.
Majone, G, *Rethinking the Union of Europe Post-Crisis: Has Integration Gone Too Far?* (Cambridge, Cambridge University Press, 2014).
——. 'The European Union Post-Brexit: Static or Dynamic Adaptation?' (2017) 23 *European Law Journal* 9.
Möllers, C, 'Pouvoir Constituant – Constitution – Constitutionalisation' in A von Bogdandy and J Bast (eds), *Principles of European Constitutional Law* (Oxford, Hart Publishing, 2006).
Mortati, C, 'Appunti sul problema delle fonti del potere costituente' (1946) 1 *Rassegna di diritto pubblico* 26.
Mortati, C, 'Voce Costituzione (dottrina generale)' in *Enciclopedia del diritto*, vol 11 (Milan, Giuffré 1961).
——. 'La teoria del potere costituente' (1972) 1 *Studi sul potere costituente e sulla riforma costituzionale dello Stato- Raccolta di Scritti* 12.
Mouffe, C, 'Deliberative Democracy or Agonistic Pluralism?' (1999) 66 *Social Research* 745.
Negri, A, *Insurgencies: Constituent Power and the Modern State* (Minneapolis, University of Minnesota Press, 1999).
Nicolaïdis, K, 'The Idea of European Demoicracy' in J Dickson and P Eleftheriadis (eds), *Philosophical Foundations of European Union Law* (Oxford, Oxford University Press, 2012) 247.
——. 'European Democracy and its Crisis' (2013) 51 *Journal of Common Market Studies* 351.
Paine, T, 'Rights of Man' in E Foner (ed), *Paine: Collected Writings*, (New York, Library of America, 1995).
Pescatore, P, 'The Context and Significance of Fundamental Rights in the Law of the European Communities' (1981) 2 *Human Rights Law Journal* 295.
Romano, S, 'L'instaurazione di fatto di un ordinamento costituzionale e la sua legittimazione' in *Scritti minori*, vol 1 (Milan, Giuffré, 1950).
Scharpf, F, 'Democratic Policy in Europe' (1996) 2 *European Law Journal* 136.

——. 'Legitimacy in the Multi-level European Polity' in P Dobner and M Loughlin (eds), *The Twilight of Constitutionalism* (Oxford, Oxford University Press, 2010).

Schmitt, C, *The Nomos of the Earth* (New York, Telos, 2003).

——. *Constitutional Theory* (Durham, NC, Duke University Press 2008).

Sieyès, E and Zapperi, R (eds), *Qu'est-ce le Tiers état*? (Paris, Librarie Droz, 1970).

Starr, P, *Freedom's Power: The History and Promise of Liberalism* (Cambridge, Basic Books, 2007).

Tizzano, A, 'The Role of the ECJ in the Protection of Fundamental Rights' in A Arnull, P Eeckhout and T Tridimas (eds), *Continuity and Change in EU Law: Essays in Honour of Sir Francis Jacobs* (Oxford, Oxford University Press 2008).

Torfing, J, 'Discourse Theory: Achievements, Arguments, and Challenges' in D Honneth and J Torfing (eds), *Discourse Theory in European Politics. Identity, Policy and Governance* (New York, Palgrave Macmillan, 2005).

Tuori, K, *European Constitutionalism* (Cambridge, Cambridge University Press, 2015).

Tuori, K and Tuori, K, *The Eurozone Crisis: A Constitutional Analysis* (Cambridge, Cambridge University Press, 2014).

Van Djik, TA, 'Principles of Critical Discourse Analysis' (1993) 4 *Discourse & Society* 249.

Van Middelaar, L, *The Passage to Europe* (New Haven, Yale University Press, 2011).

Vauchez, A, 'The Transnational Politics of Judicialization: *Van Gend en Loos* and the Making of the EU Polity' (2010) 16 *European Law Journal* 1.

Weiler, J, 'The Transformation of Europe' (1992) 100 *Yale Law Journal* 2403.

——. 'Individual and Rights: The Sour Grapes' (2010) 21 *European Journal of International Law* 277.

Wilkinson, MA, 'Political Constitutionalism and the European Union' (2013) 76 *Modern Law Review* 191.

——. 'The Reconstitution of Post-War Europe: Liberal Excesses, Democratic Deficiencies' in M Dowdle and M Wilkinson (eds), *Constitutionalism beyond Liberalism* (Cambridge, Cambridge University Press, 2017).

Von Bogdandy, A and Schill, S, 'Overcoming Absolute Primacy: Respect for National Identity under the Lisbon Treaty' (2011) 48 *Common Market Law Review* 1417.

6

The National Security Challenge to EU Legal Integration

ANNA JONSSON CORNELL

I. INTRODUCTION

THE IMPORTANCE OF joint judicial and police cooperation, together with the sharing of resources and information was made evident by the terror attacks at the beginning of the twenty-first century. And it is clear that European integration in relation to what can be termed national security as a policy and interest has made important progress.[1] Joint declarations, framework decisions, conventions and programmes have played an important role. Still, the former pillar structure and the impact it had on the role played by the Court of Justice of the European Union (CJEU) held back the process of legal integration in areas of relevance to national security. This all changed with the Treaty of Lisbon and the removal of the pillar structure, although the Area of Freedom, Security and Justice (AFSJ) still holds important traits of state sovereignty and transnationalism.[2]

The main purpose of this chapter is to discuss what role national security, understood as an EU constitutional law concept, might play for EU legal integration in the future. In order to fulfil this purpose, it will be necessary to map out national security[3] as an EU constitutional law concept. This will be

[1] For a chronological overview of the measures taken, see C Harding, 'EU Criminal Law under the Area of Freedom, Security and Justice' in A Arnull and D Chalmers (eds), *The Oxford Handbook of European Union Law* (Oxford, Oxford Handbooks Online, 2015); and S Peers, *EU Justice and Home Affairs Law*, 4th edn (Oxford, Oxford University Press, 2016).

[2] K Tuori, *European Constitutionalism* (Cambridge, Cambridge University Press, 2015) ch 8.

[3] For the purposes of this chapter, public security and internal security are included in the EU law analysis. As will be shown below, national security does not appear frequently in EU law and nor does it dominate the CJEU case law; rather, it is public security and internal security that prevails. Moreover, the WP 29 argued in its *Opinion on Surveillance of Electronic Communications for Intelligence and National Security Purposes* that national security should be distinguished from internal and public security when trying to identify the scope of Member States' retained powers; see *Working Document on Surveillance of Electronic Communications for Intelligence and National Security Purposes, Adopted on 5 December 2014.*

done by an analysis of the wording of relevant parts of the Treaties, especially Article 4(2) of the Treaty on European Union (TEU) and Title V of the Treaty on the Functioning of the European Union (TFEU), which is followed by an analysis of the case law of the CJEU of relevance to national security. In order to add to our understanding of how national security can be a driver for, or pose a hindrance to, EU legal integration, I will conduct two case studies: the first is Schengen and the temporary closing of borders; and the second is privacy rights in a national security context.[4] This will reveal if there are any differences as to how the concept of national security is understood and hence what role it is allowed to play in these two areas.

Initially, my main focus was not on the relationship and potential tension between rights protection and security at a general EU law level. Much has been written on this topic already.[5] Rather, my focus was on national security as a competence-deciding (horizontally and vertically) concept.[6] However, as will become evident, the dividing line between national security as a competence-deciding concept and as a justification for derogation and limitation of fundamental rights is difficult to obtain in the EU law context. This is mainly due to the impact of internal market case law on the AFSJ and the national security derogation, which among other things states that the retained powers argument does not equal non-application of EU law.[7] Therefore, a substantial part of this chapter will be devoted to the CJEU's case law on rights restrictions in the national security context. Several of these cases have been dealt with elsewhere, but mostly from the rights-paradigm angle.[8] Clearly, my ambition

[4] The retention of data for intelligence purposes falls at the core of the responsibilities and activities of state bodies devoted to national security, which is why this is an interesting case study for national security as a competence-deciding and rights-infringing constitutional law concept. My main focus will not be on the balancing between rights and security per se, but rather the effect of the balancing exercise on the powers of the EU and the Member States, and hence the definition of national security as a competence-deciding norm.

[5] See, eg, S Carrera and V Mitsilegas (eds), *Constitutionalising the Security Union: Effectiveness, Rule of Law and Rights in Countering Terrorism and Crime* (Brussels, Centre for European Policy Studies, 2017); M Tzanou, *The Fundamental Right to Data Protection: Normative Value in the Context of Counter-terrorism Surveillance* (Oxford, Hart Publishing, 2017); J Kremer, 'The End of Freedom in Public Places? Privacy Problems Arising from the Surveillance of the European Public Space' (Helsinki, 2017), https://helda.helsinki.fi/bitstream/handle/10138/176300/TheEndof.pdf?sequence=1&isAllowed=y.

[6] Influenced by Tuori's analysis of the high degree of tension between the transnational, European and the Member State levels within the security dimension. Another important tension within the security dimension is that between security and fundamental rights; Tuori (n 2) 301. The latter will not be the main focus on this chapter.

[7] See, eg, ibid 274 concerning arts 36 and 45 TFEU as a security exception to freedom of movement within the internal market and as part of economic constitutional law. The purpose of this exception was to uphold the sovereignty for Member States within the area of national security. See also M Claes and B de Witte, 'Competences: Codification and Contestation' in A Lazowski and S Blockmans (eds), *Research Handbook on EU Institutional Law* (Cheltenham, Edward Elgar, 2016).

[8] See, eg, T Ojanen, 'Rights-Based Review of Electronic Surveillance after *Digital Rights Ireland* and *Schrems*' in D Cole, F Fabbrini and S Schulhofer (eds), *Surveillance, Privacy and Transatlantic Relations* (Oxford, Hart Publishing 2017).

is not to put forward an argument or conclusion that aims to backtrack on the progress made concerning rights protection in the security context. Nor is my ambition to contribute to the vast debate on how rights and security are to be balanced.[9] My ambition is to map out how EU constitutional law deals with national security matters from a competence-deciding point of view, in order to draw conclusions as to how it impacts on Member States' national security prerogative.

The national security context brings with it specific constitutional and legal traits. From a constitutional law point of view, national security generally means more powers and discretion for the executive, lack of transparency, lack of legal remedies and a limited role for courts in rights protection. When it comes to EU law, national security displays additional specific traits. National security could be seen as a competence-deciding concept, leaving national security exclusively to the Member States' competence.[10] At the same time, the AFSJ is regulated in the Treaties and the overlap between this policy area and what could be termed national security proper is obvious, especially taking border control and anti-terrorism matters into account.[11] Still, and as pointed out by Kaarlo Tuori, state sovereignty remains strong within the AFSJ and focus remains on cooperation rather than legal integration. For analytical purposes, I will, as far as possible, try to uphold the difference between national security as a competence-deciding concept and national security as a justification for restricting fundamental rights protection. However, as we shall see in the CJEU's ruling in the *Tele2* decision,[12] this dividing line is increasingly difficult to uphold.

Traditionally, matters of national security referred to the protection of territorial integrity and sovereignty of states. From this point of view, external threats, primarily from other states, dominated the security mindset, and national security in constitutional law was basically treated as a matter of war powers and possibly emergency powers. Two developments have contributed to challenging this approach in Europe: first, the establishment of the internal market and freedom of movement leading up to the Schengen cooperation; and, second, the terrorist attacks on 11 September 2001 in the US and the subsequent

[9] See, eg, R A Epstein, 'The ECJ's Fatal Imbalance: Its Cavalier Treatment of National Security Issues Poses Serious Risk to Public Safety and Sound Commercial Practices' and a response by M Scheinin, 'Towards Evidence-Based Discussion on Surveillance: A Rejoinder to Richard A. Epstein' (2016) 12 *European Constitutional Law Review* 330 and 341 respectively.

[10] Which is also illustrated by the national security exception as expressed in the General Data Protection Regulation [2016] OJ L119/1 and the Law Enforcement Data Protection Directive [2016] OJ L119/89. See A Jonsson Cornell, 'Privacy Rights and Data Protection in Law Enforcement Cooperation: Comparing the US and EU' in A-S Lind, J Reichel and I Österdahl (eds), *Information and Law in Transition: Freedom of Speech, the Internet, Privacy and Democracy in the 21st Century* (Stockholm, Liber, 2015) 179.

[11] V Mitsilegas, 'The Security Union as a Paradigm of Preventive Justice: Challenges for Citizenship, Fundamental Rights and the Rule of Law' in Carrera and Mitsilegas (n 5).

[12] Joined Cases C-203/15 and C-698/15 *Tele2 Sverige AB v Post- och telestyrelsen and Secretary of State for the Home Department v Tom Watson and Others* [2016] ECLI:EU:C:2016:970.

attacks in Madrid, London, Paris and Brussels. Following these terrorist attacks, a systemic shift occurred: international terrorism was labelled a threat to international peace and (national) security. UN Security Council Resolution 1373 set in motion substantive changes to international and national law, which Kim Scheppele has termed 'global security law'.[13] There were also substantial developments within EU law in order to counter terrorism. The blurring of the line between internal and external security has resulted in difficulties in obtaining a clear line between defence, security and criminal law, a line that is especially important for the level of protection of constitutional rights and the division of powers and functions (competence-deciding norms). To this should be added the distorted line between administrative and criminal law in the anti-terrorism and migration context.[14] As a result, there are concerns of a permanent state of emergency and preventionism[15] coming to define states' response to threats to national security. Basically, it means that criminal, and occasionally administrative, law measures are used to prevent threats to national security, such as terrorist acts, and that national security, criminal and migration policy are intertwined. There is an obvious danger in this development, especially taking into account the implications of national security, as it has been understood traditionally, on constitutional law, and that risk prevention has an 'inherent expansionism', as expressed by Tuori.[16]

II. LEGAL INTEGRATION AND NATIONAL SECURITY

One of the main implications of the AFSJ not being part of the first pillar before the Treaty of Lisbon is that the role of the CJEU has been limited. Hence, legal integration at the hands of the CJEU has not, historically, been a decisive factor in this particular area. However, the vast understanding of national security, as described above in section I, in combination with the absence of a clearly defined national security competence-dividing concept in EU constitutional law, has left the door open for the CJEU to also expand its powers into the field that has traditionally been considered to be within the national security field proper and hence within the exclusive competence of Member States, such as intelligence-gathering. This, together with the constitutionalisation of EU law in general, including the growing impact of the EU Charter of Fundamental

[13] KL Scheppele, 'Global Security Law and the Challenge to Constitutionalism after 9/11' [2011] *Public Law* 352.

[14] See T Ojanen, 'Administrative Measures in Counter-terrorism Activities: More Leeway for the Imperatives of Security at the Expense of Human Rights?' in M Fichera and J Kremer (eds), *Law and Security in Europe: Reconsidering the Security Constitution* (Cambridge, Intersentia, 2013).

[15] See V Mitsilegas, 'The Security Union as a Paradigm of Preventive Justice: Challenges for Citizenship, Fundamental Rights and the Rule of Law' in Carrera and Mitsilegas (n 5).

[16] Tuori (n 2) 292.

Rights (CFR), will have implications on the size of Member States' national security prerogative and the extent of rights protection within the national security context. It could be argued that the Member States' national security prerogative is shrinking and that rights protection to the benefit of individuals is increasing.

It is clear that the security situation globally, and especially in Europe, has been an important driver of increased cooperation between Member States within the national security context, broadly defined. The AFSJ has specific traits that impact on the character of legal integration. It still has important traits of intergovernmentalism and state sovereignty. And as Tuori points out, the 're-surfacing of state-sovereignist concerns, reliance on the international law system, opt-ins and opt-outs, reflects an exceptionally high tension between the transnational, European and national'.[17] The main tools for integration in the AFSJ are coordination and cooperation, mutual recognition and legal harmonisation, in that order; thus, cooperation rather than integration remains the prevailing principle within the AFSJ.[18] At the same time, legal integration has come a long way in fundamental rights protection, especially due to the CJEU case law after the entry into force of the CFR. Add to this the blurred line between national security, criminal, migration and administrative law measures, the complexity of the question as to how national security might restrict or advance legal integration becomes clear. One of the main questions is what impact will EU legal integration in fundamental rights protection have on the national security prerogative of Member States? Will it only have an effect when national security is invoked as a justification for derogating from or limiting rights, or might it also impact the competence-deciding norm in Article 4(2) TEU? What is the spillover effect on EU legal integration concerning fundamental rights on issues of national security that fall under the exclusive competence of Member States?

III. NATIONAL SECURITY AS AN EU CONSTITUTIONAL LAW CONCEPT

A. Introduction

As stated above, national security as a constitutional law concept can have two clearly defined, and separate, traits: first, it is a competence-deciding concept (both in EU and in national constitutional law); and, second, it is a concept that can allow for derogations from and limitations of fundamental rights. For example, in both national constitutional law and the European Convention on Human Rights (ECHR), security (national and public security) is an explicit

[17] Tuori (n 2) 301.
[18] ibid 314.

ground for limiting rights.[19] Individual rights serve to control measures that aim to achieve security (the collective good) and a constitutional law concept of security enters the constitution as a ground for restricting fundamental rights.[20] Security could in itself also be a fundamental individual right – see, for example, Article 6 of the CFR (the individual right to liberty and security of person).[21] The AFSJ as laid down in Title V of the TFEU provides public goods, not individual rights.[22] Although the CFR does not explicitly mention security as a ground for limiting rights (see Article 52(1)), the CJEU has elaborated on what could be termed an objective of general interest within the meaning of Article 52(1). The fight against terrorism constitutes such an interest.[23]

While the competence-deciding or rights-restricting constitutional concepts of national security are, for analytical purposes, separate, they may nevertheless be difficult to separate taking into account the CJEU's broad interpretation of when EU law is applicable.[24] This is especially the case in the light of the absence of any clear EU law definition of national security as competence-deciding concept and the broad reach of the CFR as a result of the CJEU case law. *Digital Rights Ireland* and the subsequent decisions on data protection 'may prove to be a milestone in asserting fundamental rights as a restriction on security-motivated measures'.[25]

In this context, the *Tele2* decision[26] is crucial if we want to understand how the CFR might have an impact on national law of great importance for the protection of national security. The *Tele2* case illustrates well how interlinked EU and national security-motivated laws are and the conundrum that this might pose for the dividing line between national and EU competence in areas of direct or indirect relevance to national security. The case concerned Directive 2002/58,[27] which provides for the harmonisation of national provisions

[19] On the derogation in the ECHR, see I Cameron, *National Security and the European Convention on Human Rights* (Uppsala, Iustus, 2000); and on art 15 ECHR in particular, see B van der Sloot, 'Is All Fair in Love and War? An Analysis of the Case Law of Article 15 ECHR' (2014) 53 *Military Law and the Law of War Review* 319.

[20] According to Tuori ((n 2) 302): 'In constitutional doctrine national security can be treated either as an individual right or as a collective good.'

[21] Compare Case C-601/15 *JN v Staatssecretaris van Veiligheid en Justitie* [2016] ECLI:EU:C:2016:84, where the CJEU states that art 6 of the Charter requires a balancing between one person's right to liberty and another person's right to security.

[22] Tuori (n 2), referring to J Monar.

[23] Joined Cases C-293/12 and C-594/12 *Digital Rights Ireland Ltd v Minister for Communications, Marine and Natural Resources* [2014] ECR I-238 para 41-42.

[24] Coined as the 'retained competences formula'; see Claes and de Witte (n 7) 77, referring to L Azoulai, 'The "Retained Powers" Formula in the Case Law of the European Court of Justice: EU Law as Total Law?' (2011) 4 *European Journal of Legal Studies* 192, 196. Case C-300/11 *ZZ v Secretary of State for the Home Department* ECLI:EU:C:2013:363 is of particular interest to this chapter and will be dealt with in more detail below.

[25] Tuori (n 2) 312.

[26] *Tele2 Sverige AB* (n 12).

[27] Directive 2002/58/EC of the European Parliament and of the Council of 12 July 2002 concerning the Processing of Personal Data and the Protection of Privacy in the Electronic Communications Sector [2002] OJ L201/37.

required to ensure an equivalent level of protection of fundamental rights and freedoms, and in particular the right to privacy and confidentiality, with respect to the processing of personal data in the electronic communication sector and to ensuring the free movement of such data and of electronic communication equipment and services in the Community (Article 1(1)). The Directive does not apply to activities concerning public security, defence or state security, including the economic well-being of the state and the activities of the state in areas of criminal law (Article 1(3)). According to Article 15(1) of the Directive, restrictions to the right to privacy and confidentiality of communication are allowed in order to protect national security, provided that the measures are necessary, appropriate and proportionate within a democratic society. Still, the CJEU ruled that the Directive *does* apply to national law that aims to limit rights protection in order to safeguard national security and in matters of criminal law. It stated that any other conclusion would be impossible when reading Articles 3 and 15(1) of the Directive in conjunction,[28] since any legislative measure according to Article 15(1) would require providers of communication services to *process* data in order for them to meet the demands of the state.[29] Thus, the CJEU put Article 1(3) of the Directive, and hence the national security exception, aside.[30] The CJEU then stated that national legislation, which, for the purpose of fighting crime, provides for the general and indiscriminate retention of all traffic and location data of all subscribers and registered users relating to all means of electronic communication, is in violation of Article 15(1) of the Directive read in conjunction with Articles 7, 8, 11 and 52(1) CFR.[31] In conclusion, the CJEU's decision means that any national law providing an exception to the right to privacy and the principle of confidentially of communication must meet the requirements set out in Articles 7, 8, 11 and 52(1) CFR, even if it could be argued that it falls under the exception for national security and serious crime, since, according to the Court, any other interpretation would render the protection offered by the Directive meaningless.[32]

B. National Security in Primary EU Law

The constitutionalisation of security activities is difficult due to the nature of these activities. This is because 'they belong to the executive domain, consist

[28] Article 3: 'This Directive shall apply to the processing of personal data in connection with the provision of publicly available electronic communications services in public communications networks in the Community, including public communications networks supporting data collection and identification devices.'

[29] *Tele2 Sverige AB* (n 12) para 78.

[30] ibid paras 73–74, 81.

[31] ibid para 112.

[32] ibid para 125.

of factual rather than normative measures and seem to escape the legislative function'.[33] This is also true for EU law.[34] The main purpose of this chapter is not to debate whether there is an EU security constitution as understood by Tuori or whether the AFSJ is just another policy area without any constitutional significance.[35] In the following, we will turn to the Treaties to see if their wording provides any guidance as to the scope of the national security exception as a competence-deciding concept, to be followed by a short account of the case law of the CJEU of relevance for the national security exception.

Article 3(2) TEU states that the EU shall offer its citizens an area of freedom, security and justice without internal frontiers. It is noteworthy that the AFSJ comes before the internal market, which is regulated in Article 3(3) TEU,[36] although this is not surprising, taking into account the importance of safety and security for the internal market to function. According to Article 4(2) TEU, national security remains within the sole responsibility of the Member States. Moreover, the EU shall respect Member States' essential state functions, including territorial integrity, maintaining law and order, and safeguarding national security.

The *meaning and scope* of Article 4(2) TEU is difficult to assess for the following reasons: first, there is no EU law definition of national security; second, the line between external and internal security is difficult to uphold; third, the AFSJ falls under the shared competence between the EU and its Member States;[37] and, fourth, the AFSJ (as well as other policy areas) allows for EU legislative measures, which are of direct relevance to national security, which makes it difficult to uphold a clear boundary as to the division between national and EU competence in this context. The *aim* of Article 4(2) is to hold back the impact that the use of functional powers has or can have on policy fields that Member States consider particularly sensitive.[38]

The AFSJ is regulated in Title V of the TFEU. According to Article 67(1), the AFSJ builds on respect for fundamental rights and the different legal systems and traditions of Member States. According to Article 72, Title V should not impair the competence of the Member States to uphold and safeguard internal security. This article should be read in conjunction with Article 4(2) TEU.

[33] Tuori (n 2) 269–70.

[34] ibid.

[35] Compare ibid 272. However, individual treaty provisions do not make up a security constitution; sufficient coherence (derived from an underlying conception of security issues) in security-related constitutional law is also needed (ibid 289). Still, the treaty amendments leading up to the Treaty of Lisbon concerning the AFSJ have brought with them a body of case law, new primary and secondary EU law, and national responses to both that are indeed constitutionally significant. To this should also be added new EU agencies (ibid).

[36] See Tuori (n 2) 278 on why internal security was included on the Treaty of Amsterdam and why it is subordinated (or I would rather say a precondition for) the freedom of movement of persons.

[37] Article 4(2)(j) TFEU.

[38] Claes and de Witte (n 7) 76.

Article 72 does not restrict EU competence in the AFSJ in terms of substance.[39] In Article 73 TFEU, national security is mentioned explicitly when it is stated that Member States should be free to organise, between themselves and under their own responsibility, forms of cooperation and coordination between the relevant national departments responsible for safeguarding national security. This article could be understood as primarily focusing on the institutional, organisational and practical aspects of coordination and cooperation, ie, how such activities should be conducted and what departments and agencies that should be involved.

Article 83(1) TFEU lays down the procedure for adopting directives in accordance with the ordinary legislative procedure that defines minimum rules for the definition of serious crimes (and sanctions) with a cross-border dimension and a need to combat them on a common basis, such as terrorism. The material (substantive) aspect of police cooperation is regulated in Article 87 TFEU. For the purposes of this chapter, our interest primarily concerns Article 87(2) (the collection, storage, processing, analysis and exchange of relevant information)[40] and Article 87(3) (measures concerning operational cooperation). Terrorism is a criminal offence, which would involve the cooperation of the ordinary police and the security police. Finally, according to Article 276 TFEU, the CJEU does not have jurisdiction to review the validity or proportionality of Member States' operations in the field of law and order and internal security.

There are further restrictions to the EU's ability to dictate the actions of Member States when internal and national security is at stake. For example, according to Article 346(1)(a) TFEU, no Member State should be forced to supply information which if disclosed could be considered contrary to that state's security interests. Articles 346, 347 and 348 regulate additional circumstances when EU measures aiming primarily at upholding the internal market can be set aside in the interests of, inter alia, law and order, and national security, and the procedure to be applied if such measures are deemed necessary.

As is clear by now, the concept of national security brings with it several challenges to EU law. First, Article 4(2) TEU sets limits to EU competences in relation to Member States. However, the CJEU has ruled that although it is for Member States to take the appropriate measures to ensure their internal and external security:

> It cannot be inferred that the Treaty contains an inherent general exception excluding all measures taken for reasons of public security from the scope of Community law. The recognition of the existence of such an exception, regardless of the specific

[39] Steve Peers' argument is that art 72 is too general to be interpreted as imposing material restrictions on EU legislative powers and that it will have to be read in context of the other articles in Title V. For example, when the drafters of the Treaty wished to limit EU's competence as to substance, they have done so explicitly; compare art 79(5). See Peers (n 1) 55.

[40] Compare *Opinion 1/15 of the Court (Grand Chamber) on 26 July 2017* [2017] ECLI:EU:C:2017:592, where the CJEU stated that the joint legal basis for the EU-Canada Passenger Name Record Agreement should be arts 16 and 87(2)a TFEU.

> requirements laid down by the Treaty, would be liable to impair the binding nature of Community law and its uniform application.[41]

Second, within policy areas that fall under the EU's exclusive or shared competence, national security, as will be illustrated, can serve both as a restriction of individual rights as granted by EU law and as a means to allow for national measures derogating from EU law. This point is illustrated in *ZZ v Secretary of State for the Home Department*[42] and a request for a preliminary ruling by the Court of Appeal in England and Wales. On the question of admissibility, the Italian government argued that the question fell under the national security exception as laid down in Articles 4(2) TEU and 346(1)a TFEU. The CJEU ruled that the question concerned the interpretation of an EU Directive in light of the CFR and that it arose from a genuine legal conflict regarding the legality of a decision to refuse an EU citizen entry on grounds of public security, 'although it is for Member States to take the appropriate measures to ensure their internal and external security, the mere fact that a decision concerns State security cannot result in European Union law being inapplicable'.[43] Consequently, the request for a preliminary ruling was admissible. Third, there is no legal definition of national security as a competence-deciding concept in EU law, although activities of intelligence and security service agencies are considered by some to fall under the national security derogation.[44] Fourth, the blurring of the external and internal security assessment and strategy in combination with the EU's legislative and operational competences within criminal law and police cooperation (for example, see Article 75 TFEU) makes it difficult to uphold a clear-cut definition of national security. The Law Enforcement Data Protection Directive, which excludes activities related to national security, serves as another example. And, finally, several measures with a direct or indirect impact on national security, related for example to the four freedoms, fall under EU competence, which in its turn means that the claim of national security is under review by the CJEU and, more importantly, that the CFR is applicable.

[41] Case C-387/05 *European Commission v Italian Republic* [2009] ECLI:EU:C:2009:781, para 45.

[42] *ZZ v Secretary of State for the Home Department* (n 24).

[43] ibid paras 35, 38. The question posed was: 'Does the principle of effective judicial protection, set out in Article 30(2) of Directive 2004/38, as interpreted in the light of Article 346(1)(a) [TFEU], require that a judicial body considering an appeal from a decision to exclude a European Union citizen from a Member State on grounds of public policy and public security under Chapter VI of Directive 2004/38 ensure that the European Union citizen concerned is informed of the essence of the grounds against him, notwithstanding the fact that the authorities of the Member State and the relevant domestic court, after consideration of the totality of the evidence against the European Union citizen relied upon by the authorities of the Member State, conclude that the disclosure of the essence of the grounds against him would be contrary to the interests of State security?' (para 34).

[44] *WP 29 Opinion on Surveillance of Electronic Communications for Intelligence and National Security Purposes*, Working Document on Surveillance of Electronic Communications for Intelligence and National Security Purposes, adopted on 5 December 2014.

C. The CJEU and National Security Considerations

In a recent body of case law, the CJEU has dealt with questions related to what national security, public security and public order entail within the AFSJ. The cases referred to here deal primarily with issues of rights restrictions motivated by national security and not national security as a competence-deciding concept.

The CJEU has held that public security covers Member States' internal and external security and:

> [T]hat a threat to the functioning of the institutions and essential public services and the survival of the population, as well as the risk of a serious disturbance to foreign relations or to peaceful coexistence of nations, or a risk to military interests, may affect public security.[45]

In addition, the Court has held that:

> [T]he concept of 'public order' entails, in any event, the existence – in addition to the disturbance of the social order which any infringement of the law involves – of a genuine, present and sufficiently serious threat affecting one of the fundamental interests of society.[46]

As regards third-country nationals and their right to enter the EU, the scope for the relevant national authorities to assess whether that person poses a threat to public security is wide; it is sufficient that the national authorities can show that there is a potential threat. In *Sahar Fahimian v Bundesrepublik Deutschland*,[47] the CJEU, in a preliminary ruling, held that a Member State (in this case Germany) was granted wide discretion when assessing the facts in order to conclude whether a third-country national applying for a visa to enter the EU posed a threat to public security. The relevant national authorities can make an overall assessment of whether that person poses an actual or potential threat to public security.[48] Regarding judicial review of the contested decision, the CJEU stated that national courts must take into consideration whether the decision is based on a sufficiently solid factual basis. However, the burden of proof as to there not being sufficient grounds to refuse the application on public security grounds lies with the applicant.[49] The scope of judicial review is limited to the threat assessment, absence of manifest errors and fundamental procedural guarantees.[50] The national security issue at stake in this case was cyber-security

[45] Case C-145/09 *Land Baden-Württemberg v Panagiotis Tsakouridis* [2010] ECLI:EU:C:2010:708, paras 43–44.

[46] To my knowledge, there is no comparable attempt to clarify what national security may entail. See *JN v Staatssecretaris van Veiligheid en Justitie* (n 21) para 65.

[47] Case C-544/15 *Sahar Fahimian v Bundesrepublik Deutschland* [2017] ECLI:EU:C:2017:255.

[48] ibid paras 42, 43.

[49] ibid paras 44, 45.

[50] ibid para 46.

and the risk that the person involved would, through her studies in Germany, obtain knowledge and skills which could at a later point be used by her state of origin to bring harm to the opposition in that country and to other countries. The applicant's affiliation with a research centre funded by the state of origin was another decisive factor. The CJEU confirmed its earlier case law regarding the understanding of public security, underlining that:

> [T]he concept of 'public security' covers both the internal security of a Member State and its external security. Public security may thus be affected by a threat to the functioning of institutions and essential public services and the survival of the population, as well as by the risk of a serious disturbance to foreign relations or the peaceful coexistence of nations, or a risk to military interests.[51]

Moreover, the CJEU concluded that when the matter is related to third-country nationals who seek to enter the EU, a *potential* threat to public policy is enough. The assessment may thus take into account not only the personal conduct of the applicant but also other elements relating, in particular, to his or her professional career.[52] This is contrary to the situation when the freedom of movement of EU citizens is at stake. In these cases, measures taken in the name of public security must be based exclusively on the personal conduct of the individual concerned and that that conduct must represent a 'genuine, present and sufficiently serious threat' to that fundamental interest of society.[53]

Another category of third-country nationals is asylum seekers that are already within the EU. In February 2016, the CJEU delivered a preliminary ruling stating that an asylum seeker can be held in detention for reasons of national security and public order if it is deemed necessary after an individual assessment in the specific case and if less coercive measures cannot be applied effectively. Thus, placing an individual in detention for posing a threat to national security and public order is in line with Articles 6 and 52 CFR 'if the applicant's individual conduct represents a genuine, present and sufficiently serious threat, affecting a fundamental interest of society or the internal or external security of the Member State concerned'.[54]

A third category is long-term permanent residents. Such third-country nationals enjoy reinforced protection against expulsion on public order and security grounds, which, inter alia, includes the right to an individual assessment. Expulsion is in accordance with the applicable EU law only when that individual poses an actual and sufficiently serious threat to public policy and public security. Decisions must be taken on a case-by-case basis and the following circumstances must be taken into consideration: the length of stay, the age and family situation of the concerned and its family members, links

[51] ibid para 39.
[52] ibid para 40.
[53] ibid para 55.
[54] *JN v Staatssecretaris van Veiligheid en Justitie* (n 21) para 67.

with the country of residence and absence of links with the country of origin. It is in violation of EU law to automatically expel someone just because that person has been sentenced to imprisonment for a period exceeding one year.[55]

In June 2015, the CJEU delivered a preliminary ruling on the interpretation of Article 24(1) of Directive 2004/83/EC.[56] The issue concerned the revocation of a residence permit on the grounds of compelling reasons of national security or public order. In the decision, the CJEU referred to its earlier case law on the definition of compelling reason of national security or public order and concluded that:

> [I]n relation to Directive 2004/83 specifically, it should be pointed out that, according to recital 28 thereof, the notions of 'national security' and 'public order' cover cases where a third country national belongs to an association which supports international terrorism or supports such an association.[57]

In *ZZ v Secretary of State for the Home Department*, the CJEU gave a preliminary ruling on the right to effective judicial remedy for an EU citizen refused entry to another EU country. In this case, the responsible national authorities claimed that the reasons for refusing entry could not be revealed due to national security reasons. In its decision, the CJEU set out the minimum requirements:

> [T]he national court with jurisdiction to ensure that failure by the competent national authority to disclose to the person concerned, precisely and in full, the grounds on which a decision taken … is based and to disclose the related evidence to him is limited to that which is strictly necessary, and that he is informed, in any event, of the essence of those grounds in a manner which takes due account of the necessary confidentiality of the evidence.[58]

The Court left the threat assessment to the national authorities and the proportionality assessment to the national courts, setting the minimum standard as to procedural rights in national security related cases concerning EU citizens. Thus, measures related to national security must be in conformity with EU law, although the threat assessment and the decision to refuse entry remains within the prerogative of the Member States. However, any person subjected to such measures does have rights according to EU law.

Based on this overview, the tentative conclusion could be drawn that the scope of discretion provided to relevant national authorities when assessing threats to national security depends on the policy area concerned and the legal status of the individual affected.

[55] Case C-636/16 *Wilber López Pastuzano v Delegación del Gobierno en Navarra* [2017] ECLI:EU:C:2017:949.

[56] Council Directive 2004/83/EC of 29 April 2004 on minimum standards for the qualification and status of third country nationals or stateless persons as refugees or as persons who otherwise need international protection and the content of the protection granted [2004] OJ L304/12.

[57] Case C-373/13 *HT v Land Baden-Württemberg* [2015] ECLI:EU:C:2015:413, para 80.

[58] *ZZ v Secretary of State for the Home Department* (n 24) para 69.

D. Conclusions

According to a textual reading of the Treaties, Member States hold exclusive competence in matters of national security (retained powers). However, the case law of the CJEU is clear on the fact that EU law still applies in matters of national security as a result of the retained powers formula, especially when individual rights and freedoms are at stake. The scope of national measures and the rigidity of threat assessments – from a potential to an actual and sufficient threat – are decided by the legal status and the geographical location of the individual concerned.

Finally, it has to be recognised that legal harmonisation within the AFSJ is a matter of substantive law primarily as regards serious crimes with a cross-border dimension resulting from the nature or impact of such offences or from a need to combat them on a common basis. Terrorism is the crime that comes closest to national security in this context. Thus, when a directive has been adopted, EU law applies, meaning that the CFR must be respected and the space available to invoke national security as a competence-deciding concept is limited. Now, secondary EU law that does not fall under Article 87(2) is still of significance to the collection and storage of data which is important for the protection of national security. In these circumstances, the national security exception does not hold against EU legislative measures and hence the application of the CFR, which the *Tele2* decision testifies to. Thus, when secondary EU law exists on a matter of direct or indirect relevance to national security, Member States cannot claim that the EU is acting contra Article 4(2) TEU if the legal basis for such regulation is correct. Hence, when it comes to national security as a competence-deciding concept, an ultra vires argument can be made primarily as regards institutional and organisational design in Member States (compare Article 73 TFEU) and operational (factual) measures (compare Articles 72 and 276 TFEU).

Although the wording of Article 4(2) TEU is fairly clear as regards the national security exception, there is no clear understanding of the definition and scope of national security as a competence-deciding norm. However, in the light of the CJEU's case law on national security and public order as compelling reasons for limiting fundamental rights and freedom, which defines the scope of national security as a rights-infringing concept, one can conclude that the scope of retained powers for national security purposes is very limited and that it is restricted to institutional and organisational issues, together with operational (especially coercive) measures.

IV. NATIONAL SECURITY IN DIFFERENT POLICY AREAS

In this section the analysis will, as far as possible, follow the structure presented above: national security as a competence-deciding concept and national security as justification for restricting rights.

A. Schengen and Internal Border Control

The tension here is between the fundamental right to freedom of movement for persons on the one hand, and the desire for Member States to uphold internal security, on the other. The common policy on border checks, asylum and immigration is regulated under Part III Title V TFEU. The Schengen Borders Code adopted on 9 March 2016[59] finds its legal basis in Article 77(2)(b) and (e) TFEU. According to Article 78(3) TFEU, in the event of an emergency situation due to a large influx of nationals of third countries, the Council upon a proposal by the Commission may adopt provisional measures to the benefit of a Member State. The European Parliament shall be consulted. In the preamble to the Schengen Border Code, it is stated that, in particular, terrorist incidents or threats might pose such a threat to public policy or internal security as to justify closing the border. Still, the crossing of borders of a large number of third-country nationals should not per se be considered a threat to public policy and internal security. Nor does this in itself justify a temporary closing of borders. Derogations from the freedom of movement must be interpreted strictly and presuppose the existence of a genuine, present and sufficiently serious threat affecting one of the fundamental interests of society.

Within the Schengen *acquis*, it is the prerogative of the Member State to decide if border control needs to be reinstated, which can be justified in three different situations. The Commission cannot veto such a decision; however, it can deliver an opinion on the necessity and proportionality of the decision (Article 27(4)). This is a clear example of how state sovereignty still dominates in the AFSJ. As a main rule, the reinstatement of border control is an exceptional measure that should be adopted only as a last resort and when it is considered strictly necessary in order to respond to a serious threat to public policy or internal security. It is required that the adequateness of the measure in relation to countering the threat is assessed and that the measure is proportional in relation to the threat (Article 26). When making this assessment, Member States should balance the likely impact of such threats on public policy and internal security against the likely impact on the freedom of movement of persons (Article 26(a) and (b)). First, in foreseeable cases such as sports events, borders can be closed for a time period of 30 days or for a foreseeable duration of the threat if it exceeds 30 days. The closing of borders can be renewed for up to a maximum of six months (Article 25(4)). The Commission and other Member States should be notified four weeks before or as soon as possible (Article 27(1)). The information should be sent to the European Parliament and the Council at the same time. The notification should include information on, inter alia, the reason for and the scope of the measure, and the duration of the measure.

[59] Regulation (EU) 2016/399 of the European Parliament and of the Council of 9 March 2016 on a Union Code on the rules governing the movement of persons across borders [2016] OJ L77/1 (Schengen Borders Code).

In cases where immediate action is needed due to a threat, borders can be closed without prior notification to the Commission for 10 days. Member States and the Commission should be informed immediately and the period can be prolonged up to 20 days. The overall period must not exceed two months (Article 28(1), (4)). The third option refers to exceptional circumstances that put the functioning of the whole Schengen area at risk. In these situations, the Council may, upon the recommendation of the Commission, recommend that one or several Member States reintroduce border controls for a period of up to six months. This period can be prolonged to up to two years altogether (Article 29).

As of 6 June 2018, Norway, Sweden, Denmark, Germany, Austria and France had prolonged the closing of their borders.[60] In a report from May 2018, the European Parliament condemned the prolongations of the closing of the borders, calling them unlawful in that they were disproportional and unnecessary. It is argued that the closing of borders has become a new status quo[61] or, to put it in other words, the exceptional has become the new normal at the expense of the fundamental freedom of movement for persons.

The crux of the matter is that the CJEU has no jurisdiction to review the validity or proportionality of measures by a Member States taken in order to ensure internal security or public policy.[62] Should the Commission or another Member State disagree with the assessment of proportionality and necessity, it can issue an opinion and engage in a consultation with the Member State in question.[63] To my knowledge, there are no guidelines from the Commission as to how necessity or proportionality should be assessed and tested; this lies fully within the discretion of the Member States as a matter of national security. The Commission's sharpest weapon is the monitoring and evaluation process, without any actual sanctions for violations of the Schengen *acquis*.[64]

Thus, in this context, national security as an EU constitutional law concept is given a broad understanding and hence the scope of the Member States' national security prerogative is broad, both in terms of national security as a competence-deciding and as a rights-restricting concept.

[60] For a full list of Member States that have reintroduced border control, see https://ec.europa.eu/home-affairs/sites/homeaffairs/files/what-we-do/policies/borders-and-visas/schengen/reintroduction-border-control/docs/ms_notifications_-_reintroduction_of_border_control_en.pdf.

[61] *Report on the Annual Report on the Functioning of the Schengen Area* (2017/2256 (INI)), 3 May 2018, 6, www.europarl.europa.eu/sides/getDoc.do?pubRef=-//EP//NONSGML+REPORT+A8-2018-0160+0+DOC+PDF+V0//EN.

[62] Article 276 TFEU.

[63] Article 27 of the Schengen Borders Code.

[64] Council Regulation (EU) 1053/2013 of 7 October 2013 establishing an evaluation and monitoring mechanism to verify the application of the Schengen *acquis* and repealing the Decision of the Executive Committee of 16 September 1998 setting up a Standing Committee on the evaluation and implementation of Schengen [2013] OJ L295/27.

B. Data Protection and National Security

In a number of well-known decisions, the CJEU has assessed the right to privacy and data protection in the national security context. Although the legal background and procedures differ in these cases, they are all relevant for the discussion on national security as an EU constitutional law concept. First, it must be underlined that the CJEU recognises the fight against international terrorism and serious crimes as an objective of general interest within the meaning of Article 52(1) CFR, and that an explicit reference is made to Article 6 CFR and the individual right to security.[65] First out is the *Digital Rights Ireland* case.[66] In this case, the CJEU declared the EU Data Retention Directive to be invalid, since the EU legislature had not taken Articles 7, 8, and 52(1) CFR into account. The Directive failed to provide clear and precise rules as to the permitted extent of interference with the right to privacy and personal data.[67] In a second case, the *Safe Harbour* decision (*Schrems*),[68] the CJEU ruled that the Safe Harbour Agreement between the US and the EU failed to meet EU requirements as to the protection of EU citizens' privacy rights. The CJEU declared that the national security exception in the Safe Harbour Agreement, stating that national security has primacy over the safe harbour principles and thereby allowing US organisations to disregard privacy rights of EU citizens, failed to meet the requirements of EU law, and Articles 7 and 8 of the Charter in particular.[69]

Already, it is clear that national security per se does not provide carte blanche to unrestricted access to personal data and that mass surveillance in itself is in violation of the essence of privacy rights as protected by the CFR. According to Tuomas Ojanen, 'one of the major lessons from *Digital Rights Ireland* and *Schrems* is that a trade-off between liberty and security *in abstracto* should be rejected'.[70] What is required is instead a case-by-case assessment of surveillance measures, taking the permissible limitations test into account. In this context, the system for protecting fundamental rights provides the starting point for balancing rights and security, including the proportionality test.[71] *Digital Rights Ireland* and the *Safe Harbour* decisions not only had important ramifications for data protection and privacy rights in EU law, they also lay the foundation for the CJEU's decision in the *Tele2* case[72] and set the path to CJEU's decision on the EU-Canada Passenger Name Record (PNR) Agreement.

[65] *Digital Rights Ireland* (n 23) and *Seitlinger and Others* para 42; *Opinion 1/15* (n 40) para 149.

[66] *Digital Rights Ireland* (n 23).

[67] For an analysis, see Ojanen (n 8).

[68] Case C-362/14 *Maximillian Schrems v Data Protection Commissioner* (CJEU (Grand Chamber)) [2015] ECLI:EU:C:2015:650.

[69] ibid paras 86–91.

[70] Ojanen (n 8) 18.

[71] ibid.

[72] Joined Cases C-203/15 and C-698/15 *Tele2 Sverige AB v Post- och telestyrelsen* and *Secretary of State for the Home Department v Tom Watson and Others* [2016] ECLI:EU:C:2016:970.

In the *Tele2* decision,[73] the CJEU dealt explicitly with the national security exception as a competence-deciding concept.[74] It held that the exemption for the collection of data for national security (activities concerning public security, defence and state security, including the economic well-being of the state) and the activities of the state in areas of criminal law as laid down in Article 1(3) of Directive 2002/58 does not apply, and that national laws transposing the Directive must be in conformity with Articles 7, 8, 11 and 52(1) CFR, even if such laws are mainly concerned with national security or criminal law. Although the decision in the *Tele2* case mainly addressed national legislation regulating the collection of data for the purpose of fighting crime, it will have implications for the collection of data in the interests of national and public security due to the overlap between security and criminal law, and the broad interpretation by the CJEU as to the scope of the Directive, as was illustrated at the beginning of this chapter. Thus, as regards the retention and processing of data within the EU, the bar is set high in terms of rights protection and the scope for claiming a national security exception has been made narrower.

In its opinion on the EU-Canada PNR Agreement,[75] the CJEU found the agreement to be in violation of Articles 7, 8, 21 and 52(1) CFR. First, the Court stated that in accordance with the well-established case law of the CJEU, restrictions to the fundamental right of private life, and in observance of the principle of proportionality, 'derogations from and limitations on the protection of personal data should apply only in so far as is strictly necessary'.[76] In order to be in congruence with the CFR and the case law of the CJEU laws, restricting privacy rights must:

> [L]ay down clear and precise rules governing the scope and application of the measure in question and imposing minimum safeguards, so that the persons whose data has been transferred have sufficient guarantees to protect effectively their personal data against the risk of abuse. It must, in particular, indicate in what circumstances and under which conditions a measure providing for the processing of such data may be adopted, thereby ensuring that the interference is limited to what is strictly necessary.[77]

The data transferred according to the PNR Agreement was personal data to be used mainly for intelligence purposes and border control. Based on the data transferred, individuals can be subject to additional checks at the borders and decisions binding upon them. Furthermore, the assessment as to whether a passenger may present a risk to public security is made without there being

[73] ibid. For a case law analysis see, I Cameron, 'Balancing Data Protection and Law Enforcement Needs: *Tele2 Sverige and Watson*' (2017) 54 *Common Market Law Review* 1467.

[74] Directive 2002/58/EC of the European Parliament and of the Council of 12 July 2002 concerning the processing of personal data and the protection of privacy in the electronic communications sector [2002] OJ L201/37 (Directive on privacy and electronic communications).

[75] *Opinion 1/15* (n 40).

[76] ibid para 140.

[77] ibid para 141.

reasons based on individual circumstances.[78] Concerning the latter, a parallel can be drawn to the relevant CJEU case law as to how to conduct threat assessments in relation to EU citizens. The threat needs to be real and the assessment based on concrete circumstances assessed and evaluated in relation to the behaviour of the individual concerned. The Court further stated that:

> [T]he interferences which the envisaged agreement entails are capable of being justified by an objective of general interest of the European Union and are not liable adversely to affect the essence of the fundamental rights enshrined in Articles 7 and 8 of the Charter.'[79]

The CJEU then moved on to assess whether the measure is appropriate to achieve public security and reached the conclusion that it is.[80] When conducting the 'strictly necessary' test which entails 'clear and precise rules governing the scope and application of the measures provided for',[81] it found that as regards the PNR data to be transferred to Canada, the Agreement does 'not delimit in a sufficiently clear and precise manner the scope of the interference with the fundamental rights enshrined in Articles 7 and 8 of the Charter'.[82] Since the Agreement concerned the transfer of sensitive data and there was also a risk of violating Article 21 CFR (discrimination), the CJEU stated that the transfer of such data requires a precise and particularly solid justification based on grounds other than safeguarding public security and fighting international terrorism and transitional crime, referring to the PNR Directive. Such justifications were lacking.[83] Thus, the CJEU confirmed its case law that national security per se is not a justification for rights infringements and referred to the requirements laid down in the *Tele2* decision as to the requirement of prior review following a reasoned request submitted by competent authorities within the framework of procedures for the prevention, detection or prosecution of crime.[84]

The CJEU is exercising strict scrutiny when mass surveillance and fundamental rights are at stake (especially when EU citizens' rights are involved). The connection between the collection of personal data and the aim for which it is collected must be clearly specified and in a detailed manner. Unrestricted access to personal data for national security reasons is considered a violation of the essence of the right to privacy and personal data. It is noteworthy that the CJEU in its *EU-Canada PNR* decision clearly stated that preventing terrorism is not a solid enough justification for the transfer and process of sensitive personal data. The permissibility test developed by the CJEU is clear on what is required for a restriction to be permissible and is continuously developing its case law on the

[78] ibid para 132.
[79] *Opinion 1/15* (n 40) para 151.
[80] ibid para 153.
[81] ibid para 154.
[82] ibid para 163.
[83] ibid para 165.
[84] ibid para 202.

matter, and by doing so, it is limiting the scope of the national security exception to the benefit of fundamental rights protection.

V. CONCLUSIONS

National security as an objective and interest can serve as both an accelerator and a brake to EU legal integration. So far, it has primarily served as an accelerator. Taking the political turmoil in Europe into account, especially the growing tendencies towards nationalism and the return to the nation state as the primary actor in the wake of the so-called migration crisis and Brexit, reaching the conclusion that the national security argument will serve to slow down EU legal integration in the future is not far-fetched. This is especially the case taking into account the limited scope of the national security prerogative that remains within the Member States as a result of, for example, the *Tele2* decision and the 'retained powers formula' as developed by the earlier case law of the CJEU. Still, the scope of national security as a rights-restriction argument could be viewed from a broader point of view. For example, as shown above, the closing of borders due to national security reasons, although being regulated by the Schengen *acquis*, falls under the national security prerogative of Member States. EU law regulates when and under what conditions a decision can be taken to close the borders, but the last word lies with Member States, and the Commission does not have a veto right. Compare this with privacy rights protection in the national security context – the national security exception is interpreted strictly, hence leaving a large impact for EU law and a small space for manoeuvre at the national level. In terms of rights protection, it is obvious that the scope of the national security exception is limited as a result of judicial intervention by the CJEU. As concerns national security as a competence-deciding concept, it is clear that an institutional, organisational and practical understanding of national security as a competence-deciding concept predominates in EU constitutional law. Included in the competence-deciding concept are also operative measures and threat assessments in concrete cases. In conclusion, if we merge the two perspectives on national security as a competence-deciding or rights-restricting norm, what is left for Member States? Not much. Might this conclusion stir political controversies and a national backlash? Potentially in some Member States. The question is to what extent can these Member States have an effect on EU law as a constitutional order that primarily serves to protect fundamental rights?

REFERENCES

Cameron, I, *National Security and the European Convention on Human Rights* (Uppsala, Iustus, 2000).

——. 'Balancing Data Protection and Law Enforcement Needs: Tele2 Sverige and Watson' (2017) 54 *Common Market Law Review* 1467.

Carrera, S and Mitsilegas, V (eds), *Constitutionalising the Security Union: Effectiveness, Rule of Law and Rights in Countering Terrorism and Crime* (Brussels, Centre for European Policy Studies, 2017).
Claes, M and de Witte, B, 'Competences: Codification and Contestation' in A Lazowski and S Blockmans (eds), *Research Handbook on EU Institutional Law* (Cheltenham, Edward Elgar, 2016).
Epstein, RA, 'The ECJ's Fatal Imbalance: Its Cavalier Treatment of National Security Issues Poses Serious Risk to Public Safety and Sound Commercial Practices' (2016) 12 *European Constitutional Law Review* 330.
Harding, C, 'EU Criminal Law under the Area of Freedom, Security and Justice' in A Arnull and D Chalmers (eds), *The Oxford Handbook of European Union Law* (Oxford, Oxford Handbooks Online, 2015).
Jonsson Cornell, A, 'Privacy Rights and Data Protection in Law Enforcement Cooperation: Comparing the US and EU', in A-S Lind, J Reichel and I Österdahl (eds), *Information and Law in Transition: Freedom of Speech, the Internet, Privacy and Democracy in the 21st Century* (Stockholm, Liber, 2015).
Mitsilegas, V, 'The Security Union as a Paradigm of Preventive Justice: Challenges for Citizenship, Fundamental Rights and the Rule of Law' in S Carrera and V Mitsilegas (eds), *Constitutionalising the Security Union: Effectiveness, Rule of Law and Rights in Countering Terrorism and Crime* (Brussels, Centre for European Policy Studies, 2017).
Ojanen, T, 'Administrative Measures in Counter-terrorism Activities: More Leeway for the Imperatives of Security at the Expense of Human Rights?' in M Fichera and J Kremer (eds), *Law and Security in Europe: Reconsidering the Security Constitution* (Cambridge, Intersentia, 2013).
——. 'Rights-Based Review of Electronic Surveillance after *Digital Rights Ireland* and *Schrems*' in D Cole, F Fabbrini and S Schulhofer (eds), *Surveillance, Privacy and Transatlantic Relations* (Oxford, Hart Publishing, 2017).
Peers, S, *EU Justice and Home Affairs Law*, 4th edn (Oxford, Oxford University Press, 2016).
Scheppele, KL, 'Global Security Law and the Challenge to Constitutionalism after 9/11' [2011] *Public Law* 352.
Scheinin, M, 'Towards Evidence-Based Discussion on Surveillance: A Rejoinder to Richard A Epstein' (2016) 12 *European Constitutional Law Review* 341.
Tuori, K, *European Constitutionalism* (Cambridge, Cambridge University Press 2015).
Tzanou, M, *The Fundamental Right to Data Protection: Normative Value in the Context of Counter-terrorism Surveillance* (Oxford, Hart Publishing, 2017).
Van der Sloot, B, 'Is All Fair in Love and War? An Analysis of the Case Law of Article 15 ECHR' (2014) 53 *Military Law and the Law of War Review* 319.

7

Immunity or Community? Security in the European Union

EDUARDO GILL-PEDRO

I. INTRODUCTION

THE TWO PREVIOUS chapters in this volume by Fichera and by Jonsson Cornell address striking developments in the EU's Area of Freedom, Security and Justice (AFSJ), and examine some of the ways in which the EU's security strategy is implemented. In this chapter, I intend to engage with those developments[1] and frame them in a new way, which may allow for some further critical reflection on the direction in which the EU is heading and on the choices with which it is faced.

The framework that I will develop builds on two concepts which were elaborated by the Italian philosopher Roberto Esposito: the concepts of 'community' (*communitas*) and 'immunity' (*immunitas*). The point of this chapter is not to give a detailed exposition of Esposito's philosophy;[2] rather, I aim to appropriate the concepts advanced by Esposito and apply them as heuristic devices in order to think about the securitisation of the EU's AFSJ.

The first part of the argument which I advance in this chapter is that the EU, as it existed prior to the development of the security agenda highlighted by the previous two chapters, could be understood as being based on a logic of

[1] I was invited to the Conference which formed the genesis of this book as a commentator and my contribution here is offered in same spirit. I wish to thank the editors for their helpful comments and feedback, and Markus Gunneflo, who read and commented on an earlier draft. Any errors are of course mine.

[2] Esposito himself has outlined what he has called a 'philosophy for Europe' (R Esposito, *A Philosophy for Europe*, Z. Hanafi (trans) (London, Polity Press, 2018) However, my reliance on Esposito's concepts as heuristic devices does not entail a commitment to Esposito's 'philosophy for Europe'.

'community'. This logic of community represented the EU's 'special path',[3] to borrow Weiler's term, and this special path justified the EU project vis-a-vis both the Member States and the citizens. The EU was not a state and did not need to be legitimated as a state, but could be understood as a unique constitutional[4] arrangement, which followed its own particular path, justified by the logic of community.

The second and central part of the argument advanced here is that the securitisation of the EU, as highlighted by Fichera and Jonsson Cornell, has transformed the EU project and has moved it away from a logic of community to a logic of immunity. As an immunitarian project, the EU left its 'special path' and can no longer be justified to the Member States or to the citizens under a logic of community. I conclude by observing that there is an inherent contradiction in a project which seeks to further European integration by adopting a logic of immunity.

II. ESPOSITO'S COMMUNITY AND IMMUNITY

In order to engage with the arguments set out in this chapter, it will be necessary first to give a brief overview of the concepts of 'community' and 'immunity' as understood by Esposito.

A. Community

Esposito begins his elaboration of the term 'community' with an etymological investigation of the word,[5] which he traces back to the Latin word *communitas*, a word which contains two elements – *cum*, with or together, and *munus*. The focus of Esposito investigation is on *munus*, a term which has a 'complex, bivalent meaning of "law" or "gift"'.[6] The origin of this term goes even further back in antiquity and is linked by Esposito to the Greek myth of creation. According to this myth, when Prometheus creates man, he steals fire from heaven and gives it to man. The gift of fire is the gift of community – the *munus* that man received

[3] This term is borrowed (and anglicised) from J Weiler, 'Federalism without Constitutionalism: Europe's *Sonderweg*' in K Nicolaïdes and R Howse (eds), *The Federal Vision* (Oxford, Oxford University Press, 2001).

[4] The term 'constitutional' is used here in the broad sense, which does not entail a commitment to an understanding of the EU as having a 'constitution' in the sense of a legal order built on a single constituent power. This is in order to be faithful to Weiler's understanding of the EU's *Sonderweg*, which, as the title of his work indicates, entails federalism without constitutionalism.

[5] I will not be able to go into detail on Esposito's elaborate etymological investigation. For a careful overview of this aspect of Esposito's work, see R Bonito Oliva 'From the Immune Community to Communitarian Immunity' (2006) 36 *Diacritics* 70.

[6] R Esposito 'Community, Immunity, Biopolitics' (2013) 18 *Angelaki* 83, 84.

in common. *Communitas* is given to humanity at the time of its creation and is something which is given as a compensation for an original lack in the nature of humanity.[7]

By conceiving of community as a gift, Esposito distances his understanding of community from much of modern political philosophy from Hobbes onwards, which understands community as something artificial, something which humans create together.[8] According to Esposito, we do not make community; community is given to us, and it is given to us at the moment of our creation. But while community is something that is given to us to compensate for an original lack in our nature, it is not an ineluctable part of our nature. Gifts can be refused and can be lost. By understanding community as a gift, Esposito positions community in the realm of the contingent.

On the other hand, by understanding community as something which is not of man's own making, but is given to him at the time of his creation, Esposito removes community from the realm of the proper. Community is not a property that we possess in common, nor is it something which we own or to which we belong. There is, on this understanding, no 'community' that is immanent in society. Because the gift that we received is a condition, a condition of exposure to others, it is, paradoxically, the gift of not being whole unto ourselves.[9] And because we are not whole unto ourselves, we must seek wholeness through exposure to, and engagement with, others.

An important component in this understanding of community is that it refers not to some entity, or even some end point, but to a process, a praxis. As Bird and Short put it:

> For Esposito, [the common] is neither 'la chose publique' the 'common wealth' nor a 'common good' because the common is not a property or a common good, because the common is nothing but exposure to common being.[10]

This theoretical move, which removes community from the realm of the proper and which focuses not on what community *is*, as an end product or an artefact, but on what community *does*, as a condition or praxis which shapes the way in which we interact with each other, has profound implications for how we can think about the political. The political is no longer the site where we determine what the authentic, proper, essential community is. Esposito's community is not a definite entity or even a reified end point. His understanding of community is neither a Weberian *Gemeinschaft* nor a neo-communitarian community of values.[11] But on the other hand, the gift of community is essential for us to be

[7] 'The original defect for which the divine gift was compensation' is translated (by Esposito) into the immanent lack of human nature. See Bonito Oliva (n 5) 73.

[8] Bonito Oliva (n 5).

[9] In this way, Esposito emphasises that the gift of community entails a lack or a deficiency.

[10] G Bird and J Short, 'Community, Immunity and the Proper' (2013) 18 *Angelaki* 1, 10.

[11] In Esposito's critique, both of these strands of political thought understood community 'as a substance that connected certain individuals to each other through the sharing of a common identity'.

truly human – without this gift, we are incomplete, stunted beings. In Esposito's words:

> We need community because it is the very locus, or better, the transcendental condition of our existence, given that we have always existed in common.[12]

Esposito therefore rejects the understanding of the individual as self-sufficient, capable of determining his own ends autonomously. The thing that unites the 'members of a community'[13] is that they are bound by the common law according to which they are 'obligated not to lose this originary condition'[14] – the condition of being in a community, and being vulnerable and exposed to the other.

B. Immunity

Esposito's understanding of community is very challenging. There is no community which is united by a common property or a common identity; rather, community is understood negatively: 'the subjects of community are united by an obligation'[15] – the obligation of openness, of exposure to others. This quality of being under an obligation to others presents a threat to the self-identity of individuals. The reaction to the threat of community is *immunity* – as Vaughan-Williams puts it,[16] it is in response to this constitutive danger of our co-living that animates immunisation as a response to that danger:

> The subject who is 'immune' does not have any obligations or duties according to the law of reciprocal giving and exchange in communitas.[17]

The relationship between community and immunity is dialectic, in that the logic of immunity is inscribed in the logic of community and vice versa.[18] In other words, community presupposes the possibility of immunity, and immunity represents the reversal or negation of community.

Community is thus conceived in the 'substantialist, subjective sense' which Esposito himself rejects. See Esposito (n 6) 83.

[12] R Esposito, *Terms of the Political: Community, Immunity, Biopolitics*, R Welch (trans) (New York, Fordham University Press, 2013) 14.

[13] And here I use scare quotes to indicate that conceiving of community as an entity with members that belong to it goes against the grain of Esposito's understanding of community, even if he himself used it in the section cited.

[14] Esposito (n 12) 14.

[15] R Esposito, *Communitas: The Origin and Destiny of Community*, T Campbell (trans) (Stanford, Stanford University Press, 2010) 6.

[16] N Vaughn Williams, 'Immunitarian Borders' in N Vaugh Williams (ed), *Europe's Border Crisis* (New York, Oxford University Press, 2015).

[17] ibid.

[18] In fact, Esposito goes further. It is not only that 'one is the contrasting background for the other but also the object and content of the other … immunity only takes relief as a negative form of community'. R Esposito, *Immunitas*, Z Hanafi (trans) (Cambridge, Polity Press, 2011) 8.

Immunity is a term which Esposito derives from the biological sciences and from medicine in particular. In that context, it refers to the capacity of a living body to:

> [I]nsulate that body from a destructive external element by identifying what is the body's *own* and eliminating or excluding that which is pathological to it.[19]

This connection with the medical realm highlights both the protective and the destructive character of the immune *dispositif*[20] – it protects the communal body by identifying that which is other and excluding or destroying it, just as the biological immune system protects the living body by destroying pathogens. But the connection with the medical should not be taken too far. Immunity also has the sense of a status, a privilege accorded to those who are exonerated from the responsibility of community.[21] What links both these senses of 'immunity' is its function as an exception to the common condition of exposure.

Immunity is necessary for life – the physical body, the social body and the political body cannot survive without mechanisms that allow them to identify extraneous entities that threaten them and to exclude or destroy these. However, and this is the key to Esposito's work:

> [W]hen driven beyond a certain threshold it forces life into a sort of cage where not only our freedom gets lost but also the very meaning of our existence – that opening of existence outside itself that takes the name of *communitas*.[22]

The need to immunise the community against the threatening other may lead to a demand that individual members of that community 'allow themselves to be appropriated by the collective intended to defend their defence'.[23] In this way, immunity, in seeking to protect community, ends up destroying it.

III. THE EU: FROM COMMUNITY TO IMMUNITY?

Having set out this brief sketch of Esposito's concepts of community and immunity, I turn now to the central argument advanced by this chapter – that the development of a security agenda as highlighted by Fichera and Jonsson Cornell indicates a shift in the EU from a community-based logic to an immunity-based logic. As I set out in section I, the concepts of community and immunity are relied on as heuristic devices, which provide us with a frame[24] with which to critically engage with particular developments in the EU. My claim is not that

[19] Bird and Short (n 10) 7, Emphasis in the original.
[20] Esposito, 'Community, Immunity, Biopolitics' 86.
[21] ibid.
[22] Esposito (n 6) 84.
[23] Esposito (n 18) 26.
[24] And there are other frames through which we can see the EU, as well as other logics which we can see enacted in its activities.

the EU, as a political project, corresponds precisely to the logic of community as elaborated by Esposito[25] or that the developments we see happening in the securitisation of the EU can be understood solely by reference to Esposito's concept of immunity.

A. The EU as (Potentially) a Communitarian Project

In this section, I argue that the EU can be conceived as a political project that follows a logic of community. I will recall three aspects of Esposito's understanding of community which I will test for 'fit' with the project of European integration. First, community exists in a dialectic relationship to immunity. Community and immunity presuppose each other, but each is, to some degree, a negation of the other. Second, community is understood by Esposito not as property that we own or an entity to which we belong and which is immanent in society, but as an obligation which we are under. Third, the condition which community imposes on us is that of being exposed to others and of not being sufficient unto ourselves. Community obliges us to allow ourselves to be exposed to others. I will take each of these aspects in turn.

i. The EU as a Reaction to Immunitarian Excesses

As already alluded to above, the forces that gave the impetus for the creation of what has become the EU were various and multi-faceted. However, there is historical evidence[26] that one of those forces emerged as a reaction to the dangers to peace and well-being of the peoples of Europe posed by totalitarian regimes – both the totalitarian regimes that had just been defeated in the bloodiest war in human history and the different kind of totalitarian regime[27] that was represented by the Soviet Union and the large part of Eastern Europe that was now under the control of that regime.

For Esposito, twentieth-century totalitarianism represents the apex of immunitarian logic. In particular, Nazi Germany saw the 'absolute convergence of the protection and the negation of life'.[28] To immunise the body of the German

[25] The forces that led to coming into being of the EEC were many and diverse, and it is not possible to see the EU as representing one single logic or one single vision – there have been competing visions of what the EU is and what it is for from its inception to the present day.

[26] See D Urwin, *A Community of Europe*, 2nd edn (London, Routledge, 2014). But this is not an uncontroversial view. For an overview of different theories of the history of European integration, see W Loth, 'Explaining European Integration: The Contribution from Historians' (2008) 14 *Journal of European Integration History* 9.

[27] According to Esposito, there are a number of factors that cross-cut the two kinds of totalitarianism – Nazism and Soviet communism – such as 'mass society, constructivist violence, generalised terror'. Nonetheless, he notes that there is a specificity to the Nazi event that is unassimilatable to any other event in the near or remote past. See Esposito (n 12) 78.

[28] ibid 73.

people and preserve the supposed purity of the German race from contamination from the alien other entailed 'the large scale production of death: first of those others, and finally, at the moment of defeat, of their own'.[29]

While I do not claim that the founders of the EU conceived that project in terms of a reaction to immunitarian logic, there is evidence that they did regard it as a reaction to the dangers posed by an excess of nationalism.[30] In the Schuman Declaration, which first proposed what was to become the European Coal and Steel Community, Robert Schuman argued that such a community would realise the 'fusion of interest', which in turn would be 'the leaven from which may grow a wider and deeper community between countries long opposed to one another by sanguinary divisions'.[31] In the Preamble to the Treaty of Rome of 1957, which established the European Economic Community, the founding states declared themselves '[r]esolved to strengthen the safeguards to peace and liberty' by means of creating an economic community, including a common market.

Thus, I argue that the political project of European integration can be seen[32] as reacting to, and establishing a contrast with, the immunitarian excesses of the fascist and communist political projects.

ii. The EU as an Obligation

I argue that, ontologically, there are parallels between the EU as a political project[33] and Esposito's understanding of community.[34] As set out above, 'community' is not a property, or a good, or a reified entity, immanent in society. Community refers to a condition, the condition of being under an obligation. Under the logic of community:

> The stability of one's identity is secondary to a fundamental obligation to (respectively) be responsible for something, to be in service to another, and to give something (back) to others.[35]

[29] ibid 75.

[30] Although, as Judt notes at the time of the signing of Treaty of Rome, 'very few Europeans, and none in positions of powers, were talking about "giving up sovereignty"'; T Judt, *A Grand Illusion? An Essay on Europe* (London, Penguin, 1996). Judt also notes that there has been a reinterpretation of the 'foundations of Europe' which has become 'increasingly grandiose and anachronistic'.

[31] Declaration of 9 May 1950, delivered by Robert Schuman.

[32] And here I should clarify that I am not seeking to identify the 'true' nature of the EU from an historical perspective, but rather engage with the claims which the EU (or EEC) made for itself as a political project that presented itself as a normatively justified project. This caveat also applies to the following two sections.

[33] Again, as clarified in n 32 above, I am referring to the claims that the EU made for itself as a normatively justified political project rather than seeking to identify the 'true' nature of the EU.

[34] Though, of course, these parallels cannot be taken too far.

[35] J Short, 'An Obligatory Nothing: Situating the Political in Post-metaphysical Community' (2013) 18 *Angelaki* 239, 140.

The EU is not a state. This was expressly acknowledged by the Court of Justice of the European Union, which pointed out that the EU 'under international law, precluded by its very nature of being considered a State'.[36] Further, the EU appears characterised more by that which it is not than by that which it is. In his thoroughgoing critique of what he sees as the failure of the European project to create 'a dynamic society of the people and peoples of Europe', Allot sets out what the EU does not have – a single constitution,[37] a single demos[38] or a single economy.[39] But community, according to Esposito's understanding, is defined by a lack, by a limit, rather than by anything positively immanent in our social world. As such, the fact that the EU can be defined more easily in negative terms, as that which it is not rather than as that which it is, is consistent with this aspect of community.

'The EU is not a state, but it must be a community of law.' This point was emphasised by Jean-Claude Juncker, the President of the EU Commission, in his State of the Union speech of September 2017.[40] The ontology of the EU is normative. While there is no EU as a self-standing polity, demos or economy, there is an EU as a legal order,[41] and the project of European integration is 'integration through law'.[42] In other words, what the EU is, as the outcome of international treaties, is a set of obligations agreed to by the states that are parties to those treaties, and through which those states acquire obligations which bind them to each other and to the citizens of all of them.[43]

Weiler[44] draws an interesting parallel between the obligations which states agree to be placed under as members of the EU and the submission by observant

[36] *Opinion 2/13 of the Court (Full Court) of 18 December 2014 on the Agreement on Accession of the EU to the European Court of Human Rights*, ECLI:EU:C:2014:2454.

[37] According to Allott: '"European Integration" is a normative order without a *grundnorm*.' See P Allott, 'Europe and the Dream of Reason' in J Weiler and M Wind (eds), *European Constitutionalism beyond the State* (Cambridge, Cambridge University Press, 2003) 219.

[38] 'The general will is more than the aggregation of the national will-forming process. It is the universalizing of the interests of all the people and peoples of Europe through law-making and law-applying in the common interest' (ibid 220). Allott goes on to point out that no such mechanisms exist in the EU.

[39] According to Allott, 'the EU economy has no … integrative totality. It is a piece-meal and artificial aggregation of parts of the national economies' (ibid 221).

[40] President Juncker's State of the Union speech, 13 September 2017 (SPEECH/17/3165), www.europa.eu/rapid/press-release_SPEECH-17-3165_en.htm.

[41] This was already noted by Hallstein in 1972, who claimed that: 'The [EU] … is a creation of law; is a source of law and is a legal system.' Instead of armies and weapons, the EU has law and 'the majesty of law is to achieve that which centuries of "blood and iron" could not'. See W Hallstein, *Europe in the Making*, C Roeder (trans) (New York, Norton, 1972) 30.

[42] The term was coined in M Cappelletti, M Seccombe and J Weiler, *Integration through Law* (Berlin, de Gruyter, 1986).

[43] Law in this way functions as 'the natural cement that holds the member states, their peoples, and social and legal structures together'. See L Azoulai, '"Integration through law" and Us' (2016) 14 *I-Con*, 449, 462. However, Azoulai goes on to observe that this is a role which law can no longer perform.

[44] J Weiler, 'In Defence of the Status Quo: Europe's Constitutional *Sonderweg*' in J Weiler and M Wind (eds), *European Constitutionalism Beyond the State* (Cambridge, Cambridge University Press, 2003).

Jews to the Mosaic Law.[45] The commitment to accept constraints on our actions by a higher authority, or at least by an authority which is independent of our own individual will, may have an intrinsic value and may even be an act of liberation. By accepting the authority of something which is not solely of their own making and which derives from something that is not fully equitable with their own sovereign will, Member States may be seen as liberating themselves from the need to always pursue their own immediate self-interest.

It is important to note that Weiler uses the Mosaic Law as a simile, but neither Weiler nor Esposito[46] should be seen as advancing an understanding of law as something which is predetermined and given to us from above in the way that God gave the law to Moses and the Israelites.[47] The point of connection between these two thinkers which I am seeking to highlight here is this idea of *insufficiency*. We, as human beings, are insufficient in ourselves and can only try to be whole when we open ourselves up to the authority of something which is not a product of our own will. Thus, law is not something which is given to us fully formed, but is a condition of our existence: 'law creates an opening in immanence, a play of alteration that cuts through being'.[48] Because we are bound by a law that is not immanent to ourselves, law creates 'a gap in immanence that institutes a play of difference within Being, which prevents the subject or the community from becoming a totality'.[49]

Applying this logic by analogy, I argue that EU law, by demanding that Member States recognise the authority of something which is external to them and which is not a product of their will or immanent in their legal orders, prevents those states from becoming a totality.

iii. The EU as Exposure to the 'Other'

As set out in section III.A above, the condition of community is the condition of being vulnerable and exposed to the other. Community entails being in relation to an outside and constitutionally so – what makes us a community is our exposure to one another and the reciprocal obligations we have for each other.

It is arguable that this logic of community can be seen at play in the development of the EU.[50] Weiler argued that European Community (EC) law could and

[45] Weiler focuses in particular on the kosher laws, the Sabbath laws and the laws of purity in sexual relations.

[46] Nor I, in my application of their thinking in this chapter.

[47] And as Isaiah Berlin highlighted most forcefully, there are very serious dangers in conceiving of freedom as being bound to a higher, rational law, which will force one to be 'truly' free. See I Berlin, 'Two Concepts of Liberty' in I Berlin and H Hardy (eds), *Liberty: Incorporating Four Essays on Liberty* (Oxford, Oxford University Press, 2002).

[48] K Hole, 'The Ethics of Community' (2013) 18 *Angelakii* 103, 113. Hole refers to Nancy rather than Esposito in the passage quoted, but as the next quote will show, this logic also applies to Esposito.

[49] ibid.

[50] Originally, of course, known as the European Community.

should be seen as an expression of what he called the 'Principle of Constitutional Tolerance'. This principle is remarkable in that it requires Member States:

> [T]o accept to be bound by precepts articulated not by 'my people' but by a community composed of distinct political communities: a people, if you wish, of others.[51]

The outcome of the application of this Principle of Constitutional Tolerance in the Member States' legal orders is:

> [A] different type of political community one unique feature of which is that very willingness to accept a binding discipline which is rooted in and derives from a community of others.[52]

This community is not something fixed and determined. Community is neither a property which is owned by the Member States nor a reified entity to which they belong, but a praxis[53] – a praxis of being receptive to, and open to, the other. Weiler gives a number of examples: the example of immigration officials who are required, by EU law, to recognise the passport of a citizen of another EU Member State in the same way as those of their own nationals; the example of national legislative bodies that have to take account of the impact of their decisions not only on their national legal order, but also on the interests of others in the EU; or the national judges who are required to apply the law of another legal order in deciding the cases before them. These daily practices 'habituate [the public official] to deal with a very distinctive "other", but to treat him or her as if he/she was his own'.[54]

By being subject to the law of the European Community and required to comply with the Principle of Constitutional Tolerance, the Member State, as a subject of law, is 'insulated from self-consistency'.[55] The Member State is exposed to others, and this exposure is part of what constitutes that Member State *qua* Member State.

B. The EU as a (Budding) Immunitarian Polity

The central argument which I advance in this chapter is that the objective of creating an AFSJ in general, and the development of the security agenda as a means to achieve that objective, can be seen as bringing about a transformation in the logic governing European integration from a communitarian to an immunitarian logic. In what follows, I will try to show how.

[51] Weiler (n 3) 67.

[52] ibid 68.

[53] And this is where the parallels with the understanding of 'community' advanced by Esposito and set out in section III.A above are most obvious.

[54] Weiler (n 44) 22.

[55] A condition which Esposito attributes to the community. See Esposito (n 12) 22.

i. The AFSJ as a Space Immanent in Society

The logic of immunity results in a transformation of how the political body (the 'people' or the 'community') is conceived. In contrast to the logic of community, under the logic of immunity, the political community is seen as something concrete and immanent in society which we can possess in common or to which we can belong. The political body is seen as 'a "proper" body'.[56]

The language of the TEU, which proclaims that the AFSJ is an area that is 'offered' to the citizens of the EU,[57] reflects an understanding of a community as 'property' – something which is made whole and offered to those deemed to be its citizens. The Commission, in its Communications on issues concerning the AFSJ, refers to it as an area to be 'delivered' to its citizens[58] or to be 'consolidated', that is, to be made solid or 'shaped' through EU action.[59] In all these ways, the 'community' which is the AFSJ is presented as an artefact – something created, made and shaped by the EU, and as belonging in the realm of the proper – something which can constitute property, to be offered to a specific people.[60]

Even the understanding of 'freedom' in the AFSJ reflects this conception of the AFSJ as something that is offered to those deemed to belong. As I have argued elsewhere, the rights and freedoms guaranteed under EU law are not a reflection of the status of EU citizens as free and equal members of a political community, or the conditions which allow those citizens to regulate their life together.[61] Instead, they are what Maus described as 'legal goods (*rechtsgüter*) defined by an "expertocracy" [which are then] rationed and allocated to the subject (*untertanen*) as the state sees fit'.[62] This understanding of freedom, as something which is given to us, which we possess, something which is a 'good' to which we are entitled, also places the AFSJ in the realm of the proper.[63]

[56] Bird and Short (n 10) 7.

[57] Article 3(2) TEU.

[58] Communication from the Commission, 'Implementing the Stockholm Programme' COM [2010] 171.

[59] Communication from the Commission, 'Towards an Area of Freedom, Security and Justice' COM [1998] 459.

[60] As Lindahl notes, 'the European polity claims a right to include and exclude aliens because Europe is the own place of its citizens'; H Lindahl, 'Breaking Promises to Keep Them: Immigration and the Boundaries of Distributive Justice' in H Lindahl (ed), *A Right to Inclusion and Exclusion?: Normative Fault Lines of the EU's Area of Freedom, Security and Justice* (London, Hart Publishing, 2009).

[61] See E Gill-Pedro, *EU Law, Fundamental Rights and National Democracies* (London, Routledge, 2019).

[62] I Maus, 'On Liberties and Popular Sovereignty: Jürgen Habermas' Reconstruction of a System of Rights' (1996) 17 *Cardozo Law Review* 825, 852–53.

[63] Esposito describes the understanding of freedom under the logic of immunity as 'a quality, or a faculty, or a good, that a … subject must acquire in so far as possible'. This is in contrast to freedom under the logic of community, which is not understood as a property we possess, but as a condition we are in – we do not have freedom, we are free. Or, rather, we become free through community. Freedom is thus 'the part of community that resists immunization, that is not identical to itself, that remains open to difference'; Esposito (n 12) 53–56.

ii. The AFSJ Insulating the Other from the Own

As set out in section III.B above, the logic of immunity works as a reaction to, and an exception to, the logic of community. We are immune when we are exempt from the relationship of exposure that determines the meaning of community.[64] This means that there is a need to identify that which is own and that which is other – immunity protects the communal body by identifying that which is other and excluding or destroying it.

The process of delineating an area of freedom, security and justice entails a process of delineating that which belongs inside the area and that which belongs outside it. Where the community is conceiving a defined entity, borders are necessary as the 'container' of that community.[65] This delineation entails the normative 'marking off' of a territory (the AFSJ) and a status (EU citizen) which 'designate those beyond their bounds as qualitatively different and apart'.[66]

The EU's policies in this area have been driven in particular by security considerations; in the AFSJ, the need to protect security has been afforded particular importance.[67] The EU has thus developed what Tuori calls a 'security constitution', which 'defines membership of the polity through exclusion'.[68] The example that epitomises this phenomenon of security through exclusion of the other is the EU migration policies. As Kostakopoulou forcefully points out the EU immigration policies within the AFSJ have been marked by a definition of migration as primarily a security threat.[69] On this understanding, the community to which migrants come is seen as pre-existing, essential and unified. It is something which belongs to those who are part of it. Migrants can join it only by integrating into it – until then, they are 'the other' and therefore a threat to community.[70] In order to protect the community from that threat,

[64] M Gunneflo, 'The Life and Times of Targeted Killing' (Doctoral thesis, Lund University, 2014) 19.

[65] R Zapata-Barrero, 'Political Discourses about Borders: On the Emergence of a European Political Community' in Lindahl (ed) (n 60) 15.

[66] P Fitzpatrick 'Finding Normativity: Immigration Policy and Normative Formation' in H Lindahl (ed), *A Right to Inclusion and Exclusion?* (Oxford, Hart Publishing, 2009).

[67] See E Herlin-Karnell 'The Domination of Security and the Promise of Justice: On Justification and Proportionality in Europe's AFSJ' (2017) 8 *Transnational Legal Theory* 79, who argues that 'much of the EU's involvement in the AFSJ has been built on the concept that European security is a device for achieving further integration [and] consequently a large majority of the measures adopted … have been characterized by a strong precautionary focus' (at 86). Douglas-Scott regrets that 'it has become almost a commonplace to state that, within the AFSJ, freedom and justice have been sacrificed to security' (S Douglas-Scott, 'Human Rights as a Basis for Justice in the European Union' (2017) 8 *Transnational Legal Theory* 59, 61).

[68] K Tuori, 'The Many Constitutions of Europe' in K Tuori and S Sankari, *The Many Constitutions of Europe* (Farnham, Ashgate Publishing, 2010) 27.

[69] D Kostakoupolou 'The Area of Freedom, Security and Justice and the Political Morality of Migration and Integration' in Lindahl (ed) (n 60) 185.

[70] ibid 202.

the EU has developed an array of measures designed to identify,[71] keep out[72] or remove[73] those who do not belong, and to homogenise and 'de-other' those who are given a right to stay.[74]

But this logic of immunisation, of seeing the EU as a body which must be protected from potentially threatening external entities, can be seen not only in EU migration policies, but also in a large array of EU policies. As Fichera points out in this volume,[75] the need to ensure the security of the EU – the security of what the President of the EU called 'The European way of life'[76] – empowers and justifies the EU in pushing for further integration. The need to secure Europe against external and internal threats has become a key driver of European policies.[77]

iii. The AFSJ: Destroying Community to Protect the Community?

As set out in section II.B above, while community and immunity presuppose and require each other, the logic of immunity can lead to the destruction of community. I suggest that we can also discern this process in the way in which the immunitarian logic introduced by the need to create the AFSJ is undermining the communitarian logic of the EU.

[71] Among other policies, the European Commission prioritises the creation of 'Hotspots' 'where the European Asylum Support Office, Frontex and Europol will work on the ground with frontline Member States to swiftly *identify, register and fingerprint* incoming migrants'; Communication from the Commission 'A European Agenda on Migration' COM [2015] 240, 6 (emphasis added).

[72] The EU has developed a wide array of policies to strengthen the security of EU's external borders, both by acting directly, through EU agencies (in particular, Frontex) and indirectly, with initiatives such as the development of an EU standard for efficient border management and fostering the 'smart borders' initiative. The EU has also introduced legislation imposing duties on private actors not to facilitate the travel of undocumented migrants into the EU territory (see in particular Council Directive 2001/51/EC of June 28 2001 supplementing the provisions of Article 26 of the Convention implementing the Schengen Agreement of 14 June 1985 [2001] OJ L187/045 – the Carrier Sanctions Directive).

[73] See in particular Directive 2008/115/EC of the European Parliament and of the Council of 16 December 2008 on common standards and procedures in Member States for returning illegally staying third-country nationals [2008] OJ L348/095 (the Return Directive). For an indication of the obligations which EU law places on Member States to remove those who are not entitled to stay, see Case C-38/14 *Extranjería v Samir Zaizoune* EU:C:2015:260.

[74] And here I am referring to EU policies coordinating and supporting Member States action in integrating third-country nationals legally present in the territory (see in particular Communication from the Commission 'Action Plan on the Integration of Third County Nationals' COM [2016] 377 final).

[75] Fichera ch 5 in this volume. It should be noted that Fichera understands 'security' in a very broad sense, in that it encompasses all measures which uphold the primacy, efficacy and unity of EU law.

[76] President Juncker's State of the Union speech, 14 September 2016 (SPEECH/16/3043).

[77] As Juncker put it in his State of the Union speech of 2016: 'My Commission has prioritised security from day one – we criminalised terrorism and foreign fighters across the EU, we cracked down on the use of firearms and on terrorist financing, we worked with internet companies to get terrorist propaganda offline and we fought radicalisation in Europe's schools and prisons.'

The most obvious way in which this occurs is through the mere operation of the exclusionary and insulating processes highlighted in section III.B.ii above. By demanding that officials identify and exclude those who do not belong and by setting in place mechanisms designed to protect the security of the EU's space, the EU does not foster the 'Principle of Constitutional Tolerance' examined in section III.A.iii above, which would engender the culture of openness and acceptance of the other, but instead reinforces the immunitarian logic of the Member States, merely transferring the locus of the body to be protected from the national level to the EU level.

But the logic of immunity also has another, more profound effect on the EU legal order. As set out in section II.A above, according to Espositio, 'community' binds individuals to a common law according to which they are obliged to live in community, and to be vulnerable and exposed to the other. In effect, community imposes on us an obligation to accept a law which is not of our own making. The EU's project has had that effect, as set out in section III.A above. The point of the EU being a 'community of law'[78] is that it requires the sovereign states to be bound by a law which is not exclusively the outcome of that sovereign state's will – it creates an opening in the immanence of that state's sovereign will.[79]

The logic of immunity closes that opening or, rather, it moves the location of closure from the Member State level to the EU level. If the AFSJ is a space which is immanent in society and which must be closed off and insulated from 'the Other', and if the legitimacy of EU law is based on the need to protect the security of that space, then that EU law is self-sufficient unto itself.[80] In other words, the objective of creating an area of freedom, security and justice, and to protect that area from possible external and internal threats, is a *sufficient* ground to justify the authority of EU law.

IV. CONCLUSION

The EU is not unique in adopting an immunitarian logic based on the need to secure the polity against external and internal threats. The Member States are immunitarian polities par excellence and in many respects it is the Member States executives who have 'used' the EU in order to further their own security agendas. Nor is the logic of immunity incompatible with community – as I set

[78] As affirmed by the President of the EU Commission – see n 40 above.

[79] This requirement – that the sovereign power is not wholly self-sufficient, but is dependent on an external point of reference for its legitimacy – has been proposed as the definition of the 'rule of law' (see D Kochenov, 'EU Law without the Rule of Law: Is the Veneration of Autonomy Worth it? (2015) 34 *Yearbook of European Law* 74). My argument differs from Kochenov in that I do not claim that there is a 'higher' law to which EU law should be bound.

[80] As in *Opinion 2/13* (n 36), where the Court held that states must refrain from assessing the validity of EU law by reference to any standard external to the EU legal order if such an assessment would jeopardise the primacy, unity and efficacy of EU law.

out in section II.B above, community presupposes, and requires, immunity. But, while it is possible, as I set out in section III.A, to see how the EU, and the obligations which EU law imposes on the Member States, can be justified under a logic of community, this is not the case under a logic of immunity. Under the logic of community, the EU can be justified as a reaction to, and as a remedy against, the excessive immunitarian tendencies of the Member States. By imposing on the Member States an obligation of openness towards the other, the EU can be seen to '[preserve] difference within immanence, to resist totalization'.[81]

The same arguments cannot be advanced to justify the EU under a logic of immunity. Immunity protects the body for the sake of that body's protection. The existence of the EU justifies the measures taken in order to protect that existence.

Why is that problematic? Are the Member States not also their own justification? Here it is important to remember that the EU is not a state. States are polities which are meant to realise the self-determination of their people. The claim of legitimacy of a state is ultimately grounded on the claim that the state is an expression of the will of its people.[82] This is not to say that the state and the people are the same – as I argue elsewhere, who the people is, and what that people wants, is and must be a matter of contestation.[83] Nonetheless, the political processes in a state's[84] polity can be conceived as processes of collective will-formation: processes by which questions concerning who the people is and what the people wants can be argued out. In the context of a state, immunitarian processes aimed at securing the continued existence of the state can be seen as protecting the continued existence of the people of that state – the 'people' has no existence except through, and within, the political processes of will-formation of that polity.[85]

The EU does not have such processes of democratic will-formation.[86] It is a purposive polity, set up through international agreements between the Member States to achieve particular objectives. I cannot develop the argument fully here,[87] but as Davies points out, the purposive orientation of EU law 'prevent[s]

[81] K Hole, 'The Ethics of Community' (2013) 18 *Angelakii* 103.

[82] And here I am referring to democratic legitimacy.

[83] See Gill-Pedro (n 61).

[84] And here I am referring to EU Member States, which claim to be democracies.

[85] In fact, as I have argued elsewhere, the 'people' has no existence prior to the political community – the people are brought into being retrospectively, in the acts claiming and contesting to represent the people. See E Gill-Pedro, 'The Reflexive Identity of the People and the Act of Claiming Human Rights' in M Arvidson, L Brännström and P Minkkinen (eds) Constituent Power: Law, Popular Rule, and Politics (Edinburgh, Edinburgh University Press, forthcoming, 2019). In this I draw extensively on the thinking of Hans Lindahl; see in particular H Lindahl, 'Constituent Power and Reflexive Identity: Towards an Ontology of Collective Selfhood' in M Loughlin and N Walker (eds) *The Paradox of Constitutionalism* (Oxford, Oxford University Press, 2008).

[86] As Weiler puts it, in Europe, the presupposition of the supreme authority and sovereignty of demos 'simply does not exist'. See Weiler (n 44) 57.

[87] For an elaboration on this argument, see Gill-Pedro (n 61).

meaningful democratic processes from taking place because they render certain goals non-negotiable, and thereby pre-empt essential choices of policy direction'.[88] Without those democratic processes, there is no possibility for a 'European people' to come into being.

If there is no European people who are to be immunised from the 'other', what then constitutes this 'body' which is being protected? I argue that the 'body' which is being secured and insulated from the threatening other is an idea[89] – the idea of European integration. It is in the name of this idea, and not of a European people, that the EU claims the authority to impose obligations on the Member States to further the EU's objectives. This echoes Somek's description of *authoritarian liberalism*, according to which:

> A government possesses authority to the extent that it succeeds at presenting itself as representative of the leading idea of an institution.[90]

The exercise of power, in authoritarian liberalism, is done 'not on behalf of a subject, but of an idea'.[91] I suggest that, similarly, Member States are required to comply with their obligations to give effect to EU law in order to further the realisation of this idea of European integration. The 'body' which needs to be immunised against possible threats is 'nothing more than the concept of European integration'.[92] The EU deploys immunitarian logic to protect European integration from that which might threaten it.

This results in a paradox. As set out in section III.A above, we can understand the idea of European integration as imposing an obligation of community on the Member States, that is, as an obligation to be open to 'the other'. But this very idea of European integration is in turn deployed as the idea that justifies the immunitarian logic which imposes on Member States the obligation to identify and exclude 'the other'.

This paradox cannot be answered by pointing to the excellence of the idea. However good the idea of European integration might be, however worthwhile the achievements of the EU, this idea cannot, on its own, carry the weight of binding together a community to its service. If the peoples of Europe are to offer up their political freedom to the idea of European integration, there must be processes by which those people feel that this idea is in some sense also their idea.

[88] G Davies, 'Democracy and Legitimacy in the Shadow of Purposive Competence' (2015) 21 *European Law Journal*, 2.

[89] This was affirmed by the Court of Justice, which held that the raison d'etre of the EU is the process of integration itself. See *Opinion 2/13* (n 36) para 172.

[90] A Somek, 'Delegation and Authority: Authoritarian Liberalism Today' (2015) 21 *European Law Journal* 340, 355.

[91] ibid.

[92] P Agha, 'The Empire of Principle' in J. Přibáň (ed), *Self-Constitution of the European Society* (London, Routledge, 2016). I should add that Agha does not frame his argument within Esposito's framework of community/immunity.

And it should be remembered that there are other, more dangerous ideas in Europe: the idea of 'the people-as-one', the idea of a glorious national past and the idea of a racially pure ethnic group. These are all ideas which have found, and continue to find, dangerous traction among the peoples of Europe[93] and which are capable of harnessing immunitarian logic to their service, with tragic consequences. The 'special path' that justified the EU was that it acted as counter to this immunitarian logic. If instead the EU reinforces and legitimises immunitarian logic, then it may happen that the peoples of Europe chose to deploy that logic not to immunise European integration, but instead to immunise ideas that they may consider more important and more relevant to them – the idea of their 'people', their 'nation', their 'race'.

I suggest that we are at a crossroads. If the EU continues to develop the logic of immunity in the service of the idea of European integration, but there are no meaningful processes by which the peoples of Europe can see themselves as authors of that integration, then the growing rift between the EU, as a political project, and its putative citizens becomes ever wider.

REFERENCES

Agha, P, 'The Empire of Principle' in J Přibáň (ed), *Self-Constitution of the European Society* (London, Routledge, 2016).

Allott, P, 'Europe and the Dream of Reason' in J Weiler and M Wind (eds), *European Constitutionalism beyond the State* (Cambridge, Cambridge University Press, 2003).

Azoulai, L, '"Integration through Law" and Us' (2016) 14 *I-Con* 449.

Berlin, I, 'Two Concepts of Liberty' in I Berlin and H Hardy (eds), *Liberty: Incorporating Four Essays on Liberty* (Oxford, Oxford University Press 2002).

Bird, G and Short, J, 'Community, Immunity and the Proper' (2013) 18 *Angelaki* 1.

Bonito Oliva, R 'From the Immune Community to Communitarian Immunity' (2006) 36 *Diacritics* 70.

Cappelletti, M, Seccombe, M and Weiler, J, *Integration through law* (Berlin, de Gruyter, 1986).

Davies, G, 'Democracy and Legitimacy in the Shadow of Purposive Competence' (2015) 21 *European Law Journal* 2.

Douglas-Scott, S, 'Human Rights as a Basis for Justice in the European Union' (2017) 8 *Transnational Legal Theory* 59.

Esposito, R, *Communitas: The Origin and Destiny of Community*, T Campbell (trans) (Stanford, Stanford University Press, 2010).

——. *Immunitas*, Z Hanafi (trans) (Cambridge, Polity Press, 2011).

——. 'Community, Immunity, Biopolitics' (2013) 18 *Angelaki* 83.

[93] And there has in fact been a surge of support for nationalist and regionalist movements, as well as movements that are overtly racist (see A Chakelean, 'Rise of the Nationalists: A Guide to Europe's Far-Right Parties', *New Statesman* (8 March 2017), https://www.newstatesman.com/world/europe/2017/03/rise-nationalists-guide-europe-s-far-right-parties).

——. *Terms of the Political: Community, Immunity, Biopolitics*, R Welch (trans) (New York, Fordham University Press, 2013).

Fichera, M, 'Discursive Constituent Power and European Integration' (2017) 47 *Helsinki Legal Studies Research Paper*.

Fitzpatrick, P, 'Finding Normativity: Immigration Policy and Normative Formation' in H Lindahl (ed), *A Right to Inclusion and Exclusion?: Normative Fault Lines of the EU's Area of Freedom, Security and Justice* (London, Hart Publishing, 2009).

Gill-Pedro, E, *EU Law, Fundamental Rights and National Democracies* (London, Routledge, 2019).

——. 'The Reflexive Identity of the People and the Act of Claiming Human Rights' in M Arvidson, L Brännström and P Minkkinen (eds), *'The People': Democracy, Populism, and the Constituent Popular Sovereign* (Edinburgh, Edinburgh University Press, forthcoming, 2019).

Gunneflo, M, 'The Life and Times of Targeted Killing' (Doctoral thesis, Lund University, 2014).

Hallstein, W, *Europe in the Making*, C Roeder (trans) (New York, Norton, 1972).

Herlin-Karnell, E, 'The Domination of Security and the Promise of Justice: On Justification and Proportionality in Europe's AFSJ' (2017) 8 *Transnational Legal Theory* 79.

Hole, K, 'The Ethics of Community' (2013) 18 *Angelakii* 103.

Judt, T, *A Grand Illusion? An Essay on Europe* (London, Penguin, 1996).

Kochenov, D, 'EU Law without the Rule of Law: Is the Veneration of Autonomy Worth it? (2015) 34 *Yearbook of European Law* 74.

Kostakoupolou, D, 'The Area of Freedom, Security and Justice and the Political Morality of Migration and Integration' in H Lindahl (ed), *A Right to Inclusion and Exclusion?: Normative Fault Lines of the EU's Area of Freedom, Security and Justice* (London, Hart Publishing, 2009).

Lindahl, H, 'Constituent Power and Reflexive Identity: Towards an Ontology of Collective Selfhood' in M Loughlin and N Walker (eds), *The Paradox of Constitutionalism* (Oxford, Oxford University Press, 2008).

——. 'Breaking Promises to Keep Them: Immigration and the Boundaries of Distributive Justice' in H Lindahl (ed), *A Right to Inclusion and Exclusion?: Normative Fault Lines of the EU's Area of Freedom, Security and Justice* (London, Hart Publishing, 2009).

Loth, W, 'Explaining European Integration: The Contribution from Historians' (2008) 14 *Journal of European Integration History* 9.

Maus, I, 'On Liberties and Popular Sovereignty: Jürgen Habermas' Reconstruction of a System of Rights' (1996) 17 *Cardozo Law Review* 825.

Short, J, 'An Obligatory Nothing: Situating the Political in Post-metaphysical Community' (2013) 18 *Angelaki* 239.

Somek, A, 'Delegation and Authority: Authoritarian Liberalism Today' (2015) 21 *European Law Journal* 340.

Tuori, K, 'The Many Constitutions of Europe' in K Tuori and S Sankari, *The Many Constitutions of Europe* (Farnham, Ashgate Publishing, 2010).

Urwin, D, *A Community of Europe*, 2nd edn (London, Routledge, 2014).

Vaughn Williams, N, 'Immunitarian Borders' in N Vaugh Williams (ed), *Europe's Border Crisis* (New York, Oxford University Press, 2015).

Weiler, J, 'Federalism without Constitutionalism: Europe's *Sonderweg*' in K Nicolaïdis and R Howse (eds), *The Federal Vision* (Oxford, Oxford University Press, 2001).

——. 'In Defence of the Status Quo: Europe's Constitutional *Sonderweg*' in J Weiler and M Wind (eds), *European Constitutionalism beyond the State* (Cambridge, Cambridge University Press, 2003).

Zapata-Barrero, R, 'Political Discourses about Borders: On the Emergence of a European Political Community' in H Lindahl (ed), *A Right to Inclusion and Exclusion?: Normative Fault Lines of the EU's Area of Freedom, Security and Justice* (London, Hart Publishing, 2009).

Part III

Rule of Law in the Member States

8

The Rule of Law in Contemporary Finland
Not Just a Rhetorical Balloon

JUHA RAITIO

I. INTRODUCTION

WHAT DOES THE rule of law (*oikeusvaltio*) mean in Finland? After posing this question, one might expect a list of various elements of the rule of law[1] and some practical examples of the legal system at hand. Instead, I propose an answer that provides a relatively theoretical overview of the Finnish conceptions of the rule of law, mainly on the basis of Finnish legal literature. Yet, in doing so, I do not try to avoid the question. I simply think Finnish legal theory provides reflections and findings that are applicable and will be of interest not only in Finland. As far as the state of the rule of law in Finland is concerned more specifically, the practical problems are not many, but a few of them will nevertheless be discussed in section IV below.

The rule of law in Finland is here also studied from the perspective of EU law, since Finland has been a Member State since 1995. In general, the EU has no such tensions with Finland as regards the rule of law as it has with Poland and Hungary. It currently appears that Poland in particular has partially returned to the old authoritarian administrative 'rule by law' culture, which makes it pertinent to study issues such as the rule of law or mutual trust in the EU.[2]

[1] On the elements of rule of law, see, eg, T Bingham, *The Rule of Law* (London, Allen Lane, 2010) 37–129.

[2] In Poland, the Law and Justice party has enacted legislative changes that questioned the independence of Poland's Constitutional Court. For this reason, the EU introduced the procedure under art 7 of the Treaty on European Union (TEU), on which see Commission Recommendation 2016/1374 of 27 July 2016 regarding the rule of law in Poland [2016] OJ L217/53-68. There is also case law as regards the rule of law in Poland, for example C-216/18 LM, ECLI:EU:C:2018:586 and

During the Communist administration, courts were not independent from the political exercise of power in the way required by the current European concept of the rule of law. Under the Communist regime, law was understood in its relation to the state. Its purpose was to discipline people and create some kind of bureaucratic consistency in the administration of state affairs.[3] As is well known, this development in Poland, as well as in Hungary, has recently been referred to as 'illiberal democracy' both in legal literature and in the political discourse.[4]

The emphasis in this chapter is on the definition of the rule of law, although any attempt to define 'rule of law' is most likely doomed to fail, at least to a certain extent. The starting point is that the rule of law is not only a normative but also a legal cultural concept.[5] In Finland, the interpretation of the rule of law principle has been especially characterised by the comparison to the Anglo-American concept of the rule of law and the German *Rechtsstaat* concept.[6] Recently, the principle of the rule of law has also been considered from a global trade and comparative law viewpoint.[7] Yet, there is still reason to study the rule of law from a more theoretical point of view, since I argue that it contains a substantive element. So, in the contemporary world, one can pose the question of whether the rule of law can be said to exist in a society if, for example, the only requirement for the rule of law is a stable market and predictable norms, whereupon it would not matter how the norms have originated and what their content is.

C-619/18 R, European Commission v. Republic of Poland, ECLI:EU:C:2018:1021. In Hungary, for its part, the government led by the Fidesz party caused a stir in the spring of 2017 by deciding to close down a central university (Central European University (CEU)) independent of the political exercise of power through a new Universities Act. In addition, the government of Hungary has for years weakened the independence of the Constitutional Court, the freedom of the media and the freedom of the civil society.

[3] On rule by law thought in Eastern Europe, see A Sájo, 'Rule by Law in East Central Europe' in V Gessner, A Hoeland and C Varga (eds), *European Legal Cultures* (Dartmouth, Aldershot, 1996) 471–73.

[4] See, eg, B Bugariĉ, 'Protecting Democracy inside the EU: On Article 7 TEU and the Hungarian Turn to Authoritarianism' in C Closa and D Kochenov (eds), *Reinforcing Rule of Law Oversights in the European Union* (Cambridge, Cambridge University Press, 2016) 82–101.

[5] See K Tuori, *Oikeuden ratio ja voluntas* (Helsinki, WSOYpro, 2007) 222; and K Tuori, *Ratio and Voluntas: The Tension between Reason and Will in Law* (Farnham, Ashgate, 2011) 208. Tuori has somewhat similarly separated the Constitution into explicit, written norms and constitutional culture, which refers to constitutional theories, concepts and principles, as well as ways of dealing with these, ie, patterns of constitutional argumentation.

[6] See, eg, A Jyränki, *Presidentti, Tutkimus valtionpäämiehen asemasta Suomessa v. 1919–1976* (Vammala, Suomalainen lakimiesyhdistys, 1978) 41–42; K Tuori, 'Oikeusvaltiokäsite – vielä kerran' in *Foucault'n oikeus, Kirjoituksia oikeudesta ja sen tutkimisesta* (Vantaa, WSOY, 2002) 49–65; J Raitio, *The Principle of Legal Certainty in EC Law* (Dordrecht, Kluwer Academic Publishers, 2003) 134–146; and Tuori, *Oikeuden ratio ja voluntas* (n 5) 221–47.

[7] See J Husa, 'Nordic Law and Development: See No Evil, Hear No Evil?' (2015) 60 *Scandinavian Studies in Law* 1 and J. Husa, Advanced Introduction to Law and Globalisation, (Cheltenham, Edward Elgar Publishing, 2018) 49–63.

II. IS AN ATTEMPT TO DEFINE RULE OF LAW MERELY A WASTE OF TIME?

Based on the legal literature, the content of the concept of the rule of law seems to be contested, especially in relation to how the material dimension of the concept should be regarded. Already in the 1990s in Sweden, Frändberg described the concept of the rule of law as a 'rhetorical balloon' that one can, in a way, fill up, including in it everything possible that is perceived to be positive.[8] Frändberg's argument reflects a fear that the rule of law is in danger of becoming blurred as a concept and losing some of its expressiveness if it is interpreted too broadly. He compared the rule of law (or *Rechtsstaat*) with other value-laden concepts such as liberty, legal certainty or democracy. In his more recent works, he has studied 'law-state thinking' and clarified his idea of the 'watering-down of language'. According to him, this tendency manifests itself mainly in the smoothing over of tensions and conflicts between different values and principles. He finds that by including two or more different values or principles in one and the same concept, one hides the fact that they might be potentially contradictory. He advocates a 'minimal law state-thinking' in which only a few narrowly defined values are set out and applied in practice.[9] In a similar vein, Raz has warned against confounding the concept of the rule of law with a wide range of values, principles or goals that are characteristic of a good legal system.[10]

Tuori, in turn, describes the problem to interpret the rule of law with an example presented by Bingham about a legal case in which both parties appeal to the principle of the rule of law in such a way that it barely means anything other than 'Hooray for our side'.[11] On the one hand, he points out that many commentators tend to interpret the English rule of law doctrine as relating to the problem of how to prevent the exercise of arbitrary power by the government and to safeguard individual rights. Additionally, Tuori has aptly observed that the rule of law has been treated as an ideal of a good legal system as well as a legal principle of existing law.[12] Indeed, it is indisputable that the concept of the rule of law is ambiguous, but on the other hand, I think that a legal interpretation is always contextual in such a way that labelling the concept of the rule of law as a rhetorical balloon is a hyperbole.

[8] See Å Frändberg, 'Begreppet rättsstat' in F Sterzel (ed), *Rättsstaten – rätt, politik, moral* (Stockholm, Rättsfonden, 1996) 22–23.

[9] See Å Frändberg, *From Rechtsstaat to Universal Law-State: An Essay in Philosophical Jurisprudence* (Dordrecht, Springer, 2014) 30–32.

[10] See J Raz, *The Authority of Law: Essays on Law and Morality* (Oxford, Clarendon Press, 1979) 211.

[11] See Tuori, *Ratio and Voluntas* (n 5) 210–11.

[12] ibid; similarly, see Frändberg (n 9) 6, in which he states that the nucleus of his law-state thinking is that the individual enjoys legal protection against violations caused by the exercise of power on the part of the public power.

Another issue is related to the challenges transnational law and globalisation pose to the concept of the rule of law. What if there is no sovereign (nation) state at all in a certain field of law and the question of democracy seems not to be as relevant as in the traditional rule of law discourse? Salonen, for one, has recently studied how many corporations across various business areas develop industry-wide standards, recommendations, standardised contracts and even rules to address industry-specific problems. For example, in the derivative markets, the International Swaps and Derivatives Association (ISDA) is the dominant source of such private regulation. This kind of private norm creation by non-state actors may constitute a kind of contemporary *lex mercatoria*.[13]

This is interesting, since the traditional Western rule of law doctrine tends to require democratic legitimacy for the rules at hand, which in turn illustrates the context of a nation state. Democratic legitimacy on its own is not enough, since some sort of substantive acceptability for the legal rules is also a prerequisite for legitimacy. In Finland, one tends to refer to human rights and to legal principles in this context. The substantive acceptability of law is obviously difficult to describe or define, but I think Fuller has succeeded in illustrating its main features by using the fascinating allegory of King Rex, who failed to make law in eight different ways.[14] For example, laws cannot be obscure or require an impossibility. They cannot be changed frequently, since the lack of stability causes many problems. This reference to Fuller is not as novel an idea as it may seem, since Kilpatrick has recently referred to Fuller in her article, which relates to the managerialism connected to the taming of the sovereign debt crisis in the EU.[15] Thus, I think the outcome is that trying to define the rule of law is not merely a waste of time, but instead seems to be an always topical task, which is worth studying from various angles.

III. HOW HAS THE RULE OF LAW BEEN DEFINED BY SOME FINNISH SCHOLARS?

In Finland, Tuori has striven to avoid defining material content for the rule of law concept. He has utilised the term 'rhetorical balloon' in different contexts and, like Frändberg, warned about a conceptual idyll in which the concept of the rule of law contains mutually conflicting principles.[16] This observation assumes significance, for example, by referring to the German Third Reich's 'National Socialist rule of law', in which the concept of the rule of law was given material

[13] A Salonen, 'Kansainvälisen rahoituksen *lex mercatorian* ja sen lähteet Euroopan unionin kontekstissa' (2016) 97 *Defensor Legis* 86.

[14] L Fuller, *The Morality of Law* (New Haven, Yale University Press, 1969) 33–38.

[15] C Kilpatrick, 'On the Rule of Law and Economic Emergency: The Degradation of Basic Legal Values in Europe's Bailouts' (2015) 35(2) *Oxford Journal of Legal Studies* 325, 345–47.

[16] See, for example, Tuori, 'Oikeusvaltiokäsite' (n 6) 49.

and political content in a way that was far from the democratic rule of law ideal.[17] He has also referred to Schmitt, who did not want to include material content in the concept of the rule of law because 'all kinds of propagandists like to rely on it to denounce their opponent as an enemy of the rule of law'.[18]

Tuori has recently presented a definition of the concept of the rule of law in the EU context, in which he emphasises protecting the powers of the Member States, the principle of legality and accountability, ie, the responsibility for and controllability of the exercise of power.[19] By contrast, the democratic rule of law outlined at the time for a nation state context seems to him to be the concept pair that ensures individual legal protection and the substantive validity of law through human and fundamental rights. In the same vein, Paunio has analysed Tuori's conception of the rule of law in her dissertation about legal certainty and has noted the dangers of a 'thicker' or substantive concept of the rule of law. She concludes that the rule of law escapes any precise definition, but it nevertheless forms an umbrella principle under which legal certainty can be posited.[20]

On the other hand, the concept of the rule of law has been presented as also having substantive content by some Finnish scholars. For example, Jyränki has pointed out that human rights that are binding on all activities protect the individual's position and thus belong to the sphere of substantive concept of the rule of law.[21] It is notable that Jyränki does not mention the democratic rule of law at all in this context. Instead, he leads us to the interpretation of the Finnish concept of the rule of law through the Anglo-American concept of the rule of law, which, like the common law legal culture more generally, is characterised by the fact that as many societal conflicts as possible can be converted into a court case and that the law is not perceived primarily as a positive right set by a democratic legislator in a continental European sense.[22] It is thus essential to separate the *Rechtsstaat* discourse intertwined with the German legal culture[23] from the Anglo-American *rule of law* discourse.

[17] See Tuori, *Oikeuden ratio ja voluntas* (n 5) 177–78. Concepts used in constitutional law are time-bound and Tuori has illustrated this aptly by referring to Carl Schmitt's sociology of concepts.

[18] ibid; see also C Schmitt, *Legalität und Legitimität*, 4th edn (Berlin, Duncker & Humblot, 1988) 19. Schmitt was influential in Nazi Germany and presented, for example, an idea of a National Socialist rule of law, which certainly encourages one to interpret the concept of the rule of law in a very formal manner, as Frändberg does, so that it is not distorted by factors contrary to basic and human rights.

[19] See K Tuori, *European Constitutionalism* (Cambridge, Cambridge University Press, 2015) 214, in which the three normative elements are 'protection of Member State powers, the principle of legality and accountability'. For these, see arts 5(2) and 13(2) TEU.

[20] See E Paunio, *Legal Certainty in Multilingual EU Law: Language, Discourse and Reasoning at the European Court of Justice* (Farnham, Ashgate, 2013) 54–56.

[21] See A Jyränki, 'Oikeusvaltio ja demokratia' in A Aarnio and T Uusitupa (eds), *Oikeusvaltio* (Helsinki, Lakimiesliiton kustannus, 2002) 23.

[22] ibid 21–22.

[23] See, eg, K Tuori, 'Four Models of *Rechtsstaat*' in W Krawietz and G Henrik von Wright (eds), *Öffentliche oder Private Moral, Festschift für Ernesto Garzón Valdes* (Berlin,

Jyränki's way of interpreting the rule of law is strengthened by Nieminen, who has defined the modern concept of the rule of law in such a way that it includes both the formal and the substantive side. With the substantive side, she refers above all to the requirement of the realisation of justice. According to her, we seek justice by having state bodies separated from each other, exemplifying the separation of powers, and thus bound to ensure the substantive fundamental rights of citizens.[24]

In addition, one may compare this problem of defining the rule of law to the relatively similar Nordic debate concerning the formal and substantive elements of legal certainty. According to both Aarnio and Peczenik, the expectation of legal certainty contains two important elements: the demands that arbitrariness must be avoided (formal legal certainty) and that the decision must be proper and thus acceptable (substantive legal certainty).[25] On the other hand, there are many legal positivists who would like to emphasise formal legal certainty and fear the inclusion of substantive elements in the concept of legal certainty.[26] For example, it has been argued that substantive elements might obscure the meaning and applicability of the concept.[27] However, even more elaborated conceptions of substantive legal certainty have been presented in Nordic jurisprudence during the last few decades. For example, Gustafsson has presented an idea of social acceptability and moral acceptability in the context of substantive legal certainty, which in turn resembles my idea of formal, factual and substantive legal certainty.[28]

One may then pose the question as to whether the debate on the various elements of the concept of the 'rule of law' or 'legal certainty' does not direct attention to irrelevant issues. For example, Hallberg has studied the rule of law not as a concept, but rather as a kind of development process.[29] He has brought

Duncker & Humbold, 1992) 451; and ML Fernandez Esteban, *The Rule of Law in the European Constitution* (The Hague, Kluwer Law International, 1999) 82. Tuori has divided the development of the *Rechtsstaat* concept into four phases, which Fernandez Esteban describes with the terms 'liberal, formal, substantial and democratic'.

[24] See L Nieminen, *Eurooppalaistuva valtiosääntöoikeus – valtiosääntöistyvä Eurooppa* (Helsinki, Suomalainen lakimiesyhdistys, 2004) 107.

[25] See A Aarnio, *The Rational as Reasonable: A Treatise on Legal Justification* (Dordrecht, D Reidel Publishing Company, 1987) 3; A Peczenik, *On Law and Reason* (Dordrecht, Kluwer Academic Publishers, 1989) 32; and A Peczenik, *Vad är rätt?: Om demokrati, rättssäkerhet, etik och juridisk argumentation* (Stockholm, Nordsteds Juridik, 1995) 97–98. Peczenik has illustrated the importance of substantive legal certainty by referring to the 'Hitler argument'. Accordingly, the laws and decisions against Jews were predictable, but they were not acceptable in the light of generally agreed moral norms.

[26] See, eg, N Jareborg, *Straffrättsideologiska fragment* (Uppsala, Iustus Förlag, 1992) 90; and P Asp, *EG:s Sanktionsrätt. Ett Straffrättsligt Perspektiv* (Uppsala, Iustus Förlag, 1998) 31–37.

[27] See, eg, K Tuori, 'On rättssäkerhet och sociala rättigheter (samt mycket annat)' (2003) 115 *Tidskrift för Rättsvitenskapen* 360.

[28] See H Gustafsson, *Rättens polyvalens: En rättsvetenskaplig studie av sociala rättigheter och rättssäkerhet* (Lund, Media-Tryck, 2002) 1 ff; and Raitio (n 6) 347–87.

[29] See, eg, P Hallberg, *Rule of Law and Sustainable Development* (Tallinn, ROLFI, 2017) 27–33. The interpretation is based on my discussion with Hallberg at the launch of the book *Rule of Law and Sustainable Development* on 25 April 2017 at the University of Helsinki.

new content to the Finnish definition of the concept of the rule of law, which cannot be derived from German legal science in the way in which, for example, the concept of the democratic rule of law can. His dynamic concept of the rule of law can be fleshed out by including the principle of legality, the balanced separation of powers, fundamental and human rights, as well as the rule of law as a functional entity (functionality).[30] He builds his concept of the rule of law by moving from the local level to the international level and from there onwards taking into account regional integration and finally globalisation. In addition, the citizen's viewpoint and along with it the emphasis on fundamental and human rights are characteristics of his wide-ranging concept of the rule of law. He refers to the interaction between public administration and civil society, whereupon a discussion on the functionality of social order and citizens' experiences of the realisation of justice can be included in the rule of law discourse. He does not emphasise the differences between the Anglo-American concept of the rule of law and the German *Rechtsstaat* concept, but rather looks for their shared features to form a kind of a synthesis of the modern principle of the rule of law.[31] He emphasises that one should not adhere to an examination that is too normative when defining the concept of the rule of law, but rather that it is important in the interpretation to take into account the empirical evidence related to the content of the concept of the rule of law.[32]

In Hallberg's interpretation, I think it is essential to emphasise the rule of law's global nature, which becomes apparent especially in contexts concerning the functionality of the rule of law. In the interpretation of modern law, one must take into account the relativised sovereignty of states, which Hallberg describes as a transition from political constitutionalism to economic constitutionalism.[33] As the role of states has changed along with globalisation, it has, according to him, also unavoidably impacted administrative structures and practices of nation states, and the functioning of the judiciary. At the same time, the impact of globalisation also extends to the concept of the rule of law in such a way that it receives substantive content especially through fundamental and human rights.

IV. PROBLEMS IN FINLAND IN RELATION TO THE RULE OF LAW

As stated in section I above, the main emphasis in this chapter is on the lively theoretical debate in Finland as regards the concept of the rule of law and

[30] ibid 6, 57 and 70–90; see also P Hallberg, *Rule of Law: Prospects in Central Asia Rural Areas and Human Problems* (Keuruu, Edita, 2016) 136–45. The capacity of the rule of law to operate is related, eg, to obligations to ensure the realisation of fundamental and human rights and enable citizens to access their rights without unnecessary delay.

[31] See P Hallberg, *The Rule of Law* (Helsinki, Edita, 2004) 5–6 and 11–70. Pekka Hallberg is the former President of the Finnish Supreme Administrative Court.

[32] ibid 41.

[33] ibid 190.

whether it should be understood as a development process. Therefore, in the remainder of the chapter, only a cursory overview of the practical problems and developments in relation to the rule of law in Finland will be offered. The starting point is that the rule of law requires compliance by the state with its obligations in international law and EU law, as well as in national law.[34]

To begin with, it is safe to say that the Finnish judiciary has not opposed the preliminary rulings of the Court of Justice of the European Union (CJEU) in the same way as the Danish Supreme Court has recently done in the (in)famous *Ajos* case.[35] On the contrary, Finland has relied on the EU legal system and the preliminary rulings procedure. For example, it is notable that the Finnish Supreme Administrative Court (Korkein hallinto-oikeus) already applied the doctrine of supremacy of EU law in 1996.[36] Therefore, I do not find it relevant to concentrate on the judiciary, although one could point out that the European Court of Human Rights has on several occasions found Finnish courts to be in violation of the European Convention on Human Rights (ECHR) on the grounds of court proceedings lasting too long.[37] In my opinion, it is also problematic that many judges work only on a temporary basis.

What I think is the most problematic feature of the Finnish legal system from a rule of law perspective is the former government's strict adherence to its political program, giving detailed guidelines for legislation and policy issues. Such a political document is naturally based on compromises between various political parties and its legal status should in any case not supersede the Constitution or human rights. However, sometimes it seems that the politics reflected in the government's programme was given more weight than, for example, human or fundamental rights. For example, Finnish legislation (Law 563/2002) requires that transsexuals must be infertile before they can legally have their legal status as man or woman changed.[38] This is clearly against a recent ruling of the European Court of Human Rights,[39] but nevertheless the former Prime Minister Sipila's

[34] See, eg, Bingham (n 1) 110.

[35] See European Court of Justice (ECJ) Case C-441/14 *Ajos* ECLI:EU:C:2016:278, as well as U Neergaard and KE Sørensen, 'Activist Infighting among Courts and Breakdown of Mutual Trust? The Danish Supreme Court, the CJEU, and the *Ajos* Case' (2017) 36 *Yearbook of European Law* 1; and R Nielsen and C Tvarnø, 'Danish Supreme Court Infringes the EU Treaties by its Ruling in the *Ajos* Case' (2017) 20 *Europarättslig Tidskrift* 303, at 303, in which it has been stated: 'In its judgment in the *Ajos*-case, the Court of Justice of the European Union (CJEU) upheld its findings in *Mangold* and *Kücükdeveci*. The Danish Supreme Court defied the CJEU and did the opposite of what the CJEU had held it was obliged to do.'

[36] See Case KHO 1996 B 577, which was published at 31 December 1996.

[37] See, eg, J Niemi, *Civil Procedure in Finland* (Alphen aan den Rijn, Kluwer Law International, 2010) 18; and *Riihikallio et al v Finland* App No 25072/02 (ECtHR, 31 May 2007) and *Rangdell v Finland* App No 23172/08 (ECtHR, 19 January 2010).

[38] For more details on the legal status of transsexuals in Finland, see, eg, M Rantala, 'Sukupuoleen sopeutetut – intersukupuolisten ja transsukupuolisten henkilöiden oikeusasema Suomessa' (2016) 45 *Oikeus* 8.

[39] See *Garcon et Nicot v France* App Nos 79885/12, 52471/13 and 52596/13 (ECtHR, 6 April 2017).

government did not do anything about this violation of human rights, mainly due on the relatively conservative government's programme. Maybe this minority is so small that it remains politically insignificant, but from a rule of law perspective, the political weight of the minority at hand is not a tenable argument. I think that this example illustrates how the rule of law requires human rights to be interpreted as part of it. This is not a novel idea at all, bearing in mind the European values reflected in Article 2 TEU.[40]

Another issue is how well Finland has complied with its legal obligations based on EU law. This question would require a lengthy study, but for the purposes of this chapter, I would like to give only a few examples, which are often regarded as typically Finnish problems. It is well known that the taxation of motor vehicles[41] and the importation of alcohol[42] in particular have triggered court proceedings in Finland based on non-compliance with EU law. Alcohol seems to be a topical issue, since the Finnish alcohol legislation was altered in 2017 and there has been discussion as to whether the new legislation contains too stringent restrictions as regards ordering alcohol via the internet from another Member State.[43] Perhaps a much more serious example is the Finnish debate as to whether the Finnish healthcare system and regional government reorganisation[44] contain elements of state aid and should be notified to the Commission on the grounds of Article 108(3) of the Treaty on the Functioning of the European Union (TFEU). The Former Finnish government never issued this notification, although the Finnish Supreme Administrative Court had stated that parts of the proposed legislation requires notification.[45] However, the government resigned in March 2019 and the reorganisation plan never became reality.

In order to provide a more nuanced overview of the state of Finnish compliance with EU law, one could also refer to the enforcement actions the Commission has initiated on the grounds of Article 258 TFEU between the years 1995 and 2016.[46] Only 12 enforcement actions led to judgments according to which Finland had breached its obligations. Most of the enforcement actions (30) dealt with the postponed implementation of a directive. Thus, one might conclude that Finland has been able to comply with EU law obligations

[40] See, eg, A Rosas and L Armati, *EU Constitutional Law: An Introduction* (Oxford, Hart Publishing, 2010) 42–43.

[41] See, eg, Case C-101/00 *Siilin* [2002] ECR I-7487; and Case C-10/08 *Commission v. Finland* [2009] ECR I-39.

[42] See, eg, Case C-434/04 *Ahokainen and Leppik* [2006] ECR I-9171; and Case C-198/14 *Visnapuu* [2015] ECLI:EU:C:2015:751.

[43] See Government's proposal 100/2017.

[44] See Government's proposal 16/2018.

[45] See Statement of the Supreme Administrative Court, 13 December 2017, H 567/17. In addition, a recent case Case T-216/15 *Dôvera zdravotná poisťovňa, a.s.*, judgment 5 February 2018, ECLI:EU:T:2018:64) has actually even strengthened the opinion according to which notification is needed.

[46] See the statistics in the report *Åtgärder av Finlands regering I EU-domstolsärenden och I EU-överträdelseärenden* 1 January–31 December 2016, Ministry of Foreign Affairs.

relatively well and, as such, there are no significant problems as regards the rule of law or mutual trust[47] from the EU law perspective in that sense.

V. CONCLUSIONS

The bone of contention in the academic discussion seems to have been for a long time the question of the relationship between democracy and the rule of law. As an illustrative example, one can cite the German legal theorist Radbruch, who stated:

> Though democracy is certainly a praiseworthy value, the *Rechtsstaat* is like a daily bread, the water we drink and the air we breathe; and the greatest merit of democracy is that it alone is adapted to preserve the *Rechtsstaat*.[48]

A little later, Hayek not only referred to this sentence by Radbruch, but also added that democracy will not exist for long unless it preserves the rule of law.[49]

Also in Finland, it is often emphasised that the fields of application for the democracy principle and the principle of the rule of law 'overlap', ie, the fields merge in certain sections.[50] I find that this stance is not as self-evident in the EU Member States as it may seem from the Finnish standpoint. For example, the British rule of law-related problems in the framework of Brexit seem rather distant from the Finnish perspective.[51] It was puzzling that during the court proceedings concerning the UK government's prerogative powers in the context of Brexit, the judges were mocked in a tabloid newspaper as the enemies of the state after they had merely interpreted the unwritten constitution and defended the status of Parliament.[52] Eventually the UK Supreme Court had to confirm that the UK government could not trigger an Article 50 TEU procedure without

[47] On the concept of mutual trust, see K Lenaerts, '*La Vie Après L'Avis*: Exploring the Principle of Mutual (Yet Not Blind) Trust' (2017) 54 *Common Market Law Review* 805.

[48] See G Radbruch, *Rechtsphilosophie* (Stuttgart, KF Köhler, 1950) 357.

[49] See FA Hayek, *The Constitution of Liberty* (London, Routledge & Kegan Paul, 1960) 248.

[50] See A Jyränki, 'Oikeusvaltio ja demokratia' in A Aarnio and T Uusitupa (eds), *Oikeusvaltio* (Helsinki, Lakimiesliiton kustannus, 2002) 24–25.

[51] See, eg, J Raitio and H Raulus, 'The UK EU Referendum and the Move towards Brexit' (2017) 24(1) *Maastricht Journal of European and Comparative Law* 25. The UK government argued forcefully that it had the royal prerogative to trigger art 50 in the EU. The royal prerogative is often used for matters relating to international affairs, but it was questioned whether there were constitutional restraints based on the very core of the concepts of parliamentary sovereignty and even the rule of law. As a consequence, several court proceedings were raised to protect parliamentary involvement.

[52] See *Daily Mail* (4 November 2016). The headline 'Enemies of the People' referred to the three High Court judges who had ruled that the UK government would require the consent of Parliament to give notice of Brexit. The *Daily Mail*'s website also initially described one of the judges as 'openly-gay ex-Olympic fencer', so the judges received extraordinary criticism, which was alarming from the perspective of the independence of the judiciary.

an authorising Act of Parliament, which in a way illustrates the overlapping relationship between the rule of law and parliamentary democracy.[53]

My recommendation for defining the concept of the rule of law starts quite pragmatically from the fact that the EU Member States are obligated to take into account the interpretations that the concept of the rule of law has received within EU law. It is essential that the EU legal concept of the rule of law be interpreted in close contact with the democracy principle and fundamental and human rights.[54] Democracy cannot exist and human rights cannot be respected if the principle of the rule of law is not adhered to;[55] that is, the concept of the rule of law is an inseparable part of the fundamental values the EU is based on.[56] In this regard, one should also refer to a report by the so-called Venice Commission concerning the principle of the rule of law,[57] in which the rule of law is strongly connected to democracy and the demand for the realisation of human rights. Thus, when in the EU the discourse concerning the rule of law cannot be separated from democracy, the separation of powers, and legal principles and human rights that legitimise the legal system and create a context for the observation of the rule of law, we can present a rhetorical question: is the concept of the rule of law a rhetorical balloon after all?

To conclude, I do not consider the kind of thinking according to which the concept of the rule of law is so ambiguous and vague that it has lost its meaning in legal argumentation to be justified. In contemporary legal literature, especially in the field of EU law, one can refer to the 'thick' conception of the rule of law, which contains both formal and substantive elements.[58] This interpretation is tenable in EU law, since there are already indications in the early case law of the CJEU that the concept of the rule of law includes certain substantive prerequisites for legal decision-making.[59] The protection of individual rights in

[53] See the judgment given on 24 January 2017, *R (Miller and Dos Santos) v Secretary of State for exiting the European Union* [2017] UKSC 5.

[54] See art 2 TEU; and, eg, Cases C-402/05 P and C-415/05 P, *Kadi* and *Al Barakaat* [2008] ECR I-6351, para 284.

[55] See, eg, JM Broekman, *The Philosophy of European Union Law* (Leuven, Peeters, 1999) 205.

[56] See Rosas and Armati (n 40) 41–43.

[57] See European Commission for Democracy through Law (Venice Commission), Report on the Rule of Law, Adopted by the Venice Commission at its 86th plenary session, Venice, 25–26 March 2011, Strasbourg, 4 April 2011, Study No 512/2009, CDL-AD(2011)003rev.

[58] See, eg, L Pech, 'Promoting the Rule of Law Abroad: On the EU's Limited Contribution to the Shaping of an International Understanding of the Rule of Law' in D Kochenov and F Amtenbrink (eds), *The European Union's Shaping of the International Legal Order* (Cambridge, Cambridge University Press, 2013) 118: 'EU publications tend to illustrate a "substantive/thick" rather than "formal/thin" understanding of the rule of law.' See also R McCorquodale, 'Defining the International Rule of Law: Defying Gravity?' (2016) 35 *International & Comparative Law Quarterly* 277, 284–85: 'The definition offered in this article of the international rule of law is a "thick" one and includes the following elements or objectives: legal order and stability; equality of application of the law; protection of human rights; and the settlement of disputes before an independent legal body.'

[59] See Case 8/55 *Fédéchar* [1954–56] ECR-245; and cases related to the concept of rule of law concerning EU law's external liability: Case 5/71 *Schöppenstedt* [1971] ECR 975; Case 59/72 *Wünsche Handelsgesellschaft* [1973] ECR-791; Case 20/88 *Roquette frères*, [1989] ECR 1553; Case C-152/88 *Sofrimport* [1990] ECR I-2477; and Case C-282/90 *Vreugdenhill* [1992] ECR I-1937.

particular seems to strengthen the interpretation of the rule of law as a 'thick' concept.[60] One might even pose the question as to whether the contemporary discussion of the thick rule of law is in line with the so-called *Radbruch formula*. Soon after the Second World War, Radbruch stressed that unbearably unjust laws should not be applied at all; for example, if a statute disregards human equality before the law, it should not be applied.[61]

Then again, as a counter-argument, one may ask whether I have been able to describe the Finnish conception of the rule of law at all. To this, my reply is that this chapter is mainly based on my personal conception of the rule of law. I think that it holds true that one cannot avoid personal values and legal theoretical background affecting one's understanding of the rule of law. For example, my references to Radbruch or Fuller may reveal that I am inclined to advocate for the basic tenets of natural law theory.[62] To be more precise, my intention has been to find a balance between legal positivism, legal realism and natural law theories when I stress the substantive elements of both the rule of law and legal certainty.[63] Surely, this kind of emphasis is not shared by all in Finnish academic circles. However, I find it tenable to hold that nowadays in any EU Member State, the 'triangle of democracy, human rights and rule of law' should be the intellectual framework to approach the concept of the rule of law. Therefore, my conclusion would be that the 'thick' concept of the rule of law would be the most balanced interpretation of the rule of law not only in contemporary Finland, but also within the EU.

REFERENCES

Aarnio, A, *The Rational as Reasonable: A Treatise on Legal Justification* (Dordrecht, D Reidel Publishing Company, 1987).

Asp, P, *EG:s Sanktionsrätt. Ett Straffrättsligt Perspektiv* (Uppsala, Iustus Förlag, 1998).

Bingham, T, *The Rule of Law* (London, Allen Lane, 2010).

Broekman, JM, *The Philosophy of European Union Law* (Leuven, Peeters, 1999).

Bugariĉ, B, 'Protecting Democracy inside the EU: On Article 7 TEU and the Hungarian Turn to Authoritarianism' in C Closa and D Kochenov (eds), *Reinforcing Rule of Law Oversights in the European Union* (Cambridge, Cambridge University Press, 2016).

[60] See, eg, A von Bogdandy, C Antpöhler and M Ioannidis, 'Protecting EU Values: Reverse *Solange* and the Rule of Law Framework' in A Jacab and D Kochenov (eds), *The Enforcement of EU Law and Values* (Oxford, Oxford University Press, 2017) 226: 'This general orientation towards a "thick" concept of Rule of Law is in principle reaffirmed in the decision to submit Poland to the Framework, which notes that the Rule of Law is a constitutional principle with both formal and substantive components. Nevertheless, when it comes to the actual reprimands against Polish reforms, priority is accorded to the formal dimension.'

[61] See G Radbruch, 'Gesetzliches Unrecht und übergesetzliches Recht' (1946) 1 *Süddeutsche Juristen-Zeitung* 105.

[62] For more on the natural law philosophy, see, eg, R Siltala, *Law, Truth and Reason: A Treatise on Legal Argumentation* (Dordrecht, Springer, 2011) 201–37.

[63] See Raitio (n 6) 368–76.

Fernandez Esteban, ML, *The Rule of Law in the European Constitution* (The Hague, Kluwer Law International, 1999).

Frändberg, Å, 'Begreppet rättsstat' in F Sterzel, (ed), *Rättsstaten – rätt, politik, moral* (Stockholm, Rättsfonden, 1996).

——. *From Rechtsstaat to Universal Law-State: An Essay in Philosophical Jurisprudence* (Dordrecht, Springer, 2014).

Fuller, L, *The Morality of Law* (New Haven, Yale University Press, 1969).

Gustafsson, H, *Rättens polyvalens: En rättsvetenskaplig studie av sociala rättigheter och rättssäkerhet* (Lund, Media-Tryck, 2002).

Hallberg, P, *The Rule of Law* (Helsinki, Edita, 2004).

——. *Rule of Law: Prospects in Central Asia Rural Areas and Human Problems* (Keuruu, Edita, 2016).

——. *Rule of Law and Sustainable Development* (Tallinn, ROLFI, 2017).

Hayek, FA, *The Constitution of Liberty* (London, Routledge & Kegan Paul, 1960).

Husa, J, 'Nordic Law and Development: See No Evil, Hear No Evil?' (2015) 60 *Scandinavian Studies in Law* 1.

Jareborg, N, *Straffrättsideologiska fragment* (Uppsala, Iustus Förlag, 1992).

Jyränki, A, *Presidentti, Tutkimus valtionpäämiehen asemasta Suomessa v. 1919–1976* (Vammala, Suomalainen lakimiesyhdistys, 1978).

——. 'Oikeusvaltio ja demokratia' in A Aarnio and T Uusitupa (eds), *Oikeusvaltio* (Helsinki, Lakimiesliiton kustannus, 2002).

Kilpatrick, C, 'On the Rule of Law and Economic Emergency: The Degradation of Basic Legal Values in Europe's Bailouts' (2015) 35(2) *Oxford Journal of Legal Studies* 325.

Lenaerts, K, '*La Vie Après L'Avis*: Exploring the Principle of Mutual (Yet Not Blind) Trust' (2017) 54 *Common Market Law Review* 805.

McCorquodale, R, 'Defining the International Rule of Law: Defying Gravity?' (2016) 35 *International & Comparative Law Quarterly* 277.

Neergaard, U and Sørensen, KE, 'Activist Infighting among Courts and Breakdown of Mutual Trust? The Danish Supreme Court, the CJEU, and the *Ajos* Case' (2017) 36 *Yearbook of European Law* 1.

Nielsen, R and Tvarnø, C, 'Danish Supreme Court Infringes the EU Treaties by its Ruling in the *Ajos* Case' (2017) 20 *Europarättslig Tidskrift* 303.

Niemi, J, *Civil Procedure in Finland* (Alphen aan den Rijn, Kluwer Law International, 2010).

Nieminen, L, *Eurooppalaistuva valtiosääntöoikeus – valtiosääntöistyvä Eurooppa* (Helsinki, Suomalainen lakimiesyhdistys, 2004).

Paunio, E, *Legal Certainty in Multilingual EU Law: Language, Discourse and Reasoning at the European Court of Justice* (Farnham, Ashgate, 2013).

Pech, L, 'Promoting the Rule of Law Abroad: On the EU's Limited Contribution to the Shaping of an International Understanding of the Rule of Law' in D Kochenov and F Amtenbrink (eds), *The European Union's Shaping of the International Legal Order* (Cambridge, Cambridge University Press, 2013).

Peczenik, A, *On Law and Reason* (Dordrecht, Kluwer Academic Publishers, 1989).

——. *Vad är rätt?: Om demokrati, rättssäkerhet, etik och juridisk argumentation* (Stockholm, Nordsteds Juridik, 1995).

Radbruch, G, 'Gesetzliches Unrecht und übergesetzliches Recht' (1946) 1 *Süddeutsche Juristen-Zeitung* 105.

——. *Rechtsphilosophie* (Stuttgart, KF Köhler, 1950).
Raitio, J, *The Principle of Legal Certainty in EC Law* (Dordrecht, Kluwer Academic Publishers, 2003).
Raitio, J and Raulus, H, 'The UK EU Referendum and the Move towards Brexit' (2017) 24(1) *Maastricht Journal of European and Comparative Law* 25.
Rantala, M, 'Sukupuoleen sopeutetut – intersukupuolisten ja transsukupuolisten henkilöiden oikeusasema Suomessa' (2016) 45 *Oikeus* 8.
Raz, J, *The Authority of Law: Essays on Law and Morality* (Oxford, Clarendon Press, 1979).
Rosas, A and Armati, L, *EU Constitutional Law: An Introduction* (Oxford, Hart Publishing, 2010).
Sájo, A, 'Rule by Law in East Central Europe' in V Gessner, A Hoeland and C Varga (eds), *European Legal Cultures* (Darthmouth, Aldershot, 1996).
Salonen, A, 'Kansainvälisen rahoituksen *lex mercatorian* ja sen lähteet Euroopan unionin kontekstissa' (2016) 97 *Defensor Legis* 86.
Schmitt, C, *Legalität und Legitimität*, 4th edn (Berlin, Duncker & Humblot, 1988).
Siltala, R, *Law, Truth and Reason: A Treatise on Legal Argumentation* (Dordrecht, Springer, 2011).
Tuori, K, 'Four Models of *Rechtsstaat*' in W Krawietz and GH von Wright (eds), *Öffentliche oder Private Moral, Festschift für Ernesto Garzón Valdes* (Berlin, Duncker & Humbold, 1992).
——.'Oikeusvaltiokäsite – vielä kerran' in *Foucault'n oikeus, Kirjoituksia oikeudesta ja sen tutkimisesta* (Vantaa, WSOY, 2002).
——. 'On rättssäkerhet och sociala rättigheter (samt mycket annat)' (2003) 115 *Tidskrift för Rättsvitenskapen* 360.
——. *Oikeuden ratio ja voluntas* (Helsinki, WSOYpro, 2007).
——. *Ratio and Voluntas: The Tension between Reason and Will in Law* (Farnham, Ashgate, 2011).
——. *European Constitutionalism* (Cambridge, Cambridge University Press, 2015).
Von Bogdandy, A, Antpöhler, C and Ioannidis, M, 'Protecting EU Values: Reverse *Solange* and the Rule of Law Framework' in A Jakab and D Kochenov (eds), *The Enforcement of EU Law and Values* (Oxford, Oxford University Press, 2017).

9

Institutional Alcoholism in Post-socialist Countries and the Cultural Elements of the Rule of Law

The Example of Hungary

ANDRÁS JAKAB

INSTITUTIONS ARE MADE up of the interplay of three components: (1) formal rules; (2) actual practices; and (3) narratives. However, lawyers in post-socialist countries do not see law through institutionalist lenses, but often nurture a false and simplistic idea of the law; they consider it to be the sum of rules, often disregarding the actual practices of the rules' addressees and narratives attached to the law (encompassing everything from the raison d'etre and goal of the institution to its symbolism, the public discourse surrounding it and social attitudes towards the institution). This restricted view makes Hungarian lawyers blind and to a certain extent also defenceless against recent authoritarian tendencies. Institution-building has been a moderately successful feat in Hungary. To put it more pessimistically, it has partially failed since the end of socialism, in particular when it comes to actual practices and narratives. In the Hungarian context, consideration of the problems of institution-building suggests two general conclusions: on the one hand, the lack of unison among the individual elements (rules, practices and narratives) renders institutions less stable and consequently less capable of inducing compliance with the law; on the other hand, the institutions that have been established have failed to deliver prosperity to the political community. This chapter describes the constitution-making of 2010/11 from the perspective of institution-building. This institutionalist view of the law yields two main specific findings: (1) historical experience shows that besides honest determination, the radical institutional overhaul of a complete legal system can only be successful in the presence of external pressure, the effect of which has unfortunately decreased with Hungary's accession to the EU – in other words, institution-building should go hand in hand with effective international and EU obligations undertaken in more sober political moments to guarantee that the political community will not enter into a self-destructive mode later; and (2) taking elements beyond mere rules more consciously into account, such as actual practices and narratives in the realm of legislation, the application of the law and legal training would ideally result in the gradual reinforcement of substantive cultural elements. This, however, requires political action – more precisely the adjustment of formal rules. Since this is not in the interests of the incumbent decision-makers, overcoming the impasse seems unlikely for the time being.

I. INTRODUCTION

Hungarian legal thinking suffers from a special disease, which, for lack of a better term, I will refer to as rule-fixation.[1] This means that the vast majority of legal scholars, practising lawyers and the public at large in Hungary perceive law as a mere jumble of rules, or perhaps a system of rules; in other words, they completely ignore *actual practices*. By this I do not necessarily mean the interpretative judicial practice, although on occasions this is also disregarded; rather, I am referring to the actual practices of the rules' addressees, as well as the *narratives* underpinning these rules, broadly comprising everything from the raison d'etre and goal of the institution to its symbolism, the public discourse surrounding it and social attitudes towards the institution.[2] Rule-fixation as criticised in this chapter therefore does not refer to absolute compliance with

[1] This chapter is based on A Jakab, 'Miért nem működik jól a magyar jogrend és hogyan javíthatjuk meg?' (2018) 1 *MTA Law Working Papers*, https://jog.tk.mta.hu/uploads/files/2018_01_Jakab.pdf; A Jakab and G Gajduschek (eds), *A magyar jogrendszer állapota* (Budapest, MTA TK, 2016); and A Jakab and L Urbán (eds), *Hegymenet. Társadalmi és politikai kihívások Magyarországon* (Budapest, Osiris, 2017). For their valuable suggestions and critical comments, I am indebted to Krisztina Arató, Majtényi Balázs, Zoltán Balázs, Mátyás Bencze, Péter Béndek, Botond Bitskey, Zsolt Boda, Eszter Bodnár, Kriszta Bodnár, András Bozóki, Petra Burai, Nóra Chronowski, László Csaba, György Csepeli, Lóránt Csink, Balázs Fekete, János Fiala-Butora, Nóra Forgács, Csaba Földvári, Johanna Fröhlich, György Gajduschek, Fruzsina Gárdos-Orosz, Dóra Győrffy, Csaba Győry, Tamás Győrfi, János Gyurgyák, Iván Halász, Tamás Hoffmann, Attila Horváth, János Jany, Béla Janky, Erzsébet Kadlót, Klára Katona, András Körösényi, Zsolt Körtvélyesi, Sebastian Krempelmeier, Herbert Küpper, Róbert László, John Morijn, Krisztián Orbán, András László Pap, András Schiffer, Balázs Schanda, Valerie Schwarzer, István Somogyvári, Pál Sonnevend, László Sólyom, Miklós Szabó, Ákos Szalai, Zoltán Szente, Péter Takács, Csaba Tordai, István György Tóth, Péter Tölgyessy, Bernát Török, Krisztián Ungváry, Balázs Váradi, Benedek Varsányi and Attila Vincze, as well as the participants of the workshop organised at the MTA TK Institute of Legal Science on 26 October 2017, the Stockholm conference of the Swedish Network for European Legal Studies held on 17 November 2017, the workshop of the ELTE TáTK Sociology Doctoral School organised on 4 December 2017 and the joint workshop of Yale Law School and the European University Institute held in Florence on 10–11 January 2018. I am thankful to Kriszta Bodnár for her careful editing, and to Petra Lea Láncos and Lisa Giles for their linguistic help.

[2] Narratives in the sense used here also include unwritten rules of legal interpretation; see, eg, J Bell, 'The Importance of Institutions' in M Adams and D Heirbaut (eds), *The Method and Culture of Comparative Law* (Oxford, Hart Publishing, 2015) 211.

the law (in fact, what happens is very often quite the opposite), but rather a *conscious blindness* towards the actual practices and narratives affecting the operation of the legal order. By abandoning the rule-fixation perspective and giving consideration to the consequences of this approach, the situation can be seen more clearly (an accomplishment in its own right), and in the medium term, this may also strongly promote a willingness to comply with the law.

Of course, the current problems present in the Hungarian legal system are not primarily caused by rule-fixation. They are in fact partly a result of general cultural problems (of which rule-fixation is only a small part, which is characteristic of lawyers) and partly a result of the concrete individual or collective decisions taken by politicians; I will come back to this point later in more detail. However, blindness to these problems and the ensuing intellectual defencelessness of lawyers may largely be explained through the phenomenon of rule-fixation.

I will elaborate on this below, discussing the institutional nature of the law, focusing on the informal elements of institution-building and then taking the problems of the 2010/11 constitution-making as an example. Finally, I make some proposals for a possible way out of this impasse.

II. INFORMAL INSTITUTIONAL ELEMENTS: PRACTICES AND NARRATIVES

There are various definitions for the concept of 'institution'. For the purposes of the present inquiry, the most suitable definition describes institutions as consisting of three components or, more precisely, an interplay of these components: (1) formal rules; (2) actual practices; and (3) narratives.[3] The latter two are referred to jointly as 'informal' components when juxtaposed with 'formal' rules. Such informal elements may operate (unwritten) institutions, which may prove to be even more powerful than formal institutions. A typical example would be institutionalised corruption. While the different components may mutually reinforce one another, producing resilient institutions, in the case of discrepancy between formal and informal elements, they may actually weaken each other, leading to weak institutions. Since informal elements are slower to change (this phenomenon is often referred to as a typical example of *path dependence*), significant changes to formal elements – for example, in connection with a regime change – will in all likelihood result in the weakening of institutions.[4] Such weakening will generally exacerbate uncertainty and

[3] V Lowndes and M Roberts, *Why Institutions Matter: The New Institutionalism in Political Science* (Basingstoke, Palgrave Macmillan, 2013) 46, 77: 'power is exercised through regulation, practice and storytelling'. Thus, by 'institution', we do not mean the mere sum of different legal rules about a social issue, but emphatically more than that.

[4] P Sztompka, *The Sociology of Social Change* (Oxford, Blackwell, 1993); P Sztompka, *Trust: A Sociological Theory* (Cambridge, Cambridge University Press, 1999); J Elster, C Offe and UK

unpredictability, inducing short-term thinking and rule evasion.[5] Institution-building is particularly difficult in societies marked by strong value divisions, for narratives are already fraught by contradictions and will resist new formal rules more than in societies boasting a more homogeneous value order.[6] Discussing how divided societies produce weak constitutional institutions and what the resulting consequences are, Daren Acemoglu writes the following (he speaks of division along ethnic lines, but his observations may be generalised, vividly portraying ideological opposition between social groups defined by twentieth-century history, like the case of the Hungarian left-wing and right-wing elites):

> [W]hen [constitutional] institutions are strong, citizens have the power to punish politicians by voting them out of power; when institutions are weak, politicians pursue clientelistic policies that punish citizens who fail to support them … many disastrous kleptocracies last for long periods; Mobutu ruled for thirty-two years, Trujillo for thirty-one, and the Somozas for forty-two years. This longevity is made even more surprising by the fact that many kleptocratic regimes lack both a core constituency of supporters and a firm command of the military … owing to the absence of strong [constitutional] institutions, rulers can deploy strategies, in particular 'divide-and-rule' to defuse opposition to their regime. The logic of the divide-and-rule strategy is to enable a ruler to bribe politically pivotal groups off the equilibrium path, ensuring that he can remain in power against challenges. By providing selective incentives and punishments, the divide-and-rule strategy exploits the fragility of social cooperation in weakly-institutionalised polities: when faced with the threat of being ousted, the kleptocratic ruler intensifies the collective action problem and destroys the coalition against him by bribing the pivotal [social] groups … Ethnic divisions are the key feature in [this] model. Each ethnic group is afraid of replacing their own leader when in power, because this increases the probability of a switch of power from their own ethnic group to a rival group. This makes the standard method of controlling political elites … ineffective, and enables leaders to not only exploit other ethnic groups but also their own ethnic group.[7]

Both the entire legal system and its individual elements (eg, constitutional jurisdiction or property) may be conceptualised as institutions. These institutions do not exist in isolation, but instead reinforce, complement or even weaken each

Preuss, *Institutional Design in Post-Communist Societies: Rebuilding the Ship at Sea* (Cambridge, Cambridge University Press, 1998).

[5] For more details and examples, see D Győrffy, *Trust and Crisis Management in the European Union: An Institutionalist Account of Success and Failure in Program Countries* (Basingstoke, Palgrave Macmillan, 2018).

[6] E Ostrom, *Understanding Institutional Diversity* (Princeton, Princeton University Press, 2005) 27.

[7] D Acemoglu, 'Constitutions, Politics and Economics: A Review Essay on Persson and Tabellini's *The Economic Effects of Constitutions*' (2005) 43 *Journal of Economic Literature* 1025, 1046. Even in societies which have strong institutions, strong ideological divides can have distructive effects (see the example of the US); GC Layman, TM Carsey and J Menasce Horowitz, 'Party Polarization in American Politics: Characteristics, Causes, and Consequences' (2006) 9 *Annual Review of Political Science* 83.

other ('institutional environment').[8] An institution will be considered 'strong' when it is capable of efficiently influencing human behaviour in a permanent and predictable manner. While this, on its own, is not a sufficient condition for the state's (economic) success, strong institutions bolstering the rule of law and democracy (both referred to here as constitutional institutions) will significantly contribute to economic success.[9]

From an institutionalist perspective, the constitution is not merely a sum of constitutional rules, but also the actual practice of constitutional bodies and narratives surrounding the constitution (the latter can be, for example, that the 'purpose of the constitution is to restrict the power of the state' or that 'the purpose of the constitution is to guarantee human rights').[10] It is typical for lawyers around the world to focus primarily on the first, formal element of institutions – the rules – yet it is a Hungarian or rather post-socialist trait to consider it a virtue to proudly ignore the other elements (for reasons explained in detail below in section III.C). The failures of institution-building in Hungary experienced in the past three decades shed light on the downsides of this approach.[11] This may also be discerned in Hungarian legal training,

[8] E Ostrom, 'An Agenda for the Study of Institutions' (1986) 1 *Public Choice* 3, 7–8; G Helmke and S Levitsky, 'Informal Institutions and Comparative Politics: A Research Agenda' (2004) 2 *Perspectives on Politics* 725.

[9] This chapter does not deal in detail with theories of democracy. By 'democracy' we simply mean here the possibility of making elected officials responsible for not promoting the citizens' interests (by not re-electing them, ie, by making them compete on the basis of who could promote the citizens' interests best). Governments could be forced by their electorate to change measures that are harmful to their interests (trial and error). This eventually also made these communities economically stronger, which was necessary for successfully fighting international conflicts. Empirical studies have confirmed that (except for extremely poor countries) democracy makes economic growth more likely (all other factors being equal). The idea of equal freedom itself also has economic implications, as it helps competition. Non-discrimination means that the most capable should do the job and that only his or her individual achievements count. Protection of private property is necessary for capitalist economic growth. Protection of privacy and freedom of thought contribute to a fearless and creative working environment. Political freedoms ensure democracy, so their economic impact is relatively indirect. For a deep analysis of these questions with further references, see RC Cooter, *The Strategic Constitution* (Princeton, Princeton University Press, 2000); SA Koob et al, *Human Rights and Economic Growth* (Copenhagen, Danish Institute of Human Rights, 2017).

[10] The so-called institutionalist legal theories (Savigny, Santi Romano, Hauriou, Schmitt, Weinberger and MacCormick) show a very diverse picture, partly criticising each other as well. These use a terminology different from the one of the present chapter in order to describe the nature of law. For more details, see M La Torre, *Law as Institution* (Dordrecht, Springer, 2010) 98–121. A typical tenet in many of these theories is that besides the concepts of positive law, there are also metaphysical 'institutions' (eg, marriage) that are realised through positive law (this tenet has no necessary connection to our considerations in the present chapter). For more details and criticism, see B Rüthers, *Institutionelles Rechtsdenken im Wandel der Verfassungsepochen* (Berlin, Gehlen, 1970) 33–37. As the focus of this chapter is not the history of legal theories, but the current Hungarian situation, I am not going to critically analyse these legal theories. The concept of institution that is used here does not stem from any of these institutionalist legal theories (and it is also not a doctrinal concept), but rather from political science.

[11] For these phenomena in Hungarian parliamentary law see, eg, P Smuk, 'Az Országgyűlés' in Jakab and Gajduschek (n 1) 617: 'In several cases, we cannot blame the respective rules of the Standing Rules, but the [lack of] democratic and constitutional culture of the actors responsible for

where legal education is confined to reciting existing legislation or reproducing legal-doctrinal constructs.[12] The same goes for the realm of legislation, where narratives ('what is the true purpose and the public policy aim of legislation?') are largely neglected, and ex ante and ex post impact studies on actual practices are not carried out, thereby reducing the task of legislation to the adoption of a formal act.[13] In György Gajduschek's words:

> [T]he specification of public policy goals [in our terminology, legislative narratives] is almost completely missing, questioning the rationality of the whole process. The way these tools are employed – which are almost exclusively of legalistic nature, or are considered as such – is ill-conceived. The shortcomings of implementation are particularly striking. With no planning or allocation of necessary resources, implementation is doomed to fail already from the outset. Public policies change so rapidly and to such a great degree, often taking a complete U-turn, that they have no time to 'run their course'. At times the system for implementing the policy has not even been set up and is already subject to change, but in general, there is hardly ever enough time for the impact and results of policies to take effect.[14]

Institution-building is a more complex process than envisaged by the majority of lawyers (this is true everywhere, but especially in post-socialist countries). Lawyers will generally concentrate on formal elements (ie, written rules and perhaps the relevant implementing acts) which, however essential, are not sufficient to ensure the successful operation of legal institutions. The failure of numerous well-crafted constitutions may be explained by the naivety of the legal profession.[15] At the same time, it is also true that unsophisticated constitutions may be successful if the right social practices and narratives replace and correct faulty formal rules. Until recently, the constitutions of the US[16] and the UK[17] were good examples of systems where patchy formal

running the legal institutions.' For post-Soviet failures, see DJ Galligan and M Kurkchiyan (eds), *Law and Informal Practices: The Post-communist Experience* (Oxford, Oxford University Press, 2003).

[12] A Jakab, 'A magyar jogi oktatás megújításához szükséges lépések: Reformjavaslat összehasonlító áttekintésre alapozva' (2010) 4 *Magyar Jog* 204.

[13] G Gajduschek, 'Előkészítetlenség és utólagos hatásvizsgálat hiánya' in Jakab and Gajduschek (n 1) 796–822.

[14] G Gajduschek, 'A közpolitikai célok megjelenése a jogban' in Jakab and Gajduschek (n 1) 43.

[15] In certain situations, institution-building is an impossible mission. See, eg, the Transitional Constitution of the Republic of South Sudan (2011), which was a well-crafted text that also tried to consider the local social reality, but which due to the civil war environment sadly failed. Despite the Constitution containing smart formal rules, South Sudan is a typical example of what we would call a failed state. For more details, see T Marauhn and H Elliesie (eds), *Legal Transformation in Northern Africa and South Sudan* (The Hague, Eleven International Publishing, 2015).

[16] The US Constitution is a very imperfect legal document, containing plenty of contradictions and loopholes; for more details, see WN Eskridge and S Levinson (eds), *Constitutional Stupidities, Constitutional Tragedies* (New York, New York University Press, 1998).

[17] In the UK, some of the informal components of constitutional institutions are called 'consitutional conventions'; see A Jakab, *European Constitutional Language* (Cambridge, Cambridge University Press, 2016) 78, 147, 200–01, with further references.

rules are supplemented by informal institutional elements. Since these institutions have multiple components, they more often than not depart from the ideals envisioned by the makers of the formal rules (in other words, due to this complexity, legislation often takes recourse to the method of *trial-and-error*), and they therefore cannot actually be precisely traced back to the will of a single policy-designer, but instead combine several, in part contradictory visions.[18] While this is bad news for the incumbent constitutional founding fathers at the time that policy is conceived, they may later deny responsibility, and rightly so, in the event that the constitution fails.

Institutions are systems of different manmade, non-physical factors that 'generate regularities of behaviour'.[19] From among these, some (indeed, perhaps even the majority) are unwritten and presupposed, stemming from narratives about actual practices – for example, when playing chess, one shall not punch one's opponent, pour boiling soup on his chess pieces, spit on the clock etc. A formal description of possible chess moves is not enough to thoroughly know the game as there is much more involved. We must adhere to certain civilisational customs, which make the game even possible. This involves not only intellectual but also moral – or, to use a less emotionally charged concept, cultural – knowledge. Poorly designed formal rules may of course result in weak institutions, but – and this seems to be more relevant here – officials' cultural shortcomings may contribute just as much. A republic without republicans or a bureaucracy without (Weberian) bureaucrats is simply not going to measure up.

Cultural traits are slow to change and there are no 'amendment procedures' available.[20] There are, however, some successful examples that are worth noting: namely, institutions are capable of gradually shaping culture.[21] Perhaps the most widely known example is the cultural transformation that took place

[18] RE Goodin, 'Institutions and Their Design' in RE Goodin (ed), *The Theory of Institutional Design* (Cambridge, Cambridge University Press, 1996) 28.

[19] A Greif, *Institutions and the Path to the Modern Economy: Lessons from Medieval Trade* (Cambridge, Cambridge University Press, 2006). For a somewhat different terminology (institutions as a combination of formal and informal rules), though with a similar content, see DC North, *Institutions, Institutional Change and Economic Performance* (Cambridge, Cambridge University Press, 1990) 3. It would be possible to introduce a fourth component of institutions between formal rules and actual practices: informal (unwritten) rules. This would definitely be more precise, but for the actual points that I would like to make in this chapter, it did not seem necessary and, at the same time, it would have considerably complicated the explanations. Therefore, for the sake of simplicity, this conceptual component has not been introduced here.

[20] On the difficulties of the Hungarian situation from this perspective, see IG Tóth, 'Turánbánya? Értékválasztások, beidegződések és az illiberalizmusra való fogadókészség Magyarországon' in Jakab and Urbán (n 1) 37–50.

[21] JG March and JP Olsen, *Rediscovering Institutions* (New York, Free Press, 1989) 17. 'Not only are institutions man-made, but also men institution-made'; see C Offe, 'Designing Institutions in East European Transitions' in Goodin (ed) (n 18) 208.

in Germany following the Second World War, a success story bolstered by the following elements (without providing an exhaustive list):

(1) German legal scholarship, traditionally of a high standard, contributed greatly to the creation of well-designed formal legal rules. Although this was not a decisive factor (it is possible to design excellent constitutional systems built on the rule of law upon a relatively weak legal scholarship background, as evidenced by the example of the Scandinavian states), this intellectual matrix certainly helped to build the *Rechtsstaat*.

(2) Instead of indulging in self-pity, Germans confronted – albeit with a considerable delay, from the 1960s onwards – their mistakes and sins (*Vergangenheitsbewältigung*). Of course, populists and demagogues are always quick to offer simplistic narratives, serving up excuses instead of the painful truth. However, after the Second World War (somewhat belatedly, also facilitated by the ageing of the previous generation, but nevertheless), both the West German elite and society at large chose honesty. This moral stance towards the past helped forge a *credible* narrative for the legal order (and, in particular, the *Grundgesetz*), for the new regime built on human dignity, democracy and the rule of law.[22] The honesty and credibility of the social and political order further increased – as a self-reinforcing process – the social trust that was essential for success. Although facing the past in this way is not an indispensable condition for successful constitutional institution-building, it certainly helps to achieve it.

(3) External pressure and, to a considerable degree, military occupation of the country made a backlash to authoritarianism impossible (although, admittedly, on its own this would not have been enough). While erstwhile Nazi views were not eradicated – in fact, some former Nazis kept their high offices and helped each other as a network (a notorious example would be the West German Ministry of Foreign Affairs until as late as the 1970s, or certain university faculties of law) – new political values became unquestionable in public debates; that is, there was no public counter-narrative rejecting the rule of law and democracy. Germans were afraid of themselves or their dark side and consciously undertook international obligations (while also trying to pacify other Western European nations with their eagerness to comply). European integration – including the conception of the European Court of Human Rights – may partly be explained by this very conscious German approach. Taking their cue from Ulysses, who tied himself to the mast for fear he should yield to the temptation of the Sirens, the Germans set to work on building supranational European institutions with great fervour.

[22] For a discussion of the role of moral legitimacy in making legal systems more efficient (as shown by the example of the Hungarian legal system), see B Zsolt, 'Bizalom, legitimitás és jogkövetés' in Jakab and Gajduschek (n 1) 837–55.

(4) Economic success, that is, the output greatly contributed to legitimising these values as well as their internalisation by society (economic success was of course not unrelated to the democratic and rule of law institutions enshrined in formal rules). Daron Acemoglu (cited above) has already written extensively about this in his bestselling book *Why Nations Fail*.[23]

(5) There was a *consensus* among the German elite to adhere to democracy and the rule of law. Indeed, without the self-restricting consensus of the elite, liberal democracies will be dysfunctional.[24] This consensus was underpinned by the physical extinction of former opposing elites (including the partial exclusion of Nazis from public life), American pressure, fear of the Soviet Union and the taste of economic success.

When looking at examples of successful constitutional institution-building from the recent past, it is clear that some form of external pressure played a part in this success.[25] In some cases, such as Austria and Japan, this took the form of direct military pressure, while in others, it was the fear of possible foreign occupation that changed the mindset of local elites (and pushed them towards a consensus), as in the case of Estonia, which had its well-founded fear of the Russians to thank for its success story that began in the 1990s.[26] One should consider corrupt and authoritarian practices and narratives as being similar to alcoholism; in theory, it is possible for the patient to cure himself or herself, but normally complete recovery requires not only the will to get better, but also external support.[27] Moreover, once the patient seems to have recovered, he or

[23] D Acemoglu and J Robinson, *Why Nations Fail: The Origins of Power, Prosperity and Poverty* (New York, Random House, 2012). For a methodologically more sophisticated analysis with similar results, see R Rigobon and D Rodrik, 'Rule of Law, Democracy, Openness, and Income: Estimating Interrelationships' (2004) *National Bureau of Economic Research (NBER)* 2: 'democracy and the rule of law are both good for economic performance, but the latter has a much stronger impact on incomes. Openness (trade/GDP) has a negative impact on income levels and democracy, but a positive effect on rule of law. Higher income produces greater openness and better institutions, but these effects are not very strong. Rule of law and democracy tend to be mutually reinforcing'. On the effect of liberal democracies in helping economic growth, see, eg, M Yanovskiy and T Ginker, 'A Proposal for a More Objective Measure of De Facto Constitutional Constraints' (2017) 28 *Constitutional Political Economy* 311.

[24] J Higley and M Burton, *Elite Foundations of Liberal Democracy* (Oxford, Rowman & Littlefield, 2006).

[25] M J Gorges, 'New Institutionalist Explanations for Institutional Change: A Note of Caution' (2001) 21 *Politics* 137.

[26] However, this also had the negative consequence of excluding the local Russian population from Estonian democracy. See, with reference to the ethnic background of the local communist elite before 1990, D Bohle and B Greskovits, *Capitalist Diversity on Europe's Periphery* (Ithaca, Cornell University Press, 2012) 99. The relatively good performance of the Baltic states (as compared to other post-Soviet states) can partly be explained by the consensus of the local elite; see M Mendelski, 'The EU's Rule of Law Promotion in Post-Soviet Europe: What Explains the Divergence between Baltic States and EaP Countries?' (2016) 7 *Eastern Journal of European Studies* 111.

[27] On the necessity of international pressure in order to successfully clamp down on institutionalised corruption, see, eg, A Mungiu-Pippidi, 'Corruption: Diagnosis and Treatment' (2006) 17 *Journal of Democracy* 86. For the metaphor of alcoholism in a narrower context ('fiscal alcoholism'),

she still needs supervision so as not to regress. This is exactly what is happening in several former socialist countries, which, after having joined the EU, are no longer subject to the strict and continuous supervision ('pre-accession conditionality') that they experienced before accession, with the result that they no longer feel like they need to adhere to the civilisational norms of Western liberal democracies.[28]

A successful learning process takes considerable time, the consistent control of requirements and also a positive affirmation (experiences of economic and moral success); however, in the case of Hungary (and most other socialist countries), these (or, in fact, any of these) were not given. To put it another way: the scaffolding was dismantled too early and the half-ready institutions of the rule of law partially collapsed in several post-socialist countries. This is clearly shown by the different rule of law indices (Bertelsmann, the World Justice Project, Freedom House), which all indicate a slow erosion in former socialist countries since their accession to the EU. While this is most apparent in the case of Hungary, Croatia and Poland, it is discernible in other states as well.[29] A Western-style legal order can only function successfully in the long run if those operating the system also internalise these Western values. Such cultural conditions may be established, but only *painstakingly* slowly, and the mere adoption of new laws will, in itself, most certainly not suffice. When the internalisation of such values does not take place and the citizens do not feel invested in the new system, meaning they have nothing to win by it, then as soon as the external pressure lapses, the (pre-rule of law and pre-democratic) pagan reflexes resurface and the mask falls: first, on the level of narratives (rhetoric) and practice, with the destruction of formal institutions following soon after.[30]

Romania is a positive counter-example in this respect: here, the institutions or certain aspects of the rule of law became stronger following EU accession (although this strengthening is minimal, taking into consideration the general decline in the region, it is still relatively significant). However, this improvement is not down to the sudden enlightenment of the Romanian elite or their lesser affinity for corruption, but much rather to the fact that the accession treaty

see G Kopits, 'Saving Hungary's Finances: Budapest's Four-Step Plan for Fiscal Alcoholics' (2008) *Wall Street Journal Europe*, 4 December.

[28] On the deficiencies of EU enforcement mechanisms, see A Jakab and D Kochenov (eds), *The Enforcement of EU Law and Values* (Oxford, Oxford University Press, 2017).

[29] For similar considerations, see J Dawson and S Hanley, 'What's Wrong with East-Central Europe? The Fading Mirage of the "Liberal Consensus"' (2016) 27 *Journal of Democracy* 20. On the erosion of Slovenian constitutionalism (explaining it with inherited cultural deficiencies and hoping for external, mainly EU, help), see M Avbelj, 'The Sociology of (Slovenian) Constitutional Democracy' (2017) 10 *The Hague Journal on the Rule of Law* 1. For a general overview, see M Brusis, *Illiberale Drift und Proliferation – BTI-Regionalbericht Ostmittel- und Südosteuropa* (Gütersloh, Bertelsmann, 2018).

[30] *cf* T Snyder, *On Tyranny: Twenty Lessons from the Twentieth Century* (New York, Duggan Books, 2017) 32: 'The symbols of today enable the reality of tomorrow.'

of Romania includes a clause concerning the period following accession.[31] Namely, it introduces a so-called 'cooperation and verification mechanism', which basically means that Romania will be evaluated annually based on a set of predefined criteria and should Romania fail to take the necessary measures against corruption, the Commission will adopt 'appropriate measures'. While the specific substance of such measures (eg, cancelling payments) has not been determined and, indeed, such measures have never been applied, it is actually not the possibility of formal sanctions that has rendered this mechanism so effective, but the informal tying of entry into the Schengen zone by certain Western states to the results reflected in the annual reports and the high prestige of the EU – and consequently of these annual reports – in the eyes of the Romanian public.[32] Annual reports are a point of reference in Romanian public discourse, and their content and recommendations carry significant weight. For example, when the Romanian elite sought to relax corruption rules in February 2017, mass demonstrations erupted. Perhaps even more important for abandoning the amendment (although it was less spectacular and received less coverage in the media) was a formal condemnation of the planned amendment by the European Commission, which expressly referred to the cooperation and verification mechanism.[33]

III. THE 2010/11 HUNGARIAN CONSTITUTION-MAKING FROM THE PERSPECTIVE OF INSTITUTION-BUILDING

In light of the above, it is worth considering how the constitutional changes of the past few years in Hungary may be evaluated from the point of view of institution-building. To what extent do these three components reinforce one another, ie, do formal rules, actual practices and narratives result in stable (resilient, persistent) and strong (capable of determining human behaviour)

[31] R Carp, 'The Struggle for the Rule of Law in Romania as an EU Member State: The Role of the Cooperation and Verification Mechanism' (2014) 10 *Utrecht Law Review* 1.

[32] This mechanism also applies to Bulgaria (according to its EU accession treaty), but because of the unfortunate developments in Bulgarian domestic politics, it seems less effective. There is no guarantee that the Romanian improvement will persist, the attempts to curb anti-corruption measures continue – the improvement has been the result of a lucky *constellation* of Romanian domestic politics (power balance, personal relationships and mass protests) and external pressure from the EU. For more details, see I Iusmen, 'EU Leverage and Democratic Backsliding in Central and Eastern Europe: The Case of Romania' (2015) 53 *Journal of Common Market Studies* 593; U Sedelmeier, 'Anchoring Democracy from Above? The European Union and Democratic Backsliding in Hungary and Romania after Accession' (2014) 52 *Journal of Common Market Studies* 105; U Sedelmeier and C Lacatus, 'Compliance with the European Union's Anti-corruption Conditions in the 'Cooperation and Verification Mechanism: Why is Romania Better than Bulgaria?' (2016) 28 *MAXCAP Working Papers*.

[33] Joint Statement of President Juncker and First Vice-President Timmermans on the fight against corruption in Romania, 1 February 2017, www.europa.eu/rapid/press-release_STATEMENT-17-195_en.htm.

institution(s) or do they much rather weaken each other owing to their irreconcilability? Do the new institutional characteristics actually improve predictability, prompting long-term thinking and abidance by the law? And if they do, does this lead to prosperity for the nation on a societal level? I will elaborate on this issue in detail below, but to summarise the answer here: sadly, it does not. Unfortunately, the constitution-making of 2010/11 may be considered a failure for two reasons: (a) due to the lack of consistency between the individual elements (rules, practices and narratives), the institutions are less stable, making them less capable of promoting law abidance; and (b) the institutions ultimately established are less suitable for contributing to the prosperity of the political community.

A. The Formal Text: Relatively Few Changes, Partly Improving, Partly Worsening the Text

Compared with the large amount of institutional changes, the changes made to formal rules were relatively minor, with a new Fundamental Law basically following the regulatory system and text of the previous Constitution[34] with some codification upgrades, also including a few positive substantive changes, such as the provision on the debt break. Perhaps the decision-makers realised that it would be too risky for them to start experimenting, so they abandoned regulatory ideas to introduce a semi-presidential or bicameral system (Hungary continues to be a unicameral parliamentary system).

However, beyond rules of mere symbolic relevance, the text was scattered with ad hoc exceptions, the drafters tinkering with the rules on both state organisation and fundamental rights to align them with their real or perceived daily party interests (see in particular the provisions governing the ordinary courts, the Constitutional Court or churches). Sometimes the desired outcome was not achieved on the first attempt, so even exceptions had to be amended and then re-amended. These embarrassing repetitions were actually due to the fact that the majority of constitutional law experts informing the constitution-making project simply fled the decision-making process in close procession. This was down to the fact that, on the one hand, their opinions were not really taken into consideration and, on the other hand, they faced a situation where their ethos of restricting state power conflicted with the line they were asked to take.

[34] On the one hand, this was favourable, as liberal democratic traditions (especially case law) had a higher chance of survival. On the other hand, this was also unfavourable, because superficial observers (ie, those who only considered the legal norms, but not the actual practices and narratives) might have a false impression that the changes were only minor. For more details, see A Jakab, P Sonnevend and L Csink, 'The Constitution as an Instrument of Everyday Party Politics: The Basic Law of Hungary' in A von Bogdandy and P Sonnevend (eds), *Constitutional Crisis in the European Constitutional Area* (Oxford, Hart Publishing, 2015) 33; A Vincze and M Varju, 'Hungary: The New Fundamental Law' (2012) 18 *European Public Law* 437.

In this context, all intellectual checks placed on the decision-makers gradually melted away, and the pressure exerted by the EU institutions and foreign actors (mainly the US and international financial markets) constituted the only form of restraint on the exercise of the power of the constitution-making majority existing up to 2015 (in April 2018, the governing parties regained the two-thirds constitution-making majority).[35] This trend was already visible at the time of the 2010/11 process, becoming particularly conspicuous with the Fifth Amendment to the Fundamental Law, forced upon the government by Brussels, Venice, Strasbourg and Luxembourg, seeking to remedy the gravest constitutional flaws affecting European norms. In fact, this was even acknowledged in the official reasoning attached to the amendment: 'Therefore, in order to prevent certain constitutional issues to be used as a pretext for attacks against Hungary, the Government, without abandoning its original intentions ... proposes a different solution.'

B. Actual Practices: Gradual Erosion of the Rule of Law

Following 2010, the actual operation of the legal order was marked by an increased instrumentalisation of legislation – that is, the use of law-making as a power politics tool – as well as unpredictability, undermining legal certainty.[36] (From a constitutional perspective, the way in which laws are in fact made is part of actual practice.) Since then, the number of laws enacted has been continuously growing, with increasingly shorter timeframes being dedicated to their adoption, which is unfavourable from the point of view of legal certainty,[37] but this also has a negative impact on the quality of legislation, making frequent amendments necessary, which has a particularly adverse effect on legal certainty.[38] This is clearly reflected in the following two figures.[39]

[35] The 2018 elections were heavily criticised by the OSCE; see www.osce.org/odihr/elections/hungary/377410?download=true: 'The 8 April parliamentary elections were characterised by a pervasive overlap between state and ruling party resources, undermining contestants' ability to compete on an equal basis. Voters had a wide range of political options but intimidating and xenophobic rhetoric, media bias and opaque campaign financing constricted the space for genuine political debate, hindering voters' ability to make a fully-informed choice.'

[36] On the lack of legal certainty, see the following chapters in Jakab and Gajduschek (n 1): P Tölgyessy, 'Politika mindenekelőtt: Jog és hatalom Magyarországon'; Á Szalai and A Jakab, 'Jog mint a gazdasági fejlődés infrastruktúrája'; G Gajduschek, 'Előkészítetlenség és utólagos hatásvizsgálat hiánya'; C I Nagy, 'Esettanulmány a jogbiztonsággal kapcsolatos problémákról: a választottbíráskodásra vonatkozó szabályozás változásai'.

[37] This is not a general tendency in the world – see, eg, the British data. See M Zander, *The Law-Making Process* (Cambridge, Cambridge University Press, 2004) 1.

[38] For the statistics of the modifications of freshly adopted statutes, see M Sebők, B Kubik and C Molnár, 'A törvények formális minősége – egy empirikus vázlat' in Z Boda and A Szabó (eds), *Trendek a magyar politikában 2. A Fidesz és a többiek: pártok, mozgalmak*, (Budapest, MTA TK Politikatudományi Intézet, 2017) especially 300 and 304.

[39] The source of the graphs is (without trend lines): A magyar törvényhozás minősége 1998–2012 – leíró statisztikák. Előzetes kutatási eredmények, Corruption Research Center Budapest, www.crcb.eu/wp-content/uploads/2014/02/trvh_2013_riport_140214_1410.pdf.

Figure 9.1 The average number of laws adopted per year and per government (with trend line)

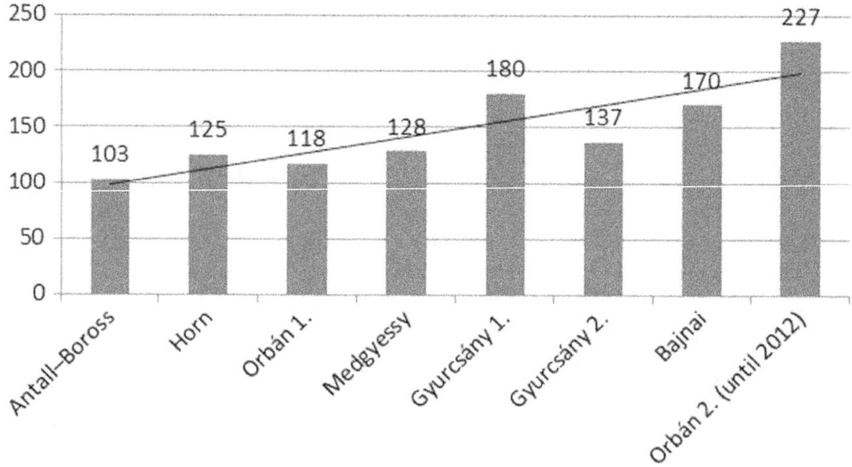

Figure 9.2 The number of days passed between submitting the legislative bill and the promulgation of the law (median)[40]

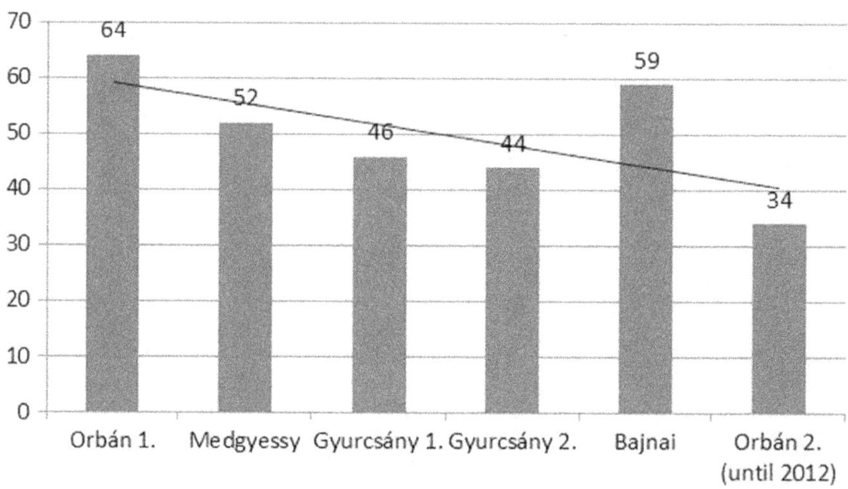

Actual practices, particularly in the ambit of constitutional law, increasingly deviate from what is set forth under formal rules. However, these practices are difficult to pin down with traditional legal methods.[41] Infringements manifested

[40] The median is more robust in case there are outliers in the sample.

[41] The discrepancy is most likely programmed into the nature of the regime: if the formal rules (and in certain cases also the political rhetoric) more or less conform to the ideas of constitutional-

in actual practices will be destructive for institutions when they reach a critical level, or where these may be explained by reference to an implicit exception, or where the rule is challenged on the level of the narrative. Although several murders occur in Hungary every year, we do not question the strength of the protection of human life as an institution.[42] Yet, if we were to witness a huge increase in homicide numbers – such as in Mexico or in the Philippines, supported by official government narratives – or the routine murder of opposition journalists (with the murderers unknown and never tracked, as is the case in Russia), this would indicate a weakening of the institution.

Unfortunately, in the past few years, we have witnessed several instances of weakening constitutional institutions in Hungary. The following list is not exhaustive, providing merely a few examples:

(1) While the Constitutional Court continues to show minor signs of life by deciding non-priority cases or cases of relatively small significance, for lawyers, and by now even for laypersons, it is clear that in certain cases, the Court is simply afraid or unwilling to render a decision that would necessarily follow from the Fundamental Law. A most vivid and recent example would be the use of in the strict sense lawful but hitherto never used delay tactics (eg, the setting-up of special analysis groups of law clerks to prepare a lengthy preliminary report on the case, while practically suspending the procedure) in respect of the manifestly unconstitutional *lex CEU*.[43] Although from a formal legal point of view this cannot be objected to, on the level of actual practices, it definitely amounts to institutional destruction. It undermines the belief in the independence of the Constitutional Court (and rightly so), gradually discrediting the narrative of the separation of powers.[44]

(2) There are a host of credible accounts, some of them also reported by the media, regarding the selection of court leaders (who continue to play an important role in allocating cases within the respective court), evidencing that at the level of actual practices, a personal relationship with the head of the National Office for the Judiciary was considered as being more important than the official criteria of merit. This practice, in the majority of cases,

ism, then this can give legitimacy to the regime, so their total disappearance seems currently unlikely, whereas in actual practice, we are finding more and more exceptions. The tension between formal and informal elements is therefore not a defect, but is quite logical from a practical political perspective in this regime.

[42] *cf* Offe (n 21) 206.

[43] For an empirical analysis of government influence on the Hungarian Constitutional Court, see Z Szente, 'The Political Orientation of the Members of the Hungarian Constitutional Court between 2010 and 2014' (2016) 1 *Constitutional Studies* 123.

[44] For the latest move by the Constitutional Court, this time clearly also a breach of its own procedural rules, see G Halmai, 'The Hungarian Constitutional Court Betrays Academic Freedom and Freedom of Association' *Verfassungsblog*, www.verfassungsblog.de/the-hungarian-constitutional-court-betrays-academic-freedom-and-freedom-of-association.

does not breach the relevant procedural rules (although in some exceptional cases it does); since these were largely drafted by the National Office for the Judiciary, it much rather infringes unenforceable general principles. This painfully corrodes the informal elements of judicial independence.[45]

(3) While the Fundamental Law formally upholds the idea of self-government, this is actually hollowed out in service of the complete and general centralisation of the state partly through formal statutory implementing rules and the re-regulation of competences, and partly through the practice of financing (discretional or non-transparent distribution of funds).[46]

(4) While formal rules on corruption have been maintained, the prosecuting services continue to operate without transparency or guarantees. Meanwhile, a string of unrefuted press reports have been published indicating that the Chief Prosecutor's Office fails to take action or delays and/or spectacularly blunders the indictment when the suspicion of the committance of a crime arises in respect of a person close to the government. Indeed, corruption in a broader sense may even appear on the level of legislation, as in the regulation of gambling and tobacco retail.[47]

(5) Although formal legal provisions stipulate that it is one of the goals of the National Media and Infocommunications Authority and of the Media Council to promote media pluralism, at the level of actual practices, they are visibly working on steering the entire media landscape into the government's fold, partly through an incomplete application of legal rules, but partly also through overt breaches, as established by an administrative tribunal.[48]

(6) Formally, the protection of private property continues to form part of the Hungarian legal order, yet this has significantly deteriorated or has at least become patchy on several points. Besides the fact that (since 2010) the relevant competences of the Constitutional Court remain incomplete to this day (the Court is barred from reviewing tax or budgetary laws from the perspective of the right of private property), one may repeatedly read about instances where a company is stripped of its market share through state efforts by first introducing legislative amendments (which on its own cannot be formally objected to), then passing them on to private persons at

[45] M Bencze and A Badó, 'A magyar bírósági rendszer hatékonyságát és az ítélkezés színvonalát befolyásoló strukturális és személyi feltételek' in Jakab and Gajduschek (n 1) 441: 'A bírói önigazgatás kiüresedése, a politikai befolyás lehetősége, konformitási kényszer megjelenése.'

[46] I Pálné Kovács, 'Modellváltás a magyar önkormányzati rendszerben' in Jakab and Gajduschek (n 1) 583–99.

[47] With detailed documentation, see M Ligeti, 'Korrupció' in Jakab and Gajduschek (n 1) 727–57. Moreover, as to the narrative, the obvious systemic corruption is openly defended by some intellectuals near to the government in friendly media outlets as building a new national capitalist class; see the infamous interview with A Lánczi in *Magyar Idők*, www.magyaridok.hu/belfold/lanczi-andras-viccpartok-szinvonalan-all-az-ellenzek-243952.

[48] G Polyák and K Nagy, 'A médiatörvények kontextusa, rendelkezései és gyakorlata' (2014) 20 *Jura* 127, www.mediakutato.hu/cikk/2016_03_osz_tel/10_frekvenciaosztogatas.

the level of actual practices (see, for example, the case of laws on gambling) and finally introducing strict formal rules as a next step to protect the new incumbent. In fact, *it is the very concept of private property that becomes relative when trying to get a clear picture of the true financial situation of senior politicians*. And not just because of the different contract options, but also because of the political dependency of certain types of private property ownership, it is a mere formality as to who happens to be registered as the owner.[49] Thanks to the tragicomic way in which politicians' asset declarations are handled, we also do not have a clear picture of politicians' wealth, even where assets are held in their name (while there is nothing new about this, the degree and the conspicuousness of the disparities nowadays go way beyond what was experienced before).

(7) Finally, as a new development from the perspective of the departure of actual practices from formal rules, the parliamentary majority took things to a new level by adopting the law on political posters in 2017 in a conscious breach of procedural (majority) rules. First, they sought to adopt provisions requiring a two-thirds majority with the necessary votes; however, when this turned out to be impossible (the government did not have a two-thirds majority between 2015 and 2018), they repackaged the bill into another law and declared that passing the concerned provisions merely required a simple majority.[50] Such overt breaches of constitutional rules governing legislative procedures (these breaches are overt, since the first time around, efforts were made to adopt the provisions with a two-thirds majority) are only one step away from a situation where the incumbent majority amend the Constitution by a simple majority.

Decision-makers completely lack the sense of responsibility to resist such temptations, even though this would be in their long-term interests, and, as such, they are actively dismantling constitutionality (ie, the system of legal norms restricting government) while formally upholding constitutional rules, which they continue to pay lip service to.[51]

Without going into lengthy scholarly elaborations, such situations may be comprehensively yet briefly described by so-called rule of law indices that capture various details in a single indicator and that, more importantly, give

[49] For interviews and case studies on these issues, see D Sallai and G Schnyder, 'The Transformation of Post-socialist Capitalism: From Developmental State to Clan State?', http://gala.gre.ac.uk/18535/13/18535%20GreenwichPapersPoliticalEconomy_Cover_UoG_FEPS_SERWPv02.pdf.

[50] See Case Reg No II/01483/2017 of the Hungarian Constitutional Court on the Law CIV of 2017. The case is pending at the Constitutional Court and there is no sign that a decision will be delivered in the foreseeable future, which is again not illegal in a strict sense, as there is no statutory deadline binding the Court in this type of procedure.

[51] For these kinds of hybrid constitutional regimes (with further references), see, eg, RN Ortega, 'Conceptualizing Authoritarian Constitutionalism' (2016) 49 *Verfassung und Recht in Übersee* 339; S Levitsky and LA Way, *Competitive Authoritarianism: Hybrid Regimes after the Cold War* (Cambridge, Cambridge University Press, 2010); A Bozóki and D Hegedűs, 'An Externally Constrained Hybrid Regime: Hungary in the European Union' (2018) 25 *Democratization* 1173.

due consideration to actual practices.[52] Such indices clearly reflect the ongoing erosion of the rule of law in Hungary in recent years, and there is every reason to believe that this process will continue. Below, I briefly present the values of two indices: (a) the rule of law sub-index of the Bertelsmann Transformation Index; and (b) the World Justice Project Rule of Law Index.

The Bertelsmann Transformation Index (the so-called status index) is the average of the democracy index (this includes the rule of law according to the conceptualisation of Bertelsmann) and the market economy index. It measures four elements of the rule of law, a total of 17 rule of law criteria with 49 different (from the point of view of traditional legal doctrine) partly overlapping questions. The four elements are as follows: (1) the separation of powers; (2) judicial independence; (3) prosecution of abuse of power; and (4) fundamental rights. Figure 9.3 below clearly shows a gradual erosion of the rule of law in Hungary.

Figure 9.3 The Bertelsmann Transformation Index depicted on a diagram, data on Hungary for the period 2006–18

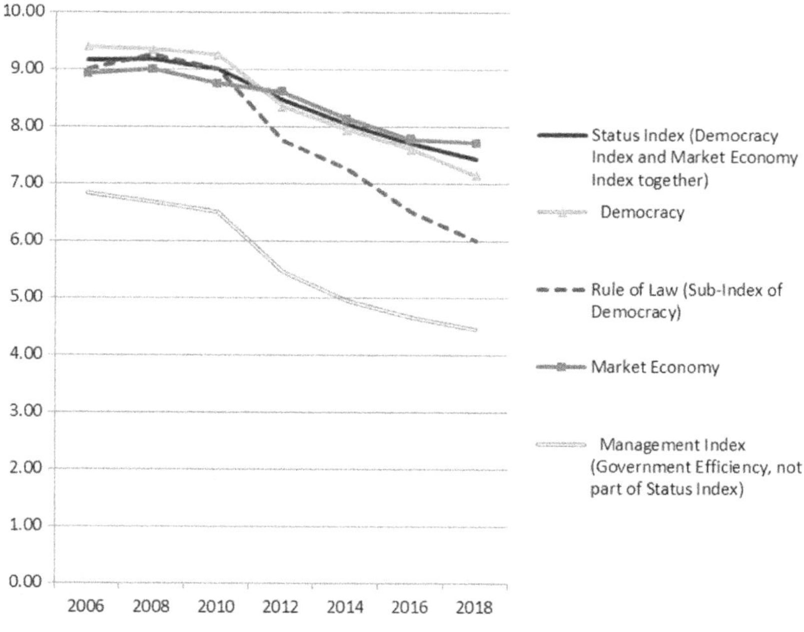

[52] For methodological details of the mentioned (and further) rule of law indexes, see A Jakab and VO Lőrincz, 'International Indices as Models for the Rule of Law Scoreboard of the European Union: Methodological Issues'(2017) *Max Planck Institute for Comparative Public Law & International Law (MPIL) Research Paper No 21*. The different rule of law indices use different data sources, namely hard data (eg, judicial budget), expert opinions (of constitutional lawyers) and/or public opinion polls (eg, corruption perception). I am grateful to Viktor Olivér Lőrincz and Nerma Taletovic for the preparation of the graphs. The use of these indices does not make traditional (doctrinal) legal analysis obsolete, but for situations with a large number of changes and for problems of growing discrepancy between facts and norms, they are particularly useful (in the expert opinions, traditional doctrinal opinions are included anyway).

Meanwhile, the management index is a different indicator, reflecting the efficiency of government. This also shows a downward trend, that is, the erosion of the rule of law did not give a boost to efficiency.

The explicit aim of the World Justice Project Rule of Law Index is to measure elements of the rule of law in operation as experienced by individuals (in other words, it measures the *actual practices* or the perception of actual practices, not primarily the body of laws). At a conceptual and methodological level, this is probably the most refined rule of law index globally. Relying primarily on UN documents, it defines the rule of law with the following four principles: (1) the government, its officials and representatives, as well as private persons and companies, are held accountable under the law; (2) laws are clear, publicised, stable and just, and serve to protect fundamental rights, including the security and property of persons; (3) processes by which the laws are enacted, administered and enforced are accessible, fair and efficient, and justice is delivered timely by competent, ethical and independent persons who are impartial, accessible, have adequate resources and reflect the makeup of the communities they serve. Based on these principles, the index measures nine factors (comprising 47 sub-factors): (1) constraints on government powers; (2) absence of corruption; (3) open government; (4) fundamental rights; (5) order and security; (6) regulatory enforcement; (7) civil justice; (8) criminal justice; and (9) informal (traditional) justice (the latter is hard to measure and is therefore is not included in the aggregate result).

Figure 9.4 Data of the World Justice Project Rule of Law Index for Hungary 2012/13–18

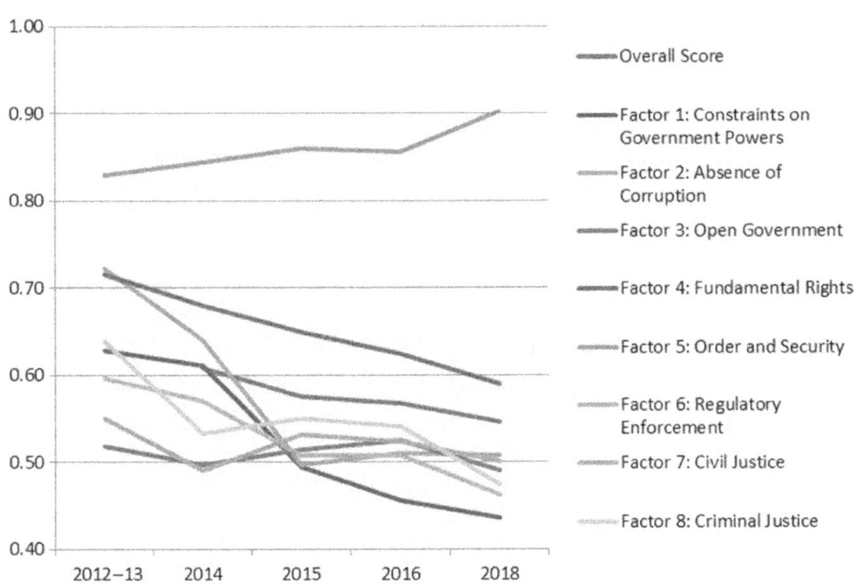

The higher the points achieved, the better; the maximum is one, while the minimum is zero. The Hungarian results reflect a gradual decline in the constraints on government power (separation of powers), absence of corruption, open government, fundamental rights, regulatory enforcement and criminal justice. The results for civil justice have largely remained the same and the points for order and security have shown a slight improvement. However, the aggregate result of these changes shows a clear downward trend (we have no data for the period preceding 2012/13 since the project is relatively new).

C. A Dishonest Narrative: Or Why Did Hungary Need a New Constitution?

At the time that the Fundamental Law was drafted, several different official reasons were given as to why Hungary needed a new constitution.[53] In the end, two main arguments prevailed. The first argument claimed that the 'Communist Constitution of 1949' had to be replaced, while the other argued that the new Constitution would mark the closure of two decades of 'confusion' following the end of socialism in 1989/90.

The argument relating to the closure of confusion following the socialist period does not hold water either formally or substantively: in terms of content, the 1949 Constitution was replaced in 1989/90 and apart from a few insignificant phrases which could have been weeded out with a simple constitutional amendment, there were no socialist remnants left in the text by 2010/11. The main formal argument was that the Constitution's title still contained a reference to the year 1949 (it was entitled 'Law No XX of 1949'). In this respect, it is worth recalling that the governing party had already proposed to remedy this problem in 2000 by way of a simple amendment, which was not accepted at the time – that is, the rewriting of the title also did not make the adoption of a new constitution necessary. A further formal argument referred to the 'patched up' character of the old text, while another claimed that instead of the existing long and technical text, containing highly detailed rules, there was a need for a 'short and likeable' constitution. However, the same objections may be raised against the current Fundamental Law: compared to the status of the text in April 2011, the ensuing seven amendments changed the original text on several points, resulting in its growth by 30 per cent, or to put it another way, the text is now just as patched up as its predecessor. At present, the Fundamental Law is already one and a half times longer than the 2010 text of the old Constitution, and therefore the brevity requisite was also not met.

However, the symbolic closure of the previous two decades (from 1989/90 until 2010) was an argument that the governing parties may have taken at least

[53] Narratives are 'not just of *how* we do things around here, but also *why* we do things the way we do'. See Lowndes and Roberts (n 3) 64.

partially seriously.[54] These two decades (and in particular the second decade) were in fact less of a success for the country: the neighbouring countries in the Central European region caught up with the once leading Hungary, some even outperforming it in terms of economic indicators. Even though politicians should have in fact been taking a closer look at themselves in the mirror, blaming the Constitution (or pointing the finger at each other) seemed to be a more comfortable solution for them. Hungarian society got stuck and sank deeper and deeper into this national version of a cold war where victory over the opposition justified all the means: corruption, running the country into debt, low-quality government or even a lack of governing. This troubled and unsuccessful period was to be closed by the new Constitution. Yet the problems have persisted after 2010/11, with some of them even becoming greater: corruption has not decreased, it has increased and it has become centralised and well organised, state debt has not been substantially lowered (although Hungary has nationalised private pension funds and has introduced growth-suppressing special taxes), and the quality of governance has not improved either. On the contrary, in certain areas (for example, in the field of public education),[55] it has spectacularly and dramatically deteriorated. Hence, the Fundamental Law was incapable of becoming the symbolic dividing line that the governing parties had intended it to be; in fact, it instead symbolises the erosion of the rule of law and, as is often the case, it has become a symbol of the whole regime (with its systemic corruption and authoritarian tendencies). Indeed, on some issues, it actually perpetuates the unsuccessful and clearly dishonest approach taken to deep-seated moral and intellectual problems – for example, there has been a clear continuity in the refusal to disclose secret service files since the end of socialism (Hungary continues to treat communist secret service information in the most intransparent way), but the problems of public procurement corruption have also been pervasive since 1990.

The opposition often critically claims that the true reason for the constitution-making was to cement the political power of the government. However, this perception is misguided, first, because it is not necessary to adopt a new constitution to enforce constitutional provisions serving the goals of everyday party politics: this is well evidenced by the events of 2010 and 2011 under the former Constitution (when the same governing parties kept amending the old Constitution for a number of different ad hoc reasons), as well as the different amendments made to the Fundamental Law since then. The tool of amendment is just as viable, if not an easier means of implementing political will, and would have surely made the formal adoption of an entirely new document obsolete. While it is true that cementing the government's power

[54] For its symbolism, see L Sólyom, *Das Gewand des Grundgesetzes: Zwei Verfassungsikonen – Ungarn und Deutschland* (Berlin, BWV, 2017).

[55] I Polónyi, 'Oktatáspolitikai kísérletek és kudarcok' in Jakab and Urbán (n 1) 379–400.

has been an obvious goal in the last few years, this has been more efficiently pursued through staffing policies and statutes than through a new constitutional document.

From the outset, the governing parties abandoned the plan to persuade opposition voters and to create a text that could be 'likeable' for them, functioning as a symbol for the entire political community. They chose not to overcome the 20-something years fraught by political fighting through reconciliation or some favourable compromise. Instead, they opted for total victory, of which the Fundamental Law has now become a symbol. Yet without open violence (something that is not characteristic of the present Hungarian regime), total victory cannot be achieved; the embers will continue to smoulder under the ashes. Even if an opposition party disappears, it will be replaced by a new one, perhaps one that is even without the historical (post-socialist) baggage. Comprehensive empirical analyses show that only those constitutions that are more or less based on a compromise between the entire political elite survive in the long term, that is, for at least two decades.[56] The Fundamental Law definitely lacks this support, and were we to accept the findings of the analyses cited, it is most likely that the text would not survive a change of government.

With the rhetorical excuse of protecting national sovereignty and national interests, the government made a constitution that threw the country off-course from the traditional principles of democracy and the rule of law. However, it would be misguided to conceive of the problem as a 'national interest versus rule of law/democracy' equation. Namely, the prosperity of the nation hinges on the prevalence of democracy and rule of law conditions.[57] While there is no such country where the operation of these institutions is ideal, market economies encouraging work, efficiency and innovation – that is, capitalist economies, a term highly unpopular in Hungarian public discourse – are all based on these premises. Well-designed institutions respecting the separation of powers are a reliable basis for a country's prosperity, and luckily, the European institutions and international pressure on Hungary are trying to protect them from their own government, or at least slow down their erosion.[58] Thus, external pressure should not be perceived as foreign dictates, but rather as a way out of self-destruction.

Ever since the times of Hungary's founding father St Stephen, the Hungarian community's political programme has been to successfully integrate into Western culture and to embrace its value system. Today, this value system is not conveyed by Christianity, but rather takes the form of a conscious choice

[56] Z Elkins, T Ginsburg and J Melton, *The Endurance of National Constitutions* (Cambridge, Cambridge University Press, 2009). More generally, for the success of a liberal democracy, a certain degree of consensus of the elite is needed, see the case studies in Higley and Burton (n 24).

[57] See n 9 above.

[58] For a chronology of international pressure about the Hungarian Fundamental Law of 2011, see, eg, K Kelemen, 'The New Hungarian Constitution: Critiques from Europe' (2017) 42 *Review of Central and East European Law* 1.

to protect human rights and promote democracy following the catastrophic political experiments of the twentieth century. While this has been on the political compass of the more fortunate half of Europe following the Second World War, Hungary could only begin to effectively follow this direction after the fall of socialism. There is now a comprehensive system of European institutions for the interpretation and enforcement of these values (aphoristically put, 'the Vatican of today is in Strasbourg'). If Hungary is to remain loyal to this 1,000-year-old agenda, instead of defiantly fighting these institutions like some kind of modern-day pagan rebels, it should embrace them as its own. In fact, Hungary's constitutional autonomy should not be conceived as being opposed to, but much rather as being helped by these institutions.

We can conclude that the reasons quoted in support of the adoption of a new constitution were unfounded. The whole process lacked a narrative that those in the know could wholeheartedly espouse. It is often the case that grounds that at first sight appear plausible for laypersons later turn out to be highly problematic upon deeper scrutiny. The drafters of the Fundamental Law were most likely aware of this; this means that the different reasons raised were not rooted in genuine conviction. The 'necessity' of constitution-making was not triggered by external factors, but was much rather the product of an artificially created, endogenous crisis, a situation consciously staged by leading politicians to score a victory (ie, to give the country a new constitution).[59]

Since then, a new general and official narrative of the legal order has emerged, namely the idea of the 'illiberal state'.[60] The Prime Minister launched this concept at his notorious Tusványos speech in 2014 and although its precise substance – apart from it being national and based on labour – is unknown, it is presented as an alternative to (liberal) Western democracies built on the protection of fundamental rights (meanwhile, the Fundamental Law formally continues to guarantee fundamental rights conducive to a democracy).[61]

Some claim that the legal system is increasingly reminiscent of that preceding 1945, at least in its rhetoric/narrative. However, this is not convincing. Namely, the most important and genuinely promoted narrative of that time related to the historical (pre-Second World War) Constitution, to which only a few, unsystematic, dishonest and unfounded references are made today, with the sole aim of historicising.[62] Meanwhile, the real – albeit restricted – similarities between current and pre-war actual practices are not sufficient to prove the analogy.

[59] On endogenously created crises from the perspective of political leadership, see A Körösényi, G Illés and R Metz, 'Contingency and Political Action: The Role of Leadership in Endogenously Created Crises' (2016) 4 *Politics and Governance* 91.

[60] For the concept, see F Zakaria, 'The Rise of Illiberal Democracy' (1997) 76 *Foreign Affairs* 22.

[61] AL Pap, *Democratic Decline in Hungary* (New York, Routledge, 2017) 47–65, with further references.

[62] See, eg, Const Court 22 December 2016 (XII. 5.) AB. For more details, see T Drinóczi, 'Hungarian Constitutional Court: The Limits of EU Law in the Hungarian Legal System' (2017) 11 *Vienna Journal on International Constitutional Law* 139; Z Szente, 'A historizáló alkotmányozás problémái – a történeti alkotmány és a Szent Korona az új Alaptörvényben' (2011) 4 *Közjogi Szemle* 1.

When looking for an archetype that best describes the narrative of the current legal system, it is more fitting to turn to the socialist era. This is all the more surprising, since the most important reason put forward for adopting the new Fundamental Law was to overcome the previous (1949/1989) socialist (or even 'communist') Constitution. At a political level, the present Hungarian government consistently employs an anti-communist political rhetoric, yet its implied and sometimes also explicit ideas of the law are in fact highly reminiscent of socialist legal doctrine. This is no simple and coincidental similarity, but much rather a clear and identifiable continuity of Marxist legal theory, which had in part survived the political change and persisted in Hungarian legal thinking.[63] It became visibly dominant after 2010, having partly been elevated to the level of official narrative.[64] This continuity is not merely a simple remnant of the past, but the reinforcement of certain characteristics – in part induced by the similarity of political operation (in particular, statism and voluntarism) and in part by the bits and pieces of socialist theory that survived as mental residues.[65]

The official Marxist-Leninist legal doctrine (and, in particular, constitutional doctrine) at the time of socialism may be briefly summarised in a few simplified assumptions (see below).[66] While I am not claiming that these would form the essence of Marxist legal or constitutional theory *in abstracto* and a Marxist legal scholar would most probably reconstruct his theses in a different way, the points listed below seem to be the most relevant for understanding the contemporary legacy of these views in Hungary. The government's approach to the law visibly shuns theoretical underpinnings, and when fragments of it accidentally emerge, it is difficult to piece them together into a consistent, abstract legal doctrine.[67] Meanwhile, different elements of Marxist legal theory still tend to resurface, of which I will highlight a few below. Following the description of the different theses, I will briefly outline how and to what extent they continue to live on today:[68]

(1) *Law is only a technical impediment and is not a real barrier to politics; it reflects the will of the ruling class – legal instrumentalism, which essentially denies the idea of constitutionalism.* Infamous examples are the unbridled use of legislation, including constitution-making for the concrete

[63] For more details, see, eg, A Jakab and M Hollán, 'Socialism's Legacy in Contemporary Law and Legal Scholarship: The Case of Hungary' (2004) 2–3 *Journal of East European Law (Columbia University)* 95.

[64] See Tölgyessy (n 36).

[65] The expression 'mental residues' has been borrowed from Offe (n 21) 210.

[66] As regards the use of Marxist legal theory in this chapter, I mean the socialist normativism of Soviet origin or, to put it differently, Marxist-Leninist legal theory. For more details, see, eg, J N Hazard, *Communists and Their Law* (Chicago, University of Chicago Press, 1969); WE Butler, *Soviet Law* (London, Butterworths, 1988).

[67] As to the 'illiberal state', see below.

[68] On the continuing influence of the socialist legacy, with further references, see Jakab and Hollán (n 63).

aims of power politics (eg, the laws on the media, on the election procedure and on political advertising in public spaces) or for the economic benefit of a restricted interest group (eg, the regulation of gambling, tobacco retail or different tax laws). But the blatantly unconstitutional (and probably EU law-violating) *lex CEU* is another clear example of instrumentalised legislation,[69] which probably sought to divert public discourse and distract from uncomfortable issues, such as corruption, the state of public health services and the education system. The instrumentalist concept of the law has only changed in the sense that 'working class' has been replaced by 'nation', whose interests may even legitimise formal violations of the law and in whose interests legislation must be passed in contravention with the principles of Western constitutionalism.

(2) *From among the methods of interpretation, textual approaches are given preference, since more creative solutions such as referring to the general aims of the legal text would provide judges with too much leeway, amounting to anti-democratic methods, in breach of legal certainty*. Actually, the original text of the Fundamental Law would have signalled a step forward by encouraging purposive interpretation, which is customary in Western legal cultures and even in Hungary before the Second World War.[70] However, the Fourth and the Seventh amendments of the Fundamental Law were largely aimed at curbing judicial power (both of the Constitutional Court and the ordinary courts) by rewriting the formal rules.[71]

(3) *Rejecting the idea of the separation of powers, in preference for the unity of power, or 'democratic centralism'*. Officially and somewhat pharisaically, the principle of the separation of powers has been spelled out in the text of the Fundamental Law (ie, it is formally part of the Constitution); however, at the level of actual practice, we are witnessing a clear erosion of the separation of powers. This is hard to pin down with traditional legal methods focusing on formal legal rules, often happening through staffing and informal pressures. In socialist times, constitutional courts were described as elitist and anti-democratic institutions with no original legitimacy, which therefore should not interfere with political processes, while judges were considered to be mere bureaucrats. Similar views had also been present in Hungarian public discourse and legal thought after the end of socialism, but the openly hostile stance and the tone in which this was voiced

[69] See, eg, www.theguardian.com/world/2018/may/15/central-european-university-ready-to-move-out-of-hungary; L Sólyom, M Lévay, Z Szente and A Jakab, *Amicus Curiae a Lex Ceu ügyében* (*Amicus Curiae in the Case of Lex CEU*) (2017).

[70] A Jakab, 'A bírói jogértelmezés az Alaptörvény tükrében' (2011) 2 *Jogesetek Magyarázata* 86.

[71] On the fading but still-persisting post-socialist traditions of judicial formalism, see M Matzak, M Bencze and Z Kühn, 'EU Law and Central European Judges: Administrative Judiciaries in the Czech Republic, Hungary and Poland Ten Years after Accession' in M Bobek (ed), *Central European Judges under European Influence* (Oxford, Hart Publishing, 2015).

(eg, referring to constitutional jurisprudence as 'haruspicy') on the highest political levels was unprecedented.[72]

(4) *The force of international law is derived from state sovereignty and is secondary to it.* This is also something that we are experiencing on a daily basis, from the statements portraying the Venice Commission as being part of an international conspiracy led by the Jewish financier of Hungarian origin George Soros, to the state's poster campaigns inciting hate against migrants, the UN(!) and the EU (only referred to as 'Brussels'). But recent years have also seen a parliamentary resolution that harshly criticised a Strasbourg judgment, even though the imposed fine of the judgment was later actually paid to the claimant.[73] Meanwhile, this stance even appears in certain Constitutional Court decisions, with total disregard to the relevant provisions of the Fundamental Law.[74]

While the similarities are apparent, one or two elements may stem from other sources, eg, from authoritarian concepts of the law or simply from old-style legal positivism.[75] However, taken together, their origins may clearly be traced back to socialism, and if we take a closer look at how these ideas manifest themselves, the Marxist source often reveals itself.

Resistance towards judicial review of parliamentary acts, for example, is also characteristic of classical British constitutionalism (which no longer exists in its original form since the Human Rights Act 1998 and since a moderate fundamental rights-oriented constitutional jurisprudence was introduced). However, paying lip service to the British example for the benefit of the Hungarian audience disregards the fact that in the lack of a formal constitution, the British system allows for the adoption of any law with a simple majority, that is, it differs greatly from the Hungarian system. Any effort at transplanting the British concept of 'political constitutionalism' would fail in the context of the different institutional environment.[76] Also, rejecting judicial creativity was not only characteristic of Marxist legal theory, but was also an important branch

[72] The changes in the legal rules relating to the Constitutional Court since 2010 can largely be explained by the aim of the constitution-maker to distance the Court from politically relevant law-making. See F Gárdos-Orosz, 'Alkotmánybíróság 2010–2015' in Jakab and Gajduschek (n 1) 442.

[73] Parl Dec 58/2012 (VII. 10.) OGY hat.

[74] Article Q of the Fundamental Law contains the obligation of conformity with international law. For attempts to neutralise the provision, see Const Court Dec 34/2013 (XI. 22.) AB, sep op by Justice Béla Pokol [83]–[85]; Const Court Dec 7/2014 (III. 7.) AB, sep op by Justice Béla Pokol [113].

[75] B Pokol, 'Separation of Power and Parliamentarism in Hungary' (2003) 37 *East European Quarterly* 67; B Pokol, *The Juristocratic State: Its Victory and the Possibilities of Taming* (Budapest, Dialóg Campus, 2017).

[76] On political constitutionalism see, eg, R Bellamy, *Political Constitutionalism* (Cambridge, Cambridge University Press, 2007). For a critical review of the Hungarian reception of the concept, see A Antal, 'Politikai és jogi alkotmányosság Magyarországon' (2013) 22 *Politikatudományi Szemle* 48, with further references; I Stumpf, *Erős állam – alkotmányos korlátok* (Budapest, Századvég, 2014).

of American scholarly literature, the originalists, which hold a similar view.[77] However, while originalists are trying to unearth the original meaning of certain specific terms, there is no actual sign of this approach in Hungarian practice. A number of proponents of the current government from amongst the legal scholarly community actually started their careers as Marxist legal theorists and some even continue to work (among others) with Marxist terminology.[78]

D. The Joint Effect of the Components

In 2011, László Sólyom (the first President of the Hungarian Constitutional Court (1990–98) and also a former President of the Republic (2005–10)) wrote that he believes in the survival of institutions of constitutionalism, despite both the objectionable provisions of the new Fundamental Law and government practices, through the constitutional culture and future Constitutional Court case law.[79] Unfortunately, however, his optimistic vision did not become a reality. While constitutional culture did in fact succeed in toning down some gross amendments to formal rules, the Fourth Amendment in 2013 made it blatantly clear that all this can do is merely delay, but not prevent decline. Since then, it is not only the practices of the government and the legislator that give rise to concern, but also the actual practice of the Constitutional Court (particularly the delaying tactics employed in respect of politically sensitive cases). Existing institutions have been measurably weakened – according to the indices described above – and no new resilient institutions have been established to take their place. One of the main functions of any institution is to increase predictability, to reinforce law-abiding behaviour and thus promote long-term thinking. This, however, stands in stark contrast to the current regime's ad hoc, short-term driven, pragmatic power politics which almost completely neglects actual public policy considerations. On several occasions, the government has violated the formal rules of the very legal order that it runs. Hence, an actual practice which is focused on completely 'controlling the political moment' resists any substantive narrative (in this case, theoretical foundation).[80]

[77] See, eg, A Scalia, *Reading Law: The Interpretation of Legal Texts* (St Paul, Thomson/West, 2012).

[78] C Varga, 'A joguralom és színeváltozásai idealizáció és ideokratikus nyomásgyakorlás között' *Pázmány Law Working Papers No 12*, www.plwp.eu/evfolyamok/2016/170-2016-12 (one of the most well-known Marxist legal theorists before 1990); P Béla, *Globális uralmi rend* (Budapest, Kairosz, 2008) (working with the neo-Marxist theses of Hardt and Negri).

[79] L Sólyom, 'Előszó: Az alkotmányos kultúra szerepe' in A Jakab (ed), *Az Alaptörvény keletkezése és gyakorlati következményei* (Budapest, HVG ORAC, 2011) 11–14.

[80] Theoretical foundations are, by their nature, futile in this regime. However, for such attempts, see, eg, ZA Varga, *Eszményből bálvány? A joguralom dogmatikája* (Budapest, Századvég, 2015); Á Rixer (ed), *Állam és közösség: Válogatott közjogi tanulmányok Magyarország Alaptörvénye tiszteletére* (Budapest, Károli Gáspár Református Egyetem Állam- és Jogtudományi Kar, 2012).

IV. WHAT TO DO: A MANUAL FOR INSTITUTION-BUILDING IN THE CONTEMPORARY HUNGARIAN CONTEXT

The greatest difficulty of institution-building lies in the fact that informal elements are not directly accessible, ie, there is no applicable amendment procedure; furthermore, they may even sabotage the effects of formal amendments. Some of the challenges of institutional-building in Hungary originate from the socialist legacy, while others are determined by cultural traits that even pre-date the socialist era.[81]

While informal elements may be changed with the help of institutions – a strategy highly reminiscent of the notorious attempt of Baron von Munchhausen,[82] the success of institution-building actually hinges on proper practices/narratives, which in turn rely on the right institutions.[83] The solution lies in the combination of a will to recover and the acceptance of external help. It is crucial for Hungary to abandon the mirage of sovereignty and adapt to Western civilisation by undertaking commitments which are concluded in the more sober moments of a nation's history, thereby providing a guarantee that even in less sober times, its political elite will not deviate from this course and will not give free rein to its pagan instincts. Unfortunately, such a scenario where political elites come to a compromise is rarely successful and usually follows grave upheavals. Indeed, this also bears the risk of putting the country on the wrong course instead of sobering up elites: an example would be the Trianon Peace Treaty for Hungary (in which Hungary lost two-thirds of its territory after the First World War and after which liberalism was blamed for the misery of the nation) or the centuries-old struggles and even decline of several Latin American states (where crises only resulted in new crises).[84] So what shall we do?:

(1) Unfortunately, there is no magic recipe for institution-building; nevertheless, we may formulate several conclusions that are worth considering. When it comes to *formal rules*, we should learn from the lessons of the recent past and amend the constitutional or legislative rules governing the most important constitutional institutions.[85] Instead of comprehensive recodification,

[81] On the authoritarian traditions of Hungarian constitutional law before the Second World War, see L Péter, *Hungary's Long Nineteenth Century: Constitutional and Democratic Traditions in a European Perspective* (Leiden, Brill, 2012).

[82] For similar considerations, with a somewhat more optimistic terminology, see A Alessina and P Giuliano, 'Culture and Institutions' (2015) 53 *Journal of Economic Literature* 898, 928 and 938, on two-way effects, interdependence and mutual feedback effects.

[83] Offe (n 21) 200: 'Thus good citizens make good institutions, and good institutions are "good" to the extent that they generate and cultivate good citizens or the "better selves" of citizens.'

[84] The consensus of the elite can develop in an evolutive manner (eg, in Italian and in Belgian politics in the decades following the Second World War) or through explicit symbolic agreements (eg, the English Bill of Rights of 1689 or the Spanish Moncloa Pact of 1978). For a number of examples, see Higley and Burton (n 24) 55–106 and 139–80.

[85] For many examples and suggestions in this sense, see Jakab and Gajduschek (n 1).

the course to take would be a series of small steps.[86] Grand recodifications may have unforeseeable consequences, precisely because institutions are not the sum of their rules, and at the same time, such recodifications exacerbate uncertainty, decreasing trust in these institutions.[87] Hence, the success of institutional reforms depends much more on the trust and the actual practices of those concerned than on the quality of individual (otherwise important) detailed rules.[88]

I cannot proceed to go into the details of these small steps here, but I will highlight some of the main abstract elements that require legislative or, better yet, constitutional underpinnings: institutional autonomies, transparency, rule-based governance, stability, meritocracy, predictability, slowing down legislation, more stringent rules for preparing legislative bills, constitutional financing guarantees and funds for universities and other educational institutions (with a prohibition on individual aid), constitutional guarantees of internal party democracy, and making the financing of churches and foundations/civil society organisations independent from government decisions. Among others, the reinforcement of these areas through the adoption of formal rules may break down current practices. Opportunities offered by means of closer European integration may play a key role in building formal guarantees, such as integration into the most stringent system of the European Public Prosecutor's Office (*cf* the famous metaphor about self-binding: 'The Sirens and Ulysses').

We must also acknowledge that transplanting formal Western regulatory solutions to other countries in an identical form may turn out to be a spectacular failure.[89] This is not to say that 'Hungary is not cut out for the rule of law'. Exactly the opposite is true: the cultural elements presupposed by Western states based on the rule of law must be consciously built step by step, if necessary, through the adoption of formal rules that may or may not exist in Western model states. In other words, where the necessary cultural components are missing, formal rules may have to deviate from those we would otherwise adopt to support an optimal cultural component,[90] and we may have to opt for the *second-best* rule. This holds true for the entire population where dependency on political powers and, in particular, the state must be significantly decreased (eg, hospitals', schools' universities', and other cultural and social establishments' independence from party

[86] For similar conclusions, see A Sajó, 'Az állam működési zavarainak társadalmi újratermelése' (2008) 55 *Közgazdasági Szemle* 690, 710.

[87] On the dangers of 'designer activism', see D Stark, 'Path Dependence and Privatization Strategies in East Central Europe' (1992) 6 *East European Politics and Societies* 17.

[88] Offe (n 21) 215.

[89] S Holmes, 'Can Foreign Aid Promote the Rule of Law?' (1999) 8 *East European Constitutional Review* 68.

[90] For similar considerations about the formal and informal elements of a constitution, see A Vermeule, 'System Effects and the Constitution' (2009) 123 *Harvard Law Review* 4.

politics, enshrining concrete personal and financial guarantees in different constitutional rules). But it also applies to the elite, where attitudes towards fostering compromise should be strengthened (eg, with an election system which allows particularly controversial politicians to be voted out by the negative vote of citizens who are otherwise voting for other parties).[91]

(2) At the level of *actual practices*, the imperative of re-staffing key constitutional organs (the Court of Auditors, the Constitutional Court, leaders of the prosecuting services etc through transparent procedures) is often mentioned. Getting rid of obvious party soldiers of the current authoritarian regime (who also in practice have been behaving like party soldiers) would most certainly increase the credibility of the legal order; however, by itself, it will not solve existing problems (in fact, it may even exacerbate them by deepening the sharp division between 'us' and 'them'). What is more important is strict compliance with and enforcement of formal rules. Even the best formal guarantees will fail where officials are seeking to circumvent them or do nothing in the face of their breach. Stability of formal rules (except for the moment of regime change) is also important – in fact, in some cases even more important – than the content of rules.[92]

(3) Finally, perhaps the most important prerequisite is to find an honest and credible *narrative* for the legal system which is acceptable to the entire society. The way in which Hungarian society perceives and speaks of the legal system is highly contradictory and this is not just a product of the past few years. In György Gajduschek's words:

> While citizens do not trust the state or the law, they nevertheless rely on these to solve all their problems. They demand extremely detailed regulation and the severe sanctioning of any deviation from the law, however, when it comes to their person, they will gladly circumvent the rules and expect equitable treatment. All this is coupled with a social culture of exceptional pessimism, cynicism and anomie. What we are missing is a consistent value system that is shared by the majority of citizens – even when it comes to the most basic elements of the law (role of fundamental rights and duties, the presumption of innocence). In fact, individuals will often profess values that stand in stark contrast with each other. Members of society agree that society is unfair, yet they are not ready to do anything to change this. Almost every individual is of the view that s/he is better, more moral and law abiding than everyone else.[93]

[91] See n 56 above. On the advantageous effect of negative votes (and plural votes) in electoral systems in an easily comprehensible form, see www.d21.me/en; or in a more academic style with detail, see D Cahan and A Slinko, 'Electoral Competition under Best-Worst Voting Rules', www.ssrn.com/abstract=2850683; M Gregor, 'The Optimal Ballot Structure for Double-Member Districts' *CERGE-EI Working Paper Series No 493*, www.ssrn.com/abstract=2347118.

[92] Foreign direct investment in Central Eastern Europe correlates more with the *stability* of tax rules than with their actual content; see K Edmisto, S Mudd and N Valev, 'Tax Structures and FDI: The Deterrent Effects of Complexity and Uncertainty' (2003) 24 *Institute for Fiscal Studies* 341.

[93] G Gajduschek, 'Jogtudat és értékvilág – mint a magyar jogrendszer környezete' in Jakab and Gajduschek (n 1).

The fabric of society is glued together with values and prohibitions that may not be directly questioned, but will be cautiously reinterpreted: from an anthropological perspective, these are taboos. In medieval times, Christianity played this role and heretics payed a heavy price. In Western Europe since the end of the Second World War and following the fall of socialism, on the entire continent, this framework of integration has been made up of the secular taboos of constitutionalism. The twentieth century may be read as the history of experimenting and failing with different secular taboo systems, such as nationalism or socialism. Today, democracy and the protection of fundamental rights (the very reason why the Council of Europe was established in 1949) seem to be the only rational narrative for organising society. No sustainable alternative has emerged, notwithstanding the fact that this narrative has clearly been shaken and has experienced crises, yet these have only served to pinpoint the existence of extremely diverse sources of discontent and frustration. In recent times, the government invoked sovereignty as an argument to justify corruption cases and to reject without further scrutiny all foreign (including EU and international) criticism regarding the violation of fundamental rights. These references to the people and/or sovereignty are a mere rhetorical tool in the hands of the government to justify its own corruption and violations of the law. Hence, the notion of sovereignty should be redefined by the new narrative or, alternatively, references to it should possibly be avoided.[94]

The Hungarian experiment of the illiberal state will only be sustainable in the long run in the event that the grand narrative of the European integration project itself breaks down, either formally or at the level of actual practices. Fortunately, despite all challenges, this does not seem to be a realistic scenario, but whether or not the rebuilding of the Hungarian legal system will be successful depends largely on whether Hungary will be capable of carrying out the necessary tasks of institution-building. This implies not only elevating the narrative of democracy and the rule of law (including the protection of fundamental rights) to the level of taboo,[95] but also securing the moral foundations of the legal order. Citizens cannot be expected to consider secular constitutional values to be credible and profess them to be their own, if earlier violations and betrayals are left unnamed and unsanctioned.[96] The crucial problem of

[94] A Jakab, 'Neutralising the Sovereignty Question: Compromise Strategies in Constitutional Argumentations about the Concept of Sovereignty before European Integration and since' (2006) 2 *European Constitutional Law Review* 375.

[95] *cf* denouncing liberal values, especially the protection of fundamental rights by Prime Minister Viktor Orbán; eg, www.kormany.hu/en/the-prime-minister/the-prime-minister-s-speeches/prime-minister-viktor-orban-s-speech-at-the-25th-balvanyos-summer-free-university-and-student-camp; www.kormany.hu/en/the-prime-minister/the-prime-minister-s-speeches/viktor-orban-s-speech-at-the-14th-kotcse-civil-picnic.

[96] According to empirical studies, the payment of taxes is more likely in a morally acceptable regime; see L Feld and B Frey, 'Tax Compliance as a Result of a Psychological Tax Contract: The Role of Incentives and Responsive Regulation' (2007) 29 *Law and Policy* 102; V Braithwaite, *Defiance in Taxation and Governance: Resisting and Dismissing Authority in a Democracy* (Cheltenham,

institution-building in the 1989/90 constitutional system (besides corrupt practices) was that issues of justice, of dealing with the past (ie, the narrative) were swept under the carpet following a peculiar interpretation of the formal rules.[97]

Where legal and moral expectations clearly collide – as in the times of socialism, but to a certain degree also during the transition from socialism to the rule of law in 1989/90 and often even after that – both legal and moral norms will be weakened, leading to some degree of anomie.[98] To put it more provocatively and comprehensibly, Hungarian society is in a moral crisis.[99] Therefore, it seems particularly pertinent that the files of the secret services from the time of socialism are dealt with[100] and that corrupt officials are held accountable, so that public trust can be rebuilt in the constitutional institutions underlying the legal order.[101] We must consciously express moral expectations both towards members of society and public figures in public discourse,[102] thereby

Edward Elgar, 2009). On the issue that at the end of communism the economic elite was able to acquire major wealth in ways which were considered by the vast majority of the population to be immoral (for which, however, there was no legal punishment), resulting in a loss of trust in the rule of law, see G Gajduschek, *Rendnek lenni kellene: Tények és elemzések a közigazgatás ellenőrzési és bírságolási tevékenységéről* (Budapest, KSZK-MK, 2008) 220–237; and G Gajduschek, 'A közigazgatási bírságolás eredménytelenségéről' (2009) 1 *Jogtudományi Közlöny* 9. See also G Gajduschek, 'Measuring Cross-sectorial Law Enforcement Capacity of Regulatory Agencies in Hungary' (2015) 11 *Transylvanian Review of Administrative Sciences* 108, 122: 'In the end, those following rules may be considered as "losers", and breaking norms may become a norm itself.'

97 According to G Halmai, 'Rise and Fall of Constitutionalism in Hungary' in P Blokker (ed), *Constitutional Acceleration within the European Union and Beyond* (New York, Routledge, 2017) 220–23, the main reasons for the failure of liberal democracy in Hungary are the following: lack of human rights culture and liberal democratic traditions, victim culture in the national narrative, lack of economic success, loss of civic or participatory constitutionalism (and too much emphasis on judicial solutions), and a disproportionate electoral system.

98 Hungarian society is not only characterised by a low level of trust, but it is also anomic: even if normative expectations are clear, in the case of own interests, people easily defy these expectations (more than usual in an international comparison). See IG Tóth, 'A társadalmi kohézió elemei: bizalom, normakövetés, igazságosság és felelősségérzet – lennének …' in T Kolosi and IG Tóth (eds), *Társadalmi riport 2010* (Budapest, TÁRKI, 2010); T Keller, 'A gazdasági erkölcsösséget szabályozó társadalmi normákról – normakövetés és normaszegés' in IG Tóth (ed), *Európai Társadalmi Jelentés 2. Gazdasági attitűdök* (Budapest, TÁRKI, 2009).

99 With a sociologically more precise expression: 'amoral'. See the classic description of the southern Italian situation ('amoral familism') by EC Banfield, *The Moral Basis of a Backward Society* (New York, Free Press, 1958). In Banfield's work, this means the inability of collective action in the public interest, the irrelevance of any goal beyond the immediate material advantages of the nuclear family, the lack of social trust, nepotism, envy and suspicion. See also the general attitude in Hungarian society towards corruption, which is more lenient not only than the average European, but also the average of Hungary's neighbouring countries; *Special Eurobarometer 470. Corruption* (Brussels, European Commission, 2017).

100 On the unresolved nature of this issue, see, eg, L Varga, *Világ besúgói, egyesüljetek!* (Budapest, PolgArt, 2006); and K Ungváry, *A szembenézés hiánya* (Budapest, published by the author, 2017).

101 On this possibility, see T Hoffmann, 'Az állami közreműködéssel szerzett tulajdon elvonásának lehetősége a nemzetközi és európai emberi jogi sztenderdek fényében' (2017) *MTA Law Working Papers No 17*, www.jog.tk.mta.hu/uploads/files/2017_17_Hoffmann.pdf.

102 See S Bowles and H Gintis, *A Cooperative Species: Human Reciprocity and its Evolution* (Princeton, Princeton University Press, 2011) on a game theoretical analysis which shows that a low level of altruism and a lack of institutions enforcing altruism lead to weaker communities in conflict situations.

going against some know-all political commentators often appearing in the Hungarian media who interpret violations of various norms by public figures as successfully following the 'logic of politics'. Not only are these *destructive to institutions*, but they also reflect a lack of scholarly understanding of how institutions work.

In order for this to be successful, it is important to provide new generations of lawyers with the necessary theoretical toolbox.[103] Law is not just a sum of rules to be learned by heart. Currently, law students passing their final exams have a precise knowledge of administrative procedure. However, if you ask them why a state based on the rule of law is superior or what is the point of democracy, they will rattle off a brief truism (perhaps formulated in legalese), but most will not be able to make a solid case for it.[104] If these are the people who will operate the legal system in the future, they will not be able to lead the way or prevent the erosion of institutions. This is because they do not understand what it is that must be protected and supported beyond the realm of formal rules.[105] Yet, institutions must be continuously cared for and nurtured every day, otherwise they will gradually fall into disrepair.[106] Lawyers must constantly be aware of this and must not be satisfied by the thought that 'we are only interested in the legal rules as that is our job'.[107]

The bad news is that from among the three main components of institutions, it is the system of formal rules that is the easiest to change; however, this necessitates political action, that is, legislation. Unfortunately, as evidenced by the mechanisms described in the longer quote from Acemoglu given at the beginning of this chapter, we can hardly expect such action from a political elite that benefits from this situation, where the interplay of weak institutions, circumvention of rules and distrust are mutually disruptive.[108]

*

This overview of the institutionalist perception of law yields two findings. The first is that historical experience shows that besides honest determination, a radical institutional overhaul of the complete legal system can only be successful in the presence of external pressure, the effect of which had

[103] Snyder (n 30) 27: 'eternal vigilance is the price of liberty'.

[104] Z Fleck et al, *Technika vagy érték a jogállam? A jogállami értékek átadása és az előítéletek csökkentése a jogászok és a rendőrtisztek képzésében* (Budapest, L'Harmattan, 2012).

[105] On the negative picture of lawyers as command followers and enforcers, see Snyder (n 30) 41.

[106] Lowndes and Roberts (n 3) 171.

[107] Strangely, in written rules on legal education, we already have this requirement; see Ministerial Reg 18/2016 (VIII. 5.) EMMI, pt 7.1.1.c. In reality, however, it is hardly happening. Thus again, making the formal rule is insufficient, but the law-maker (out of comfortable blindness) considered the job to be done. The rule about overcoming rule-fixation became a victim of rule-fixation itself – how ironic.

[108] On the relationship between social trust and institutions, see, eg, B Rothstein and EM Uslaner, 'All for All: Equality, Corruption, and Social Trust' (2005) 58 *World Politics* 41.

unfortunately decreased with Hungary's accession to the EU. In other words, institution-building should go hand in hand with effective international and EU law obligations undertaken in more sober political moments, in order to guarantee that the political community does not enter into self-destructive mode at a later point in time (in a similar fashion to an alcoholic person engaging in self-destruction). The second finding is that, taking elements beyond mere rules more consciously into account, such as actual practices and narratives in the realm of legislation, the application of the law and legal training would ideally result in the gradual reinforcement of the substantive cultural elements necessary for the rule of law and democracy. This, however, requires political action – more precisely, the adjustment of formal rules. Since this is not in the interests of the incumbent decision-makers, for the time being, overcoming the impasse seems, sadly, unlikely.

REFERENCES

Acemoglu, D, 'Constitutions, Politics and Economics: A Review Essay on Persson and Tabellini's *The Economic Effects of Constitutions*' (2005) 43 *Journal of Economic Literature* 1025.

Acemoglu, D and Robinson, J, *Why Nations Fail: The Origins of Power, Prosperity and Poverty* (New York, Random House, 2012).

Alessina, A and Giuliano, P, 'Culture and Institutions' (2015) 53 *Journal of Economic Literature* 898.

Antal, A, 'Politikai és jogialkotmányosság Magyarországon' (2013) 22 *Politikatudományi Szemle* 48.

Avbelj, M, 'The Sociology of (Slovenian) Constitutional Democracy' (2017) 10 *The Hague Journal on the Rule of Law* 1.

Banfield, EC, *The Moral Basis of a Backward Society* (New York, Free Press, 1958).

Béla, P, *Globális uralmi rend* (Budapest, Kairosz, 2008).

Bell, J, 'The Importance of Institutions' in M Adams and D Heirbaut (eds), *The Method and Culture of Comparative Law* (Oxford, Hart Publishing, 2015).

Bellamy, R, *Political Constitutionalism* (Cambridge, Cambridge University Press, 2007).

Bencze, M and Badó, A, 'A magyar bírósági rendszer hatékonyságát és az ítélkezés színvonalát befolyásoló strukturális és személyi feltételek' in A Jakab and G Gajduschek (eds), *A magyar jogrendszer állapota* (Budapest, MTA TK, 2016).

Bohle, D and Greskovits, B, *Capitalist Diversity on Europe's Periphery* (Ithaca, Cornell University Press, 2012).

Bowles, S and Gintis, H, *A Cooperative Species: Human Reciprocity and its Evolution* (Princeton, Princeton University Press, 2011).

Bozóki, A and Hegedűs, D, 'An Externally Constrained Hybrid Regime: Hungary in the European Union' (2018) 25 *Democratization* 1173.

Braithwaite, V, *Defiance in Taxation and Governance: Resisting and Dismissing Authority in a Democracy* (Cheltenham, Edward Elgar, 2009).

Brusis, M, *Illiberale Drift und Proliferation – BTI-Regionalbericht Ostmittel- und Südosteuropa* (Gütersloh, Bertelsmann, 2018).

Butler, WE, *Soviet Law* (London, Butterworths, 1988).
Carp, R, 'The Struggle for the Rule of Law in Romania as an EU Member State: The Role of the Cooperation and Verification Mechanism' (2014) 10 *Utrecht Law Review* 1.
Cooter, RC, *The Strategic Constitution* (Princeton, Princeton University Press, 2000).
Dawson, J and Hanley, S, 'What's Wrong with East-Central Europe? The Fading Mirage of the "Liberal Consensus"' (2016) 27 *Journal of Democracy* 20.
Drinóczi, T, 'Hungarian Constitutional Court: The Limits of EU Law in the Hungarian Legal System' (2017) 11 *Vienna Journal on International Constitutional Law* 139.
Edmisto, K, Mudd, S and Valev, N, 'Tax Structures and FDI: The Deterrent Effects of Complexity and Uncertainty' (2003) 24 *Institute for Fiscal Studies* 341.
Elkins, Z, Ginsburg, T and Melton, J, *The Endurance of National Constitutions* (Cambridge, Cambridge University Press, 2009).
Elster, J, Offe, C and Preuss, U, *Institutional Design in Post-communist Societies: Rebuilding the Ship at Sea* (Cambridge, Cambridge University Press, 1998).
Eskridge, WN and Levinson, S (eds), *Constitutional Stupidities, Constitutional Tragedies* (New York, New York University Press, 1998).
Feld, L and Frey, B, 'Tax Compliance as a Result of a Psychological Tax Contract: The Role of Incentives and Responsive Regulation' (2007) 29 *Law and Policy* 102.
Fleck, Z et al, *Technika vagy érték a jogállam? A jogállami értékek átadása és az előítéletek csökkentése a jogászok és a rendőrtisztek képzésében* (Budapest, L'Harmattan, 2012).
Gajduschek, G, *Rendnek lenni kellene: Tények és elemzések a közigazgatás ellenőrzési és bírságolási tevékenységéről* (Budapest, KSZK-MK, 2008).
——. 'A közigazgatási bírságolás eredménytelenségéről' (2009) 1 *Jogtudományi Közlöny* 9.
——. 'Measuring Cross-sectorial Law Enforcement Capacity of Regulatory Agencies in Hungary' (2015) 11 *Transylvanian Review of Administrative Sciences* 108.
——. 'A közpolitikai célok megjelenése a jogban' in A Jakab and G Gajduschek (eds), *A magyar jogrendszer állapota* (Budapest, MTA TK, 2016).
——. 'Előkészítetlenség és utólagos hatásvizsgálat hiánya' in A Jakab and G Gajduschek (eds), *A magyar jogrendszer állapota* (Budapest, MTA TK, 2016).
——. 'Jogtudat és értékvilág – mint a magyar jogrendszer környezete' in A Jakab and G Gajduschek (eds), *A magyar jogrendszer állapota* (Budapest, MTA TK, 2016).
Galligan, DJ and Kurkchiyan, M (eds), *Law and Informal Practices: The Post-communist Experience* (Oxford, Oxford University Press, 2003).
Gárdos-Orosz, F, 'Alkotmánybíróság 2010–2015' in A Jakab and G Gajduschek (eds), *A magyar jogrendszer állapota* (Budapest, MTA TK, 2016).
Goodin, RE, 'Institutions and Their Design' in RE Goodin (ed), *The Theory of Institutional Design* (Cambridge, Cambridge University Press, 1996).
Gorges, MJ, 'New Institutionalist Explanations for Institutional Change: A Note of Caution' (2001) 21 *Politics* 137.
Greif, A, *Institutions and the Path to the Modern Economy: Lessons from Medieval Trade* (Cambridge, Cambridge University Press, 2006).
Győrffy, D, *Trust and Crisis Management in the European Union: An Institutionalist Account of Success and Failure in Program Countries* (Basingstoke, Palgrave Macmillan, 2018).
Halmai, G, 'Rise and Fall of Constitutionalism in Hungary' in P Blokker (ed), *Constitutional Acceleration within the European Union and Beyond* (New York, Routledge, 2017).

Hazard, JN, *Communists and Their Law* (Chicago, University of Chicago Press, 1969).
Helmke, G and Levitsky, S, 'Informal Institutions and Comparative Politics: A Research Agenda' (2004) 2 *Perspectives on Politics* 725.
Higley, J and Burton, M, *Elite Foundations of Liberal Democracy* (Oxford, Rowman & Littlefield, 2006).
Hoffmann, T, 'Az állami közreműködéssel szerzett tulajdon elvonásának lehetősége a nemzetközi és európai emberi jogi sztenderdek fényében' (2017) *MTA Law Working Papers No 17*.
Holmes, S, 'Can Foreign Aid Promote the Rule of Law?' (1999) 8 *East European Constitutional Review* 68.
Iusmen, I, 'EU Leverage and Democratic Backsliding in Central and Eastern Europe: The Case of Romania' (2015) 53 *Journal of Common Market Studies* 593.
Jakab, A, 'Neutralizing the Sovereignty Question: Compromise Strategies in Constitutional Argumentations about the Concept of Sovereignty before European Integration and since' (2006) 2 *European Constitutional Law Review* 37.
——. 'A magyar jogi oktatás megújításához szükséges lépések: Reformjavaslat összehasonlító áttekintésre alapozva' (2010) 4 *Magyar Jog* 204.
——. 'A bírói jogértelmezés az Alaptörvény tükrében' (2011) 2 *Jogesetek Magyarázata* 86.
——. *European Constitutional Language* (Cambridge, Cambridge University Press, 2016).
——. 'Miért nem működik jól a magyar jogrend és hogyan javíthatjuk meg?' (2018) *MTA Law Working Papers* No 1.
Jakab, A and Gajduschek, G (eds), *A magyar jogrendszer állapota* (Budapest, MTA TK, 2016).
Jakab, A and Hollán, M, 'Socialism's Legacy in Contemporary Law and Legal Scholarship: The Case of Hungary' (2004) 2–3 *Journal of East European Law (Columbia University)* 95.
Jakab, A and Kochenov, D (eds), *The Enforcement of EU Law and Values* (Oxford, Oxford University Press, 2017).
Jakab, A and Lőrincz, VO, 'International Indices as Models for the Rule of Law Scoreboard of the European Union: Methodological Issues' (2017) *Max Planck Institute for Comparative Public Law & International Law (MPIL) Research Paper No 21*.
Jakab, A, Sonnevend, P and Csink, L, 'The Constitution as an Instrument of Everyday Party Politics: The Basic Law of Hungary' in A von Bogdandy and P Sonnevend (eds), *Constitutional Crisis in the European Constitutional Area* (Oxford, Hart Publishing, 2015).
Jakab, A and Urbán, L (eds), *Hegymenet. Társadalmi és politikai kihívások Magyarországon* (Budapest, Osiris, 2017).
Kelemen, K, 'The New Hungarian Constitution: Critiques from Europe' (2017) 42 *Review of Central and East European Law* 1.
Keller, T, 'A gazdasági erkölcsösséget szabályozó társadalmi normákról – normakövetés és normaszegés' in IG Tóth (ed), *Európai Társadalmi Jelentés 2. Gazdasági attitűdök* (Budapest, TÁRKI, 2009).
Körösényi, A, Illés, G and Metz, R, 'Contingency and Political Action: The Role of Leadership in Endogenously Created Crises' (2016) 4 *Politics and Governance* 91.
Koob, SA et al, *Human Rights and Economic Growth* (Copenhagen, Danish Institute of Human Rights, 2017).

Kopits, G, 'Saving Hungary's Finances: Budapest's Four-Step Plan for Fiscal Alcoholics' (2008) *Wall Street Journal Europe*, 4 December.

La Torre, M, *Law as Institution* (Dordrecht–London, Springer, 2010).

Layman, GC, Carsey, TM and Menasce Horowitz, J, 'Party Polarization in American Politics: Characteristics, Causes, and Consequences' (2006) 9 *Annual Review of Political Science* 83.

Levitsky, S and Way, LA, *Competitive Authoritarianism: Hybrid Regimes after the Cold War* (Cambridge, Cambridge University Press, 2010).

Ligeti, M, 'Korrupció' in A Jakab and G Gajduschek (eds), *A magyar jogrendszer állapota* (Budapest, MTA TK, 2016).

Lowndes, V and Roberts, M, *Why Institutions Matter: The New Institutionalism in Political Science* (Basingstoke, Palgrave Macmillan, 2013).

Marauhn, T and Elliesie, H (eds), *Legal Transformation in Northern Africa and South Sudan* (The Hague, Eleven International Publishing, 2015).

March, JG and Olsen, JP, *Rediscovering Institutions* (New York, Free Press, 1989).

Matzak, M, Bencze, M and Kühn, Z, 'EU Law and Central European Judges: Administrative Judiciaries in the Czech Republic, Hungary and Poland Ten Years after Accession' in M Bobek (ed), *Central European Judges under European Influence* (Oxford, Hart Publishing, 2015).

Mendelski, M, 'The EU's Rule of Law Promotion in Post-Soviet Europe: What Explains the Divergence between Baltic States and EaP Countries?' (2016) 7 *Eastern Journal of European Studies* 111.

Mungiu-Pippidi, A, 'Corruption: Diagnosis and Treatment' (2006) 17 *Journal of Democracy* 86.

Nagy, CI, 'Esettanulmány a jogbiztonsággal kapcsolatos problémákról: a választottbíráskodásra vonatkozó szabályozás változásai' in A Jakab and G Gajduschek (eds), *A magyar jogrendszer állapota* (Budapest, MTA TK, 2016).

North, DC, *Institutions, Institutional Change and Economic Performance* (Cambridge, Cambridge University Press, 1990).

Offe, C, 'Designing Institutions in East European Transitions' in RE Goodin (ed), *The Theory of Institutional Design* (Cambridge, Cambridge University Press, 1996).

Ortega, RN, 'Conceptualizing Authoritarian Constitutionalism' (2016) 49 *Verfassung und Recht in Übersee* 339.

Ostrom, E, 'An Agenda for the Study of Institutions' (1986) 1 *Public Choice* 3.

——. *Understanding Institutional Diversity* (Princeton, Princeton University Press, 2005).

Pálné Kovács, I, 'Modellváltás a magyar önkormányzati rendszerben' in A Jakab and G Gajduschek (eds), *A magyar jogrendszer állapota* (Budapest, MTA TK, 2016).

Pap, AL, *Democratic Decline in Hungary* (New York, Routledge, 2017).

Péter, L, *Hungary's Long Nineteenth Century: Constitutional and Democratic Traditions in a European Perspective* (Leiden, Brill, 2012).

Pokol, B, 'Separation of Power and Parliamentarism in Hungary' (2003) 37 *East European Quarterly* 67.

——. *The Juristocratic State: Its Victory and the Possibilities of Taming* (Budapest, Dialóg Campus, 2017).

Polónyi, I, 'Oktatáspolitikai kísérletek és kudarcok' in A Jakab and L Urbán (eds), *Hegymenet. Társadalmi és politikai kihívások Magyarországon* (Budapest, Osiris, 2017).

Rigobon, R and Rodrik, D, 'Rule of Law, Democracy, Openness, and Income: Estimating Interrelationships' (2004) *National Bureau of Economic Research (NBER)* 2.

Rixer, Á (ed), *Állam és közösség: Válogatott közjogi tanulmányok Magyarország Alaptörvénye tiszteletére* (Budapest, Károli Gáspár Református Egyetem Állam- és Jogtudományi Kar, 2012).

Rothstein, B and Uslaner, EM, 'All for All: Equality, Corruption, and Social Trust' (2005) 58 *World Politics* 41.

Rüthers, B, *Institutionelles Rechtsdenken im Wandel der Verfassungsepochen* (Berlin, Gehlen, 1970).

Sajó, A, 'Az állam működési zavarainak társadalmi újratermelése' (2008) 55 *Közgazdasági Szemle* 690.

Scalia, A, *Reading Law: The Interpretation of Legal Texts* (St Paul, Thomson/West, 2012).

Sebők, M, Kubi, B and Molnár, C, 'A törvények formális minősége – egy empirikus vázlat' in Z Boda and A Szabó (eds), *Trendek a magyar politikában 2. A Fidesz és a többiek: pártok, mozgalmak* (Budapest, MTA TK Politikatudományi Intézet, 2017).

Sedelmeier, U, 'Anchoring Democracy from Above? The European Union and Democratic Backsliding in Hungary and Romania after Accession' (2014) 52 *Journal of Common Market Studies* 105.

Sedelmeier, U and Lacatus, C, 'Compliance with the European Union's Anti-corruption Conditions in the 'Cooperation and Verification Mechanism': Why is Romania Better than Bulgaria?' (2016) 28 *MAXCAP Working Papers*.

Smuk, P, 'Az Országgyűlés' in A Jakab and G Gajduschek (eds), *A magyar jogrendszer állapota* (Budapest, MTA TK, 2016).

Snyder, T, *On Tyranny: Twenty Lessons from the Twentieth Century* (New York, Duggan Books, 2017).

Sólyom, L, 'Előszó: Az alkotmányos kultúra szerepe' in A Jakab (ed), *Az Alaptörvény keletkezése és gyakorlati következményei* (Budapest, HVG ORAC, 2011).

——. *Das Gewand des Grundgesetzes: Zwei Verfassungsikonen – Ungarn und Deutschland* (Berlin, BWV, 2017).

Stark, D, 'Path Dependence and Privatization Strategies in East Central Europe' (1992) 6 *East European Politics and Societies* 17.

Stumpf, I, *Erős állam – alkotmányos korlátok* (Budapest, Századvég, 2014).

Szalai, Á and Jakab, A, 'Jog mint a gazdasági fejlődés infrastruktúrája' in A Jakab and G Gajduschek (eds), *A magyar jogrendszer állapota* (Budapest, MTA TK, 2016).

Szente, Z 'A historizáló alkotmányozás problémái – a történeti alkotmány és a Szent Korona az új Alaptörvényben' (2011) 4 *Közjogi Szemle* 1.

——. 'The Political Orientation of the Members of the Hungarian Constitutional Court between 2010 and 2014' (2016) 1 *Constitutional Studies* 123.

Sztompka, P, *The Sociology of Social Change* (Oxford, Blackwell, 1993).

——. *Trust: A Sociological Theory* (Cambridge, Cambridge University Press, 1999).

Tölgyessy, P, 'Politika mindenekelőtt: Jog és hatalom Magyarországon' in A Jakab and G Gajduschek (eds), *A magyar jogrendszer állapota* (Budapest, MTA TK, 2016).

Tóth, IG, 'A társadalmi kohézió elemei: bizalom, normakövetés, igazságosság és felelősségérzet – lennének …' in T Kolosi and IG Tóth (eds), *Társadalmi riport 2010* (Budapest, TÁRKI, 2010).

——. 'Turánbánya? Értékválasztások, beidegződések és az illiberalizmusra való fogadókészség Magyarországon' in A Jakab and L Urbán (eds), *Hegymenet. Társadalmi és politikai kihívások Magyarországon* (Budapest, Osiris, 2017).

Ungváry, K, *A szembenézés hiánya* (Budapest, published by the author, 2017).

Varga, C, 'A joguralom és színeváltozásai idealizáció és ideokratikus nyomásgyakorlás között' (2016) *Pázmány Law Working Papers No 12.*

Varga, L, *Világ besúgói, egyesüljetek!* (Budapest, PolgArt, 2006).

Varga, Z A, *Eszményből bálvány? A joguralom dogmatikája* (Budapest, Századvég, 2015).

Vermeule, A, 'System Effects and the Constitution' (2009) 123 *Harvard Law Review* 4.

Vincze, A and Varju, M, 'Hungary: The New Fundamental Law' (2012) 18 *European Public Law* 437.

Yanovskiy, M and Ginker, T, 'A Proposal for a More Objective Measure of De Facto Constitutional Constraints' (2017) 28 *Constitutional Political Economy* 311.

Zakaria, F, 'The Rise of Illiberal Democracy' (1997) 76 *Foreign Affairs* 22.

Zander, M, *The Law-Making Process* (Cambridge, Cambridge University Press, 2004).

Zsolt, B, 'Bizalom, legitimitás és jogkövetés' in A Jakab and G Gajduschek (eds), A Magyar jogrendszer állapota (Budapest, MTA TK, 2016).

10

'A More United Union' and the Danish Conundrum

ULLA NEERGAARD*

I. FLYING HIGH

[T]he moment you doubt whether you can fly, you cease forever to be able to do it.[1]

THE ABOVE SENTENCE encapsulates the essence of the mantra to which the EU has dedicated itself because, from the moment it flew for the first time, it has been progress-orientated in nature. This orientation has most clearly found its expression in the phrase 'Ever Closer Union', which has its origin in the Preamble to the Treaty of Rome (1957), where the original wording was simply that the founding fathers were: 'Determined to lay the foundations of an ever closer union among the peoples of Europe.' Furthermore, in Article 2 of that Treaty, there was a reference to 'closer relations between the States belonging to it'.[2] Recently, in the high-profile speech regarding the State

* The chapter builds on the author's presentations on the following two conferences: 'In the Maelstrom of Crises. European Solidarity under Pressure', Vienna, 29–30 June 2017 ('Challenges to the Legitimacy of European Integration/European Solidarity under Pressure – The State of Play in Denmark'); and 'The Future of Europe: Political and Legal Integration beyond Brexit', Stockholm, 16–17 November 2017 ('A Tale of Challenges to Legal Integration – A Danish Perspective'). Inspiration has also been taken in the presentations and discussions at the conference: 'Legal Disintegration in the European Union', Copenhagen, 15–16 March 2018. The author warmly wishes to thank Christopher Muttukumaru and Peter Biering for substantive comments, and the former also for excellent language editing. The usual disclaimer applies.

[1] JM Barrie, the author of *Peter Pan, or The Boy Who Wouldn't Grow Up* (1904) and *The Little White Bird* (1902); see https://en.wikiquote.org/wiki/J._M._Barrie.

[2] In the Treaty of Lisbon, the wording was slightly changed as the wording of the Preamble became that the signing parties are '*resolved* to continue the process of creating an ever closer union among the peoples of Europe, in which decisions are taken as closely as possible to the citizen in accordance with the principle of subsidiarity' (emphasis added). In a similar vein, in art 1 of the Treaty on European Union (TEU), it was stated: 'This Treaty marks a new stage in the process of

of the Union by Commission President Jean-Claude Juncker, which was introduced in a document embellished with an image of what seems to be a colourful 'paper bird' – apparently symbolising the flight being taken – there was a significant heading which used a similar phrase, namely 'a more united Union' in the following context:

> If we want the euro to unite rather than divide our continent, then it should be more than the currency of a select group of countries. The euro is meant to be the single currency of the European Union as a whole. All but two of our Member States are required and entitled to join the euro once they fulfil the conditions. Member States that want to join the euro must be able to do so. This is why I am proposing to create a Euro-accession Instrument, offering technical and even financial assistance.[3]

By using the phrase 'a more united Union', a more symbolic and controversially perceived phrase, 'an ever closer union', was left out, but the use of this 'new' phrase does not really change the essence of what is meant, although it could be claimed that it is even stronger because one may associate it with a 'United States of Europe'. In all circumstances, what both terms have in common is that they describe an evolving process towards a common goal. Further integration is still a key aim of the EU, now clearly also expressed as a desire eventually to include as many Member States as possible in the European Monetary Union (EMU).

The many challenges currently facing Europe have strongly increased the interest in the phenomenon of further integration. As to such challenges, the European Commission has recently in its 'White Paper on the Future of Europe' – filled with illustrations of simplistic, flying, blue 'paper birds' – pointed out that:

> [M]any Europeans consider the Union as either too distant or too interfering in their day-to-day lives. Others question its added-value and ask how Europe improves their standard of living. And for too many, the EU fell short of their expectations as it struggled with its worst financial, economic and social crisis in post-war history. Europe's challenges show no sign of abating. Our economy is recovering from the global financial crisis but this is still not felt evenly enough. Parts of our neighbourhood are destabilised, resulting in the largest refugee crisis since the Second World War. Terrorist attacks have struck at the heart of our cities. New global powers are emerging as old ones face new realities. And last year, one of our Member States voted to leave the Union.[4]

creating an ever closer union among the peoples of Europe, in which decisions are taken as openly as possible and as closely as possible to the citizen.' The Preamble to the Treaty on the Functioning of the European Union (TFEU) was similarly drafted.

[3] European Commission, 'President Jean-Claude Juncker's State of the Union Address 2017', Brussels, 13 September 2017, www.europa.eu/rapid/press-release_SPEECH-17-3165_en.htm.

[4] European Commission, *White Paper on the Future of Europe. Reflections and Scenarios for the EU 27 by 2015*, COM [2017] 2025, 6.

As to the process of integration and the difficulties in that regard, the European Commission in this significant *White Paper on the Future of Europe* not only explained but also warned that:

> The EU is a unique project in which domestic priorities have been combined and sovereignty voluntarily pooled to better serve national and collective interests. It has not always been an easy journey, it has never been perfect, but it has shown its capacity to reform itself and has proven its value over time. Following the motto of 'unity in diversity', the EU and its Member States have been able to draw on the unique strengths and richness of their nations to achieve unprecedented progress. In an uncertain world, the allure of isolation may be tempting to some, but the consequences of division and fragmentation would be far-reaching. It would expose European countries and citizens to the spectre of their divided past and make them prey to the interests of stronger powers.[5]

Several other important political statements as to future developments have recently been launched. As a significant example, reference may be made to the Rome Declaration on the occasion of the sixtieth anniversary of the EU, where an aim of an 'even greater unity' was stated in the following context:

> We will make the European Union stronger and more resilient, through even greater unity and solidarity amongst us and the respect of common rules. Unity is both a necessity and our free choice. Taken individually, we would be side-lined by global dynamics. Standing together is our best chance to influence them, and to defend our common interests and values. We will act together, at different paces and intensity where necessary, while moving in the same direction, as we have done in the past, in line with the Treaties and keeping the door open to those who want to join later. Our Union is undivided and indivisible.[6]

As a final recent example of significance, reference may be made to one of the many recent speeches by the French President Emmanuel Macron, namely his 'Speech for Europe in Athens' in which, among other things, he stated:

> Europe is one of the last havens where we collectively continue to harbour a certain idea of humanity, law, freedom and justice. We need Europe now more than ever. The world needs Europe. Organizing its dismantlement would therefore make no sense. It would be a sort of political and historical suicide. That is why … I want us collectively to get back that primary energy, the force to rebuild our Europe, not to continue what does not work or try to tweak it, but to start with an uncompromising critical assessment of these last years, to give us the primary strength, the primary ambition … We must bring back the primary force of hope which led certain individuals in Europe, despite the divisions of the post-war period, to desire a bigger story, more beautiful than themselves.[7]

[5] ibid 26.

[6] Council of Europe, 'The Rome Declaration. Declaration of the Leaders of 27 Member States and of the European Council, the European Parliament and the European Commission', 25 March 2017, www.consilium.europa.eu/en/press/press-releases/2017/03/25/rome-declaration.

[7] E Macron, 'A Speech for Europe', Athens, 2017, www.ellopos.com/blog/4471/em-macron-a-speech-for-europe-athens-2017-full-text-in-english-and-video/3.

These initiatives clearly show that there are significant expressions of intention to develop an intensification of integration or – to return to the image of a bird in flight – a continuation of the flight to even greater heights.[8] Yet, at the same time, opposite forces exist. The aim of the present chapter is to analyse how, having regard to the situation in Denmark, these different forces have materialised in various ways in a legal context.

In more than one respect, this Member State is situated at the margins of the EU in more ways than simply geographically. Paradoxically, it is a country that now belongs to the group of longest-lasting members of the EU, as it became a full member back in 1973 (together with Ireland and the UK). Perhaps it ought by now to have become accustomed to it, but nevertheless it may be considered to have one of the most puzzling stances towards it. In fact, after the in/out referendum in the UK ('Brexit') on 23 June 2016 and the consequential expected exit from the EU, Denmark will be the country with the most numerous explicit standalone arrangements. Thus, rather unsurprisingly, the country has, for instance, been referred to as 'an awkward European partner',[9] 'a reluctant European',[10] 'an outlier when it comes to European integration'[11] and 'a state suffering from an "integration dilemma"'.[12] It has also (together with the other Scandinavian countries) been referred to as only a 'soft euro-sceptic',[13] as well as 'a smart state handling a differentiated integration dilemma'.[14] At the same time, its relationship with the EU has been characterised by what looks like a paradox.[15] Thus, with regard to its relations to the EU, Denmark somehow constitutes something of a conundrum as a country having a problematic or differentiated relationship to the EU, yet combined with more 'comforting' behaviour traits.[16]

Although this phenomenon to some degree has already been analysed in the literature, the perspectives developed so far have mainly been from that of

[8] See also J-C Piris, *The Future of Europe: Towards a Two-Speed Europe?* (Cambridge, Cambridge University Press, 2012).

[9] A Wivel, 'As Awkward as They Need to Be: Denmark's Pragmatic Activist Approach to Europe' in M Stegmann McCallion and A Brianson (eds), *Nordic States and European Integration: Awkward Partners in the North* (London, Palgrave Macmillan, 2018) 14.

[10] L Miles and A Wivel, 'Introducing Denmark and the European Union' in L Miles and A Wivel (eds), *Denmark and the European Union* (New York, Routledge, 2014) 1.

[11] L Miles and A Wivel, 'A Smart State Handling a Differentiated Integration Dilemma? Concluding on Denmark in the European Union' in Miles and Wivel (eds) (n 10) 228.

[12] Miles and Wivel, 'Introducing Denmark and the European Union' (n 10) 1.

[13] J Hassing Nielsen, 'The Pragmatic Euroscepticism of Scandinavia' in B Leruth et al (eds), *The Routledge Handbook of Euroscepticism* (London, Routledge, 2018) 231.

[14] Miles and Wivel (n 11) 228.

[15] M Marcussen, 'Denmark and the Euro Opt-out' in Miles and Wivel (eds) (n 10) 74.

[16] According to R Adler-Nissen, *Opting out of the European Union: Diplomacy, Sovereignty and European Integration* (Cambridge, Cambridge University Press, 2014) 2: 'Differentiation is the collective term for rejecting common rules and moving towards a form of co-operation where various member states have different rights and obligations within specific policy areas.'

political science or from a more fragmented legal point of view.[17] Accordingly, the objective here is rather to provide a more legally based analysis of the most significant deviating elements in Danish membership and behaviour, thereby providing a kind of mini-case study of a country seemingly not wanting to fly as high as the majority. Against this background, I do not intend to adopt a normative approach.[18] More specifically, the following topics will be covered: the overall relationship with the EU (section II); the EU citizenship opt-out (section III); the EMU opt-out (section IV); the defence policy opt-out (section V); the Area of Freedom, Security and Justice (AFSJ) opt-out (section VI); the 'second home' protocol (section VII); other areas of differentiation (section VIII); and conclusions – not completely wanting to fly along (section IX).

II. THE OVERALL RELATIONSHIP WITH THE EU

If a formal context for Denmark's independent behaviour were needed, it is mainly a consequence of the initial so-called Danish 'No' in 1992 to the Treaty of Maastricht (with only 50.7 per cent in favour of a 'No').[19] This led to the Edinburgh Agreement of 1992, the purpose of which was to assist in approval in a second referendum.[20] Thus, four opt-outs were stipulated in the so-called Edinburgh Decision.[21]

Accordingly, in a new referendum, which took place in 1993, the Danes accepted the Treaty of Maastricht (with 56.7 per cent in favour thereof), which was subsequently ratified. In other word, these opt-outs have now been in force for a quarter of a century and their practical importance has steadily increased over the years. On the one hand, they have, for example, been seen as implying that Denmark has less influence in important matters.[22] On the other hand,

[17] See. eg. ibid; J Hassing Nielsen, 'The Pragmatic Euroscepticism of Scandinavia' in Leruth et al (n 13); Miles and Wivel (eds) (n 10); and Wivel (n 9).

[18] In the current Danish political fora, the issue of whether the opt-outs should be given up continuously play a very central role. However, the intention of the present analysis is not to contribute with inputs either in favour of or in opposition to this.

[19] On this referendum and more generally about the Danish relation to the EU, see M Kelstrup, 'Denmark's Relation to the European Union: A History of Dualism and Pragmatism' in L Miles et al (eds), *Denmark and the European Union* 14–29. See also Wivel (n 9) 13 f.

[20] Included in Part B, 'Denmark and the Treaty on European Union', of the Conclusions of the Presidency, European Council in Edinburgh, 11–12 December 1992, www.europarl.europa.eu/summits/edinburgh/default_en.htm.

[21] More precisely, the agreement consists of the following set of arrangements: (a) a decision concerning certain problems raised by Denmark on the Treaty on European Union (Annex 1); (b) two declarations from the European Council (Annex 2; one on social policy, consumers, environment and distribution of income and one on defence); (c) two unilateral declarations from Denmark (Annex 3); and (d) a final declaration. In the latter, it is stated that as far as Denmark is concerned, the Edinburgh Decision is compatible with the Treaty of Maastricht and does not call its objectives into question.

[22] See, eg, Dansk Institut for Internationale Studier, *De danske forbehold overfor den europæiske union. Udviklingen siden 2000* (Copenhagen, Dansk Institut for Internationale Studier, 2008) 22.

they have, for instance, been interpreted as bulwarks against European integration and symbolising 'the preservation of national sovereignty – emphasising an image of the state with full political and legal authority over people, territory and currency – which makes them seem almost sacrosanct'.[23]

The Edinburgh Decision constitutes an international law decision and has the status of a legally binding instrument, complementing EU Treaty law.[24] It is not in itself subject to the jurisdiction of the Court of Justice of the European Union (CJEU).[25] Pursuant to Section E, No 1, of the decision, it took effect on the date of entry into force of the Treaty on European Union and without any prior ratification in the individual Member States.[26] Therefore, it was only in Denmark that the Decision became an element in the Danish ratification of the Treaty of Maastricht.[27]

The Decision can be said successively to have been upheld when Treaty amendments have taken place.[28] Thus, the Decision is considered not to be in conflict with the Treaty of Lisbon, but rather as complementing it.[29] There is in Protocol No 22 of the Treaty of Lisbon a reference to the Decision.[30] Here, it is also stipulated that Denmark will not prevent the other Member States from further developing their cooperation with respect to measures that are not binding on Denmark. Since the Treaty of Amsterdam, due to the adoption of that Protocol, the opt-outs may be viewed as having moved from only having the status of international law to also having the status of EU law, and thus subject to interpretation not only by Denmark but also by the EU as such.[31] On that basis, the CJEU may also now be considered competent in this regard.

[23] Adler-Nissen (n 16) 8.

[24] Udenrigsministeriet, *Notat til Udenrigspolitisk Nævn om Edinburgh-aftalen*, 2008, www.eu.dk/samling/20072/almdel/EUU/bilag/364/580364.pdf.

[25] Dansk Institut for Internationale Studier (n 22) 37.

[26] Udenrigsministeriet (n 24).

[27] See C Thorning, 'Forsvarsforbeholdet' in BE Olsen and KE Sørensen (eds), *EU-retten i Danmark* (Copenhagen, DJØF, 2018). It is also explained here that the second referendum accordingly concerned a legislative proposal to accede to both the Edinburgh Decision and the Treaty of Maastricht, namely L177/1992-93, adopted as Act No 355 of 9 June 1993, and that the Edinburgh Decision and the associated act of amendment to the Act of Accession added to that Act's § 4, which lists those treaties which constitute the foundation of the Danish EU membership (ie, Act No 289 of 28 April 1993).

[28] See, eg, Folketinget, *Lissabontraktaten sammenskrevet med det gældende traktatgrundlag* (Copenhagen, Folketingets EU-Oplysning, 2018).

[29] Thorning (n 27).

[30] See also Protocols 16 and 17 as of relevance to the Danish situation; and 'Politisk aftale af 2008-02-21 mellem Regeringen (Venstre og Det Konservative Folkeparti), Socialdemokraterne, Socialistisk Folkeparti, Det Radikale Venstre og Ny Alliance om dansk europapolitik i en globaliseret verden', which according to *EU-Karnov* is printed in FT 2007-08, 2. samling, ad L 53, in 'Europaudvalgets betænkning af 2008-03-14'.

[31] Thorning (n 27). See also more generally AG Toth, 'The Legal Effects of the Protocols Relating to the United Kingdom, Ireland and Denmark' in T Heukels, N Blokker and M Brus (eds), *The European Union after Amsterdam: A Legal Analysis* (The Hague, Kluwer Law International, 1998).

The term 'opt' derives from the Latin term 'optare' and means to select or to choose.[32] Importantly and as has been put forward by Adler-Nissen: 'At first glance, a national opt-out is simply a legal protocol attached to a treaty, which usually implies that a member state will not formally participate in the decision-making process and will not adopt or implement EU legislation in the area covered by the opt-out. In practice, however, Danish and British officials participate in meetings where new legislation covered by their protocols is discussed, only without always casting their formal vote.'[33] The Danish opt-outs may be viewed as not only having a function vis-a-vis the EU – in simplified terms – in the shape of a right not to participate in the specified areas of law, but by nature presumably also an obligation vis-a-vis the Danish electorate, as they may also be interpreted as a promise to respect this approach, namely, that the areas covered by the opt-outs are protected from action.[34]

According to Section E, No 2, Denmark can give up its opt-outs at any time. More precisely, according to Section E, No 2, Denmark may at any time, in accordance with its constitutional requirements, inform other Member States that it no longer wishes to avail itself of all or part of this decision. In that event, Denmark will apply in full all relevant measures then in force taken within the framework of the EU. However, to give up one or all of the Danish opt-outs is considered to require a referendum.[35] That said, it is considered unlikely that the Danish electorate at present would vote for such a change. By now, mainly in light of that fact, changing Danish governments seem to have become more hesitant regarding such referenda on EU matters.[36]

The four Danish treaty-based opt-outs more specifically concern 'Citizenship', 'Economic and Monetary Union', 'Defence Policy' and 'Justice and Home Affairs' (ie, the AFSJ).[37] In general terms, they imply that in the areas of law at stake, Denmark cannot participate.

[32] See, eg, *Webster's Encyclopedic Unabridged Dictionary of the English Language*.

[33] Adler-Nissen (n 16) 15.

[34] See also the not legally binding 'Danish Compromise', 27 October 1992, www.retsforbehold.eu.dk/da/folkeafstemning/lovstof/eu/nationale_kompromis.

[35] On the legal details in that regard, see Thorning (n 27).

[36] Three out of eight times, referenda ended with a 'No' vote and generally it is a rather tight vote in the cases leading to a 'Yes'. The figures are as follows: 1972: Treaty of Rome (accession) => Yes (63.3 vs 36.7); 1986: European Single Act => Yes (56.2 vs 43.8); 1992: Treaty of Maastricht => No (49.3 vs 50.7); 1992: Treaty of Maastricht and the Edinburgh Agreement => Yes (56.3 vs 43.3); 1998: Treaty of Amsterdam => Yes (55.1 vs 44.9); 2000: The Euro (one of the opt-outs) => No (46.8 vs 53.2); 2014: Patent Court => Yes (62.5 vs 37.5); 2015: Change of the opt-out regarding police and judicial collaboration => No (46.9 vs 53.1).

[37] According to Tænketanken Europa, 'Forbeholdslandet Danmark. De mange aktiveringer af forbeholdene – og det voksende tab af suverænitet', Report (2017) 14, www.thinkeuropa.dk/sites/default/files/notat.forbehold.2017.endelig0206_1.pdf, a majority would vote 'no' to give up all four opt-outs.

III. THE UNION CITIZENSHIP OPT-OUT

In Section A of the Edinburgh Decision, the following is stated:

> No provisions of Part Two of the Treaty establishing the European Community relating to citizenship of the Union give nationals of the Member States additional rights and protection as specified in that Part. They do not in any way take the place of national citizenship. The questions whether an individual possesses the nationality of a Member State will be settled solely by reference to the national law of the Member State concerned.[38]

This is further expanded upon in the first of the two unilateral declarations of Denmark (Annex 3).[39] Here, most importantly, it is emphasised that nationals of the other Member States enjoy the right to vote and to stand as a candidate at municipal elections, and that Denmark would introduce legislation to the same effect with regard to elections for the European Parliament.

Today, the opt-out is generally perceived as having no real impact, mainly because in 1999, the Treaty of Amsterdam stipulated in what is now Article 20 TFEU that: 'Citizenship of the Union shall be additional to and not replace national citizenship.'[40] Importantly, the opt-out was essentially stipulated rather narrowly. The subsequent significant development of the concept of EU citizenship, which has taken place, mainly driven forward by the CJEU, was in all likelihood not foreseen 25 years ago and is generally not caught by the opt-out.[41] Nevertheless, a majority of the electorate would vote 'no' if invited to give up the opt-out.[42]

IV. THE EMU OPT-OUT

The opt-out regarding the euro gives Denmark the right to decide if, and when, to join the euro.[43] In other words, it implies that Denmark is never obliged to enter the third phase of the EMU. The original fear behind the opt-out is closely related to an overall fear of a federal Europe with loss of a Danish national

[38] Denmark and the Treaty on European Union [1992] OJ C348/1.

[39] Included in Part B, Denmark and the Treaty on European Union, of the Conclusions of the Presidency, European Council in Edinburgh, 11-12 December 1992, www.europarl.europa.eu/summits/edinburgh/default_en.htm.

[40] See also art 9 TEU.

[41] See, eg, U Neergaard, 'Europe and the Welfare State – Friends, Foes, or …?' (2016) 35 *Yearbook of European Law*, 1–41.

[42] Tænketanken Europa (n 37) 17.

[43] This section draws on parts of U Neergaard, 'The European Exchange Rate Mechanism II' in F Amtenbrink and C Herrmann (eds), *The EU Law of Economic and Monetary Union* (Oxford, Oxford University Press, forthcoming); and U Neergaard, 'Euro-forbeholdet' in Olsen and Sørensen (n 27).

identity.[44] More specifically, in Section B of the Edinburgh Decision, the following is stated:

1. The Protocol on certain provisions relating to Denmark attached to the Treaty establishing the European Community gives Denmark the right to notify the Council of the European Communities of its position concerning participation in the third stage of Economic and Monetary Union. Denmark has given notification that it will not participate in the third stage. This notification will take effect upon the coming into effect of this decision.
2. As a consequence, Denmark will not participate in the single currency, will not be bound by the rules concerning economic policy which apply only to the Member States participating in the third stage of Economic and Monetary Union, and will retain its existing powers in the field of monetary policy according to its national laws and regulations, including powers of the National Bank of Denmark in the field of monetary policy.
3. Denmark will participate fully in the second stage of Economic and Monetary Union and will continue to participate in exchange-rate cooperation within the European Monetary System (EMS).[45]

In addition, reference may be made to Protocol No 16, the so-called special Danish EMU protocol, whose origins lie in the Treaty of Maastricht.[46] The following is stated in the Treaty of Lisbon:

> The high contracting parties, taking into account that the Danish Constitution contains provisions which may imply a referendum in Denmark prior to Denmark renouncing its exemption, given that, on 3 November 1993, the Danish Government notified the Council of its intention not to participate in the third stage of economic and monetary union, have agreed upon the following provisions, which shall be annexed to the Treaty on European Union and to the Treaty on the Functioning of the European Union:
>
> 1. In view of the notice given to the Council by the Danish Government on 3 November 1993, Denmark shall have an exemption. The effect of the exemption shall be that all Articles and provisions of the Treaties and the Statute of the ESCB referring to a derogation shall be applicable to Denmark.
> 2. As for the abrogation of the exemption, the procedure referred to in Article 140 shall only be initiated at the request of Denmark.
> 3. In the event of abrogation of the exemption status, the provisions of this Protocol shall cease to apply.[47]

[44] See, eg, Dansk Institut for Internationale Studier (n 22) 35–36.

[45] Denmark and the Treaty on European Union [1992] OJ C348/1.

[46] ie, in Protocol No 12 and thereby originating from before the 1992 referendum.

[47] A Danish government interpretation of this provision may be found here: Justitsministeriet, 'Notat om visse forfatningsretlige spørgsmål i forbindelse med Danmarks ratifikation af traktaten om stabilitet, samordning og styring i Den Økonomiske og Monetære Union (den såkaldte finanspagt)', 22 February 2012, 10, www.ft.dk/samling/20111/almdel/euu/bilag/304/1086616/index.htm.

Any change with regard to this opt-out, as well as the others, will (as mentioned above) require a referendum.[48] In fact, in 2000, the Danish electorate – despite the fact that only six months earlier, a fairly large proportion of the population was in favour of voting in the positive – voted against joining the euro in a referendum (a rejection by 53.2 per cent of voters). Public support in favour of the euro itself is still rather weak, which also supports the view that it would not be realistic to expect a new referendum to be launched in the near future.[49] Therefore, it can reasonably be predicted that the Danish euro opt-out will stand for many years to come.

Somehow in spite of the opt-out, it is noteworthy that Denmark follows a fixed-exchange-rate policy vis-a-vis the euro, which was agreed upon nearly 20 years ago.[50] More specifically, the decision was made at an informal meeting of the Ecofin Council on 25–27 September 1998 in Vienna between the ministers for economy and finance and the central bank governors of the EU Member States.[51] A narrow fluctuation band of +/−2.25 per cent around the central rate in the European Exchange Rate Mechanism II (ERM II) was the decision made at that time.[52] In the circumstances, Denmark keeps the exchange rate within a much narrower range than is required by the system itself (as a currency here is allowed to float within a quite wide range of +/−15 per cent). In practice, since the fixed-exchange-rate policy ensures that fluctuations in the 'krone' rate against the euro are kept at such a very modest level, the 'krone' will match the euro's fluctuations vis-a-vis other currencies.[53] Even today, the ERM II still constitutes the formal framework for the Danish fixed-exchange-rate policy.[54] The Danish Central Bank's assessment is that this policy has provided an anchor for low and stable inflation expectations.[55] Thus, rather remarkably,

[48] See the account of the relevant literature and the Ministry of Justice's assessments in that regard in the following Memorandum: 'NOTAT om hvorvidt dansk deltagelse i det styrkede banksamarbejde forudsætter anvendelse af proceduren i grundlovens § 20', 29 April 2015, www.justitsministeriet.dk/sites/default/files/media/Arbejdsomraader/Vaaben/Notat%20om%20visse%20statsretlige%20sp%C3%B8rgsm%C3%A5l.pdf.

[49] See, eg, Tænketanken Europa (n 37) 15.

[50] Danmarks Nationalbank, *Monetary Policy in Denmark* (Copenhagen, Rosendahls-Schultz Grafisk, 2009) 9. Importantly, again before joining the ERM II, Denmark had conducted a fixed-exchange-rate policy. This policy was initiated back in the early 1980s, initially against the Deutsche Mark and then against the euro. See further Danmarks Nationalbank, 'Foreign-Exchange-Rate Policy and ERM 2', www.nationalbanken.dk/en/monetarypolicy/fixed_exchange_rate_and_ERM2/Pages/default.aspx.

[51] Danmarks Nationalbank, *Monetary Policy in Denmark* (n 50) 9.

[52] ibid 9.

[53] ibid 120.

[54] See www.nationalbanken.dk/da/pengepolitik/fastkurserm2/Sider/default.aspx.

[55] See ibid. For further details, see M Spange et al, 'Fastkurspolitik i Danmark' in Danmarks Nationalbank, 'Kvartalsoversigt' (2014), www.nationalbanken.dk/da/publikationer/Documents/2014/03/Fastkurspolitik_KVO1_2014.pdf. Importantly, the European Central Bank can choose not to support the 'krone'; see Agreement of 16 March 2006 between the European Central Bank and the national central banks of the Member States outside the euro area laying down the operating procedures for an exchange rate mechanism in stage three of Economic and Monetary Union [2006] OJ C73/08, art 3.1: 'Intervention at the margins shall in principle be automatic and unlimited.

since Denmark joined ERM II back in 1999 when the euro was introduced, its participation has been long-lasting and compliant. Perhaps even more remarkably, the country has for many years been able to fulfil the convergence criteria and is thus qualified to join the euro.[56]

Formally viewed, the euro-opt-out has only been activated once, namely in relation to the decision of Denmark not to join the euro when it was first set up.[57] Nevertheless, it has been pointed out that in reality, there have been several legal acts in which Denmark has had to abstain from participating as a consequence of the opt-out.[58]

At the same time, there are important initiatives in which Denmark did decide to take part. Among these, in particular, there are two intergovernmental agreements which may be referred to as important examples, namely the Stability and Growth Pact from 1997 (and revised at a later stage)[59] and the Treaty on Stability, Coordination and Governance in the EMU (also called the 'TSCG' and the fiscal part thereof for the 'Fiscal Compact') from 2012.[60] In addition, it is worth mentioning that Denmark has entered an important soft law instrument, the Euro Plus Pact, in 2011, and also becomes subject to review pursuant to the so-called European Semester.

Moreover, it is the intention that those Member States which are outside the eurozone can enter the Banking Union. The Ministry of Justice has estimated that joining would not, pursuant to the Danish Constitution, require a referendum. But this conclusion should perhaps be problematised in the light of the following point of view: 'Banking union signifies a further transfer of sovereign powers from the national to the supranational arena.'[61] Although no decision has been made yet, the present government is positive towards the idea.[62]

However, the ECB and the participating non-euro area NCBs could suspend automatic intervention if this were to conflict with their primary objective of maintaining price stability.'

56 See Marcussen (n 15) 53, who explains that Denmark, like most other countries in the EU in 2014, was no longer able to fulfil the convergence criteria.

57 Tænketanken Europa (n 37).

58 ibid 15.

59 European Council, Resolution of the Amsterdam European Council on the Stability and Growth Pact [1997] OJ C236/01.

60 It can be found at: www.eur-lex.europa.eu/legal-content/EN/TXT/HTML/?uri=LEGISSUM:1403_3&from=EN. As to the possible 'repatration' of the TSCG into EU law, see JG von Luckner, 'How to Bring it Home: The EU's Options for Incorporating the Fiscal Compact into EU Law' *European Law Blog* (9 April 2018), www.europeanlawblog.eu/2018/04/09/how-to-bring-it-home-the-eus-options-for-incorporating-the-fiscal-compact-into-eu-law/#more-4048.

61 Justitsministeriet, 'Notat om hvorvidt dansk deltagelse i det styrkede banksamarbejde forudsætter anvendelse af proceduren i grundlovens § 20' (2015), www.justitsministeriet.dk/sites/default/files/media/Arbejdsomraader/Vaaben/Notat%20om%20visse%20statsretlige%20sp%C3%B8rgsm%C3%A5l.pdf; and Arbejdsgruppen vedrørende analysearbejdet ift. dansk deltagelse i det styrkede banksamarbejde, 'Rapport om mulig dansk deltagelse i det styrkede banksamarbejde' (2015), www.evm.dk/publikationer/2015/15-04-30-rapport-omstyrket-banksamarbejde.

62 See Folketingets EU-Oplysning: www.eu.dk/da/fakta-om-eu/politikker/oekonomisk-politik/banker.

V. THE DEFENCE POLICY OPT-OUT

The opt-out regarding defence is placed in Section C of the Edinburgh Decision with the following content:

> The Heads of state and Government note that, in response to the invitation from the Western European Union (WEU), Denmark has become an observer to that organisation. They also note that nothing in the Treaty on European Union commits Denmark to become a member of the WEU. Accordingly, Denmark does not participate in the elaboration and the implementation of decisions and actions of the Union which have defence implications, but will not prevent the development of closer cooperation between Member States in this area.[63]

The overall intentions behind the opt-out are perhaps best understood by reference to the so-called 'National Compromise' in which it is stated that Denmark should stay outside the 'defence political dimension', which is viewed as including membership of the WEU and common defence policy or common defence.[64] The concern then was mainly that of the establishment of a 'Defence Union' as such, including, eg, an EU army competent to require the deployment of Danish soldiers to a war zone. Naturally, the term 'defence implications' included in the opt-out itself is crucial. In contrast to the AFSJ opt-out, the defence opt-out is understood as a reservation with regard to the substantive area in question rather than to the rules on cooperation.[65] Accordingly, Denmark is considered – unlike the AFSJ opt-out – not to be allowed to enter into parallel agreements in the substantive areas covered by the opt-out.[66]

Certain changes in relation to the opt-out have over the years taken place to ensure that it is continuously respected.[67] An important step in that regard occurred with the new protocol on the position of Denmark, which, as pointed out above, was first adopted in connection with the Treaty of Amsterdam. Article 5 of Protocol No 22 of the Treaty of Lisbon states:

> With regard to measures adopted by the Council pursuant to Article 26(1), Article 42 and Articles 43 to 46 of the Treaty on European Union, Denmark does not participate in the elaboration and the implementation of decisions and actions of the Union which have defence implications. Therefore Denmark shall not participate

[63] Denmark and the Treaty on European Union [1992] OJ C348/1. Also, in the second of the two declarations of the European Council, the following is stated: 'The European Council takes note that Denmark will renounce its right to exercise the Presidency of the Union in each case involving the elaboration and the implementation of decisions and actions of the Union which have defence implications. The normal rules for replacing the President, in the case of the President being indisposed, shall apply. These rules will also apply with regard to the representation of the Union in international organisations, international conferences and with third countries'.

[64] 'Danish Compromise', 27 October 1992, www.retsforbehold.eu.dk/da/folkeafstemning/lovstof/eu/nationale_kompromis.

[65] Thorning (n 27).

[66] ibid.

[67] ibid.

> in their adoption. Denmark will not prevent the other Member States from further developing their cooperation in this area. Denmark shall not be obliged to contribute to the financing of operational expenditure arising from such measures, nor to make military capabilities available to the Union. The unanimity of the members of the Council, with the exception of the representative of the government of Denmark, shall be necessary for the acts of the Council which must be adopted unanimously. For the purposes of this Article, a qualified majority shall be defined in accordance with Article 238(3) of the Treaty on the Functioning of the European Union.

The defence element of Protocol No 22 should be viewed as an EU Treaty-based supplement to the Edinburgh Decision and of central contemporary importance in relation to the regulation of Denmark's special position.[68] Thus, important clarifications in that regard have been stipulated.

Significantly, the opt-out is interpreted as including within its scope only legal acts – a term that does not, for instance, include Communications or Conclusions – having their legal base in the EU Treaty (ie, in provisions expressly mentioned in the defence element of Protocol No 22).[69] Also, the condition as to 'defence implications' should self-evidently be fulfilled. This in particular implies that various military actions including those having a peace-orientated or humanitarian purpose are included, thereby preventing Denmark from participating.[70] Denmark has also been prevented from participating in the important Permanent Structured Cooperation on Security and Defence (PESCO) provided for by the Treaty of Lisbon.[71] Only Malta (and in principle also the UK) also stands outside the scope of cooperation under PESCO. The European Defence Fund has been viewed as not constituting problems in relation to the Danish defence opt-out.[72]

[68] ibid.
[69] ibid.
[70] ibid.
[71] Decided by the European Council on 22 June 2017. See Press Release 403/17, www.consilium.europa.eu/en/press/press-releases/2017/06/22/euco-security-defence/pdf, where it is stated that: 'To strengthen Europe's security and defence in today's challenging geopolitical environment and to help reach the level of ambition of the EU expressed in the EU Global Strategy, the European Council agrees on the need to launch an inclusive and ambitious Permanent Structured Cooperation (PESCO). A common list of criteria and binding commitments, fully in line with Articles 42(6) and 46 TEU and Protocol 10 to the Treaty – including with a view to the most demanding missions – will be drawn up by Member States within three months, with a precise timetable and specific assessment mechanisms, in order to enable Member States which are in a position to do so to notify their intentions to participate without delay. This work has to be consistent with Member States' national defence planning and commitments agreed within NATO and the UN by Member States concerned. Concrete collaborative projects and initiatives should also be identified in support of PESCO's common goals, commitments and criteria.'
[72] Thorning (n 27). The finding is mainly supported by the kind of measures and legal basis applied. On the fund, see, eg, Press Release 403/17, where, among other things, it is stated that: 'The joint development of capability projects commonly agreed by Member States to fill the existing major shortfalls and develop the technologies of the future is crucial to fulfil the level of ambition of the EU approved by the European Council in December 2016. The European Council welcomes the Commission's communication on a European Defence Fund, composed of a research window and a capability window, and is looking forward to its swift operationalisation. It calls for rapid agreement

For a fuller picture, it may be added that the interpretation by the Danish political and administrative elite of the defence opt-out has, in a rather thought-provoking manner, been summed up by Wivel as follows:

> The defence opt-out limited Danish participation in the development of the EU as a military actor and reduced Danish action space with regard to pursuing an activist foreign policy agenda more generally. The effects of this development have been cushioned by the permissive interpretation of the Danish defence opt-out by Danish foreign policy-makers. This interpretation has allowed them to engage in debates in the Council of Ministers with possible implications for defence, allowing (and expecting) civil servants to engage actively in EU security and defence discussions on all issues except those with direct consequences for the operational level. Thus, the Danish political and administrative elite has continued to focus on influence by allocating resources for active participation in EU foreign, security and defence policy-making, and by using the formal channels for influence available in the EU system (such as working group participation) despite the domestically induced priority given to autonomy. The result has been a structural change in day-to-day Danish political and administrative practices, which have been Europeanized in the sense that EU policies have been downloaded … increasing attention and awareness on the part of domestic actors towards the EU as well as adaptation of domestic institutional structures and processes.[73]

Towards the end of 2017, the opt-out was considered to have been activated 141 times and to a continuously intensified degree over the years.[74] Its practical importance has – even though there are limitations to its application by virtue of the abovementioned conditions for its application and general approach – thereby grown significantly since it was originally adopted. This may, by some, be viewed as paradoxical in the light of the greatly increased Danish engagement in international military actions under alternative organisational arrangements, such as NATO in particular.[75] This may be one, among several, explanatory factors which appear to suggest that today, there may be a majority in the Danish electorate to give up the opt-out.[76]

VI. THE AFSJ OPT-OUT

The background for the adoption of the AFSJ opt-out is viewed as being a worry by the Danish electorate that the EU would eventually develop a federal

on the proposal for a European Defence Industrial Development Programme with a view to its swift implementation, before more comprehensive programmes can be envisaged in the medium term.' See further Communication from the Commission, 'Launching the European Defence Fund' COM [2017] 295.

[73] See generally on the Danish defence policy A Wivel, 'A Pace-Setter out of Sync? Danish Foreign, Security and Defence Policy and the European Union' in Miles and Wivel (eds) (n 10) 93.

[74] Tænketanken Europa (n 37).

[75] See generally on Danish defence policy Wivel (n 73) 80–94.

[76] According to Tænketanken Europa (n 37) 16.

police force à la American Federal Bureau of Investigation (FBI), as well as a system of European criminal law.[77] Section D of the Edinburgh Decision states in that regard that: 'Denmark will participate fully in cooperation on Justice and Home Affairs on the basis of the provisions of title VI of the Treaty on European Union.'[78]

Moreover, the previously mentioned Protocol No 22 is of significance here. Thus, it is of particular interest that in Article 1, it is stated that Denmark shall not take part in the adoption by the Council of proposed measures pursuant to Title V of Part 3 TFEU. At the overall level, this opt-out is therefore concerned with three main areas, namely: (1) border control, asylum and immigration; (2) civil law; and (3) police and criminal law cooperation.[79] What is decisive in terms of assessing whether the opt-out is applicable is whether a given legal act is to be enacted with a legal basis in one of the provisions in the Treaty's Title V (the AFSJ part).[80] In that regard, it is also worth mentioning that, in Article 2 of Protocol No 22, it is stated that:

> None of the provisions of Title V of Part Three of the Treaty on the Functioning of the European Union, no measure adopted pursuant to that Title, no provision of any international agreement concluded by the Union pursuant to that Title, and no decision of the Court of Justice of the European Union interpreting any such provision or measure or any measure amended or amendable pursuant to that Title shall be binding upon or applicable in Denmark; and no such provision, measure or decision shall in any way affect the competences, rights and obligations of Denmark; and no such provision, measure or decision shall in any way affect the Community or Union *acquis* nor form part of Union law as they apply to Denmark. In particular, acts of the Union in the field of police cooperation and judicial cooperation in criminal matters adopted before the entry into force of the Treaty of Lisbon which are amended shall continue to be binding upon and applicable to Denmark unchanged.

Originally, the opt-out was designed as an exemption from supranational cooperation in the specified substantive areas, implying that Denmark was free to participate as long as the cooperation remained intergovernmental.[81] With the adoption of the Treaty of Amsterdam, the nature of the cooperation underwent change – a change that came to its fruition with the Treaty of Lisbon and the restructuring of the so-called pillar structure, as all parts of the AFSJ then became supranational. This had severe consequences and increasing complexity

[77] Tænketanken Europa (n 37) 32.

[78] In addition, see the second of the two unilateral declarations of Denmark (Annex 3), included in Part B, 'Denmark and the Treaty on European Union', of the Conclusions of the Presidency, European Council in Edinburgh, 11–12 December 1992, www.europarl.europa.eu/summits/edinburgh/default_en.htm.

[79] Regeringen, *Samarbejdet om retlige og indre anliggender: En analyse af EU-lovgivning omfattet af retsforbeholdet* (Stockholm, Regeringen, 2015) 11.

[80] ibid 12 f.

[81] Adler-Nissen (n 16) 117.

for Danish participation. Significantly, this opt-out is viewed as not hindering Denmark in participating in the AFSJ in substance and so it is 'only' a reservation as to the mode of cooperation, namely hindering Denmark in participating in supranational cooperation.[82]

This is the reason why it is possible for Denmark, in spite of the opt-out, to enter intergovernmental agreements in the areas in question.[83] The implications of the opt-out may thus appear to have been minimised. The main differences between supranational and intergovernmental cooperation may be that the latter requires unanimity, that the competence of the CJEU is limited, and that the principles of supremacy and direct effect are not applicable.[84] However, the complexity of this 'solution' is rather high and at times may lack transparency. The willingness of the other party (ie, the EU Member States/the EU) to negotiate and reach an acceptable result for both sides is obviously also an issue which has to be taken into consideration.

The opt-out is considered to imply that Denmark stands outside approximately a quarter of the areas of relevance.[85] However, it is unlikely that a referendum will be planned in the near future – a stance which is further supported by the negative result (rejection by 53 per cent of voters) on the most recent referendum on the opt-out to convert Denmark's current full AFSJ opt-out (but not the other opt-outs) into an opt-out with a case-by-case opt-in, which took place on 3 December 2015.[86] Approval by the Danish electorate was in particular needed in order for Denmark to remain in Europol under the new rules.[87] Consequently, an alternative solution was considered desirable, resulting in Denmark recently succeeding in entering an agreement with the EU on participation in Europol. Also, Denmark takes part in the Schengen cooperation, but under a rather specific arrangement, the contours of which date much further back.[88]

It would be beyond the scope of this chapter to present and analyse the many special arrangements in this area, such as those of relevance in relation

[82] Thorning (n 27).

[83] ibid; and Regeringen (n 79) 1289 f.

[84] T Elholm, 'Det retlige forbehold og strafferetten' in Olsen and Sørensen (n 27).

[85] Tænketanken Europa (n 37) 33.

[86] See in that regard, eg, Folketingets EU-Oplysning, 'De danske EU-forbehold', www.eu.dk/danmark%20i%20eu/de%20danske%20forbehold; and Regeringen (n 79) 17 f.

[87] See the proposal itself at: www.retsinformation.dk/forms/R0710.aspx?id=93871&exp=1; 'Forslag til Lov om Danmarks deltagelse i den fælles valuta, Vedtaget af Folketinget ved 3. behandling den 6. september 2000'.

[88] Even by 1998, the position of Denmark with regard to the Schengen *acquis* was described as rather confusing and determined by 'a number of (perhaps deliberately) opaque and seemingly contradictory provisions'; see AG 'Toth, The Legal Effects of the Protocols Relating to the United Kingdom, Ireland and Denmark' in Heukels, Blokker and Brus (n 31) 16; Adler-Nissen (n 16) 133 f; and art 4 of Protocol No 22 of the Treaty of Lisbon, often referred to as the 'Schengen technicality'.

to the prominent Dublin III Regulation[89] and the European Arrest Warrant.[90] However, it is essential to stress that, generally, reflecting the growing complexity of the AFSJ itself, including in particular the change of mode of cooperation, Denmark's position due to the opt-out has equally grown in terms of complexity and lack of transparency. Nevertheless, the country as far as possible contributes and participates collaboratively, and, at times, according to Vedsted-Hansen, to a much larger degree than anticipated by the Danish population and media, and in all likelihood also by many of the politicians.[91]

VII. THE 'SECOND HOME' PROTOCOL

Protocol No 32 of the Treaty of Lisbon, entitled 'On the Acquisition of Property in Denmark', provides that: 'Notwithstanding the provisions of the Treaties, Denmark may maintain the existing legislation on the acquisition of second homes.' The protocol originates in the Treaty of Maastricht and so pre-dates the referendum resulting in the Danish 'No'.[92] Having regard to the Danish legislation at stake, it implies that Denmark, in principle, is permanently permitted to prohibit the acquisition of second homes in Denmark by nationals of other Member States;[93] thereby, a derogation from the fundamental principle of non-discrimination in such situations has been allowed for. In particular, this allows for 'protection' from the Treaty provisions on free movement of capital and services, which in principle would otherwise have the effect of ensuring that EU nationals can buy property in other Member States. Therefore, the protocol is often referred to as Denmark's 'fifth opt-out', but it is in nature and origin obviously rather different.

[89] Regulation (EU) No 604/2013 of the European Parliament and of the Council of 26 June 2013 establishing the criteria and mechanisms for determining the Member State responsible for examining an application for international protection lodged in one of the Member States by a third-country national or a stateless person (recast) [2013] OJ L180/31.

[90] Framework Decision 2009/299/JHA of 26 February 2009 amending Framework Decisions 2002/584/JHA, 2005/214/JHA, 2006/783/JHA, 2008/909/JHA and 2008/947/JHA, thereby enhancing the procedural rights of persons and fostering the application of the principle of mutual recognition to decisions rendered in the absence of the person concerned at the trial [2009] OJ L81/24. However, see in that regard in particular the following works: Elholm (n 84); PA Nielsen, 'Det retlige forbehold og civilretten' in Olsen and Sørensen (n 27); and J Vedsted-Hansen, 'Det retlige forbehold og personers mobilitet' in Olsen and Sørensen (n 27).

[91] Vedsted-Hansen (n 90).

[92] Then numbered Protocol No 16. Already in 1988, when the capital markets were about to be opened, a reference protecting the Danish rule was inserted into the legal act of relevance, namely art 6(4) in Directive 88/361/EEC for the implementation of art 67 of the Treaty, stating that: 'Existing national legislation regulating purchases of secondary residences may be upheld until the Council adopts further provisions in this area in accordance with Article 69 of the Treaty. This provision does not affect the applicability of other provisions of Community law.'

[93] The law in question encompasses a 'package' a regulation of relevance.

According to Danish law, it is possible to buy a second home, ie, a so-called 'summerhouse', if the interested person has lived in the country for at least five years.[94] Nevertheless, in other instances, it may also be possible for a non-national to buy a Danish summerhouse provided that the Ministry of Justice is willing to grant a dispensation, which in practice is said to require a close relationship to the country.[95] Even though the number of granted permissions steadily increases, it is still only a minority of summerhouses that are owned by non-nationals.[96]

As reservation of ownership of land to own nationals has been of long-lasting interest to many states, it may be viewed by some as an attractive situation for Denmark to enjoy; for instance, Greece had sought an identical protocol for its own territory, but was turned down.[97] Especially with regard to agricultural property, many countries including Denmark have operated with similar discriminatory measures. Yet, as a point of departure, they are not considered as being in conformity with EU law.[98] However, certain countries have temporarily, or subject to certain conditions, been permitted to have similar arrangements.[99] In the Danish case, the law dates back to 1959 and was adopted in order to address a concern that, if non-nationals were allowed to buy summerhouses, it could lead to higher prices, thus preventing Danes themselves from being able to afford them. In addition, the concern was that the summerhouse areas, typically situated by the coasts, would become nearly abandoned, because non-nationals would in all likelihood be less in residence than Danes.[100] Much less 'officially', it might be thought that this was a measure to prevent Germans buying property in Denmark, as this would have been a sensitive issue in the years following the Second World War.

As understood from the text of the protocol, Denmark may only maintain the legislation as it applied and was in force on 1 November 1993 when the Treaty of Maastricht entered into force. It must thus be considered as largely 'frozen'.[101] Therefore, Denmark cannot adopt alterations changing the fundamental nature of the legislation. Since a summerhouse in Denmark was originally

[94] Lov om erhvervelse af fast ejendom, jf. lovbekendtgørelse nr. 566 af 28. august 1986, med den ændring, der følger af lov nr. 1102 af 21. december 1994 § 1(1). A similar principle is in force in relation to undertakings, institutions etc; see § 1(2). Regarding permanent housing and EU citizens, see Bekendtgørelse 764 af 18/09/1995 om erhvervelse af fast ejendom for så vidt angår visse EF-statsborgere og EF-selskaber samt visse personer og selskaber fra lande, der har tiltrådt aftalen om Det Europæiske Økonomiske Samarbejdsområde.

[95] Tænketanken Europa (n 37) 54.

[96] ibid.

[97] D Curtin, 'The Constitutional Structure of the Union: A Europe of Bits and Pieces' (1993) 30(1) *Common Market Law Review* 22, 47. However, Greece was successful in getting a declaration as to Mount Athos; see Kammeradvokaten, 'Redegørelse for Planlovens § 41 og Sommerhusprotokollen', 20 October 2004, 30, www.ft.dk/samling/20041/almdel/mpu/bilag/54/114490.pdf.

[98] In that regard, as to Denmark, see in particular Case C-370/05 *Festersen* [2007] EU:C:2007:59.

[99] See Kammeradvokaten (n 97) 30 f.

[100] Tænketanken Europa (n 37) 54.

[101] In the same direction, see, eg, Case C-452/01 *Ospelt* [2003] EU:C:2003:493.

defined as a house in which no one was allowed to live all year round, a recent change permitting retired persons to live in their summerhouse – after a year of ownership – all year round, it has been questioned whether such a softening implies that it is no longer possible for the protocol to be upheld.[102] By the same token, it has more generally also been argued that the protocol is untimely, unjustified and/or hypocritical, since many Danes own second homes (and other kinds of property) in other Member States.[103]

VIII. OTHER AREAS OF DIFFERENTIATION

Besides the above-mentioned Danish Treaty-based kinds of differentiation, there are further areas where Denmark may be viewed as – in legal terms – 'flying' in directions other than that of the EU, which is directing itself towards 'more unity'. The country's differing behaviour in such respects will be briefly dealt with in relation to the following three significant examples of recent developments: the 'European Pillar of Social Rights'; the Danish Chairmanship of the Committee of Ministers of the Council of Europe; and Danish courts' relationship with the CJEU.

In November 2017, the 'European Pillar of Social Rights' was proclaimed at the Social Summit for Fair Jobs and Growth.[104] It is said to be an attempt to address the doubts among many citizens as to whether the EU – since the financial crisis began and the EU's response to it included wider austerity in a number of countries – is still committed to prosperity and rising living and working standards.[105] It consists of 20 key principles divided into three chapters, namely, first, on equal opportunities and access to the labour market, second, on fair working conditions and, finally, on social protection and inclusion. In the preamble, there is a reference to a competitive social market economy. It is also stated that: 'A stronger focus on employment and social performance is particularly important to increase resilience and deepen the Economic and Monetary Union. For this reason, the European Pillar of Social Rights is notably conceived

[102] See Lov om ændring af lov om planlægning, lov om naturbeskyttelse og lov om aktindsigt i miljøoplysninger, adopted on 1 June 2017. Previously, the requirement as to length of ownership was eight years. For a critical analysis, see Kammeradvokaten (n 97) 30 f.

[103] Tænketanken Europa (n 37) 55.

[104] European Parliament, the Council and the Commission, *European Pillar of Social Rights* (2017) www.ec.europa.eu/commission/sites/beta-political/files/social-summit-european-pillar-social-rights-booklet_en.pdf. See also Z Rasnača, '(Any) Relevance of the European Pillar of Social Rights for EU Law?' *European Law Blog* (17 November 2017), www.europeanlawblog.eu/2017/11/17/any-relevance-of-the-european-pillar-of-social-rights-for-eu-law.

[105] In this connection, see also European Commission, 'Social Dimension of Europe – Overview of Initiatives since the Start of the Juncker Commission', www.ec.europa.eu/commission/sites/beta-political/files/social_dimension_of_europe_overview_of_initiatives_en.pdf; and F Vandenbroucke, C Barnard and De Baere (eds), *A European Social Union after the Crisis* (Cambridge, Cambridge University Press, 2017).

for the euro area but it is addressed to all Member States.' Thus, while it is aimed at the eurozone countries, other Member States can also participate. Although normally considered as one of the forerunners of action in relation to social welfare, Denmark has decided to distance itself from it.[106] It is notable that this stands in contrast to Sweden's standpoint in particular, a country with which Denmark has traditionally compared itself.[107] The Danish concern is likely to stem from a fear of further transfer of competences in the social area and in that regard a desire to protect the so-called Danish model. Having regard to the Danish position, it might be thought that this constituted yet another Danish opt-out.[108]

Although Denmark did not (as the UK, Poland and the Czech Republic did) secure exemptions from the Charter of Fundamental Rights of the European Union, it has recently, in connection with the Danish Chairmanship of the Committee of Ministers of the Council of Europe, demonstrated what by some could be seen as a certain hesitation towards human rights and perhaps to some degree even towards one of the founding values of the EU, namely the rule of law.[109] More specifically, in April 2018, the visible outcome of the Danish presidency became the adoption of the so-called Copenhagen Declaration.[110] The role of the European Court of Human Rights had been the subject of strong debate. In particular, this debate had focused on the supposed dynamic interpretational style, which it had become common to criticise.[111] It is in this light that the declaration in that regard should be read, although it did not go as far as originally proposed by Denmark:

> Welcomes efforts taken by the Court to enhance the clarity and consistency of its judgments. Appreciates the Court's efforts to ensure that the interpretation of the Convention proceeds in a careful and balanced manner.
>
> Welcomes the further development of the principle of subsidiarity and the doctrine of the margin of appreciation by the Court in its jurisprudence. Welcomes the Court's continued strict and consistent application of the criteria concerning admissibility and jurisdiction, including by requiring applicants to be more diligent in raising

[106] See, eg, the letter from the Danish Minister for Employment, T Lund Poulsen, to the Commissioner for Employment, Social Affairs, Skills and Labour, M Thyssen, 1 March 2018, www.eu.dk/samling/20171/almdel/EUU/bilag/444/1862796.pdf.

[107] According to D Schraad-Tischler, C Schiller SM Heller and N Siemer, *Social Justice in the EU: Index Report 2017 Social Inclusion Monitor Europe* (Gütersloh, Bertelsmann Stiftung, 2017). Denmark ranked top with 7.39, followed by Sweden (7.31) and Finland (7.14). In contrast, Greece had the worst score with 3.7, followed by Romania (3.99) and Bulgaria (4.19).

[108] See, eg, Tænketanken Europa, 'EU's sociale søjle – endnu et dansk forbehold' (2017), www.thinkeuropa.dk/sites/default/files/social_soejle_notat.25042017.pdf.

[109] This is, eg, expressed in the Preamble to the TEU: 'Drawing inspiration from the cultural, religious and humanist inheritance of Europe, from which have developed the universal values of the inviolable and inalienable rights of the human person, freedom, democracy, equality and the rule of law.'

[110] Copenhagen Declaration, www.regeringen.dk/media/5101/koebenhavn-erklaering-13-4.pdf.

[111] See further, eg, Danish Institute for Human Rights, www.menneskeret.dk/emner/danmarks-formandskab-europaradet.

their Convention complaints domestically, and making full use of the opportunity to declare applications inadmissible where applicants have not suffered a significant disadvantage.[112]

It had, for a long time, been widely claimed that Danish courts over the years had not been too eager to refer cases pursuant to Article 267 TFEU to the CJEU.[113] More recently, this tendency seems to have changed and Danish courts are, according to Pagh, no longer seen as necessarily differing from other Member States in that regard.[114] Whether scepticism among Danish courts in other respects might exist is not easy to measure, but it is worth drawing attention to the recent *Ajos* cases.[115] Here, the Danish Supreme Court in its combative *Ajos* judgment openly and controversially challenged the authority of the CJEU.[116] In the preliminary ruling by the CJEU preceding it, the CJEU had continued to develop the controversial general principle prohibiting age discrimination. This issue lay at the heart of the dispute and it seems very likely that the Danish Supreme Court felt that the CJEU had been too activist when it originally 'launched' this general principle. Indeed, the reasoning of the Danish Supreme Court gives the impression that the CJEU had itself created it out of nowhere. In turn, this appeared to be an implicit reference to the widely criticised interpretative approach of the CJEU, resulting in a far-reaching willingness to espouse judicial activism. But in acting as it did, it seems ironic that the Danish Supreme Court itself showed that it too had an activist streak.

[112] Copenhagen Declaration (n 110) paras 29–31.

[113] See, eg, M Wind, 'The Scandinavians: The Foot-Dragging Supporters of European Law' in M Derlén and J Lindholm (eds), *The Court of Justice of the European Union: Multidisciplinary Perspectives* (Oxford, Hart Publishing, 2018) 199.

[114] See P Pagh, 'Præjudicielle søgsmål: Danske domstoles præjudicielle forelæggelser for EU-Domstolen' in Olsen and Sørensen (n 27).

[115] For the Danish Supreme Court judgment, see UfR 2017.824H (Case No 15/2014, DI, acting on behalf of *Ajos A/S v Estate of A*). A translation from Danish into English is available at: www.supremecourt.dk/supremecourt/nyheder/pressemeddelelser/Pages/TherelationshipbetweenEUlawandDanishlawinacaseconcerningasalariedemployee.aspx. The judgment was given on 6 December 2016. As for the CJEU judgment, see Case C-441/14 *Ajos* [2016] EU:C:2016:278. The judgment was given on 19 April 2016.

[116] For an in-depth analysis, see U Neergaard and KE Sørensen, 'Activist Infighting among Courts and Breakdown of Mutual Trust? The Danish Supreme Court, the CJEU, and the *Ajos* Case' (2017) 36 *Yearbook of European Law* 275. See also, eg, O Garner, 'The Borders of European Integration on Trial in the Member States: *Dansk Industri*, *Miller*, and *Taricco*' (2017) 9 *European Journal of Legal Studies* 1; SW Haket, 'The Danish Supreme Court's *Ajos* Judgment (*Dansk Industri*): Rejecting a Consistent Interpretation and Challenging the Effect of a General Principle of EU Law in the Danish Legal Order' (2017) 10(1) *Review of European Administrative Law* 135; R Holdgaard and GK Schaldemose, 'From Cooperation to Collision: The ECJ's *Ajos* Ruling and the Danish Supreme Court's Refusal to Comply' (2018) 55(1) *Common Market Law Review* 17; J Kristiansen, 'Grænser for EU-rettens umiddelbare anvendelighed i dansk ret – om Højesterets dom i Ajos-sagen' (2017) *Ugeskrift for Retsvæsen*, U.2017B.75–84; MR Madsen, HP Olsen and U Sadl, 'Competing Supremacies and Clashing Institutional Rationalities: The Danish Supreme Court's Decision in the *Ajos* Case and the National Limits of Judicial Cooperation' (2017) 23 *European Law Journal* 140; and R Nielsen and C Tvarnø, 'Danish Supreme Court Infringes the EU Treaties by its Ruling in the *Ajos* Case' [2017] *Europarättsligt Tidsskrift* 303.

As a consequence, currently parts of EU law are not fully part of Danish law. Naturally, there is considerable importance in understanding how a country's highest court behaves in relation to EU law and the CJEU, and the signal given here seems rather significant. It may thus be viewed as the culmination of an implied development – and at times expressly articulated restiveness – among constitutional and supreme courts across Europe challenging the authority of the CJEU. Most dramatically, it seems that the *Ajos* judgment may have the consequence that general principles other than that of age discrimination and in particular relevant Charter provisions do not have (horizontal?) direct effect in Denmark. Until 6 December 2016, the Danish Supreme Court had, followed a pragmatic and careful approach towards the CJEU and EU law, and it appears startling that it has now chosen not to comply with a ruling of the CJEU, thus undermining a cornerstone of the EU *acquis* by failing to apply the principle of the supremacy of EU law.

IX. CONCLUSIONS: NOT COMPLETELY WANTING TO FLY ALONG

Undoubtedly, rather than flying high as an 'EU paper bird', Denmark at times appears to be much closer to the soil, going its own way and perhaps resembling a rogue elephant, separating from the herd and roaming alone. This has been most obvious by virtue of the shape of the above-mentioned Treaty-based special arrangements allowing for deviation from the direction of travel taken by the majority. However, for the sake of the full picture, it is also essential to note that the official policy of successive Danish governments has apparently been to go as far as possible to support 'a more united Europe' and thereby to limit the impact of the opt-outs whenever there is adequate room for manoeuvre.[117] This policy may have led to a diminishment of the fuller effect of the special arrangements. Importantly, the Danish opt-outs imply that Denmark on the one hand has a right towards the EU, but on the other hand, in principle, also has an obligation towards the Danish electorate, whose preference is that the EU should stay out of the areas in question.

Twenty-five years ago, not many could have predicted the development of EU competence in the areas of the EMU, the AFSJ and defence, where in particular the two former categories have become some of the fastest-growing areas in the EU, but in fact also among the most politically sensitive ones. The degree of complexity has simultaneously increased.

The 'second home' protocol's importance in the bigger picture is not as great as those three opt-outs and its practical importance may cease little by little due

[117] In this regard, see also, eg, Adler-Nissen (n 16) 20: 'There is little written material on opt-outs in the archives of British and Danish ministries, as the management of the exemptions is based on tacit knowledge. Due to the secretive and sensitive nature of Council of Ministers negotiations, the informal norms and strategies are not directly accessible to the outsider.'

to above-mentioned choice taken by the Danish legislator. In contrast, the opt-out on EU citizenship, which had been narrowly constructed, does not have any practical implications.

Twenty-five years ago, Curtin analysed the then newly adopted Treaty of Maastricht and concluded that the picture that emerged was one of fragmentation rather than unity, of bits and pieces rather than singleness.[118] Today, the development of the Danish 'otherness' only adds further to that picture and it will be difficult to change, especially the Treaty-based choices of differentiation, where most of the opt-outs have grown in their importance because the areas of law that they concern have in themselves become of increased significance (yet not necessarily in the way originally feared). Recent developments in other fields, such as comity between the national courts and the CJEU, social policy and human rights, also seem to point to some degree of differentiation or at least to signify some scepticism towards the entire project. Certain trends in developments may be thought to result in a lack of solidarity with other Member States (in particular in relation to the economic and refugee crises, but also in light of a desire to protect the Danish welfare state). Thus, the Danish situation may also be seen as fitting well (perhaps too well) into the motto of the EU, 'United in diversity'.[119] Yet, according to all recent polls, the Danes are among the most eager supporters of remaining in the EU and a 'Dan-exit' is not at present a likely scenario.[120]

REFERENCES

Adler-Nissen, R, *Opting out of the European Union: Diplomacy, Sovereignty and European Integration* (Cambridge, Cambridge University Press, 2014).

Curtin, D, 'The Constitutional Structure of the Union: A Europe of Bits and Pieces' (1993) 30(10 *Common Market Law Review* 22.

Elholm, T, 'Det retlige forbehold og strafferetten' in BE Olsen and KE Sørensen (eds), *EU-retten i Danmark* (Copenhagen, DJØF, 2018).

Garner, O, 'The Borders of European Integration on Trial in the Member States: *Dansk Industri*, *Miller*, and *Taricco*' (2017) 9 *European Journal of Legal Studies* 1.

Haket, SW, 'The Danish Supreme Court's *Ajos* Judgment (*Dansk Industri*): Rejecting a Consistent Interpretation and Challenging the Effect of a General Principle of EU Law in the Danish Legal Order' (2017) 10(1) *Review of European Administrative Law* 135.

Hassing Nielsen, J, 'The Pragmatic Euroscepticism of Scandinavia' in B Leruth et al (eds), *The Routledge Handbook of Euroscepticism* (London, Routledge, 2018).

[118] Curtin (n 97).

[119] The motto was included in the ill-fated Constitutional Treaty of 2004, but is now only to some degree an element in the Treaty of Lisbon; see Declaration 52.

[120] For the recent results on the 'Eurobarometer', where 76 per cent of the population finds the EU to be 'a good thing', see: www.thinkeuropa.dk/vaerdier/rekordhoej-opbakning-til-dansk-eu-medlemskab.

Holdgaard, R and Schaldemose, GK, 'From Cooperation to Collision: The ECJ's *Ajos* Ruling and the Danish Supreme Court's Refusal to Comply' (2018) 55(1) *Common Market Law Review* 17.

Kelstrup, M, 'Denmark's Relation to the European Union: A History of Dualism and Pragmatism' in L Miles and A Wivel (eds), *Denmark and the European Union* (New York, Routledge, 2014).

Kristiansen, J, 'Grænser for EU-rettens umiddelbare anvendelighed i dansk ret – om Højesterets dom i Ajos-sagen' (2017) *Ugeskrift for Retsvæsen*, U.2017B.75.

Madsen, MR, Olsen, HP and Sadl, U, 'Competing Supremacies and Clashing Institutional Rationalities: The Danish Supreme Court's Decision in the *Ajos* Case and the National Limits of Judicial Cooperation' (2017) 23 *European Law Journal* 140.

Marcussen, M, 'Denmark and the Euro Opt-out' in L Miles and A Wivel (eds), *Denmark and the European Union* (New York, Routledge, 2014).

Miles, L and Wivel, A, 'Introducing Denmark and the European Union' in L Miles and A Wivel (eds), *Denmark and the European Union* (New York, Routledge, 2014).

Neergaard, U, 'Europe and the Welfare State: Friends, Foes, or …?' (2016) 35 *Yearbook of European Law* 1.

——. 'Euro-forbeholdet' in BE Olsen and KE Sørensen (eds), *EU-retten i Danmark* (Copenhagen, DJØF, 2018).

——. 'The European Exchange Rate Mechanism II' in Amtenbrink, F and Herrmann, C (eds), *The EU Law of Economic and Monetary Union* (Oxford University Press, forthcoming).

Neergaard, U and Sørensen, KE, 'Activist Infighting among Courts and Breakdown of Mutual Trust? The Danish Supreme Court, the CJEU, and the Ajos Case' (2017) 36 *Yearbook of European Law* 275.

Nielsen, PA, 'Det retlige forbehold og civilretten' in BE Olsen and KE Sørensen (eds), *EU-retten i Danmark* (Copenhagen, DJØF, 2018).

Nielsen, R and Tvarnø, C, 'Danish Supreme Court Infringes the EU Treaties by its Ruling in the Ajos Case' [2017] *Europarättsligt Tidsskrift* 303.

Pagh, P, 'Præjudicielle søgsmål: Danske domstoles præjudicielle forelæggelser for EU-Domstolen' in BE Olsen and KE Sørensen (eds), *EU-retten i Danmark* (Copenhagen, DJØF, 2018).

Piris, J-C, *The Future of Europe. Towards a Two-Speed Europe?* (Cambridge, Cambridge University Press, 2012).

Schraad-Tischler, D, Schiller, C, Heller, SM and Siemer, N, *Social Justice in the EU – Index Report 2017 Social Inclusion Monitor Europe* (Gütersloh, Bertelsmann Stiftung, 2017).

Thorning, C, 'Forsvarsforbeholdet' in BE Olsen and KE Sørensen (eds), *EU-retten i Danmark* (Copenhagen, DJØF, 2018).

Toth, AG, 'The Legal Effects of the Protocols Relating to the United Kingdom, Ireland and Denmark' in T Heukels, N Blokker and M Brus (eds), *The European Union after Amsterdam: A Legal Analysis* (The Hague, Kluwer Law International, 1998).

Vandenbroucke, F, Barnard, C and de Baere, G (eds), *A European Social Union after the Crisis* (Cambridge, Cambridge University Press, 2017).

Vedsted-Hansen, J, 'Det retlige forbehold og personers mobilitet' in BE Olsen and KE Sørensen (eds), *EU-retten i Danmark* (Copenhagen, DJØF, 2018).

Wind, M, 'The Scandinavians: The Foot-Dragging Supporters of European Law' in M Derlén and J Lindholm (eds), *The Court of Justice of the European Union: Multidisciplinary Perspectives* (Oxford, Hart Publishing, 2018).
Wivel, A, 'A Pace-Setter out of Sync? Danish Foreign, Security and Defence Policy and the European Union' in L Miles and A Wivel (eds), *Denmark and the European Union* (New York, Routledge, 2014).
——. 'As Awkward as They Need to Be: Denmark's Pragmatic Activist Approach to Europe' in M Stegmann McCallion and A Brianson (eds), *Nordic States and European Integration: Awkward Partners in the North* (London, Palgrave Macmillan, 2018).

Part IV

Epilogue

11

EU and Member State Constitutionalism

Complementing and Conflicting

KAARLO TUORI

I. THE SETTING

IN THIS CHAPTER, I want to make two points. First, the relationship between EU constitutionalism and Member State constitutionalism is not only about conflicts; it is also about dialogue and cooperation, as well as complementarity. Second, the relationship that EU constitutionalism maintains with Member State constitutionalism should not be discussed only within the juridical and political constitutions but also within the sectoral constitutions, such as the economic, social and security constitutions. Discussion of EU constitutionalism should always include its interaction with national constitutionalism and should attend to not only the juridical and political constitutions, but also the sectoral constitutions.

I shall elaborate upon my two points through the criticism of two influential portrayals of EU constitutionalism and Member State constitutionalism: constitutional pluralism[1] and the proposal to locate the constitutional aspect exclusively on the Member State side and approach the EU in terms of administrative law. My concern with constitutional pluralists lies in their overblown emphasis on the conflictual nature of the relationship between European and Member State constitutionalism and their focus on what I call the juridical constitution. Constitutional pluralists approach both sides of the relationship in constitutional terms. In turn, Peter Lindseth, in his *Power and Legitimacy*,

[1] The scholarly debate was initiated by Neil MacCormick's influential articles put together in his *Questioning Sovereignty: Law, State and Nation in the European Commonwealth* (Oxford, Oxford University Press, 1999).

refuses to recognise the constitutional aspect of the EU and its legal system. Lindseth uses 'constitutionalism' in a thick normative sense, referring to vital elements of the American notion of a constitutional democracy and the European notion of a democratic *Rechtsstaat*, such as democracy and fundamental rights.[2] In this conceptual setting, 'constitutionalism' is intimately linked to legitimacy; it implies that the legitimacy of a polity and its law should be achieved through democratic procedures and fundamental rights.

Such a thick concept of constitutionalism reflects the persistent dominance of the state template in constitutional theory and, hence, risks blocking the view to the specificity of European constitutionalism. It focuses on the juridical and political constitutions, and tends to neglect sectoral constitutionalisation, a distinct feature of European constitutionalism which corresponds to the basic teleological, policy orientation of the EU and its law. To use 'constitutionalism' in a normatively more neutral sense does not entail denying the relevance for European constitutionalism of the normative ideas of a constitutional democracy (a democratic *Rechtsstaat*) or the conception of legitimacy they imply. I subscribe to the premise that where there is power, it must be legitimated and restricted, and where there is law – which always implies power too – it must also be legitimated and restricted. But in the European context, efforts to secure democratic constitutional legitimacy should be examined through the interaction between the transnational and national levels of constitutionalism. In some crucial respects, European constitutionalism has been, and still is, parasitic on national constitutionalism. Most importantly, this also holds for constitutional and democratic legitimacy.

The European transnational constitution shares certain basic features with Member State national constitutions, such as the status of constitutional law as higher law. But it also shows certain peculiarities which should be taken into account in an analysis of its relations with Member State constitutions, but which both constitutional pluralists and administrative law theorists tend to ignore. These peculiarities include the multi-dimensional nature of the European constitution.

In a typical state setting, the constitution addresses the national political and legal systems. The political and juridical constitutions frame sectoral policies and legislation, which, however, are usually left to the province of ordinary politics and law-making. By contrast, in a functionally oriented transnational polity such as the EU, which raises a substantively limited claim to political and juridical authority, even central sectoral policies are constitutionally anchored. Hence, in addition to the two framing constitutions – the juridical and the political constitutions – I have proposed that we distinguish between three sectoral constitutions, all of them possessing a distinct constitutional object to which

[2] P Lindseth, *Power and Legitimacy: Reconciling Europe and the Nation-State* (Oxford, Oxford University Press, 2010).

constitutional law relates: the economic, social and security constitutions. Furthermore, economic constitutionalisation in the EU has proceeded in two sub-dimensions which merit separate analysis: a micro-economic and a macro-economic one.[3]

II. CONSTITUTIONAL PLURALISM

During the last 20 years, constitutional pluralism has dominated scholarly discussion on the relations between the European constitution and its national counterparts. The debate does address an important aspect in the relations that the European transnational constitution entertains with Member State national constitutions: the fact that these constitutions raise overlapping and rival claims of authority. Indeed, I would suggest that we define the very concept of legal or constitutional pluralism as a constellation where two legal regimes raise such overlapping and conflicting claims of authority. Pluralist constellations are typical of our age of postnational law. Conflicts of authority seem to be inevitable between transnational law (such as EU law) and national law (such as Member State law). Transnational and national law follow different principles of authority; the scope of their authority is circumscribed through different criteria. National law adheres to the territorial principle of authority and claims universal jurisdiction in in its territory. By contrast, transnational law's claim to authority is substantially or functionally defined and limited. Territorial and functional principles of authority are bound to clash, producing at regular intervals what I would call fundamental conflicts of authority; that is, conflicts turning on the autonomy and identity of the colliding legal regimes. The celebrated cases involving the German Constitutional Court and the Luxembourg Court – the Outright Monetary Transactions (OMT) case[4] is the latest but will not be the last example – intimate how high the stakes are: the German Constitutional Court sees itself as the guardian of German constitutional identity and the autonomy of German law, while the European Court of Justice (ECJ) defends the autonomy and constitutional identity of EU law. Such fundamental conflicts of authority are vastly different from the border skirmishes addressed by private international law or, as the Anglo-American term goes, conflict of laws. However, the exchange of arguments between the German Constitutional Court and the Luxembourg Court in, for instance,

[3] See K Tuori, *European Constitutionalism* (Cambridge, Cambridge University Press, 2015); and K Tuori, *The Eurozone Crisis* (Cambridge, Cambridge University Press, 2014).

[4] The contributions of the German Constitutional Court are Beschluss vom 06 Juli 2014 – 2 BvR 2728/13 and Urteil vom 21 Juni 2016 – 2 BvR 2728/13, and the ECJ interventions Opinion of Advocate General Cruz Villalón delivered on 14 January 2015, case C-62/14 *Gauweiler and Others* [2015] ECLI:EU:C:2015:7.

the OMT case not only shows the inevitability of fundamental conflicts of authority under the pluralism of postnational law, but also testifies to the possibility of a dialogical resolution of these conflicts. The relationship between the function-specific EU constitution and universalist Member State constitutions is not labelled only by actual or latent conflicts, but is also marked by dialogue and cooperation, facilitated by a shared constitutional deep culture; in brief, by normative and institutional *interlegality*.

In addition to its conflictual focus, the debate on constitutional pluralism has been one-sided in another respect too. The debate on constitutional pluralism has addressed the consequences of the overlap of national and transnational claims of authority merely in the juridical dimension. However, Member States' defence of their political and legislative sovereignty – the universality of their political and legal claims to authority – has also had implications for European sectoral constitutions. Member States have raised sovereignty concerns vis-a-vis EU action with regard to fiscal and other economic policy, welfare policy and the choice of welfare regimes, and the use of the coercive power of the state, ie, the state's 'monopoly of legitimate use of violence'.

In fundamental conflicts of authority that are typical of the pluralist constellation, each party – say, the ECJ and a national constitutional court – approaches the issue from the perspective of its referential legal order – say, EU law and the national legal order, respectively. What I would call perspectivism of legal orders is inevitable. As constitutional pluralists have emphasised, no second-order legal principle or neutral arbiter exists to resolve the conflict. In this sense, the conflicts are undecidable. This observation has been picked up by theorists of federal constitutionalism, such as Robert Schütze, and related to the notion of *Staatenverbund* or – in Schütze's translation – federal union. What is considered characteristic of a federal union is the very undecidability of fundamental conflicts of authority (sovereignty). If such conflicts were to be resolved in favour of the union, it would develop into a federal state; if, in turn, they were to be resolved in favour of the states, the union would be degraded to the status of an international organisation.[5] In line with the debate on constitutional pluralism, federal constitutionalism points to an important aspect in the relationship between European and Member State constitutionalism. However, it also shares the one-sided conflictual focus and the reduction of the European constitution to its juridical and political dimensions.

III. RELATIONS OF COMPLEMENTARITY

The conflict-oriented view adopted by constitutional pluralism tends to obscure another, equally important aspect in the relationship between the transnational

[5] R Schütze, 'Constitutionalism and the European Union' in C Barnard and S Peers (eds), *European Union Law* (Oxford, Oxford University Press, 2014).

European constitution and the national Member State constitutions, namely, that of complementarity. Treaty provisions on the respective competences of the EU and the Member States may be read to imply a division of labour based on a relationship of complementarity. Yet this may be an erroneous reading. Complementarity in the sense of division of labour presupposes common objectives; only with regard to common objectives can an expedient division of labour and a corresponding allocation of competences be adopted. But division of competences, such as is enshrined in the Treaty on European Union (TEU), does not necessarily imply a division of labour: division of competences may free the EU and its Member States to pursue their distinct objectives and policies within their fields of competence. It is misleading to assume that the EU and its Member States constitute in every relevant respect a multi-level *Verfassungsbund* where relations between the transnational and the national are primarily characterised by intertwinement and complementarity.[6] In the field of shared competences, the principle of subsidiarity, as formulated in Article 5(3) TEU, does presuppose the existence of common objectives; the EU will step in only if the objective at issue cannot be better achieved by lower-level action. A presumption of common objectives, grounded in a common value basis whose existence Article 2 TEU postulates, also facilitates an understanding of the demarcation between national and EU fundamental rights review in terms of complementarity.

All the sectoral European constitutions imply relations of complementarity. Take the economic constitution. EU constitutional law does not comprise all the constitutional guarantees which must be in place to enable a European internal market based on undistorted competition. The fundamental rights that a market economy requires are mainly ensured by national constitutions – by national constitutional provisions on the right to property, freedom of contract and freedom of trade. Hence, what I have called the European micro-economic constitution, covering primarily the fundamental market freedoms and competition law, is premised on the complementary contribution of Member State constitutions. In turn, the European macro-economic constitution has presupposed, say, Member State budgetary autonomy, although its use has been subjected to European constraints. In the social dimension, the European constitution has relied on the existence of national redistributive welfare regimes. Finally, in the security dimension too, core security functions and their judicial supervision have been retained under Member State sovereignty and taken by the European security constitutions as a given premise.

The relation of complementarity is also conspicuous in the field of citizenship, which brings us to the dimension of the political constitution.

[6] The idea of a multi-level *Verfassungsverbund* was propounded, first of all, by Ingolf Pernice. See, eg, I Pernice, 'The Treaty of Lisbon: Multilevel Constitutionalism in Action' (2009) 15 *Columbia Journal of European Law* 349.

European citizenship builds on national citizenship and not only in the sense of the identification of individual citizens. Complementarity labels the participatory rights of European citizens as well. In their EU constitutional practices, in debating EU issues and in participating in the European public sphere, EU citizens rely on the public autonomy guaranteed to them as Member State citizens, such as the freedoms of assembly, association and the press enshrined in national constitutions. And if we can in general speak of European citizenship in collective terms, as European citizenry, a European demos, this collective political subject can only emerge and exist as a result of the networking of national citizenries and national public spheres.

IV. TWO-STAGE LEGITIMATION

The legitimising function belongs to the basic functions constitutions are expected to fulfil, and this also holds for the European constitution. Constitutions are expected to bestow legitimacy on the constitutional object they address, such as the national or transnational polity and legal system.

Paradoxically perhaps, the Treaties owe their original constitutional legitimacy to their international law aspect, to the fact that they have been ratified by national parliaments or in referendums, in accordance with the provisions of the national constitution. As is typical of the two-stage European legitimating mechanism, national democratic procedures have been crucial for the original legitimacy of the legal documents which today function as surface-level European constitutional law.

However, the initial legitimacy which the EU may derive from Member States acting as Masters of the Treaties does not suffice. The claim to legitimacy must be constantly re-redeemed. This concerns both system legitimacy – the overall legitimacy of the EU – and the policy legitimacy of individual policies and institutions responsible for these. Let us rely on Fritz Scharpf's distinction between democratic input legitimacy and result-based output legitimacy.[7] In state constitutions, provisions on legislative and budgetary procedures, as well as participatory citizenship rights, aim to produce democratic input legitimacy at both the system and the policy level. In turn, provisions on independent expert bodies, such as courts or central banks, seek to facilitate output legitimacy in terms of, say, impartial and reasoned adjudication or monetary policy objectives, such as monetary stability.

At the European level, the distinction between system and policy legitimacy has not always been very sharp. Especially in the early, pre-Maastricht decades, European integration as a whole could be understood as a cluster

[7] F Scharpf, *Governing in Europe: Effective and Democratic?* (Oxford, Oxford University Press, 1999) 6–8.

of specific policies[8] and assessed in terms of output legitimacy. Bracketing the second-order objective of maintaining peace in Europe, what was decisive was whether the promise of increased economic prosperity (re)distributed through national mechanisms was kept or not. However, enlargement of European competences through ECJ case law and the prominent role of the ECJ in European law-making and constitution-making in general raised concerns about the need for democratic input legitimacy. The boost to political constitutionalisation in Maastricht has, and I think rightly, been seen as a response to these concerns.

Reflecting the initial technocratic policy orientation of European integration prominent in, for instance, Jean Monnet's functionalism, the Treaty of Rome largely ignored the issue of democratic legitimacy. The Member States ratified the Treaties according to their constitutional requirements, and the democratic legitimacy this produced was considered to be sufficient. However, embryos of democratic legitimation of European policy-making too were inserted even in the Treaty of Rome through the Council and the Assembly (European Parliament). These embryos manifested the two-stage mechanism of democratic legitimacy, which is such a distinct feature of European constitutionalism and the significance of which has grown in line with the widening of European competences. The contribution of national democratic procedures to the legitimacy of European policies is a vital epitome of the complementary relation between national and European constitutionalism. Lindseth's administrative law portrayal of the EU not only ignores sectoral constitutionalisation; from its exclusive Member State perspective, it also refuses to examine putative European constitutionalism through interaction between the transnational and national levels. It declines to place national democratic procedures of control, oversight and implementation in the context of European constitutionalism.

In the course of political constitutionalisation, efforts have been made to create direct legitimating relations between European citizenry and European institutions, most notably through the direct elections of the European Parliament and the introduction of European citizenship. However, as the low turnout in European elections has most dramatically proved, the cultural and social prerequisites for the formation of a European civil society and public sphere, capable of sustaining a Europe-wide democracy, are still largely lacking. On their own, European constitutional practices, culminating institutionally in the election of the European Parliament and its legislative and supervisory powers, can hardly live up to the high expectations of the thick normative concept of constitutionalism. This has only accentuated the importance of the contribution of national constitutionalism to the democratic legitimacy of the EU.

[8] Such an understanding was implicit in Hans Peter Ipsen's often-cited characterisation of the European Communities as *Zweckverbände funktioneller Integration*. See HP Ipsen, *Europäisches Gemeinschaftsrecht* (Tübingen, JCB Mohr, 1972).

Intergovernmental EU institutions work under the guidance of national democratically legitimated bodies, and national parliaments even participate directly in EU law-making. Furthermore, the majority of EU legislative and other measures are implemented and enforced by national authorities. EU directives are transposed into the municipal legal order by the national legislator, thereby receiving an injection of democratic input legitimacy. Furthermore, nationally applicable EU law is integrated into the whole of the national legal order and, as it were, scrounges off the general legitimacy of the latter. In Jürgen Habermas' distinction between regulatory law (law as a medium) and law as an institution,[9] EU law has mainly fallen into the former category. Law as an institution is intimately related to the moral and value texture of society; hence, this department of law is vital to the overall substantive legitimacy of the legal order. Insofar as EU law enjoys substantive legitimacy, it is at least partly parasitic on the substantive legitimacy of national legal orders. In sum, the fact that the general public has primarily confronted EU measures not directly, but indirectly, through the political and administrative institutions and the legal system of the respective Member State, has been crucial for the legitimacy that the EU and its individual policies have enjoyed among European citizenry.[10]

As Lindseth has shown, Member State parliamentary oversight of European policies has intensified during recent decades.[11] Yet, contrary to what Lindseth contends, this is not an argument for rejecting the existence of European constitutionalism. Along with the importance of sectoral constitutionalisation, the interaction between the transnational and national levels belongs to the features which distinguish European from state constitutionalism. This interaction is vital for providing European institutions and policies with democratic legitimacy. Although this can hardly be seen as a decisive argument, it might still be worth mentioning that the Treaty of Lisbon explicitly recognises the role of Member State constitutionalism in realising the democratic principle. Article 10 TEU proclaims that the functioning of the EU is founded on representative democracy. Not only are citizens directly represented at the EU level in the European Parliament, but, in addition, Member States are represented in the European Council by their heads of state or government and in the Council by their governments. In turn, these representatives are themselves democratically accountable either to national parliaments or citizens. Article 10 TEU expressly confirms the complementarity of direct European democracy and the two-level mechanism which harnesses national procedures to the service of European-level democratic legitimacy.

[9] J Habermas, *The Theory of Communicative Action*, vol 2 (Cambridge, Polity Press, 1989) 365.

[10] F Scharpf, *Legitimacy Intermediation in the Multilevel European Polity and its Collapse in the Euro Crisis* (Cologne, Max Planck Institute for the Study of Societies, 2012) 19.

[11] See Lindseth (n 2) 2010.

V. CONCLUSION

The complementarity relationship between European and national constitutionalism manifests the plurality of post-national law – a plurality that can no longer be depicted in accordance with the black-box model, as a mere co-existence of self-contained and self-sufficient legal regimes, shut in their respective boxes. Another important manifestation of postnational plurality consists in the overlapping and rival claims of authority, discussed in the European context under the heading of constitutional pluralism. This discussion, initiated by the late Neil MacCormick,[12] has thematised vital issues, but appears now to have come to a standstill. New insights into the interrelationship between European and Member State constitutionalism requires overcoming the limitations of the constitutional pluralism debate. These include its one-sided conflictual emphasis and ignorance of the sectoral constitutionalisation, so characteristic of the multi-dimensional and multi-temporal European constitution.

The complementarity of transnational and national constitutionalism possesses not only scholarly but also practical significance. The crises-full last decade has only aggravated the perennial legitimacy deficit. It has also shown that the deficit cannot be mended through means presupposing European citizenry – European demos – as a collective political agent. The solution does not lie in increasing the self-sufficiency of the European polity, but in further strengthening the mechanisms of two-stage legitimation. However, the last 10 years have also provided us with examples of the pitfalls of national democracies getting caught up in a collision course. As such, the difficulty consists in reinforcing the influence of national democratic procedures while simultaneously avoiding nationalistic excesses, ensuring attention is given in national debates to the viewpoints of other Member States and the EU, and engaging national democracies in a constructive dialogue.

REFERENCES

Habermas, J, *The Theory of Communicative Action*, vol 2 (Cambridge, Polity Press, 1989).

Ipsen, HP, *Europäisches Gemeinschaftsrecht* (Tübingen, JCB Mohr, 1972).

Lindseth, P, *Power and Legitimacy: Reconciling Europe and the Nation-State* (Oxford, Oxford University Press, 2010).

MacCormick, ND, *Questioning Sovereignty: Law, State and Nation in the European Commonwealth* (Oxford, Oxford University Press, 1999).

Pernice, I, 'The Treaty of Lisbon: Multilevel Constitutionalism in Action' (2009) 15 *Columbia Journal of European Law* 349.

[12] MacCormick (n 1).

Scharpf, FW, *Governing in Europe: Effective and Democratic?* (Oxford, Oxford University Press, 1999).
——. *Legitimacy Intermediation in the Multilevel European Polity and its Collapse in the Euro Crisis* (Cologne, Max Planck Institute for the Study of Societies, 2012).
Schütze, R, 'Constitutionalism and the European Union' in C Barnard and S Peers (eds), *European Union Law* (Oxford, Oxford University Press, 2014).
Tuori, K, *European Constitutionalism* (Cambridge, Cambridge University Press, 2015).
Tuori, K and Tuori, K, *The Eurozone Crisis* (Cambridge, Cambridge University Press, 2015).

Index

www.ingramcontent.com/pod-product-compliance
Lightning Source LLC
Chambersburg PA
CBHW071352220926
51613CB00008B/113
9781509923304